THE ART AND SCIENCE OF LEADERSHIP

FIFTH EDITION

THE ART AND SCIENCE OF LEADERSHIP

Afsaneh Nahavandi

Arizona State University

PEARSON

Prentice
Hall

Upper Saddle River, New Jersey 07458

Library of Congress Cataloging-in-Publication Data

Nahavandi, Afsaneh.
  The art and science of leadership / Afsaneh Nahavandi.—5th ed.
    p. cm.
  Includes bibliographical references and index.
  ISBN 0-13-604408-5
  1. Leadership.   2. Leadership—Cross-cultural studies.   I. Title.
  BF637.L4N35 2009
  158'.4—dc22   2008000915

AVP/EIC: David Parker
VP/Editorial Director: Sally Yagen
Product Development Manager: Ashley Santora
Project Manager, Editorial: Kristen Varina
Editorial Assistant: Liz Davis
Marketing Manager: Nikki Jones
Marketing Assistant: Ian Gold
Senior Managing Editor: Judy Leale
Project Manager, Production: Ana Jankowski
Permissions Project Manager: Charles Morris
Senior Operations Specialist: Arnold Vila
Media Project Manager: Lisa Rinaldi
Cover Design: Margaret Kenselaar
Creative Director: Jayne Conte
Cover Illustration/Photo: Getty Images, Inc.
Composition/Full-Service Project Management: Bharath Parthasarathy/TexTech
Printer/Binder: R.R. Donnelley/Harrisonburg
Typeface: 10/12 New Baskerville

Credits and acknowledgments borrowed from other sources and reproduced, with
permission, in this textbook appear on appropriate page within text.

Pearson Education Ltd., London   Pearson Education Australia PTY, Limited
Pearson Education Singapore, Pte. Ltd   Pearson Education North Asia Ltd., Hong Kong
Pearson Education Canada, Inc.   Pearson Educación de Mexico, S.A. de C.V.
Pearson Education–Japan   Pearson Education Malaysia, Pte. Ltd.
                                          Pearson Education Upper Saddle River, New Jersey

10 9 8 7 6 5 4 3
ISBN-13: 978-0-13-604408-6
ISBN-10:   0-13-604408-5

To my family. Their love and happiness are the only things that truly matter.

Brief Contents

Contents

Preface

Leading people effectively is a tremendous challenge, a great opportunity, and a serious responsibility. Since the first edition of *The Art and Science of Leadership* was published, the call for leadership has been growing. Our organizations and institutions, more than ever, need effective leaders who understand the complexities of our dynamic global environment and who have the intelligence to deal with complex problems and the sensitivity and ability to empathize with their followers to motivate them to strive for excellence. We always have been interested in leadership. Leaders and followers have existed since humans first organized into groups to accomplish a task. Every civilization throughout history has focused on its leaders, revering or reviling them. Throughout history, the fate of millions has depended on the leadership qualities of emperors, kings, and queens and on their struggles for power and battles for succession. Children all over the world learn early, through listening to fairy tales, that the happiness and misery of people depend on the goodness (or evilness) of leaders.

It is no wonder then that we are fascinated by those who lead us. Some consider leadership to be a magical process. Indeed, when we read about historical figures or meet some of the leaders of our times, we can be transfixed by their seemingly magical exploits. They move armies, create new countries, and destroy whole civilizations through what often appears to be the sheer strength of their will. They affect our very existence on this planet. Although our leaders are the ones who dazzle us, we sometimes fail to consider that leaders alone can accomplish nothing. It is the strength of their followers that moves history. It is the army of foot soldiers who achieves victory. It is the hard work of employees that turns a profit in a faltering company. It is the initiative of volunteers that achieves an institution's goals. We also must remember that many extraordinary leaders found themselves shunned and rejected by the people who once admired them. President Charles de Gaulle's road to the leadership of France was long, tortuous, and fraught with failure: After coming to office as a hero after World War II, he was forced out of office twice. Winston Churchill was removed from office on two occasions and faced long periods in his life during which his leadership was neither valued nor wanted. Julius Caesar experienced many ups and downs in his battles with the Roman senate. More recently, Margaret Thatcher saw her fortunes come and go with the mood of the British public and the economic upheaval in Europe. Benazir Butto of Pakistan moved from national hero to national villain several times. Lee Iaccoca of Chrysler was not always the hero that some consider him to be today. George Watson Jr. was booted out of office after successfully leading IBM for many years. Jack Welch, recently retired from the leadership of General Electric and considered by many to be one of the most successful U.S. CEOs, was nicknamed Neutron Jack in his early days at GE for decimating the company workforce through layoffs. Megawati Sukarnoputri, former president of Indonesia, the world's fifth most populous nation and daughter of the much revered Sukarno, father of Indonesian independence, was considered a hero by some and an ineffectual decision maker by others. Many elected leaders around the world face similar challenges.

If a leader's powers are truly magical, why do they wax and wane? Why are they not effective all the time? Why are they effective with some followers and not with others? These questions, along with many others, will be addressed in this book.

For our organizations to be effective and for society to function successfully, we must be able to select, develop, and train the right leaders and help them succeed. Because the processes of leading others to achieve organizational goals are applicable in any institutional setting, this book presents a broad review and analysis of the field of leadership with application to both business and other organizations. Current research goes far in demystifying leadership and teaching it to the rest of us mortals. Although we still come across some leaders whose performance and behavior escape the bounds of scientific explanation, by and large we know a good deal about leadership and how to train people to be leaders. The cornerstone of our new knowledge is that *leaders are made, not born*; most of us can learn to become better leaders. Maybe only a few of us will someday shape human civilization, but most people are capable of improving their leadership skills, connecting with their followers, and shaping their organizations and communities.

Despite the knowledge about leadership, accumulated by various disciplines over the past 70 to 90 years, deep divisions are present in the field. Few scholars and practitioners even agree on how to define leadership and its key elements. Scholars and practitioners continue to debate whether a leader's personality or behavior should be the focus of our inquiry. In addition, they discuss at length the role of followers and their characteristics. These differences and disagreements are explored in this book; they contribute to understanding the complex process of leadership. The focus, however, is on distilling knowledge, identifying themes, and integrating concepts that can be useful to students and practitioners of leadership.

SOMETHING OLD: KEEPING THE GOOD

The fifth edition of this book builds on the strengths of the first four editions while introducing new themes and features. The many debates and controversies within the field of leadership are presented in this edition as they were in the first four. I continue to emphasize integration of the concepts and distill useful and practical concepts from each theory while taking a cross-cultural perspective. The guiding philosophy and assumption remain the same.

> ➤ *We all can learn to become better leaders.*   For some of us, the learning is easier in certain areas than in others, but with practice and support from our organizations, we all can improve our leadership capabilities. Like many readers, I occasionally come across incredibly charismatic leaders who seem to have special talents at moving others. Although it is tempting to attribute to them a special leadership "gift" that defies systematic explanation, with some effort and critical thinking, one can objectively analyze their style and the situations in which they are effective. Such analysis demystifies their performance and provides practical guidelines for understanding their effectiveness and learning from them. Through this process, the charismatic leader's actions lose their magical qualities and become understandable and predictable. Most of us are not trying to change civilizations, although maybe we should be. Instead, we are

trying to move our teams, departments, and organizations toward higher levels of effectiveness and efficiency. We want better decision making, more satisfied employees, better-quality products and services, and more satisfied constituencies and customers. These outcomes are difficult to obtain, but no magic is involved in achieving them. We can use the many existing leadership theories to achieve these goals. A new Chapter 10 discusses the tools and methods of leader development.

➤ *Application focus.*   Along with continued strong theoretical coverage and analysis and the introduction of cutting-edge research, the book continues to be application focused. The goal remains to help students of leadership understand theoretical developments and apply them to their own development and improvement of their organizations.

➤ *Cross-cultural focus.*   Leadership is not a culture-free process. Because it occurs within the context of a culture, the styles and behaviors that are considered key to effectiveness differ from one culture to the next. Some common threads do run through different cultures though. Few of the leadership theories presented in this book fully consider the cultural context, either globally or internally within the United States. Issues of race and gender also are rarely addressed. One goal for this book is to include cross-cultural, racial, and gender-based analyses of leadership as a major part of the discourse about leadership effectiveness. The changing demographics within the United States and the globalization of the world economy make such analysis essential. A new Chapter 2 focuses exclusively on culture at the national and group levels, and the concept is fully integrated in other discussion throughout the book.

➤ *Looking at changing organizations.*   This edition continues to focus on the future by addressing the dramatic changes that organizations are undergoing. A new Chapter 9 focuses specifically on the challenges of leading change. Businesses and not-for-profit organizations are being challenged continuously to be more effective. They are reorganizing and redefining the role of leaders. The reliance on teams is a mainstay of our institutions. Quality and customer focus have moved from the academic domain to the everyday language of our organizations. Flexibility and adaptability take center stage in our discussions of leadership and organizational effectiveness. These changes require a new look at the role and function of leaders. Our old theories do not explain all the current changes adequately. Throughout the chapters, establishing the link between the old and the new shows how what we have known and used can help the reader deal with the current and future trends in leadership, particularly the focus on teams and nonhierarchical organizations.

➤ *Exercises and self-assessments.*   This fifth edition continues to include many end-of-chapter exercises and self-assessments with several additions and revisions.

➤ *Pedagogical features.*   Several of the pedagogical features of the previous editions are included with new research and examples. "Leading Change" highlights examples of innovative practices in organizations. "Leadership in Action" at the end of every chapter presents a short case study of a real-life leader. "Leadership Challenge" continues to draw attention to the challenging decisions that leaders face by providing brief scenarios designed to elicit critical analysis and discussion.

NEW TO THE FIFTH EDITION

This fifth edition presents an updated structure to address several current and cutting-edge topics in leadership. Part I, The Building Blocks, still defines the concepts and reviews individual differences and power. The concept of culture, however, is now covered in a separate chapter and the history of leadership chapter includes the early contingency theories. Part II, Contemporary Concepts, now focuses on new models of charismatic and neo-charismatic leadership and includes a chapter on other leadership perspectives from the upper echelon and nonprofit organizations. Part III, Leading, addresses the practical aspects of leading, including a discussion of participative leadership and new chapters on change and development. Throughout the chapters, the new research covered in "Leadership from the Cutting Edge" in the previous edition has been integrated in the chapters and the "Leading from the Grassroots" is replaced by "Applying What You Learn."

This new edition continues to offer a test bank, a complete instructor's manual that includes many of the old cases and materials from the previous edition that are not included in this fifth edition.

Chapter 1 "Definition and Significance of Leadership" introduces the basic definitions of leadership, roles, obstacles, and importance of leadership in a changing environment. A discussion of why leadership is needed has been added. The "Leading Change" case and "Leadership Challenge" are both new. "Leadership in Action" case has been updated and revised.

Chapter 2 "The Global and Cultural Contexts" is a new chapter. The discussion of various cultural models has been revised and moved from Chapter 1 of the fourth edition and an extensive discussion of gender and diversity in leadership and ways in which organizations can better manage diversity in leaders has been added. The "Leading Change" case and the "Leadership in Action" case are both new. Two new exercises are introduced, one using national proverbs to understand leadership and one to explore the concept of sexual harassment. A new self-assessment exploring views of women has been added.

Chapter 3 "Early Theories: The Foundation of Modern Leadership" has been substantially revised to include a history of leadership (which was covered in Chapter 2 in the previous edition) and to discuss the early contingency theories of leadership that were covered in Chapters 5 and 6 in the previous edition. These include Fiedler's Contingency Model, the Normative Decision Model, Path-Goal theory, Attributional models, substitutes for leaders, and leader–member exchange. The latest research, when available has been included. The "Leading Change" case is new.

Chapter 4 "Individual Differences and Traits" includes most of the material covered in Chapter 3 in previous editions. In addition to research updates, the trait of narcissism and its links to leaders has been added. The "Leading Change" and "Leadership in Action" cases have both been updated. A new self-assessment for Narcissism has been added.

Chapter 5 "Power and Leadership" includes the material covered in Chapter 4 in previous editions. The "Leading Change" and "Leadership in Action" cases have both been updated.

Chapter 6 "New Models for Leadership" has been substantially updated. It includes updated material on charismatic and transformational leadership presented in Chapter 8 in previous editions. Discussions of spiritual, value-based, and authentic leadership have been added. The "Leading

Change" and "Leadership in Action" cases have both been updated. A new self-assessment about authentic leadership has been added.

Chapter 7 "Other Leadership Perspectives" includes the material on upper-echelon leadership presented in Chapter 9 in previous editions. A discussion of the challenges of leadership of nonprofit organizations has been added. The "Leading Change" case is new; the "Leadership in Action" case has been updated.

Chapter 8 "Participative Management and Leading Teams" includes the material presented in Chapter 7 in previous editions. The "Leading Change" case is new; the "Leadership in Action" case has been updated.

Chapter 9 "Leading Change" is a new chapter. Forces for change, types of change, models, resistance to and solutions to resistance to change are discussed. Visionary leadership previously in Chapter 8 has been moved to this chapter. The "Leading Change" and the "Leadership in Action" cases, and the "Leadership Challenge" are all new. The cases and self-assessments are new.

Chapter 10 "Developing Leaders" is a new chapter. The concepts of leader and leadership development are discussed; the criteria and methods for leader development are also discussed. The role of culture is explored and the key factors in leader development are highlighted. The "Leading Change" and the "Leadership in Action" cases, and the "Leadership Challenge" are all new. The cases and self-assessments are new.

INSTRUCTOR'S SUPPLEMENTS

At www.prenhall.com/irc, instructors can access a variety of print, digital, and presentation resources available with this text in downloadable format. Registration is simple and gives you immediate access to new titles and new editions. As a registered faculty member, you can download resource files and receive immediate access and instructions for installing course management content on your campus server.

If you ever need assistance, our dedicated technical support team is ready to help with the media supplements that accompany this text. Visit http://247. pearsoned.com for answers to frequently asked questions and toll-free user support phone numbers.

The following supplements are available to adopting instructors (for detailed descriptions, please visit www.prenhall.com/irc):

➤ Printed Instructor's Manual with Test Item File —ISBN: 0-13-604409-3
➤ PowerPoint Slides—Available online at the IRC.
➤ Videos on DVD—ISBN: 0-13- 604376-3

COURSESMART TEXTBOOKS ONLINE

CourseSmart Textbooks Online is an exciting new choice for students looking to save money. As an alternative to purchasing the print textbook, students can subscribe to the same content online and save up to 50 percent off the suggested list price of the print text. With a CourseSmart etextbook, students can search the text, make notes online, print out reading assignments that incorporate lecture notes, and bookmark important passages for later review. For more information, or to subscribe to the CourseSmart eTextbook, visit www.coursesmart.com.

WHO SHOULD READ THIS BOOK?

The Art and Science of Leadership is targeted to students of leadership—whether they are advanced undergraduate and graduate students or managers with a desire to learn and grow. It is written for those who want not only to understand the various theories and research in the field, but also to apply that knowledge to becoming leaders and to improving the leadership of their organizations. The examples and cases used are from different types of industries and from the private and public sectors. Although the theories often are developed and tested by psychology and management researchers, they include broad applicability to all students of organizations and leadership.

ACKNOWLEDGMENTS

Years after leaving graduate school, I continue to be grateful for the faculty with whom I worked. I would like to thank Marty Chemers for putting the leadership bug in my ear when I was a graduate student and Irv Altman, who taught me to look at any issue from many different perspectives. I owe Carol Werner many thanks for teaching me to organize my thoughts.

Many thanks go also to my partners at Pearson Prentice Hall. I also would like to acknowledge the reviewers for their thoughtful comments in reviewing the book.

I must thank my assistant, Sandy Chavez-Lopez at the University College, for helping me manage my time and supporting me through this revision. Finally, I sincerely appreciate my family's patience and support in completing this fifth edition. My youngest daughter, Arianne, had to come home most days to me being glued to my computer for many long hours. I could not have done it without you!

About the Author

Afsaneh Nahavandi is a professor in the School of Public Administration and the associate dean in the College of Public Programs at Arizona State University. She received her Ph.D. in social psychology from the University of Utah. Her areas of specialty are leadership, culture, ethics, and teams. She has published articles and contributed chapters on these topics in journals such as the *Academy of Management Review*, the *Journal of Management Studies*, the *Academy of Management Executive*, and the *Journal of Business Ethics*. Her article about teams won the *Academy of Management Executive*'s 1994 Best Article of the Year award. Her book *Organizational Culture in the Management of Mergers* was published in 1993. Her 1999 book *Organizational Behavior: The Person–Organization Fit* was also published by Prentice Hall. She joined Arizona State University in 1987 after teaching at Northeastern University in Boston. She has held several administrative positions, including associate dean of ASU's University College, director of the University College at the West campus of ASU, and director of that ASU West School of Management MBA program. She is the recipient of several teaching awards, including the Arizona State University Parents Association Professor of the Year in 2004.

THE ART AND SCIENCE OF LEADERSHIP

Building Blocks

Part I lays the foundation for understanding the processes of leadership. After studying Part I, you will be able to define the basic elements of leadership and be ready to integrate them to understand more complex leadership processes. Leadership involves the interaction among several key elements: a leader, followers, and the situation. Since its beginnings in the West in the late nineteenth century, the formal study of leadership has generated many definitions of the concept. As with any social phenomenon, culture strongly influences not only our definitions of leadership, but how we actually lead and what we expect of our leaders. Tracing the history of the field can inform us and not only help us understand leadership today, but also enable us to become aware of how the process of leadership and our images and expectations of effective leaders change with organizational, social, and cultural evolutions.

The first chapter provides a working definition of leadership and effectiveness, explores the reasons why we need leadership, describes the roles and functions of leaders, and discusses their impact. Chapter 2 focuses on understanding the role of culture in leadership. Several models for describing culture are presented, and the roles of gender and diversity in leadership are explored. Chapter 3 presents a history of the field of leadership and reviews the contingency theories that provide the foundation for current approaches to leadership. Individual differences that affect leadership are discussed in Chapter 4. They include demographic differences, values, abilities, skills, and several personality traits. Chapter 5 reviews the concept of power and its importance to leadership.

Definition and Significance of Leadership

An army of sheep led by a lion would defeat an army of lions led by a sheep.
—ARAB PROVERB

After studying this chapter, you will be able to:

▪ Define leadership and leadership effectiveness.

▪ Explain why people need leadership.

▪ Discuss the major obstacles to effective leadership.

▪ Compare and contrast leadership and management.

▪ List the roles and functions of leaders and managers.

▪ Summarize the debate over the role and impact of leadership in organizations.

W̲ho is a leader? When are leaders effective? These age-old questions appear simple, but their answers have kept philosophers, social scientists, scholars from many disciplines, and business practitioners busy for many years. It is easy to define bad leadership; we agree on the characteristics of a bad leader. Defining and understanding effective leadership, however, is more complex. This chapter defines leadership and its many aspects, roles, and functions and explores the impact of leaders on people and organizations.

EFFECTIVE LEADERSHIP

We recognize effective leaders when we work with them or observe them; however, many different ways exist for defining who leaders are and when they are effective.

What Is Leadership? Who Is a Leader?

Dictionaries define *leading* as "guiding and directing on a course" and as "serving as a channel." A leader is someone with commanding authority or influence. Researchers, for their part, have developed many working definitions of leadership. Although these definitions share much in common, they each consider different aspects of leadership.

3

Some define leadership as an integral part of the group process (Green, 2002; Krech and Crutchfield, 1948). Others define it primarily as an influence process (Bass, 1960; Cartwright, 1965; Katz and Kahn, 1966). Still others see leadership as the initiation of structure (Homans, 1950) and the instrument of goal achievement. Several even consider leaders to be servants of their followers (Greenleaf, 1998). Despite the differences, the various definitions of leadership share three common elements:

➤ First, leadership is a *group phenomenon*; there can be no leaders without followers. As such, leadership always involves interpersonal influence or persuasion.

➤ Second, leadership is *goal directed* and plays an active role in groups and organizations. Leaders use influence to guide others through a certain course of action or toward the achievement of certain goals.

➤ Third, the presence of leaders assumes some form of *hierarchy within a group*. In some cases, the hierarchy is formal and well defined, with the leader at the top; in other cases, it is informal and flexible.

A leader is a person who influences individuals and groups within an organization, helps them in establishing goals, and guides them toward achievement of those goals, thereby allowing them to be effective.

Combining these three elements, we can define a leader as any person who influences individuals and groups within an organization, helps them in establishing goals, and guides them toward achievement of those goals, thereby allowing them to be effective. Wendy Kopp, CEO and founder of Teach for America, considers teaching successfully to be leadership (George and Kopp, 2007). Lorraine Monroe, executive director of the School Leadership Academy in New York City, a nonprofit organization she founded in 1997, is surprised at the number of leaders who lack the basic leadership skills. She states, "The job of a good leader is to articulate a vision that others are inspired to follow" (Canabou and Overholt, 2001: 98). Mary Sammons, chairman, president, and CEO of Rite Aid Corporation, focuses on the role of followers in leadership, a view that is shared by Mitt Romney, former governor of Massachusetts and 2008 U.S. presidential candidate. Romney believes that "You have to build the right team. I look for bright people with strong personalities who will argue with me" (Prospero, 2004: 58).

What Is Effectiveness? When Is a Leader Effective?

What does it mean to be an effective leader? As is the case with the definition of leadership, effectiveness can be defined in various ways. Some researchers, such as Fred Fiedler, whose Contingency Model is discussed in Chapter 3, define leadership effectiveness in terms of group performance. According to this view, leaders are effective when their group performs well. Other models—for example, Robert House's Path-Goal Theory presented in Chapter 3—consider follower satisfaction as a primary factor in determining leadership effectiveness; leaders are effective when their followers are satisfied. Still others, namely researchers working on the transformational and visionary leadership models described in Chapter 6, define effectiveness as the successful implementation of large-scale change in an organization.

The definitions of leadership effectiveness are as diverse as the definitions of organizational effectiveness. The choice of a certain definition depends mostly on the point of view of the person trying to determine effectiveness and on the constituents who are being considered. For cardiologist Stephen Oesterle, senior vice president for medicine and technology at Medtronic, one the world's biggest manufacturer of medical devices and pacemakers, restoring lives is both a personal and an organizational goal (Tuggle, 2007). Barbara Waugh, a 1960s civil rights and antidiscrimination activist and worldwide personnel director and worldwide change manager of Hewlett-Packard Laboratories (often known as the "World's Best Industrial Research Laboratory"—WBIRL), defines effectiveness as "helping people communicate more, collaborate more, and innovate more" (Mieszkowski, 1998). The mayor of Denver, Colorado, John Hickenlooper, focuses on cooperation, aligning people's self-interest, and getting buy-in from the people who are affected by his decisions (Baker, 2006). For Father Francis Kline (1948–2006), the abbot of Mepkin monastery outside of Charleston, South Carolina, divine service, helping the community, and being self-sufficient are the indicators of effectiveness (Salter, 2000a). At Chick-fil-A, the U.S. chicken fast-food chain, effectiveness is defined as a satisfied customer, which can only be achieved by providing "attentive, sincere, memorable service" (McGregor, 2004a: 83).

Clearly, no one way best defines what it means to be an effective leader. Fred Luthans (1989) proposes an interesting twist on the concept of leadership effectiveness by distinguishing between effective and successful managers. According to Luthans, effective managers are those with satisfied and productive employees, whereas successful managers are those who are promoted quickly. After studying a group of managers, Luthans suggests that successful managers and effective managers engage in different types of activities. Whereas effective managers spend their time communicating with subordinates, managing conflict, and training, developing, and motivating employees, the primary focus of successful managers is not on employees. Instead, they concentrate on networking activities such as interacting with outsiders, socializing, and politicking.

The internal and external activities that effective and successful managers undertake are important to allowing leaders to achieve their goals. Luthans, however, finds that only 10 percent of the managers in his study are effective *and* successful. The results of his study present some grave implications for how we might measure our leaders' effectiveness and reward them. To encourage and reward performance, organizations need to reward the leadership activities that will lead to effectiveness rather than those that lead to quick promotion. If an organization cannot achieve balance, it quickly might find itself with a majority of flashy but incompetent leaders who reached the top primarily through networking rather than through taking care of their employees and achieving goals.

Ideally, any definition of leadership effectiveness should consider all the different roles and functions that a leader performs and then factor those elements into the definition. Few organizations, however, perform such a thorough analysis, and they often fall back on simplistic measures. For example, stockholders and financial analysts consider the CEO of a company to be effective if company stock prices keep increasing, regardless of how satisfied the company's employees are. Politicians are effective if the polls indicate their popularity is high and if they are reelected. A football coach is effective when the team is winning. Students' scores on standardized tests determine a school principal's effectiveness. In all cases, the definition of leadership effectiveness is highly complex and multifaceted.

Consider the challenge faced by the executives of the *New York Times*, one of the world's most respected newspapers. In 2002, the paper won a record seven Pulitzer prizes, a clear measure of success. A year later, however, the same executive editor team that had led the company in that success was forced to step down because of plagiarism scandals (Bennis, 2003). The executive team's hierarchical structure, autocratic leadership style, and an organizational culture that focused on winning and hustling were partly blamed for the scandals (McGregor, 2005a). By one measure, the *Times* was highly effective; by another, it failed a basic tenet of the journalistic profession. Politics further provide examples of the complexity of defining leadership effectiveness. Consider former U.S. President Clinton, who, despite being tried and impeached in the U.S. Senate, maintained his popularity at the polls in 1998 and 1999; many voters continued to consider him effective. Hugo Chavez, the president of Venezuela, continues his hold on power and on many of his followers' hearts. His opponents see him as a ruthless and dangerous dictator, but his supporters point to the concrete and effective social and economic programs that help the poorest in Venezuela and flood the economy with cash (Gould, 2007; Sanchez, 2004). Similarly, President Alvaro Uribe of Colombia, who took office in 2002 and currently serving his second term, has been credited with reducing crime, inflation, and unemployment, while being accused of ties to the right-wing paramilitary organizations blamed for death of labor activists (Farzad, 2007). Whether any of these leaders is considered effective or not depends on one's perspective.

The common thread in all these examples of effectiveness is the focus on outcome. To judge their effectiveness, we look at the results of what leaders accomplish. Process issues, such as employee satisfaction, are important but are rarely the primary indicator of effectiveness. The executive editorial team at the *New York Times* delivered the awards despite creating a difficult and sometimes hostile culture. Voters in the United States liked President Clinton because the economy flourished under his administration. Hugo Chavez survives challenges because he can point to specific accomplishments. Alvaro Uribe highlights to economic gains and improved security. Similarly, in a school system, faculty morale and turnover, which are keys to the facilitation of student learning, are not the primary criteria for determining effectiveness; when evaluating a school, parents look for test scores, and graduation and college admission rates.

One way to take a broad view of effectiveness is to consider leaders effective when their group is successful in maintaining internal stability and external adaptability while achieving goals. Overall, leaders are effective when their followers achieve their goals, can function well together, and can adapt to changing demands from external forces. The definition of leadership effectiveness, therefore, contains three elements:

Overall, leaders are effective when their followers achieve their goals, can function well together, and can adapt to changing demands from external forces.

1. *Goal achievement*, which includes meeting financial goals, producing quality products or services, addressing the needs of customers, and so forth
2. *Smooth internal processes*, including group cohesion, follower satisfaction, and efficient operations
3. *External adaptability*, which refers to a group's ability to change and evolve successfully

Leading Change   The Container Store

Chances are that if you have engaged in a home or office organization project, you have heard of the Container Store. The company offers creative, practical, and innovative solutions to a multitude of storage problems and has established a track record of success, having grown 15 to 20 percent a year since 1978 (Containing Culture, 2007). But storing things is not the only thing the company is known for. Being a great company to work for, having a unique culture, and treating its employees well are other areas in which the Container Store claims leadership. "It's based on communication and understanding that you're part of something larger than just moving that box. . . . You're part of a very special company that is helping customers" is how Amy Carovillano, the company's vice president of logistics, describes the culture (Drickhamer, 2005: 16). Kip Tindell, cofounder of the company, states, "At the container Store we are fond of saying communication is leadership—they are the same thing," which is part of the reason why Mellissa Reiff, who is known to be an outstanding communicator, was selected as president in 2006 (Duff, 2006: 3).

Tindell says, "We talk about getting the customer to dance . . . every time she goes into the closet . . . because the product has been designed and sold to her so carefully" (Birchall, 2006). Achieving this level of service takes a dedicated, and the company believes, happy group of employees that the company carefully recruits (often mostly through its existing employees) and trains. Whereas in comparable companies, the average salesperson gets about 8 hours of training during her first year on the job, it is not unusual for Container Store sales people to get over 200 hours of training before a new store opens (Birchall, 2006). In addition to a family-friendly work environment, the company covers close to 70 percent of its employees' health-care insurance costs, pays 50 to 100 percent higher wages than its competitors, and provides flexible shifts to accommodate its employees' work-life balance.

The investment in employees has paid off. The Container Store has an annual turnover of about 10 percent compared with 90 percent for most retail stores. Its founders, Kip Tindell and Garrett Boone, believe that the unique culture and the success of the company are inseparable. Their belief is so strong that when they were looking for investors, Boone stated, "Anyone who does not embrace our culture would be a lousy investor. Everything that we do is built on culture. How in the world would we otherwise have been able to create an environment where people love to come to work?" (Containing Culture, 2007: 24)

Sources: Birchall, J., 2006. "Training improves shelf life," *Financial Times*, March 8. http://search.ft.com/ftArticle?queryText=Kip+Tindell&y=0&aje=true&x=0&id=060307009431 (accessed July 8, 2007); Containing Culture. 2007. *Chain Store Age* (April): 23–24; Duff, M., 2006. "New president named at Container Store," *DSN Retailing Today*, January 23: 3, 21; Drickhammer, D., 2005. "The Container Store: Thinking outside the box," *Material Handling Management*, June: 16, 18.

Why Do We Need Leaders?

Leadership is a universal phenomenon across cultures. What it is about people that makes leadership necessary and possible? What problems does leadership address? What needs does it fulfill? Although these can be philosophical and even spiritual questions about the human condition, discussions that are beyond the scope of this book, there are more practical and maybe simpler reasons why we need leaders. These reasons closely fall in line with the functions and roles that leaders play and are related to the need or desire to be in collectives. Overall, we need leaders

➤ *To keep groups orderly and focused.* Human beings have formed groups and societies for close to 50,000 years. Whether the formation of groups itself is an instinct or whether it is based simply on the need to be with others to accomplish goals, the existence of groups requires some form of organization and hierarchy. Whereas individual group members may have common goals, they also have individual needs and aspirations. Leaders are needed to pull the individuals together, organize, and coordinate their efforts.

➤ *To accomplish tasks.* Groups allow us to accomplish tasks that individuals alone could not undertake or complete. Leaders are needed to facilitate that accomplishment, to provide goals and directions and coordinate activities. They are the instrument of goal achievement.

➤ *To make sense of the world.* Groups and their leaders provide individuals with a perceptual check. Leaders help us make sense of the world, establish social reality, and assign meaning to events and situations that may be ambiguous.

➤ *To be romantic ideals.* Finally, as some researchers have suggested (e.g., Meindl and Ehrlick, 1987), leadership is needed to fulfill our desire for mythical or romantic figures who represent us and symbolize our own and our culture's ideals and accomplishments.

With all its benefits, the need for leadership presents a sizeable challenge. The presence of leaders necessarily and unavoidably creates hierarchy and inequality in groups. Even though some consider any unequal relationship inherently wrong and suggest that leadership should only be used to describe egalitarian, participative, and willing relationships between leaders and followers (Hicks cited in Wren, 2006), such a view would limit who would be considered a leader. We often follow people we agree with most, but not necessarily all of the time. We are willing to tolerate some degree of inequality in exchange for the security of groups and the ability to reach our individual and collective goals. As we will discuss in Chapter 2, culture greatly impacts how much people tolerate inequality. Managing the inequality inherent in leader–follower relationships and the use of proper power by leaders are essential components of leadership. We will discuss this topic in detail in Chapter 5.

OBSTACLES TO EFFECTIVE LEADERSHIP

In any setting, being an effective leader is a challenging task. Even with a clear definition of leadership and what makes a leader effective, being effective is not easy. Meanwhile, organizations pay a heavy price for ineffective, incompetent, or unethical leadership (Bedeian and Armenakis, 1998; Kellerman, 2004). The keys to becoming an effective leader are knowledge, experience, practice, and learning from one's mistakes. Unfortunately, many organizations do not provide an environment in which leaders can practice new skills, try out new behaviors, and observe their impact. In most cases, the price for making mistakes is so high that new leaders and managers opt for routine actions.

Without such practice and without failure, it is difficult for leaders to learn how to be effective. The experience of failure, in some cases, may be a defining moment in the development of a leader (George, 2007). The question is, therefore, what are the obstacles to becoming an effective leader? Aside from different levels of skills and aptitudes that might prevent a leader from being effective, several other obstacles to effective leadership exist.

➤ First, organizations face considerable *uncertainty* that creates pressure for quick responses and solutions. External forces, such as voters and investors, demand immediate attention. In an atmosphere of crisis, there is no time or patience for learning. Ironically, implementing new methods of leadership, if they are allowed, would make dealing with complexity and uncertainty easier in the long run. Therefore, a vicious cycle that allows no time for the learning that would help current crises continues. The lack of learning and experimentation in turn causes the continuation of the crises, which makes unavailable the time needed to learn and practice innovative behaviors.

➤ Second, organizations are often *rigid and unforgiving*. In their push for short-term and immediate performance, they do not allow any room for mistakes and experimentation. A few organizations, such as Virgin Group Ltd., 3M, and Apple Computers that encourage taking risks and making mistakes, are the exception. The rigidity and rewards systems of many institutions discourage such endeavors.

➤ Third, organizations fall back on *old ideas* about what effective leadership is and, therefore, rely on *simplistic solutions* that do not fit new and complex problems. The use of simple ideas, such as those proposed in many popular books, provides only temporary solutions.

➤ Fourth, over time, all organizations develop a particular culture that strongly influences how things are done and what is considered acceptable behavior. As leaders try to implement new ideas and experiment with new methods, they may face resistance generated by the established culture. For example, as Ford Motor company struggles for survival, its new leaders face what many consider the company's dysfunctional culture (Kiley, 2007).

➤ Finally, another factor that can pose an obstacle to effective leadership is the difficulty involved in understanding and applying the findings of *academic research*. In the laudable search for precision and scientific rigor, academic researchers sometimes do not clarify the application of their research.

The complex and never-ending learning process of becoming an effective leader requires experimentation and organizational support. The inaccessibility of academic research to many practitioners and the short-term orientation of the organizations in which most managers operate provide challenging obstacles to effective leadership. Except for the few individuals who are talented and learn quickly and easily or those rare leaders who have the luxury of time, these obstacles are not easily surmounted. Organizations that allow their leaders at all levels to make mistakes, learn, and develop new skills are training effective leaders.

LEADERSHIP AND MANAGEMENT

What is the difference between a leader and a manager? Are the two basically the same, or are there sharp distinctions between them? These questions have moved to the fore-front of the discussion of leadership in the past few years. Carol Hymowitz, a writer with the *Wall Street Journal*, considers herself lucky to have worked for two bosses who were "leaders more than managers" (Hymowitz, 1998: B1). She believes leaders inspire their followers to take risks. Carol Bartz, chief executive at Autodesk, suggests that managers "know how to write business plans, while leaders get companies—and people—to change" (Hymowitz, 1998: B1). Brad Anderson, CEO of Best Buy, is an example of how leaders may be different from managers. He states, "My primary job as a leader is to provide the right sort of emotional support or relief" (McGregor, 2005b). Table 1-1 presents the major distinctions between managers and leaders. Whereas leaders have long-term and future-oriented perspectives and provide a vision for their followers that looks beyond their immediate surroundings, managers take short-term perspectives and focus on routine issues within their own immediate departments or groups. Zaleznik (1990) further suggests that leaders, but not managers, are charismatic and can create a sense of excitement and purpose in their followers. Kotter (1990) takes a historical perspective in the debate and proposes that leadership is an age-old concept, but the concept of management developed in the past 100 years as a result of the com-plex organizations created after the industrial revolution. A manager's role is to bring order and consistency through planning, budgeting, and controlling. Leadership, on the other hand, is aimed at producing movement and change (Kotter, 1990, 1996).

The debates suggest that for those who draw a distinction between leaders and managers, leaders are assigned attributes that allow them to energize their followers, whereas managers simply take care of the mundane and routine details. Both are nec-essary for organizations to function, and one cannot replace the other. By considering the issue of effectiveness, many of the arguments regarding the differences between leadership and management can be clarified. For example—because being an effec-tive manager involves performing many of the functions that are attributed to leaders with or without some degree of charisma—are managers who motivate their followers and whose departments achieve all their goals simply effective managers, or are these managers also leaders? The distinctions drawn between leadership and management may be more related to effectiveness than to the difference between the two concepts.

Table 1-1   Managers and Leaders.

Managers	Leaders
Focus on the present	Focus on the future
Maintain status quo and stability	Create change
Implement policies and procedures	Initiate goals and strategies
Maintain existing structure	Create a culture based on shared values
Remain aloof to maintain objectivity	Establish an emotional link with followers
Use position power	Use personal power

An effective manager of people motivates them and provides them with a sense of mission and purpose. Therefore, effective managers can be considered leaders.

Thus, any manager who guides a group toward goal accomplishment can be considered a leader. Much of the distinction between management and leadership comes from the fact that the title *leader* assumes competence. Therefore, an effective and successful manager can be considered a leader, but a less-competent manager is not a leader. Overall, the debate over the difference between the two concepts does not add much to our understanding of what constitutes good leadership or good management and how to achieve these goals. It does, however, point to the need felt by many organizations for effective, competent, and visionary leadership/management. This book does not dwell on the distinction between the two concepts and uses the terms interchangeably.

ROLES AND FUNCTIONS OF LEADERS

Although leaders in different organizations and different cultures may perform dissimilar functions and play different roles, researchers have identified a number of managerial roles and functions that cut across most settings.

Managerial Roles

To be effective, leaders perform a number of different roles. The roles are sets of expected behaviors ascribed to them by virtue of their leadership position. Along with the basic managerial functions of planning, organizing, staffing, directing, and controlling, leaders are ascribed a number of strategic and external roles, as well, which are discussed in detail in Chapter 7. Furthermore, one of the major functions of leaders is to provide their group or organization with a sense of vision and mission. For example, department managers need to plan and organize their department's activities and assign various people to perform tasks. They also monitor their employees' performance and correct employees' actions when needed. Aside from these internal functions, managers negotiate with their boss and other department managers for resources and coordinate decisions and activities with them. Additionally, like managers in many organizations, department managers must participate in strategic planning and the development of their organization's mission.

Researchers have developed different taxonomies of managerial activities (Komaki, 1986; Luthans and Lockwood, 1984). One of the most cited is proposed by Henry Mintzberg (1973), who adds the 10 executive roles of figurehead, leader, liaison, monitor, disseminator, spokesperson, entrepreneur, disturbance handler, resource allocator, and negotiator to an already long list of what leaders do. Mintzberg's research further suggests that few, if any, managers perform these roles in an organized, compartmentalized, and coherent fashion. Instead, a typical manager's days are characterized by a wide variety of tasks, frequent interruptions, and little time to think or to connect with their subordinates. Mintzberg's findings are an integral part of many definitions of leadership and management. The roles he defines are typically considered the major roles and functions of leaders.

Interestingly, research indicates that gender differences are evident in how managers perform their roles. In her book *The Female Advantage: Women's Way of Leadership*,

Sally Helgesen (1995) questions many myths about the universality of management behaviors. Through case studies of five female executives, Helgesen faithfully replicated the methodology used 20 years earlier by Mintzberg in his study of seven male managers. Mintzberg had found that his managers often worked at an unrelenting pace, with many interruptions and few non–work-related activities. The men felt that their identity was tied directly to their job and often reported feeling isolated, with no time to reflect, plan, and share information with others. They also reported having a complex network of colleagues outside of work and preferring face-to-face interaction to all other means of communication.

Helgesen's findings of female managers matched Mintzberg's only in the last two categories. Her female managers also were part of a complex network and preferred face-to-face communication. The other findings, however, were surprisingly different. The women reported working at a calm, steady pace with frequent breaks. They did not consider unscheduled events to be interruptions; they instead viewed them as a normal part of their work. All of them reported working at a number of non–work-related activities. They each cultivated multifaceted identities and, therefore, did not feel isolated. They found themselves with time to read and reflect on the big picture. Additionally, the female executives scheduled time to share information with their colleagues and subordinates.

The gender differences found between the two studies can be attributed partly to the 20-year time difference. Helgesen's suggestions about a female leadership style, which she calls "the web," are supported by a number of other research and anecdotal studies. Helgesen's web is compared to a circle with the manager in the center and interconnected to all other parts of the department or organization. This view differs sharply from the traditional pyramid structure common in many organizations. Chapter 2 further explores the gender differences in leadership.

Functions of the Leader: Creation and Maintenance of an Organizational Culture

One of the major functions of leaders is the creation and development of a culture and climate for their group or organization (Nahavandi and Malekzadeh, 1993a; Schein, 2004). Leaders, particularly founders, leave an almost-indelible mark on the assumptions that are passed down from one generation to the next. In fact, organizations often come to mirror their founders' personalities. Consider, for example, how Starbucks, the worldwide provider of gourmet coffee reflects the dreams and fears of its founder, Howard Schulltz. The company is known for its generous benefit package and its focus on taking care of its employees. Schulltz often repeats the story of his father losing his job after breaking his leg and the devastating and long-lasting effect this event had on him and his family (Holstein, 2007). As is the case in many other organizations, the founder's style, or in the case of Starbucks, the founder's family history, has an impact on the culture of an organization.

> Leaders, particularly founders, leave an almost-indelible mark on the assumptions that are passed down from one generation to the next. In fact, organizations often come to mirror their founders' personalities.

If the founder is workaholic and control oriented, the organization is likely to push for fast-paced decision making and be centralized. If the founder is participative and team oriented, the organization will be decentralized and open. Norm Brodsky, a

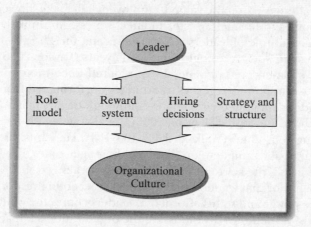

Figure 1-1   Leader's Function in Shaping Organizational Culture.

veteran entrepreneur who created several businesses, realized how much his hard-driving personality impacted the culture of his company. He also realized that his wife and partner's more caring style was having a positive impact on employees, so he worked on softening his own style and supporting her initiatives (Brodsky, 2006). The leader's passion often translates into the mission or one of the primary goals of the organization, as is the case of Howard Schulltz for Starbucks. Similarly, David Necleman's passion for customers and high-quality service (see Leadership in Action at the end of this chapter) has shaped all of JetBlue's operations. The leaders make most, if not all, of the decisions regarding the various factors that will shape the culture (Figure 1-1).

Leaders are role models for other organizational members. They establish and grant the status symbols that are the main artifacts of organizational culture. Followers take their cues from the leaders on what behaviors are and are not acceptable. For example, Stepen Oesterle of Medtronics leads by example. As a marathon runner, he promotes a healthy lifestyle and its role in restoring lives, which is the mission of his company (Tuggle, 2007). Another example is Tyler Winkler, the senior vice president of sales and business development for Secure Works, who is obsessed with improving sales numbers. One of his first statements to his employees was "Make your numbers in three months or you're out" (Cummings, 2004). He measures everything, observes employees closely, and provides detailed feedback and training, all to improve sales. His methods become the norm in the organization and create a legion of loyal employees.

Recent research about the importance of empathy in leadership suggests another function for leaders, related to cultural factors. Researchers argue that a key function of leaders is to manage the emotions of group members (Humphrey, 2002; Kellett, Humphrey, and Sleeth, 2002). Even though attention to internal process issues, such as the emotional state of followers, has always been considered a factor in leadership, it is increasingly seen not as a peripheral task, but rather as one of the main functions. This function is particularly critical to maintaining followers' positive outlook in uncertain and ambiguous situations. Followers observe their leaders' emotional reactions and take their cue from them to determine appropriate reactions (Pescosolido, 2002). Kellett and colleagues (2002) suggest that the increasing use of teams, rapid globalization, and the growing challenge to retain valued employees all make the consideration of employee emotions and feelings a factor in effectiveness. An unlikely example of the emotion management role of leaders is Bob Ladouceur, the La Salle high-school football coach whose team won every single game for 12 years (Lawlor, 2006). The California parochial school's players are not generally considered to be the most talented or the strongest. Ladouceur, however, gets extraordinary performance from them through hard training and focusing on their emotions. Although he says that an undefeated season is what he always shoots for (Lawlor, 2006), he also states, "If a team has no soul, you're just wasting your time" (Wallace, 2003: 100–104). He wants his players to get in touch with their emotions and develop "love" for their teammates. For Ladouceur, managing these emotions is the key to his teams' winning streaks.

Another behavior that leaders need to model is accepting responsibility for one's actions. With the power and status afforded to leaders comes the obligation of accepting responsibility for their own decisions and the organization's impact on others. The willingness to accept such responsibility often is lacking in many U.S. corporations, where finger pointing consumes more energy than correcting mistakes. A leader's demeanor can set the tone for others in the organization to either accept or shirk responsibility for their actions and decisions.

Other means through which the leader shapes culture are by decisions regarding the reward system (Kerr and Slocum, 1987) and by controlling decision standards. In one organization, rewards (financial and nonfinancial) go to only the highest contributors to the bottom line. In another, accomplishments such as contribution to cultural diversity or the degree of social responsibility are also valued and rewarded. Additionally, leaders are in charge of selecting other leaders and managers for the organization. Those selected are likely to fit the existing leader's ideal model and, therefore, fit the culture. Other influential members of the organization provide leaders with yet another opportunity to shape the culture. Many firms, for example, establish a nominating committee of the board of directors. In such committees, top managers nominate and select their successors. Therefore, they not only control the current culture but also exert a strong influence on the future of their organization. To select his successor, General Electric's (GE) Jack Welch carefully observed, interacted with, and interviewed many of the company's executives. He sought feedback from top company leaders, and after selecting Jeff Immelt, Welch orchestrated the transition of power. This managed succession assured that the new leader, although bringing about some new ideas, fit the existing culture of the organization (J. Useem, 2001).

The power of the leader to make decisions for the organization about structure and strategy is another effective means of shaping culture. By determining the hierarchy, span of control, reporting relationship, and degree of formalization and specialization, the leader molds culture. A highly decentralized and organic structure is likely to be the result of an open and participative culture, whereas a highly centralized structure will go hand in hand with a mechanistic/bureaucratic culture. The structure of an organization limits or encourages interaction and by doing so affects, as well as is affected by, the assumptions shared by members of the organization. Similarly, the strategy selected by the leader or the top management team will be determined by, as well as help shape, the culture of the organization. Therefore, a leader who adopts a proactive growth strategy that requires innovation and risk taking will have to create a culture different from a leader who selects a strategy of retrenchment.

Applying What You Learn
Leadership Basics

Leadership is a complex process that is a journey rather than a destination. All effective leaders continue to grow and improve, learning from each situation they face and from their mistakes. Here are some basic points that we will revisit throughout the book:

- *Find your passion*: We can be at our best when we lead others into something for which we have passion.

- *Learn about yourself*: Self-awareness of your values, strengths, and weaknesses is an essential starting point for leaders.

- *Experiment with new situations*: Learning and growth occurs when we are exposed to new situations that challenge us; seek them out.

- *Get comfortable with failure*: All leaders fail; good leaders learn from their mistakes

and consider them learning opportunities. Mistakes are more likely to happen when you are placed in new challenging situations that provide you with opportunities to learn.

- *Pay attention to your environment*: Understanding all the elements of a leadership situation, and particularly followers, is essential to effectiveness. Ask questions, listen carefully, and observe intently so that you can understand the people and the situations around you.

- *Don't take yourself too seriously*: A good sense of humor and keeping a perspective on priorities will help you. You will not never be as good as all your supporters believe and not as flawed as your detractors think!

DOES LEADERSHIP MAKE A DIFFERENCE?

Open any newspaper or business periodical and you probably will find the profile of a political, community, or business leader or a lengthy article about how an organization is likely to be greatly affected by its new leadership. Company stocks fluctuate because of changes in leadership. For example, while the board of directors of American Express was debating the fate of CEO Robinson (he was eventually replaced), the company's stock price plummeted a steep 13 percent in four days. Similarly, a new leader can affect a firm's credit rating by affecting the confidence of the financial community in this person. As Xerox weathered considerable financial and leadership problems in 2000 and 2001, the selection of Anne Mulcahy, a company veteran, as CEO helped ease stakeholders' concerns (see Leadership in Action in Chapter 10). A city or nation might feel a sense of revival and optimism or considerable concern when a new leader is elected. In 1998 Venezuelans elected Hugo Chavez, a former paratrooper and populist leader of a failed coup, as president. Despite serious concerns from the business and financial communities, Chavez energized millions of voters with a party that won 35 percent of congress a year before the presidential elections. In 2004 he survived, with a clear majority, a recall vote that was based on ongoing concerns about his authoritarian style and use of the military. Whether supporters or opponents of Chavez, Venezuelans, like many others around the world, believe that leadership is an important matter.

Although you might take this assertion for granted, considerable debate among leadership scholars addresses whether leadership actually impacts organizations. The following are the key questions:

➤ To what extent, if at all, does the leadership of an organization affect various organizational elements and organizational performance?

➤ Does leadership have more impact in certain situations than in others?

Arguments against the Impact of Leadership

Much of the research about the lack of impact of leadership has roots in the field of sociology. Such an approach asserts that organizations are driven by powerful factors other than their management (Brown, 1982; Cyert and March, 1963; Hannan and Freeman, 1977; Meindl and Ehrlick, 1987; Salancik and Pfeffer, 1977a). Suggestions that leaders are not important abound, made by many throughout history. Leo Tolstoy suggested that leaders are simply slaves of history; their presence and actions irrelevant and determined by the inevitable course of events. Karl Marx made similar assertions about the power of history and irrelevance of leaders. Modern researchers suggest that environmental, social, industrial, and economic conditions, just to name a few factors, determine organizational direction and performance to a much higher degree than does leadership. Similarly, the same external factors, along with organizational elements such as structure and strategy, are assumed to limit the leader's decision-making options, further reducing the leader's discretion. The support for this approach comes primarily from two areas:

➤ First, a group of researchers studied the impact of leadership succession in organizations. Results from studies in the private and public sectors support the notion that the change of leadership does not affect organizational performance strongly. For example, Salancik and Pfeffer (1977a), in a study of the performance of mayors, found that leadership accounted for only 7 to 15 percent of changes in city budgets. Similarly, Lieberson and O'Connor (1972) found that whereas leadership has minimal effects on the performance of large corporations (accounting for only 7 to 14 percent of the performance), company size and economic factors show considerable links to firm performance.

➤ Second, support for the lack-of-importance hypothesis is found in an area of research that focuses on the extent of managerial discretion (Finkelstein and Hambrick, 1996; Hambrick and Finkelstein, 1987). Although the goal of the research is not to show the insignificance of leadership, some of the results show that CEOs have limited discretion in their choices and activities. The lack of managerial discretion in decision making further reinforces the notion that external environmental elements and internal macro-organizational elements have more impact than does leadership.

Overall, the early evidence from the leadership succession research together with some of the managerial discretion findings can be used to support several suggestions. First, leaders have minimal impact on organizations. Second, even when leaders do make decisions that affect organizations, their decisions are determined by environmental and organizational factors and are, therefore, not a reflection of the leader's preferences or style. Additionally, some researchers consider leadership to be a simple symbol or myth rather than an objective factor in organizations (Meindl and

Table 1-2   Arguments Regarding the Impact of Leadership.

Leadership Is Insignificant	Leadership Has an Impact
• Outside environmental factors affect organizations more than leadership.	• Leadership is one of the many important factors.
• Internal structure and strategy determine the course an organization takes.	• Leadership is key in providing vision and direction.
• Leadership accounts for only 7 to 15 percent of financial performance.	• Leadership can account for up to 44 percent of a firm's profitability.
• Leaders have little discretion to really make an impact.	• Leadership is critical in orchestrating change.
• Leadership is a romantic myth rather a real organizational factor.	• Leadership's impact is moderated by situational factors.

Ehrlick, 1987). Research findings in support of such a view indicate that when asked who is responsible for a group's or an organization's success and performance, people are more likely to attribute the success to the leader than to other factors. This tendency occurs even when available data indicate that attributing success to the leader alone is not warranted. Based on these findings, researchers conclude that the effect of leaders, although interesting, is not objective and actual but rather reflects a romantic notion of the role and impact of leaders. Table 1-2 summarizes the arguments regarding the impact of leadership.

Arguments for the Impact of Leadership

Reconsideration of the data and reinterpretation of the findings point to the serious flaws in the research concerning the lack of impact of leadership. Such flaws reassert the importance of leadership in organizational performance. (See Table 1-2 for a summary.) For example, in reevaluating Lieberson and O'Connor's 1972 study, Weiner and Mahoney (1981) find that a change in leadership accounts for 44 percent of the profitability of the firms studied. Other researchers (Day and Lord, 1988; Thomas, 1988) indicate that the early results were not as strong as originally believed. Some studies of school systems show that the principal is the most important factor in the climate of a school and the success of students (Allen, 1981). Still other studies find that the leadership is critical to orchestrating and organizing all the complex elements necessary to change an organization (Burke, Richley, and DeAngelis, 1985). Recent studies suggest that leadership can have an impact by looking at the disruption that can come from changes in leadership (Ballinger and Schoorman, 2007).

Reconciling the Differences

The debates about the impact of leadership make valuable contributions to our understanding of leadership. First, it is important to recognize that leadership is one of many factors that influence the performance of a group or an organization. Second, the leader's contribution, although not always tangible, is often significant in providing a vision and direction for followers and in integrating their activities. Third, the key is to identify situations where the leader's power and discretion over the group and the organization are limited. (These situations are discussed as part of the concept of leadership substitutes in Chapters 3 and 7, which describes the role of upper-echelon leaders.) Finally, the potential lack of impact of leaders in some situations further emphasizes the importance of followers in the success of leadership and the need to understand organizations as broad systems. Some studies suggest that the two views complement each other and should be fully integrated (Osborn, Hunt, and Jauch, 2002). Overall, after years of debate, the popular view that leaders impact organizations continues to receive research support (Hambrick, 2007), as the focus shifts from whether a leader has an impact to understanding a leader's impact and its consequences.

CHANGES IN ORGANIZATIONS AND EXPECTATIONS OF LEADERS

To some, a leader is someone who takes charge and jumps in to make decisions whenever the situation requires. This view is particularly dominant in traditional organizations with a clear hierarchy in which employees and managers carry out narrowly defined responsibilities. The extent to which a leader is attributed power and knowledge also varies by culture and will be discussed in Chapter 2. In cultures where power is highly differentiated, such as in Mexico, managers are expected to provide all the answers and solutions to work problems and control the activities of their employees. Although the U.S. mainstream culture is not as authority oriented as some other cultures, a large number of our leadership theories are implicitly or explicitly based on the assumptions that leaders have to take charge and provide others with instructions. For example, the initiation-of-structure concept provides that effective leadership involves giving direction, assigning tasks to followers, and setting deadlines. These activities are considered an inherent part of an effective leader's behaviors. Similarly, the widely used concept of motivation to manage (Miner and Smith, 1982) includes desire for power and control over others as an essential component. Students of management are still told that the desire to control others might be a key factor in determining their motivation to manage, which in turn is linked to managerial success.

New Roles for Leaders

With the push for quality, continuous improvement, and the use of teams, organizations and their hierarchies are changing drastically. As a result, many of the traditional leadership functions and roles are delegated to subordinates. Figure 1-2 presents the traditional model and the new model for the role of leaders in organizations. The focus on quality and teamwork in all aspects of decision making and implementation forces us to reconsider our expectations and requirements for leadership. Effective team leaders are not necessarily in control of the group. They might need facilitation and participation skills much more than initiation-of-structure skills. For example, employees in traditional organizations are responsible only for production; the planning, leading, and controlling functions, as well as the responsibility for results, fall on the manager (see Figure 1-2). An increasing number of organizations, however, are shifting the activities and responsibilities typically associated with managers to employees. Managers are expected to provide the vision, get the needed resources to employees, act as support persons, and get out of employees' way. The employees, in turn,

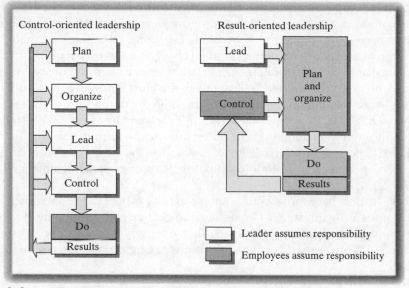

Figure 1-2   Control versus Result-Oriented Leadership.

learn about the strategic and financial issues related to their job, plan their own activities, set production goals, and take responsibility for their results.

Many executives have adopted new management techniques to help them with the challenges inherent in the new roles for leaders. When Rick Sapio was the CEO of the 37-employee New York City Mutual.com, a mutual fund advisory company, he knew that his business was high-pressure with little time to stay in touch with his employees (Buchanan, 2001). Recognizing the importance of involving employees, however, Sapio created "Hassles," an electronic mailbox through which employees can express their concerns and ideas with a guarantee from the CEO that they will be addressed within a week. For those who prefer to see the boss in person, Sapio schedules 1 hour each week in a conference room (rather than his office, which may seem inaccessible) where anyone can drop in to give him input. Jeffrey Immelt, CEO of General Electric (see Leading Change in Chapter 9), has made learning and getting to hear everybody's ideas one of his priorities. His predecessor, Jack Welch, notes that a great leader needs to "get under the skin of every person who works for the company" (Hammonds, 2004: 32). The Hay Group, a Philadelphia-based management consulting firm, conducted a study that identified elements of an effective corporate culture (Kahn, 1998). They found that "in the most admired companies, the key priorities were teamwork, customer focus, fair treatment of employees, initiative, and innovation" (Kahn, 1998: 218). Companies such as Procter & Gamble, Whole Foods, Toyota, and Best Buy practice being egalitarian and cooperative. Their priorities are fast decision making, training, and innovation.

The new leadership styles are not limited to business organizations; they can also be seen in government and other not-for-profit organizations. Harry Baxter, chairman and CEO of Baxter Healthcare in Deerfield, Illinois, likes to focus on doing the right thing instead of being right. He suggests, "I have very few definitive answers, but I have a lot of opinions" (Kraemer, 2003: 16). Philip Diehl, former director of the U.S. Mint, and his leadership team transformed the stodgy government bureaucracy into an efficient and customer-centered organization by asking questions, listening to stakeholders, creating a sense of urgency in employees, and involving them in the change (Muio, 1999). These changes also occur in local, state, and federal government agencies. For example, Ron Sims, who was recognized in 2006 as one of the most innovative public officials, was known for always looking for common ground while operating from a clear set of principles (Walters, 2006). Ron Sims is also known for leading by example. When he talked about county employees adopting a healthier lifestyle, he started eating better and biking and lost 40 pounds (Walters, 2006). Mitt Romney, the governor of Massachusetts in 2004, expects people around him to think for themselves and to challenge his ideas (Prospero, 2004).

These leaders have moved out of their top-floor offices to keep in touch with the members of their organizations. Given the rapid change and complexity of many organizations and the environment in which they operate, cultivating broad sources of information and involving many in the decision-making process are essential.

Factors Fueling Changes

A number of external and internal organizational factors are driving the changes in our organizations and in the role of leaders and managers (Figure 1-3). First, political changes worldwide are leading to more openness and democracy. These political changes shape and are shaped by images of what is considered to be appropriate leadership. With the fall of the Soviet Union at the end of the twentieth century, the world saw an increase in the use of democratic principles aimed at power sharing. In the United States, the public continues to expect openness in the affairs of both the private and the public sectors. Politicians are forced to reveal much of their past and

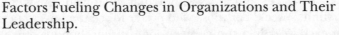

Figure 1-3   Factors Fueling Changes in Organizations and Their Leadership.

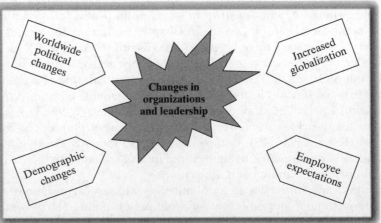

justify to the public many, if not all, of their decisions. Communities increasingly demand participation in the decisions regarding their schools, health-care systems, and environment.

Second, with increasing global and local competition and complex and fast-changing technologies, numerous organizations struggle for their survival and to justify their existence. Many are forced to reconsider how they provide goods and services to their customers and to reevaluate the assumptions they held as basic truths. For example, Bill Ford, Jr., who served as CEO of Ford for five years (Kiley, 2007), not only is an environmentalist who agreed to speak at a Greenpeace conference but also attended union contract negotiations wearing union buttons stating that he hates the "us versus them" mentality. He stayed close to employees and regularly ate at Ford's cafeteria and was interested in joining the employee hockey league (Truby, 2003).

The global competition associated with consumer demands for improved quality in products and services intensifies the need for flexibility and creativity on the part of organizations. Poor management and lack of leadership often are blamed for the problems facing U.S. organizations. The fierce international competition and perceptions of our global competitors' management practices push us to look for new solutions. Whether it is through restructuring in the private sector or through reinventing government in the public arena, our old institutions seek new vitality. Many organizations are redefining and reengineering themselves, drastically altering the way employees do their jobs. These practices demand new leadership roles and procedures.

Another key factor fueling changes in leadership are the demographic changes in the United States and many other countries (Figure 1-4 presents the ethnic diversity in the U.S. population). These demographic changes lead to increased diversity in the various groups and organizations; their leaders must consider this diversity when making

Figure 1-4   Diversity in the U.S Population.

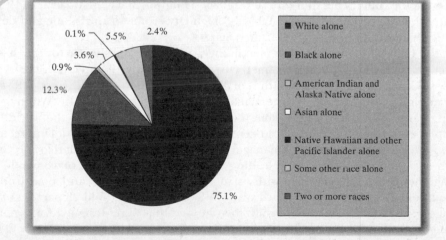

Source: U.S. Census Bureau, Census 2000: http://www.census.gov/population/.

Table 1-3   U.S Demographic Highlights and Trends.

- In 2000 over 37 million people (13% of the population) spoke a language other than English at home—over half of those speak Spanish.
- More than half of the U.S. workforce consists of women and minorities.
- By 2016, minorities will make up one third of the U.S. population.
- By 2025, the percentage of European Americans in the population will drop from 72% in 2000 to 62%.
- By 2025, Hispanics are estimated to be 18% of the population, outnumbering African Americans who will make up 13% of the population.
- By 2025, the *average* age will be close to 40, as opposed to under 35 in 2000.
- By 2025, more than 50% of the population of Hawaii, California, New Mexico and Texas will be from a minority group.
- By 2050, the Hispanic population of the U.S. will grow from 11.5% of the population in 2000 to 24.4%.
- By 2050, the average U.S. resident will be from a non-European background.
- By 2050, only about 60% of the entrants into the labor force will be white, with half that number being women.

Source: U.S. Census Bureau, Census 2000: www.census.gov/population/.

decisions. In some cases, the diversity is related to age; in others it is related to gender, ethnic background, or other factors. There are other countries that deal with similar or even greater cultural diversity. For example, Malaysia's population is highly diverse and consists of Malays, Chinese, Indians, Arabs, Sinhalese, Eurasians, and Europeans, with the Muslim, Buddhist, Daoist, Hindu, Christian, Sikh, and Shamanistic religions all practiced (*World Fact Book: Malaysia*, 2007). Although the majority of Singapore's population of more than 4 million is Chinese, it also includes Malays, Indians, and Eurasians. As a result, the country has four official languages: English, Malay, Mandarin, and Tamil (*World Fact Book: Singapore*, 2007). Table 1-3 highlights some of the ethnic and demographic changes and trends in the United States.

The increasing number of women in the workforce is another factor that has an impact on leadership. Although women currently hold only 10 percent of the executive positions in the United States, they make up over 46 percent of the general workforce and close to 51 percent of the managerial and professional ranks (Winning the waiting game for women CEOs, 2006). Similar trends exist all over the world. For example, even though progress has been slow, women make up almost 47 percent of the labor force and 36 percent of managerial positions in Canada (Tallarico and Gillis, 2007). Scandinavian countries are leading the way with the number of women in top management and leadership positions in the executive office and boardrooms: women hold 29 percent of the board seats. In Sweden women hold 23 percent of the board seats (Amble, 2006). As a result, the old ways that were designed for a gender and ethnically homogeneous population do not always work with employees and customers from varied backgrounds and cultures. Much of the burden for devising and implementing the needed changes falls on the leadership of our organizations. The demand to listen to and address the needs of nonhomogeneous groups requires skills that go beyond controlling and monitoring.

Other demographic trends in the United States include what is called the population hourglass with the largest percentage of the population being older baby boomers (born between the late 1940s and 1960s) at the top, and the millennial generation (born after the mid-1980s) at the bottom, with the generation Xers (born between the 1970s and 1980s) pinched in the middle (Zolli, 2006). This hourglass has considerable implications for those who lead organizations and what factors they must consider when leading people from different generations. We will discuss the impact of generational differences on individuals in Chapters 2 and 4. Additionally, employees attain increased levels of education today, and the younger generation enters the workplace with expectations of participation and autonomy. The younger generations entering the workforce expect fast promotions, challenging learning opportunities, training, and work-life balance. The increase in service jobs at the expense of traditional manufacturing jobs puts employees in direct contact with customers and, therefore, requires changes in how we manage and train employees. This increase in service jobs also means that employees must use judgment and make many quick decisions that previously were reserved for management.

Because of these pressures for change, many organizations find themselves rewriting their policies to address the needs of a diverse community and consumer base. Organizations are building more diversity internally and changing their practices. Ted Childs, IBM's president of global workforce diversity who has been described as the most effective diversity executive on the planet (Malveaux, 2005) states, "You're going to have to sell to people who are different from you, and buy from people who are different from you, and manage people who are different from you. . . . This is how we do business. If it's not your destination, you should get off the plane now" (Swan, 2000: 260). He views getting people to respect those who are different from them as the biggest challenge in managing diversity.

Barriers to Change

Despite the factors that fuel the need for change, few organizations and individuals have adopted new models for leadership painlessly and successfully. In part because of perceived financial pressures and attempts to find a quick way out of them, organizations turn to tough autocratic leaders whose goals are clearly not employee motivation and loyalty. For example, John Grundhofer, nicknamed "Jack the Ripper," specialized in implementing massive layoffs and found his skills in high demand. Similarly, Al Dunlap, with nicknames such as "Ming the Merciless" and "Chainsaw Al," for a long time moved successfully from the top position of one organization to another before being fired from Sunbeam Corporation in 1998. For many years, the financial community applauded him for his drastic cost-cutting strategies that involved widespread layoffs. Bill George, the highly respected former CEO of Medtronic, states that this focus on short-term and quick results cannot create the motivation necessary for the innovation and superior service that are essential to leadership and organizational effectiveness (George, 2003).

Another obstacle to implementing new models of leadership is that even though teams are fairly common in lower and middle levels of organizations, top management still remains a one-person show. The hierarchical structure of many organizations makes change difficult. Old cultures resist change. Few organizations truly reward enterprising employees and managers for crossing the traditional hierarchical barriers. Instead, most organizations continue to reward their leaders for tried-and-true approaches or sometimes for nonperformance- and nonproductivity-related behaviors, despite the lack of success (Luthans, 1989). Marcus Buckingham, a researcher at the Gallup Organization, studied global leadership practice for 15 years. According to Buckingham, "The corporate world is appallingly bad at capitalizing on the strengths of its people" (LaBarre, 2001: 90). Gallup's extensive surveys clearly show that employee engagement can have a considerable positive impact on an organization's performance. Recent surveys of employees show that job satisfaction is lower in larger companies with more bureaucracy, lower autonomy, and low responsibility (*Wall Street Journal*, 2006). Few organizations take full advantage of their employees' input. Tom Peters, the well-known management consultant, suggests that while business leaders focus on strategy they often "skip over the incredibly boring part called people," thereby failing to take advantage of one of the most important aspects of their organization (Reingold, 2003: 94). Additionally, changing the existing behaviors of management style is very difficult. John Kotter, Harvard Business School professor and noted authority on change, suggests, "The central issue is never strategy, structure, culture, or systems. The core of the matter is always about changing the behavior of people" (Deutschman, 2005).

In addition, although they might spend a great deal of time working in teams, employees are still rewarded for individual performance. In other words, our reward structures fail to keep up with our attempts to increase cooperation among employees and managers. Furthermore, many employees are not willing or able to accept their new roles as partners and decision makers even when such roles are offered to them. Their training and previous experiences make them balk at taking on what they might consider to be their leader's job. Even when organizations encourage change, many leaders find giving up control difficult. Many receive training in the benefits of empowerment, teams, and softer images of leadership, but they simply continue to repeat what seemingly worked in the past, engaging in what researcher Pfeffer calls substituting memory for thinking (1998). With all that training to be in charge, allowing employees to do more might appear to be a personal failure. Either because of years of traditional training or because of personality characteristics that make them more comfortable with control and hierarchy, managers' styles often create an obstacle to implementing necessary changes. Research with children's images of leadership indicates that the belief that leaders need to be in control develops early in life. Children, particularly boys, continue to perceive a sex-typed schema of leaders: leaders are supposed to have male characteristics, including dominance and aggression (Ayman-Nolley, Ayman, and Becker, 1993).

SUMMARY AND CONCLUSIONS

A leader is any person who influences individuals and groups within an organization, helps them in the establishment of goals, and guides them toward achievement of those goals, thereby allowing them to be effective. Leaders are often needed because they create order and organization in groups, allowing the groups to achieve their goals; they help people make sense of the world and often serve as ideal and romantic symbols for their followers. To be effective, leaders must help the organization maintain internal health and external adaptability. Despite the apparent simplicity of the definitions of leadership and effectiveness, both are difficult concepts to implement.

Various studies proposed separate definitions for leadership and management. The activities performed by leaders, however, are similar to those typically considered the domain of effective managers. Although some view the roles of leaders and managers as being different, effective, and competent, managers are often also leaders within their groups and organizations. In addition to performing the traditional managerial roles and duties, leaders also play a special role in the creation of a culture for their organizations. They can affect culture by making direct decisions regarding reward systems and hiring of other managers and employees and also by being role models for others in the organization. Notwithstanding the many roles that leaders play in an organization, in some situations their impact on group and organizational performance is limited. Therefore, it is essential to consider leadership in its proper context and to take into account the numerous factors that can affect group and organizational performance.

LEADERSHIP CHALLENGE: MOVING TO LEADERSHIP

You have been a member of a cohesive and productive department for the past three years. Your department manager has accepted a job in another organization and you have been moved into her position. You are not one of most senior members, but you have the most education, have been volunteering for many training programs, and have been an outstanding individual contributor. Over the past three years, you have developed close relationships with several of your department members who are around your age. You often go out to lunch together, have drinks after work, and get together on weekends. There are also a couple of "old-timers" who were very helpful in training you when you first came in. Although you get along with them, you feel a bit awkward being promoted to be their boss. You, however, know that neither has any formal education.

1. What are the challenges you are likely to face as the new leader?
2. What are some actions you should take to help smooth the transition?
3. What are some things you should avoid?

REVIEW AND DISCUSSION QUESTIONS

1. What are the essential components of the definition of leadership?
2. What are the essential components of the definition of leadership effectiveness?
3. Why do we need leaders?
4. Provide one example each of an effective leader and a successful leader. Consider how they differ and what you can learn from each.
5. What are the obstacles to effective leadership? How have the nature and occurrence of such obstacles changed in recent years? Why?
6. Based on your knowledge of the field of management and your personal definition of leadership, how are management and leadership similar or different? How can the differences be reconciled? How do these differences add to our understanding of leadership?
7. What are the ways in which leaders influence the creation of culture in their organizations? Are any additional methods used by top managers? Provide examples.
8. What are the basic assumptions guiding the "insignificant leadership" concept? What is your position on this issue? Document your arguments.
9. What are the elements of the emerging leadership styles? What are the factors that support such styles?
10. What obstacles do new leadership styles face in traditional organizations?
11. How can obstacles to new models be overcome?

EXERCISE 1-1:   WHAT IS LEADERSHIP?

This exercise is designed to help you develop a personal definition of leadership and clarify your assumptions and expectations about leadership and effectiveness.

1. Describe your ideal leader

Individually list five desirable and five undesirable characteristics of your ideal leader.

Desirable	Undesirable
1.	1.
2.	2.
3.	3.
4.	4.
5.	5.

2. Develop group definition

In groups of four or five discuss your list and your reasons and draw up a common definition.

3. Present and defend definition

Each group will make a 5-minute presentation of its definition.

4. Common themes

Discuss various definitions:
1. What are the common themes?

2. Which views of leadership are presented?

3. What are the assumptions about the role of the leader?

EXERCISE 1-2:   IMAGES OF LEADERSHIP

One way you can clarify your assumptions about leadership is to use images to describe your ideal leader. Through the use of such images, you can understand your views of the role of leaders in organizations and your expectations and image of leadership. These images are your personal theories of leadership. For example, viewing leaders as facilitators presents a considerably different image from viewing them as parents.

1. Select your image

   Select the image of your ideal leader. List the characteristics of that image.

2. Share and clarify

   In groups of three or four share your leadership image and discuss its implications for your own leadership style.

3. Class discussion

   Groups will share two of their individual members' images of leadership. Discuss implications of various images for the following aspects:
   1. A person's leadership style

   2. Impact on organizational culture and structure

   3. Compatibility with current or past leaders

   4. Potential shortcomings of each image

EXERCISE I-3:   UNDERSTANDING THE LEADERSHIP CONTEXT

This exercise is designed to highlight the importance and role of the context in the leadership process.

1. Individual/group work

   Select a leader and identify the contextual factors that affect his/her leadership. Consider various elements that may be relevant, such as the following:

   1. Long-term historical, political, and economic factors forces

   2. Current contemporary forces, including social values, changes, and cultural factors

   3. The immediate context, including organizational characteristics, the task, and followers

2. Discussion

   How do all these factors affect the leader? Do they hinder or help the leader achieve his/her goals?

Leadership in Action: JetBlue's David Neeleman Reinvents an Airline

"Above all else, JetBlue Airways is dedicated to bringing humanity back to air travel" (JetBlue Airways Customer Bill of Rights, 2007). "As long as we can delight our customers, there's plenty of business for us" (BW Online, 2003) states David Neeleman, founder of JetBlue, an airline that serves mostly the eastern U.S. seaboard and is fast expanding to the western United States. Neeleman, a creative entrepreneur, has successfully navigated turbulent times with a no-layoffs strategy and expansion plans that target routes that other airlines drop. JetBlue now has seven years of successful operation, a few turbulent business decisions, and a vast contingent of loyal customers under its belt (Salter, 2007). Although Neeleman is now the nonexecutive chairman rather than CEO of the company (Maurer, 2007), the way that JetBlue reacted to its own mistakes during a storm in February 2007 where it held passengers in planes on the tarmac for seven hours during a storm, is indicative of the culture Neeleman has built. With a sincere apology (posted on the Web at http://www.jetblue.com/about/ourcompany/apology/index.html) and hint of defensiveness (Salter, 2007), JetBlue quickly instituted a much publicized Passenger Bill of Rights to assure that its much-valued customers continue to remain loyal.

With 500 daily flights to 50 destinations and over 100 planes, the company continues its steady growth (JetBlue profile, 2007). JetBlue's small size, young fleet, and emphasis on teamwork allow for quick decisions and implementation. Top executives and managers consistently interact with employees and customers to listen and get feedback from them to keep addressing their concerns (Salter, 2004a). Neeleman focused on what he could control, management decisions and how customers and employees are treated (Salter, 2006). The attention to employees and customers has earned JetBlue high ratings and its CEO awards for being a visionary (www.jetblueairways.com). Programs such as generous profit sharing, excellent benefits, open communication, and extensive training all get the right employees in the company and retain them.

Neeleman not only provides the vision, but also knows to listen to his people who, on occasion, veto his decisions. Neeleman takes it in stride and says, "I'm being totally deferential and patient. . . . It's because I think the situation demands it. I have to trust the instincts of the people around me" (Judge, 2001: 131). The emphasis on employees and teamwork permeates every aspect of the company. Neeleman explains, "If you treat people well, the company's philosophy goes, they'll treat the customer well." The senior vice president of operations echoes the focus on people: "There is no 'they' here. It's 'we' and 'us' " (Salter, 2004a). "We select the best people, but we do extensive training to make sure they understand what is expected of them. . . . Our leadership are held to a very high standard as to how they treat the other crew members," says Neeleman, regarding JetBlue's commitment to its employees (Ford, 2004: 141).

Relying on creative use of technology, such as sophisticated programs to manage delays, onboard laptops that allow the crew to speed up typical paperwork, and reservation and call centers that are run out of agents' homes, provides another way for

(Continued)

Leadership in Action: (*Continued*)

JetBlue to stay ahead. In Salt Lake City, Utah, Mary Drifill, one of 700 employees who work at home serving as reservation agents for JetBlue, often takes calls in her pajamas while keeping an eye on her three children. "It's the best job I've ever had," she says (Salter, 2004a). Her supervisor makes a particular effort to get to know the telecommuting employees and keep them connected through phone calls, regular online contact, and social get-togethers (Salter, 2004b). As Drifill chats with customers while making reservations, the positive stories they tell her about Neeleman are a constant reminder about the importance of treating the customer well. Neeleman and other top executives are present at airports, on flights, and at company functions and events. Their presence and engagement with employees and customers creates opportunities to interact and get feedback.

With low fares and unusual routes such as Washington, D.C., to Oakland and Long Beach, California, the airline does things that others in its industry say it should not be doing. What other low-fare carrier provides its coach customers with individual TV sets, blue potato chips, extra leg room, chocolate chip cookies, and a highly likable crew (Donnelly, 2001)? What other airline goes against expert advice and buys a fleet of brand new Airbus planes that offer luxury but are not fuel efficient? How can JetBlue afford to be the first U.S. national carrier to install bulletproof, dead-bolted doors on cockpits even before a Federal Aviation Administration mandate? JetBlue's attitude and Neeleman's creativity make it work. As Neeleman says, "It is the people that make it happen" (Ford, 2004: 140).

QUESTIONS

1. What are the key elements of JetBlue's culture?
2. What role does the leader play in the development and maintenance of the culture?

Sources: JetBlue Airways Customer Bill of Rights. 2007. http://www.jetblue.com/p/about/ourcompany/promise/Bill_Of_Rights.pdf (accessed June 16, 2007); Salter, C., 2007. "Lessons from the Tarmac," *Fast Company*, May: 31; Maurer, H., 2007. "JetBlue changes pilots," *Business Week*, May: 28; JetBlue Profile. 2007. http://finance.yahoo.com/q/pr?s=jblu (accessed June 16, 2007); BW Online. 2003. "David Neeleman, JetBlue." http://www.businessweek.com:/print/magazine/content/03_39/b3851620.htm?mz (accessed September 16, 2004); Donnelly, S., 2001. "Blue Skies," *Time*, July 30: 24–27; Judge, P., 2001. "How will your company adapt?" *Fast Company*, 54; Ford. 2004. "David Neeleman, CEO of JetBlue Airways, on people + strategy = growth," *Academy of Management Executive* 18, no. 2: 139–143; Salter, C., 2004a. "And now the hard part," *Fast Company* 82. http://pf.fastcompany.com/magazine/82/jetblue.html (accessed October 1, 2004); Salter, C., 2004b. "Calling JetBlue," *Fast Company* 82. http://pf.fastcompany.com/magazine/82/jetblue_agents.html (accessed October 1, 2004).

Chapter 2

The Global and Cultural Contexts

"Verité en-deçà des Pyrénées, erreur au–delà"
(There are truths on this side of the Pyrenees which are falsehoods on the other)
—BLAISE PASCAL

After studying this chapter you will be able to:

■ Understand the role culture can play in leadership

■ Describe the three levels of culture

■ Discuss the models of national culture

■ Identify the impact of gender on leadership

■ Discuss the role diversity plays in leadership

Leadership is a social and an interpersonal process. As is the case with any such process, the impact of culture is undeniable. Different cultures define leadership differently and consider different types of leaders effective. A leader who is considered effective in Singapore might seem too authoritarian in Sweden. The charisma of an Egyptian political leader is likely to be lost on the French or the Germans. Additionally, gender and other cultural differences among groups impact how leaders behave and how their followers perceive them. Understanding leadership, therefore, requires an understanding of the cultural context in which it takes place.

DEFINITION AND LEVELS OF CULTURE

Culture gives each group its uniqueness and differentiates one group from the other. Our culture strongly influences us; it determines what we consider right and wrong and influences what and who we value, what we pay attention to, and how we behave. Culture affects values and beliefs and influences leadership and interpersonal styles. We learn about culture formally through various teachings and informally through observation (Hall, 1973).

Definition and Characteristics

Culture consists of the commonly held values within a group of people. It is a set of norms, customs, values, and assumptions that guides the behavior of a particular group of people. It is the lifestyle of a group and the collective programming of the group members. Culture is shared by members of a group. It has permanence and is passed down from one generation to another. Group members learn about their culture through their parents and family, schools, and other social institutions and consciously and unconsciously transfer it to the young and new members. Culture affects how people view the world and how they think and, therefore, shapes behavior. Although culture has some permanence, it is also dynamic and changes over time as members adapt to new events and their environment.

Culture affects how people view the world and how they think and, therefore, shapes behavior.

Levels of Culture

Culture exists at three levels (Figure 2-1). The first is national culture, defined as a set of values and beliefs shared by people within a nation. Second, in addition to an overall national culture, different ethnic and other cultural groups that live within each nation might share a culture. Gender differences, for example, fit into this second level of culture differences. Although these groups share national cultural values, they also develop their unique culture. Some nations, such as the United States, Canada, and Indonesia, include many such subcultures. Different cultural, ethnic, and religious groups are part of the overall culture of these nations, which leads to considerable cultural diversity. Diversity refers to the variety of human structures, beliefs systems, and strategies for adapting to situations that exist within different groups. It is typically used to refer to the variety in the second level of culture and includes such factors as race,

Figure 2-1   The Three Levels of Culture.

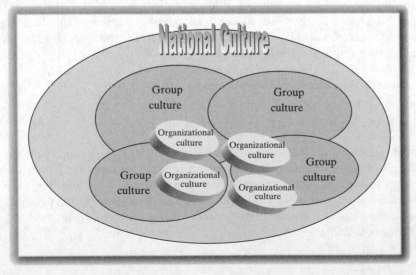

ethnicity, language, religion, or any characteristic that may differentiate one group from another and give it a unique identity. For example, as will be discussed in Chapter 6, believing in a savior contributes to the rise of charismatic leadership. Similarly, cultural differences based on gender influence our expectations of leaders and whom we consider an effective leader. In particular, widely held gender stereotypes affect our views of leadership and create significant differences in power and authority between men and women (Eagly and Carli, 2004). Many traditional male traits, such as aggression and independence, often are associated with leaders, but traditional female traits of submissiveness and cooperation are not.

The third level of culture is organizational culture—the set of values, norms, and beliefs shared by members of an organization. Given time, all organizations develop a unique culture or character whereby employees share common values and beliefs about work-related issues. These organizational values often include deeply held beliefs about leadership (Schein, 2004). In many cases, leaders, and particularly founders, are instrumental in creating and encouraging the culture. For example, the culture at Blackstone, one of the world's most prestigious venture capital organizations, is high pressure and performance oriented and highly competitive. Mark Callogly, who ran one of the company's divisions, talking about employees, states, "Each time they suit up, they expect to win. You need to bring your A-game everyday. It's not summer camp" (Schwartz, 2007). Similarly, the example of leadership team at the *New York Times* shows the critical role of organizational culture (McGregor, 2005a). Linda Greenhouse, one of the paper's senior reporters, states, "There is an endemic cultural issue at the *Times* . . . which is a top-down hierarchical structure" (Bennis, 2003). Other editors at the *Times* were reputed to focus relentlessly on the job at the expense of their employees' needs and personal life. Abe Rosenthal, who stepped in after the leadership team resigned in 2003, told one reporter, "If you are married, you don't belong in journalism!" (Bennis, 2003). Still other accounts of the culture at the *Times* indicate that leaders played favorites rather than focusing on performance (Cotts, 2003).

Another very different organizational culture that focuses on employee concerns and needs is that of the Atlanta-based consulting firm North Highland, which employs 250. The company established a "no-fly zone" when CEO David Peterson grew so tired of being constantly on the road and missing out on his family life that he created a company to serve local clients (Canabou, 2001). Peterson considers 50 miles to be the maximum distance people should have to travel for work. His company allows employees to balance their work life and home life and provides its clients with consultants who are part of their community. Richard Tuck, cofounder and CEO of Lander International, a company based in El Cerrito, California, similarly encourages his employees to spend less time at work (Fromartz, 1998). When Jon Westberg, the company's executive recruiter, hit a performance slump and sought Tuck's advice, Tuck suggested that "maybe he was spending too much time at work that he needed to devote more time to his art" (Fromartz, 1998: 125). Tuck wants his employees to have outside hobbies and commitments. He hates rules. As a result, the company's culture is loose, with an emphasis on "anything goes." Office manager Helen Winters notes, "I kept waiting for policies to be firmed up, but he just wouldn't do it" (126). Compare Lander's culture with that of the *New York Times* or the culture of Atlantic Group Furniture Procurement and Project Management, Inc., an office-furniture distributor in New York City. The company president, Roger Abramson, is obsessed with time and productivity (Fenn, 1998). He has announced, "If you are not producing revenue, do not call me during the day" (61). In Atlantic's fast-paced culture, only the highly competitive survive. The focus is on pay for performance. These different organizational cultures have different models of leadership effectiveness. At North Highland, work-life balance is key to effectiveness; at Lander's, the leader is supportive and almost spiritual; at Blackstone and Atlantic, much like the *New York Times*, the leader pushes for performance and outcomes.

Because national culture addresses many different aspects of life, it exerts a strong and pervasive influence on people's behavior in everyday activities and in organizations. The influence of organizational culture is, generally, limited to work-related values and behaviors. However, national culture strongly influences organizational culture. French companies, for instance, share some characteristics that make them different from companies in other countries. Compared with their Swedish counterparts, French companies are more hierarchical and status oriented.

All three levels of culture shape our views and expectations of our leaders. Whereas people in the United States do not expect leaders to be failure proof, in many other cultures, leaders' admission of mistakes would be intolerable and a deadly blow to their authority and ability to lead. For example, many U.S. presidents—most recently President Clinton—when faced with no other option, recognized their mistakes openly and professed to have learned from them. Many in the United States expected President Bush to admit mistakes in the war against Iraq, although no apologies have been forthcoming. Such admissions rarely happen in other countries, and, if they do, they are interpreted as signs of weakness. Former President Vincente Fox of Mexico steadfastly refused to admit any error or to change course in the handling of his country's economy. He categorically stated, "I believe there are no mistakes" (Government in Mexico, 2001: 35). When, in 1998, Indonesian president Suharto apparently admitted mistakes that contributed to his country's economic crisis, he was seen as weak. Indonesians did not forgive him, and he eventually resigned.

Each country and region in the world develops a particular organizational and management style based largely on its national culture. This style is called the *national organizational heritage* (Bartlett and Ghoshal, 1989, 1992). Although differences distinguish one organization from another and one manager from another, research indicates that national heritage is noticeable and distinct.

MODELS OF NATIONAL CULTURE

Because many researchers and practitioners believe that understanding and handling cultural differences effectively are key to organizational effectiveness in increasingly global organizations (e.g., Dupriez and Simmons, 2000), they have developed several models for understanding national cultures. This section reviews four models with direct application to organizations and understanding leadership.

Hall's High-Context and Low-Context Cultural Framework

One of the simplest models for understanding culture, Edward Hall's model, divides communication styles within cultures into two groups: high context and low context (Hall, 1976). In Hall's model, context refers to the environment and the information that provide the background for interaction and communication. Leaders from high-context cultures rely heavily on the context, including nonverbal cues and situational factors, to communicate with others and understand the world around them. They use personal relationships to establish communication. Leaders from low-context cultures focus on explicit, specific verbal and written messages to understand people and situations (Munter, 1993).

For example, Japan, Saudi Arabia, Greece, Italy, Vietnam, Korea, and China are all high-context cultures, where subtle body posture, tone of voice, detailed rituals, and a person's title and status convey strong messages that determine behavior (Figure 2-2). Communication does not always need to be explicit and specific. Trust is viewed as more important than written communication or legal contracts. In low-context cultures, such as Germany, Scandinavia, Switzerland, the United States, Great Britain, and Canada, people pay attention to the verbal message. What is said or written is more important than nonverbal messages or the situation. People are, therefore, specific and clear in their communication with others.

> **Leaders from high-context cultures rely heavily on the context, including nonverbal cues and situational factors, to communicate with others and understand the world around them. They use personal relationships to establish communication. Leaders from low-context cultures focus on explicit, specific verbal and written messages to understand people and situations.**

The difference between high and low context can explain many cross-cultural communication problems that leaders face when they interact with those of a culture different from their own. The low-context European and North American leaders might get frustrated working with followers from high-context Asian or Middle Eastern cultures because whereas low-context leaders focus on specific instructions, the high-context followers aim at developing relationships. Similarly, high-context leaders might be offended by their low-context followers' directness, which they can interpret as rudeness and lack of respect.

Figure 2-2   High- and Low-Context Cultures.

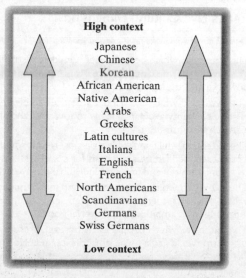

High context
Japanese
Chinese
Korean
African American
Native American
Arabs
Greeks
Latin cultures
Italians
English
French
North Americans
Scandinavians
Germans
Swiss Germans
Low context

Hofstede's Five Cultural Dimensions

Researcher Geert Hofstede developed one of the best-known classifications of culture, known as Hofstede's dimensions (Hofstede, 1992, 1997, 2001). He originally conducted more than 100,000 surveys of IBM employees in 40 countries, supplemented by another series of surveys that led to the development of Confucian dynamism (Hofstede, 1996). He used the results to develop five basic cultural dimensions along which cultures differ: power distance, uncertainty avoidance, individualism, masculinity, and time orientation (Table 2-1). According to Hofstede, the combination of these five dimensions lends each national culture its distinctiveness and unique character.

Hofstede developed five basic cultural dimensions along which cultures differ: power distance, uncertainty avoidance, individualism, masculinity, and time orientation. The combination of these five dimensions lends each national culture its distinctiveness and unique character.

For example, when compared with 40 other nations, the United States is below average on power distance and uncertainty avoidance, highest in individualism (closely followed by Australia), and above average on masculinity and has a moderate to short-term time orientation. These scores indicate that the United States is a somewhat egalitarian culture in which uncertainty and ambiguity are well tolerated; a high value is placed on individual achievements, assertiveness, performance, and independence; sex roles are relatively well defined; and organizations look for quick results with a focus on the present. Japan, on the other hand, tends to be higher than the United States in power distance, masculinity (one of the highest scores), and uncertainty avoidance but considerably lower in individualism, with a long-term orientation. These rankings are consistent with the popular image of Japan as a country in which social structures, such as family and organizations are important, their power and obedience to them tend to be absolute, risk and uncertainty are averted, gender roles are highly differentiated, and high value is placed on achievement.

Table 2-1   Hofstede's Five Cultural Dimensions.

Power distance	The extent to which people accept unequal distribution of power. In higher power-distance cultures, there is a wider gap between the powerful and the powerless.
Uncertainty avoidance	The extent to which the culture tolerates ambiguity and uncertainty. High uncertainty avoidance leads to low tolerance for uncertainty and a search for absolute truths.
Individualism	The extent to which individuals or closely-knit social structure, such as the extended family, is the basis for social systems. Individualism leads to reliance on self and focus on individual achievement.
Masculinity	The extent to which assertiveness and independence from others is valued. High masculinity leads to high sex-role differentiation, focus on independence, ambition, and material goods.
Time orientation	The extent to which people focus on past, present, or future. Present orientation leads to a focus on short-term performance.

Harry Triandis, a cross-cultural psychologist, expanded on some of Hofstede's cultural dimensions by introducing the concepts of tight and loose cultures and vertical and horizontal cultures. Triandis (2004) suggests that uncertainty avoidance can be better understood by further classifying cultures into either tight or loose categories. In tight cultures, such as Japan, members follow rules, norms, and standards closely. Behaviors are, therefore, closely regulated; those who do not abide by the rules are criticized, isolated, or even ostracized, depending on the severity of the offense. Loose cultures, such as Thailand, show much tolerance for behaviors that are considered acceptable, and although rules exist, violating them is often overlooked. Triandis (2004) places the United States in the moderate tight–loose category and suggests that the U.S. culture has moved toward becoming looser and more tolerant over the past 50 years.

Triandis further refined the concept of individualism/collectivism by arguing that there are different types of collectivist and individualist cultures (1995). He proposes that by adding the concept of vertical and horizontal, we can gain a much richer understanding of cultural values (Table 2-2). Vertical cultures focus on hierarchy; horizontal cultures emphasize equality (Triandis et al., 2001). For example, although Sweden and the United States are both individualist cultures, the Swedes are horizontal individualists (HV) and see individuals as unique but equal to others. In the United States, which is more vertical individualist (VI), the individual is viewed not only as unique, but also superior to others. Similarly, in a horizontal collectivistic (HC) culture, such as Israel, all members of the group are seen as equal. In vertical collectivistic cultures (VC) such as Japan and Korea, authority is important and individuals must sacrifice themselves for the good of the group. The horizontal–vertical dimension, because it affects views of hierarchy and equality, is likely to impact leadership.

Table 2-2   Vertical and Horizontal Dimensions of Individualism and Collectivism.

	Vertical (Emphasis on Hierarchy)	Horizontal (Emphasis on Equality)
Individualistic	Focus on the individual where each person is considered unique and superior to others, often based on accomplishments and performance, or material wealth. Example: U.S.A.	Although the focus is on each individual being unique, individuals are considered equal to others without a strong hierarchy. Example: Sweden
Collectivistic	Strong group feeling with clear rank and status differentiation among group members; members feel obligation to obey authority and sacrifice self for good of the group if needed. Example: Japan	All group members are considered equal; the group has little hierarchy and there is strong focus on democratic and egalitarian processes. Example: Israel

Source: Based on Triandis et al., 2001.

Hofstede's cultural values model along with the concepts proposed by Triandis provide a strong basis for explaining cultural differences. The model continues to be used as the basis for research on cross-cultural differences (e.g., Yan and Hunt, 2005) as well as for training leaders to work across cultures. Other researchers have provided additional means of understanding culture.

Trompenaars's Dimensions of Culture

Fons Trompenaars and his colleagues provide a complex model that helps leaders understand national culture and its effect on organizational and corporate cultures (Trompenaars and Hampden-Turner, 2001; Trompenaars and Woolliams, 2003). They developed a model initially based on 15,000 people surveyed in organizations in 47 cultures and further tested it by adding data from more than 60,000 people. The model suggests that although understanding national culture requires many different dimensions, cross-cultural organizational cultures can be classified more efficiently based on two dimensions (Trompenaars, 1994): egalitarian-hierarchical and orientation to the person or the task. When combined, they yield four general cross-cultural organizational cultures: incubator, guided missile, family, and Eiffel Tower (Figure 2-3). The four general types combine national and organizational cultures. The leader's role in each type differs, as do methods of employee motivation and evaluation.

Incubator cultures are egalitarian and focus on taking care of individual needs. Examples of incubator cultures can be found in many start-up, high-technology firms in the United States and Great Britain (Trompenaars, 1994: 173). In these typically individualist cultures, professionals are given considerable latitude to do their jobs. Leaders in such organizations emerge from the group rather than being assigned. Therefore, leadership is based on competence and expertise, and the leader's responsibility is to provide resources, manage conflict, and remove obstacles.

Figure 2-3   Trompenaars' Cross-Cultural Organizational Cultures.

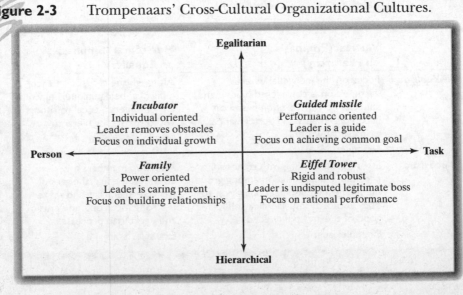

The *guided missile* is also an egalitarian culture, but the focus is on task completion rather than individual needs. As a result, the organizational culture is impersonal and, as indicated by its name, directed toward accomplishing the job. Trompenaars uses the U.S. National Aeronautics and Space Administration (NASA) as an example of the guided missile. In NASA and other guided-missile organizations, leadership is based on expertise and follower participation is expected. People work in teams of professionals who have equal status, with performance being the primary criterion for effectiveness.

The *family* and *Eiffel Tower* cultures both are hierarchical. Whereas the Eiffel Tower is focused on the task, the family takes care of individuals. As its name indicates, the family culture functions like a traditional family. The leader's role is that of a powerful father figure, who is responsible for the welfare of all members. On the one hand, Trompenaars suggests that family organizational cultures are found in Greece, Italy, Singapore, South Korea, and Japan. On the other hand, the Eiffel Tower is hierarchical and task focused. Consistent with the name—the Eiffel Tower—many French organizations have an Eiffel Tower culture, characterized by a steep, stable, and rigid organization. The focus is on performance through order and obedience of legal and legitimate authority. The leader is the undisputed head of the organization and has full responsibility for all that occurs.

Trompenaars' added dimensions and focus on culture in organizations provides a rich model for understanding culture. The most recent approach to explaining cultural differences will be presented next.

Global Leadership and Organizational Behavior Effectiveness Research

One of the most exciting and extensive research projects about cross-cultural differences and leadership was conducted by a group of researchers in 62 countries (House et al., 2004). Despite recent debates about the methodology used by researchers of Global Leadership and Organizational Behavior Effectiveness research (GLOBE) (Graen, 2006; House et al., 2006), the model is comprehensive and highly useful in understanding leadership and culture. GLOBE examines culture using nine dimensions, predicting their impact on leadership and organizational processes (House et al., 2002; Table 2-3) Although some of the dimensions proposed by the GLOBE researchers are similar to those presented by Hofstede and Trompenaars and his colleagues, others are unique and refine our understanding of culture. As with previous research, GLOBE assumes that culture affects what leaders do and how organizations are structured and managed. Based on their findings, the United States is among the highest in assertiveness and performance orientation and falls in the middle in all the other dimensions (Javidan and House, 2001). Spaniards and Germans are the most assertive and direct, while Germans also avoid uncertainty and are the lowest in valuing generosity and caring. Austrians and the Swiss, like Germans, require clear communication and will rely on rules and procedures to determine their behaviors. Russians and Italians invest the least in the future and are least likely to focus on performance and excellence. Furthermore, like the Greeks, Russians do not require much structure and can tolerate uncertainty to a greater extent than some Germanic Europeans. While differing in gender egalitarianism, the Swedes and Japanese are among the least assertive and direct. In countries with high power distance, such as

Table 2-3   Globe Dimensions.

Dimension	Description	Country Rankings
Power distance	The degree to which power is distributed equally	High—Russia, Spain, Thailand; Moderate—England, U.S.A., Brazil; Low—Denmark, Israel, Costa Rica
Uncertainty avoidance	The extent to which a culture relies on social norms and rules to reduce unpredictability (high score indicates high tolerance for uncertainty)	High—Denmark, Germany, Sweden; Moderate—Israel, U.S.A., Mexico; Low—Russia, Greece, Venezuela
Humane orientation	The degree to which a culture values fairness, generosity, caring and kindness	High—Indonesia, Egypt, Philippines; Moderate—Hong Kong, Sweden, U.S.A.; Low—Germany, Singapore, France
Collectivism I (institutional)	The degree to which a culture values and practices collective action and collective distribution of resources	High—Denmark, Singapore, Japan; Moderate—U.S., Egypt, Indonesia; Low—Greece, Germany, Italy
Collectivism II (in-group)	The degree to which individuals express pride and cohesion in their family or organizations	High—Egypt, China, Iran; Moderate—Japan, Israel, Italy; Low—Denmark, Finland, Sweden
Assertiveness	The degree to which individuals are assertive, direct and confrontational	High—U.S.A., Germany; Moderate—France, Philippines; Low—Sweden, Japan, Kuwait
Gender egalitarianism	The extent of gender differentiation (high score indicates more differentiation)	High—South Korea, Egypt, India; Moderate—Italy, The Netherlands; Low—Sweden, Poland
Future orientation	The extent to which a culture invests in the future rather than in the present or past	High—Denmark, Singapore; Moderate—Australia, India; Low—Russia, Italy
Performance orientation	The degree to which a culture values and encourages performance and excellence	High—U.S.A., Taiwan, Singapore; Moderate—Sweden, England, Japan; Low—Russia, Venezuela, Italy

Sources: Based on House et al., 2004, 2002; Javidan & House, 2001.

GLOBE assumes that culture affects what leaders do and how organizations are structured and managed. Based on their findings, the United States is among the highest in assertiveness and performance orientation and falls in the middle in all the other dimensions.

Thailand and Russia, communication is often directed one way, from the leader to followers, with little expectation of feedback. Finally, in cultures that value kindness and generosity, such as the Philippines or Egypt, leaders are likely to avoid conflict and act in a caring but paternalistic manner (Javidan and House, 2001).

GLOBE identifies several categories of leader behavior that are either universally desirable, undesirable, or whose desirability is contingent on the culture (House et al., 2004). For example, charismatic/value-based leadership is generally desirable across most cultures. Similarly, team-based leadership is believed to contribute to outstanding leadership in many cultures. Although participative leadership is seen, generally, as positive, its effectiveness depends on the culture. Autonomous leaders are desirable in some cultures but not in all, and being self-protective is seen as impeding effective leadership in most cultures. Even some behaviors that are somewhat universal reflect cultural differences. For example, Americans and the British highly value charisma whereas Middle Easterners place less importance on this behavior from their leader. Nordic cultures are less favorable toward self-protective leadership behaviors whereas Southern Asians accept it more readily (House et al., 2004).

The models of culture presented in this section provide different ways of understanding national and organizational culture. Each model is not only useful but can also be misapplied if used to stereotype national or organizational cultures. Whereas Hall and Hofstede focus primarily on national culture, Trompenaars provides a model that combines national and organizational cultural and has a strong practitioner focus. GLOBE has one of the most comprehensive models available with a strong focus on leadership characteristics across cultures. All four models are used throughout the book to provide a cross-cultural perspective on leadership.

GROUP CULTURE: GENDER AND DIVERSITY

Whereas national culture impacts us at a macro level, another strong cultural influence on individual behavior is group culture, which may consist of a number of primary factors such as gender, ethnicity, and age and other secondary factors such as income, education, and membership in various groups (Figure 2-4). The primary

Applying What You Learn
Using Culture to Be Effective

Culture at all levels can have a powerful impact on both leaders and followers. The following are some things to keep in mind to manage culture effectively:

- Be aware and conscious of your own culture and its various components. What are your values? How important are they to you? What are the conflicts you experience?

- Understand the culture of your organization. Is cooperation or competition valued? How formal is the environment? How much is performance valued? How about citizenship? What is rewarded?

- Be clear about any areas of agreement and disagreement between your culture and value system and that of your organization.

- Build on the agreements; they are likely to provide you with opportunities to shine. For example, if you value competition and high performance and so does the organization, you are likely to feel right at home.

- Carefully evaluate the disagreements. For example, you value competition and individual achievements, whereas the organization is highly team oriented. Can you adapt? Can you change the organization? A high degree of ongoing conflict among primary values is likely to lead to frustration and dissatisfaction.

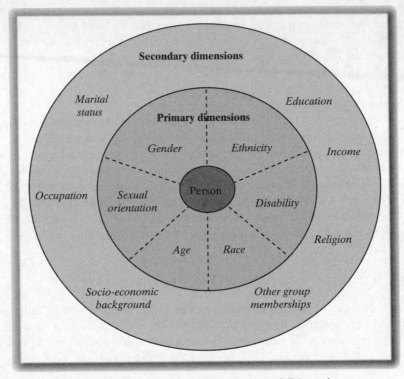

Figure 2-4   Dimensions of Group Cultures and Diversity.

dimensions of diversity are the visible and stable aspects of a person. Factors that are considered secondary are more dynamic. Group culture can affect people in two important ways. First, people's leadership style may vary based on their group membership, as some evidence regarding gender differences, for example, suggests. Second, membership in those groups impacts how others view the person and therefore how they may react to leadership from that person. We will consider gender differences in leadership and review the causes and solutions to unequal treatment based on group membership.

Gender and Leadership

Leaders such as Francis Hesselbein, chief executive of the Girl Scouts, Nancy Bador, executive director of Ford Motor Company, and Barbara Grogan, founder and president of Western Industrial Contractors, use an inclusive management style that they consider a female style of leadership. They shun the hierarchical structures for flat webs in which they are at the center rather than at the top. This structure, and their position within it, allows them to be accessible and informed. Whereas top-down and bottom-up information in a traditional hierarchy is filtered and altered as it travels, leaders at the center of the web gain direct access to all others in the organization and their employees have access to them. As a result, the web structure prevents managers from feeling isolated and out of touch with the needs of their subordinates and their organization. Meg Whitman, CEO of eBay and rated by *Fortune* as one of the most powerful woman in business in 2005, is known for her unconventional, noncommand and control use of power. She believes that having power means that you must be willing to not have any (Sellers, 2004). Gerry Laybourne, chairman and CEO of Oxygen Media, the executive who built the top-rated children's television network Nickelodeon while she was at Viacom, considers competition to be "nonfemale." When she found out that *Fortune* magazine was ranking women in business, she declared, "That's a nonfemale thing to do. Ranking is the opposite of what women are all about" (Sellers, 1998: 80). She focuses on mentoring other women and helping them balance family and work (Weiss, 2006).

Many other successful female business leaders, however, do not see their leadership styles as drastically different from that of their male counterparts. Cherri Musser, chief information officer at General Motors, recommends, "You don't focus on being female—you focus on getting the job done. If you draw too much attention to your gender, you're not a member of the team" (Overholt, 2001: 66). Darla Moore, president of investment company Rainwater, Inc., and the first woman to have a business school named after her, argues that women's worse sin is to think, "'You should be a nice girl. You ought to fit in. You should find a female mentor.' What a colossal waste of time" (Sellers, 1998: 92). She is known for her tough approach and likes to remind women that they should not take attacks personally and that they can never recover from crying in a public forum (Darla Moore's full court press, 2000).

Whether women and men lead differently or not, there are differences between them in terms of the presence and power each group has in organizations around the world.

Current State

There is no question that women in the United States, and in most other countries, have unequal access to power and that they are poorly represented in the higher levels of business, nonprofit, and governmental organizations. Although in the United States, women fill around 40 to 50 percent of supervisory and managerial jobs, they are not as well represented in top levels of organizations. Women hold only 15.6 percent of corporate officer positions (Catalyst, 2007) and only 1.5 percent of CEO positions (Paton, 2006). As of 2007, there are two female CEOs in the Fortune 100 in the United States (one is featured in the Leadership in Action case at the end of this chapter). It is estimated that if the current trends continue, by 2010 only 4.9 percent of top leadership positions will be held by women (Paton, 2006) and maybe 6 percent by 2016 (Helfat, Harris, and Wolfson, 2006). The salary gap between men and women is further evidence of the challenges women face. The compensation package of the highest-paid female executive in the United States in 2006 (Safra Catz of Oracle with $26.1 million) was 36 percent of the salary of the highest-paid male executive (Eugene Isenberg of Nabors Industries with $71.4 million). All of the ten highest-paid executives in United States in 2006 are men; their salaries are two to three times the salary of the ten top-earning women executives (Seid, 2006). The wage gap is less pronounced at lower-level managerial and other jobs, around 70 percent by most accounts; however, it is still indicative of the challenges women face.

Even though in some cases, state, local, and national governments have many female and minority leaders, the situation there is not considerably better. In 2007, out of 435 members of the U.S. House of Representatives, 70 are female, 42 are Black, 24 Hispanic, 6 Asian, and only one Native American (U.S. House of Representatives, 2007). In the U.S. Senate, only sixteen out of one hundred senators are female; one is Black; one is Asian; and three are Hispanic (U.S. Senate Biographical Directory, 2007). Only five out of the twenty-one members of the President Bush's cabinet are women (President Bush's cabinet, 2007) with twenty women ever having held ministerial positions in the United States, while the United States is yet to elect a female head-of-state. Women in Scandinavian countries have achieved higher-level positions, but the percentage of women in power is roughly the same and generally not substantially better in most other Western nations (IWDC, 2007).

The trend is similar in other areas such as education, where although women make up a large majority of teachers and students of educational leadership, the actual leadership is predominantly and consistently male. Research over an 80-year period indicates that the number of women serving in superintendent positions has decreased since 1910 (9.38 percent) with only 4.6 percent in 1990 (Dana and Bourisaw, 2006). An even more disturbing fact is that even when women are in leadership positions, they have less decision-making power, less authority, and less access to the highly responsible and challenging assignments than their male counterparts (Smith, 2002).

Causes of Gender Differences in Leadership

What factors explain the lesser roles women play in the leadership of organizations? Researchers have proposed several reasons to explain those differences (for a review see Eagly and Carli, 2004; Table 2-4).

Gender Differences in Style and Effectiveness

Researchers have identified gender differences in several areas related to leadership such as communication styles (e.g., Tannen, 1993) and negotiation styles and effectiveness

Table 2-4 Potential Cause of Poor Representation of Women in Leadership.

- Gender differences in leadership style
- Women have less experience in organizations
- Women are less committed to their work and career
- Women quit their jobs more often
- Women are less educated
- Blatant and subtle discrimination
- Persistent gender stereotypes
- Glass ceiling
- Cultural factors

(e.g., Bowles and McGinn, 2005). There is also much anecdotal evidence, such as those presented earlier in this chapter, than men and women differ in their leadership and management styles. We intuitively believe that there are clear gender differences in leadership. It, however, is not clear whether these differences benefit or disadvantage female leaders.

Researchers have found some, although not overwhelming, gender differences in leadership. Eagly and Johnson's meta analysis (1990) found that women tend to show more people-oriented and democratic styles whereas men were more likely to be task focused and autocratic. The results, however, were more pronounced in laboratory rather than organizational settings. Interestingly, the most consistent gender difference in leadership relates to change- and future-oriented leadership style, often referred to as *transformational leadership* (we discuss this topic in detail in Chapter 6). Transformational leadership focuses on establishing an emotional connection with followers and inspiring them toward implementing change. A review by Eagly and her colleagues (2003) suggests that female leaders are more transformational, show more individualized attention to their followers, and are more supportive of them than male leaders.

Given the presence of some gender differences, the question is: Do these differences handicap women, preventing them from being effective and reaching leadership positions, thus providing an explanation for the presence of fewer female leaders? Much of the focus of current leadership practice is on styles that are more stereotypically female rather than male. Management guru Tom Peters believes that the success of the new economy depends on the collaborative style that women leaders use instead of the command and control style that male leaders have traditionally used (Reingold, 2003). Among practitioners, characteristics typically associated with the female leadership style are increasingly considered necessary regardless of gender (M. Useem, 2001). The research on transformational leadership further supports the notion that transformational leadership is an effective style. Based on these assertions and research results, one would expect that organizations would seek more female leaders, that more women would be in leadership positions, and that they would be more effective than their male counterparts. That not being the case, gender differences in leadership style do not provide a clear explanation for the lesser role women play in the leadership of organizations.

Women Are Not Well-Prepared and Not as Committed as Men

Another explanation for the differential presence and role of women in leadership is that women are generally not as well prepared as men to take on leadership roles because of their lower education. They have less work experience and are less interested in investing their time and resources in reaching top levels of organizations than men. Even though one can always find anecdotal evidence of women being unprepared for and less interested in leadership, demographic information and research do not fully support this explanation. First, women have been fully engaged in organizations for over 40 years. They have occupied close to 50 percent of supervisory and managerial ranks for many years now. There are many fully qualified women ready and able to move up the ranks of our organizations. Second, women currently make up 58 percent of the undergraduate college population (Zolli, 2007) and based on the data from the 2000 U.S. Census, they are earning 45 percent of advanced degrees and

51 percent of MBAs. Women are committed to education and are bypassing men in overall numbers.

Another factor that is often mentioned is that working mothers particularly are not able to devote as much time to their careers and are more likely to quit their jobs, thereby hindering their progress. Although there have been some changes over the past few years, women still continue to carry most of the burden for child-care and household work (Bianchi, 2000), and research indicates that mothers are less employed than other women whereas fathers work more than other men (Kaufman and Uhlenberg, 2000). There, however, is no clear evidence that parenthood reduces women's commitment to their work and career or that women do not seek leadership positions because they worry about the demands of such positions (Eagly and Carli, 2004). Recent research further indicates that although many professional women do take a break from work when they start a family, over 90 percent of them try to get back in after about two years (Hewlett, 2007), further contradicting the idea that women have less commitment to their careers than men. Some women executives have even suggested that motherhood provides women with skills that can be helpful in taking on organizational leadership roles (Grzelakowski, 2005). Gerry Laybourne, founder of Oxygen states, "You learn about customer service from your 2-year-old (they are more demanding than any customer can be). You also learn patience, management skills, diversionary tactics, and 5-year planning" (*Startup Nation*, 2005).

Discrimination

The final explanation for fewer female leaders is discrimination. Discrimination would suggest that women, and members of other nondominant groups, are placed at a disadvantage not based on their abilities or actions, but based on other non–job-related factors. Women and minorities face a glass ceiling—invisible barriers and obstacles that prevent them from moving to the highest levels of organizations (Arfken, Bellar, and Helms, 2004). Some have suggested that men are fast-tracked to leadership position through a "glass elevator" (Maune, 1999), and a recent review suggests the presence of a "glass cliff," whereby successful women are appointed to precarious leadership positions with little chance of success thereby exposing them to yet another form of discrimination (Ryan and Haslam, 2007). The common theme in all these situations is the presence of invisible barriers that discriminate against women and minorities and prevent them from achieving their full potential.

Discrimination would suggest that women, and members of other nondominant groups, are placed at a disadvantage not based on their abilities or actions, but based on other non–job-related factors.

Persistent Stereotypes

Cases from organizations and academic research consistently suggest that women are caught in the double bind of having to fulfill two contradictory roles and expectations: those of being a woman and those of being a leader (Eagly and Karau, 2002). In many traditional settings, being a leader requires forceful behaviors that are more masculine (e.g., being proactive and decisive) than feminine (being kind and not appearing too competent). Women who are more masculine, however, are often not liked and not considered effective (Powell, Butterfield, and Parent, 2002). Men particularly expect women to act in ways that are stereotypically feminine and evaluate them poorly when they show the more masculine characteristics typically associated with leadership. In some cases, evidence suggests that women do not support other women in getting leadership positions (Dana and Barisaw, 2006). Further, women who actively seek leadership and show a desire to direct others are not well accepted (Carli, 1999). These stereotypes and contradictory expectations limit the range of behaviors women are "allowed" to use when leading others, further hampering their ability to be effective. As we discussed in Chapter 1, becoming an effective leader requires considerable practice and experimentation. If they want to be easily accepted, women leaders are restricted to a set of feminine behaviors characterized by interpersonal warmth as their primary, if not only, means of influence (Carli, 2001). Because of existing stereotypes, women, and in many cases minorities, are not able to fully practice to perfect their craft.

Additionally, general stereotypes of women and minorities not being as competent or able to handle challenging leadership situations as men still persist, making blatant or subtle discrimination a continuing problem. Sexual harassment, which is considered workplace discrimination, is one instance. For example, a survey done in New Zealand suggested that one in three women reported being sexually harassed (New Zealand Human Rights Commission, 2007). According to the U.S. Equal Employment Opportunity Commission 2006 report, of the 12,000 sexual harassment complaints filed in 2005, only 155 were from males with a total of $48.8 million in claims (EEOC, 2006). Surveys indicate that women are almost three times as likely as men to report that they are victims of discrimination (Wilson, 2006). Other more subtle forms include the fact that although they are in mid-management positions, women and minorities are often not mentored by the right people at the right time, a factor that is critical to success in any organization. Furthermore, women and minorities are often not exposed to the type of positions or experiences that are essential to achieving high-level leadership. For example, women and minorities may not be encouraged to take on international assignments or kept in staff rather than line positions and therefore may lack essential operational experience. Finally, subtle social and organizational culture factors, such as going to lunch with the "right" group, playing sports, being members of certain clubs, and exclusion from informal socializing and the "good old boys" network, can contribute to the lack of proportional representation of women and minorities in leadership ranks.

Real or perceived gender differences and continued used of stereotypes and discrimination all combine to prevent women from achieving their potential in organizations. Much research has been devoted to changing these situations and organizations implement a variety of programs to assure that women and minorities are well represented in their leadership ranks.

Solutions

More often than not, obstacles that women face are not immediately apparent, often not illegal, and are unwritten and unofficial policy. They are, therefore, difficult to identify and even more difficult to change. Although there are some differences, all members of nondominant groups face similar challenges. Some social factors, such as more even distribution of work at home and increased higher education, will provide a push in the right direction. The changing views of leadership and the need for leaders with strong interpersonal skills, a trait that is more *stereotypically feminine* than masculine, will also help in making leadership in organizations more accessible to women.

From an organizational point of view, the fundamental solution to addressing the challenges that women and minorities face is for organizations and their leaders to create, value, and maintain a multicultural organization where discrimination is not tolerated. Multiculturalism aims at inclusiveness, social justice, affirmation, mutual respect, and harmony in a pluralistic world (Fowers and Davidov, 2006). Rather than being viewed as an issue of quotas and percentages, diversity and multiculturalism refer to building a culture of openness and inclusiveness. The benefits of building a multicultural organization go beyond women and other minority groups; they extend to all employees, including those from another national culture. A Gallup survey suggests that organizations where diversity is valued have the most satisfied employees and better retention (Wilson, 2006).

Leadership is at the heart of building a multicultural organization (Figure 2-5). Ed Zander, CEO of Motorola, states, "Business and diversity are one and the same. Business means diversity, and diversity means business" (Winters, 2007: 7). Zander focuses on the three themes of ethics, quality, and diversity in all his meetings. Similarly, Tim Solso of Cummins addresses diversity all the time (Winters, 2007). The Gallup survey linking diversity to satisfaction further indicates that organizational leaders' commitment to diversity is linked to overall employee satisfaction (Wilson, 2006). Leaders influence the culture and organizational processes that, to a great extent, determine how decisions are made, how others behave, and what is accepted and tolerated and what is not. The leader is not only a powerful decision maker, but also exercises considerable influence through formal and informal communication, role modeling, and other powerful means. The message the leader sends through words and actions about the role of women and minorities and the importance of multiculturalism in an organization is one of the most important factors (for a discussion on the influence process used by top leaders, see Chapter 7).

> **Multiculturalism aims at inclusiveness, social justice, affirmation, mutual respect, and harmony in a pluralistic world. The benefits of building a multicultural organization go beyond women and other minority groups; they extend to all those who are different, including those from another national culture.**

Figure 2-5   Factor in Becoming a Multicultural Organization.

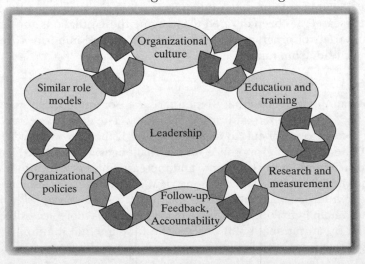

Changing the culture of an organization to address discriminatory practices, behaviors, and symbols is another powerful tool. Changing culture is one of the most difficult and lengthy processes any organization can undertake. Without a cultural change toward addressing informal discriminatory practices and attitudes, however, other improvements are not likely to be as effective. The presence of diverse role models throughout an organization is another part of the solution to providing leadership opportunities for women and minorities. By having diverse people in leadership positions, an organization "walks the talk" and can demonstrate its commitment to diversity. Toyota U.S.A. has a "diversity champion" program it started in the late 1990s. Outstanding employees with leadership skills are nominated by their colleagues to receive intensive diversity management training and return to their work units with "champion" badge and a mission to help implement changes to make the workplace more inclusive and emphasize commonalities (Wiscombe, 2007a).

Training and education can help people become aware of their biases, understand their own and others' cultural point of view, and better accept differences. When the consulting firm of Bain & Company transfers its consultants from one part of the world to another, it not only provides them with information about living in the new country, but also arms them with much cultural knowledge specific to the country to allow them to function more effectively (Holland, 2007). Other companies such as Procter & Gamble (P&G) value and encourage the development of cultural knowledge in their employees and leaders. Because their employees are as likely to work with someone from their own culture as with someone from a different culture, P&G immerses its employees in international assignments (Schoeff, 2007).

Leading Change   Lehman Bros Attracts Talent

One of the obstacles that many professionals face is not knowing how to take time off to pursue other interests or start a family and still be able to return to their careers after a short break. In some cases, organizations have cultures that consider seeking balance between life and work as a sign of disloyalty or weakness. Lehman Bros, a prestigious financial management firm well-known for its demanding work schedule, is setting a new course by implementing a program it calls "Encore." The goal is to retain and attract top talent, particularly women. A study commissioned in 2005 by Lehman found that 37 percent of its female and 24 percent of its male professional employees take a career break because their demanding and inflexible schedules do not provide them with any other option (Sellers, 2007). These professionals have a hard time getting back in. Encore addresses this problem by smoothing the way for mid-level executives to go "off-ramp" and get back "on-ramp."

Lehman's president and chief operating officer, Joe Gregory, asked Anne Erni to become the company's first chief diversity officer with a mandate,

(Continued)

Leading Change   (*Continued*)

among other things, to find, retain, and recruit women to senior leadership in the company (Marquez, 2007a).

Erni states that the company's CEO "intuitively understood that women approach their careers in a nonlinear way" (Marquez, 2007a). With Gregory's full support, Erni set out to change policies to address the needs of current employees and bring back professionals who had left. In addition to the typical flexible work schedules, options for telecommuting, reduced work hours, and job-sharing, the Lehman Encore program takes applications from both men and women (7 of this year's 50 applicants were men; Sellers, 2007) and allows current and returning professional to work fewer hours in professional capacities, for less salary and lesser titles, but with more balance. The program also provides recruiting event, opportunities for meetings with company's high-level executives, workshops, and extensive networking events. The networking program called "Women Initiative Leading Lehman" (WILL) started in 2002 with 1200 Lehman female employees and many of its top executives in attendance (Marquez, 2007b). It focuses on recruiting, networking, and personal development and has considerable support both from employees and from the leadership. Erni believes that Gregory's buy-in and support is what makes the program both successful and unique (Marquez, 2007b). Speaking about an event where Gregory addressed the importance of flexible work, Jan Hanson, who was hired to help the effort, states, "The fact that this is coming right from the president and not just an HR initiative really spoke to the women . . . It's a huge morale boost" (Marquez, 2007b).

Hanson further suggests, "Companies need to figure out how to have their best talent available 24 hours a day without burning them out. . . . There is nothing macho anymore about having a heart attack on the trading floor" (Marquez, 2007a). Although Lehman has made progress in implementing its program and has shown success, getting the organizational culture to change is not easy and continues to be a work in progress. One of the recruits of the Encore program expressed her concerns about how she would be viewed as token, but she states, "At Lehman, there is a real consciousness on the part of management to make work/life balance real" (Marquez, 2007a). The success of the program helps Lehman recruit and retain talent and allows it to build a diverse pool of leaders it can tap.

Sources: Marquez, J., 2007a. "Bringing professional women back into the workforce," *Workforce Management*, April 9: 1, 20–25; Marquez, J., 2007b. "Women's networking comes from the top at Lehman," *Workforce Management*, April 9: 24; Sellers, P., 2007. "A kinder, gentler Lehman Bros," *Fortune* 155 no. 1: 36–38.

The case of Lehman Bros in Leading Change section is an example of how organizations need to change their existing policies and implement creative new systems to support the development of their employees. Many organizational policies such as those on family leave can hinder people's changes of advancement. Similarly, traditional performance evaluation criteria, which emphasize the stereotypical male and Western characteristics associated with leaders as the basis for success, may undermine the ability of people who have other diverse characteristics and skills to rise to leadership positions. Finally, successful change requires careful measurement and monitoring. Organizations must have baseline information about the hard facts about the actual numbers of women and minorities in leadership and about the softer data related to satisfaction, attitudes, and the less-visible obstacles that may be in place. Keeping track of changes and holding decision makers accountable are essential to solidifying any improvement that may take place. For example, another indicator of Toyota's commitment to a diverse and inclusive workforce is its quick action after one of its top executives was accused of sexual harassment. Not only the executive left his position, the company created a task force to enhance training of its executives and put in place better procedures for responding to allegations and complaints (Wiscombe, 2007b).

SUMMARY AND CONCLUSION

Culture can affect whom we consider an effective leader. Several models have been proposed to increase our understanding of culture and how it may impact behavior. Hall's cultural context focuses on the communication context. People from high-context cultures rely on the environment, nonverbal cues, situational factors, and subtle signals to communicate with others. Those from low-context cultures focus on specific written or oral messages. Hofstede's cultural values suggest that culture can be understood using the five dimensions of power distance, uncertainty avoidance, individualism, masculinity, and time orientation. Additionally, whether a culture is tight, with many rules and regulations, or loose, with fewer prescriptions for behavior, further impacts how people behavior. Trompenaars further refines our understanding of culture by considering nine dimensions and providing models for cross-cultural organizational cultures. The most recent and most comprehensive model for culture has been proposed by researchers in the Global Leadership and Organizational Behavior Effectiveness (GLOBE) model.

In addition to national culture, group culture, particularly as it relates to gender and minorities, plays a role in the leadership of organizations. Although women have active roles in organizations in the West and many other parts of the world, clearly they do not have access to the same power and leadership roles as men do. Gender differences, less desire to lead, and particularly enduring stereotypes and discrimination have been proposed as the primary reasons for the presence of fewer women in leadership positions. Creating multicultural organizations where differences are valued and individuals are encouraged to thrive is the key to increasing the presence of women and minorities in organizations. Leadership plays a central role in bringing about the cultural and organizational changes necessary to achieve that goal.

LEADERSHIP CHALLENGE: JUGGLING CULTURES

Culture, gender, and leadership are closely related. In most cultures, even Western cultures, leadership is associated with males. This association is even stronger in many Arab Muslim countries, where women typically play a limited role in public and business life.

As a leader of an organization, you face the choice of selecting the leader of a negotiation team to draft a new deal with a potential Saudi Arabian client. By far, your best, most experienced, and most skilled negotiator is one of your female executives. She has, for many years, successfully negotiated deals within the United States and in several Western countries. Her second in command is a promising but relatively young male executive who still needs to develop his skills and experience.

1. Whom do you send to Saudi Arabia as head of your team?
2. What cultural factors do you need to consider?
3. What are the implications of your decision for your business and the message you send as leader?

REVIEW AND DISCUSSION QUESTIONS

1. What are the four models of culture, and how do they affect leadership?
2. How are the different models of culture similar? What unique contributions does each model make?
3. How would the definitions of leaders and effectiveness differ based on the different cultural values presented by Hofstede, Trompenaars, and the GLOBE findings?
4. How does group membership impact leaders and leadership?
5. Name some of the gender differences in leaderships.
6. What are the causes of discrimination against women and minorities in organizations?
7. What are the solutions for gender differences in leaderships?

EXERCISE 2-1:   PROVERBS AS A WINDOW TO LEADERSHIP

What do these proverbs tell us about the culture? What implications do they have for leadership in that culture?

United States (mainstream)

Proverb	Implications for Leadership
Actions speak louder than words.	
Strike while the iron is hot.	
Time is money.	
God helps those who help themselves.	

From Other Cultures

Proverb	Implications for Leadership
One does not make the wind, but is blown by it (Asian cultures).	
Order is half of life (Germany).	
When spider webs unite, they can tie up a lion (Ethiopia).	
We are all like well buckets, one goes up and the other comes down (Mexico).	
Sometimes you ride the horse; sometimes you carry the saddle (Iran).	
We will be known forever by the tracks we leave (Native American—Dakota).	
One finger cannot lift a pebble (Hopi).	
Force, no matter how concealed, begets resistance (Lakota).	

EXERCISE 2-2:   NARIAN BRIDGES

The following exercise is a cross-cultural role-play designed to allow you to experience the challenges and opportunities of interacting with people from different cultures. The setting is the fictional country of Nari. You will be asked to play the role of either an American or a Narian. Read the exercise carefully; your instructor will provide you with further information.

Background

Nari is a Middle Eastern country with an old history and a rich cultural heritage. Through judicious excavation of a number of minerals, the country has obtained considerable wealth, and the stable political and social climate has attracted many foreign investors. As a result, Nari launched a careful and well-planned development campaign in the past 20 years that allowed the country's economy to become the strongest in the region. The per capita income is the highest in the region with a literacy rate greater than 80 percent for the population under 30 (which comprises 53 percent of the population).

The political system is an authoritarian monarchy. The powers of the elected parliament are limited to its consultative role to the king. This political system has been in place for more than 1000 years, and the current dynasty began its reign 400 years ago. As compared with many of its unstable neighbors, Nari has enjoyed a calm political climate. The Western press, however, is highly critical of the lack of democracy and the authoritarian nature of the government. The king has unceremoniously dismissed the charges as cultural colonialism and emphasizes the need to preserve the Narian culture while welcoming the West's and the East's help in economic development.

The culture is warm and welcoming of outsiders. The Narian focus on politeness and kindness is easily extended to foreigners, although Narians do not accept criticism of their culture as well and do not tolerate debate about the topic, particularly with outsiders. Many younger Narians seek higher education in other parts of the world, but most return eagerly to their country. The extended family remains the core of society, with the father being the unquestioned head. Narians take pride in their family and maintain considerable commitment to it. They demonstrate a similar commitment to the organizations to which they belong; employees take pride in the accomplishments of their organizations. Although some rumblings can be heard about opening up the political systems and allowing for more democratic participation, the authority of the family, of the community, and of the monarch are rarely, if ever, questioned. Narians often mention the importance of individual sacrifice, social order, and stability and express dismay, with a smile, at how Westerners can get anything done when they behave in such unruly ways. They also contrast the inherent trust in their society, where a handshake and a person's word are as good as gold, with other countries' legalistic systems that require extensive contracts to get anything done.

Narian leaders hold total and absolute power. Although not viewed as having power derived from divine rights, leaders are assumed to be infallible. Narian leaders are confident in their complete knowledge of all that they come to face. They do not ask questions and do not seek advice, even from equals. Often autocratic, the Narian leader, however, is expected to take care of loyal followers under any circumstance. As followers owe unquestioning obedience, leaders owe them total devotion. The leaders are fully responsible for all that happens to their followers, in all aspects of their life. They are expected to help and

(Continued)

guide them and come to their rescue when needed. Leaders are expected to be caring and fair. Their primary duty is to look out for their followers.

In return, Narian followers are expected to be loyal, obedient, dutiful, and subservient. They accept their leader's orders willingly and wholeheartedly; all Narians are taught from the youngest age that leaders are infallible and that the proper functioning of the social order hinges upon obedience and loyalty to leaders and elders and upon their fulfilling their responsibility as followers. Dissent and conflict are rarely expressed in the open. People value politeness and civility and go out of their way to be kind. When mistakes are made, regardless of where the fault lies, all individuals work on correcting it without assigning blame. If the leader makes a mistake, an event rarely, if ever, brought out in the open, one of the followers openly accepts the blame to protect the leader's face and the social harmony. The person accepting that responsibility is eventually rewarded for the demonstration of loyalty.

The role of women in Narian society remains puzzling to Western observers. For more than 30 years, women have had practically equal rights with men. They can vote, conduct any kind of business transactions, take advantage of educational opportunities, file for divorce, obtain custody of their children, work in any organization, and so forth. The literacy rate for women is equal to that of men, and although fewer of them pursue higher education, it appears that most women who are interested in working outside of the home find easy employment in the booming Narian economy. The society, however, remains highly patriarchal in its traditions.

Role-Play Situation

A U.S. engineering and construction company has won its first major governmental contract for constructing two bridges in Nari. With general terms agreed upon, the company is working closely with several U.S.-educated Narian engineers employed at the Narian Ministry of Urban Development (UD) to draft precise plans and timetables. The minister of UD, Mr. Dafti, is a well-respected civil engineer, educated in Austria in the 1950s. In addition to Narian, he speaks fluent German, English, and French. He played instrumental roles in the development of his country. Although a consummate politician and negotiator and an expert on his country's resources and economic situation, he has not practiced his engineering skills for many years.

Mr. Dafti has decided on the general location and structure of the two bridges to be built. One of the locations and designs contains serious flaws. His more junior Narian associates appear to be aware of the potential problems and have hinted at the difficulties and challenges in building in that location, but have not clearly voiced their concerns to the U.S. contractors, who find the design requirements unworkable.

The role-play is a meeting with Mr. Dafti, his Narian associates, and representatives of the U.S. engineering firm. The U.S. head engineer requested the meeting, and the request was granted quickly. The U.S. team is eager to start the project. The Narians also are ready to engage in the new business venture.

Please wait for further instructions.

EXERCISE 2-3:   LEADERSHIP AND GENDER

This exercise is designed to explore the relationship between gender roles and leadership. Your instructor will assign you to one of three groups and ask you to develop a list of characteristics of a particular leader. Each group will present its list to the class. Discussion will focus on the similarities and differences between gender roles and leadership.

Now, list eight to ten characteristics associated with _____ (wait for your instructor's direction). You can use specific personality traits or behavioral descriptions.

1.

2.

3.

4.

5.

6.

7.

8.

9.

10.

EXERCISE 2-4: IS THIS SEXUAL HARASSMENT?

For each of the following scenarios, state whether you believe sexual harassment has taken place. Explain your reasoning.

1. A teacher stipulates that your grade (or participation on a team, in a play, etc.) will be based on whether you submit to a relationship.

   Is it harassment?

   Why?

2. Mary and Todd dated for a while. Mary broke off their relationship and no longer wants to date Todd and has told him so. Todd, however, continually behaves as if they are still dating. He phones her for dates. In the halls at the university, he comes up and puts his arms around her shoulders.

   Is it harassment?

   Why?

3. During a discussion at work regarding gay rights, Ricardo strongly defended the right of gays to have partner benefits at work and be able to form a civil union. He got very emotional when talking about the sadness he observed when one of his friends was not allowed to visit his partner of many years on his deathbed in the hospital because they were not legally related. Since that day, his coworkers have been making comments such as "Mama's boy," "you're such a girl," "are you going to cry now?" and insinuating that he is gay. Ricardo is heterosexual.

   Is it harassment?

   Why?

4. Tara Washington has been Peter Jacobs' assistant for over five years and they have had an excellent working relationship. Tara just found out that her father has terminal cancer, and one day recently at the office, she broke down and started crying. Peter came up to her and gave her hug.

   Is it harassment?

   Why?

5. Julie and Antonio started working at the office a few days apart. They are both recent college graduate. They immediately hit it off and soon started dating. Their supervisor talked to both of them and warned them not to let their relationship interfere with their work or affect others in the workplace. They both said that they understood the potential problems and made a commitment to keep things professional. After a couple of months, Antonio broke off the relationship. Julie was heartbroken. Both were very uncomfortable working with each other. After a few weeks, Julie talked to her supervisor about Antonio avoiding her and her belief that this may constitute sexual harassment.

   Is it harassment?

   Why?

6. Nadine is a very attractive young employee in a government office. She has developed a warm, friendly, and professional relationship with her colleagues, many of whom are males. They often joke and laugh with her, and she receives many compliments from them regarding her looks.

   Is it harassment?

   Why?

7. Nicholas is a recent immigrant from Greece who is working in a high-technology firm in Massachusetts. He really enjoys his job and likes his colleagues. They often go out to lunch and for drinks after work and play sports on weekends. Nicholas is shocked when he finds out that one of his colleagues has accused him of sexual harassment for inappropriate physical contact.

   Is it harassment?

   Why?

8. Kim is a realtor who specializes in selling homes from large developers. She shows a lot property in construction sites and has a very successful track record. Recently, she has become very uncomfortable with rude and suggestive comments from the construction workers at one of the sites; so much so that she is avoiding showing property in that location. She complained to her office manager about the problem, but she was told that they cannot really control the construction workers because they do not work for the same company.

   Is it harassment?

(Continued)

Why?

9. Gary has taken one of his company's biggest clients to dinner. The client is considering expanding her business with Gary's company. During dinner, she very clearly comes on to Gary who politely refuses her advances. The client brushes him off and says she will try again. The next day, Gary tells his supervisor about the incident and how uncomfortable he felt. His supervisor informs him that the client has specifically asked for Gary to stay on the case and has indicated that she looks forward to expanding her business with the company.

Is it harassment?

Why?

SELF-ASSESSMENT AND REFLECTION 2-1:   EXPLORING VIEWS OF WOMEN

Briefly describe the cultural views and expectations of women in your family and your culture. What are your personal views of the role of women in

Relationships

Family

Business/work

Community

How would those views facilitate or present obstacles for women in the workplace?

Leadership in Action: Indra Nooyi: The Indian-Born CEO of Pepsi Sets New Standards

Being one of two women CEOs of a Fortune 100 company is no small accomplishment. Indra Nooyi, known for having a keen business sense and an irreverent personal style, is perfect for the job. Whereas female CEOs continue to be relatively rare, female CEOs of color are even rarer (Andrea Jung of Avon is the other one; see Leadership in Action case in Chapter 6). Born and educated in South India before attending Yale University for her graduate degree, Nooyi joined PepsiCo in 1994, having worked for Motorola and the Boston Consulting group. She became chief financial officer of PepsiCo in 2001 and its first female CEO in 2006. She is credited for guiding the company through major restructuring, divesting its restaurants, and refocusing on its beverage and other food businesses with the successful multibillion dollar mergers with Tropicana and Quaker Oats (Kavilanz, 2006).

"Brilliant," "supertalented," and able to think several steps ahead of everyone else are just some of the terms people use to describe her. The former company president Enrico states, "Indra can drive as deep and hard as anyone I've ever met, but she can do it with a sense of heart and fun" (Brady, 2007). On many dimensions, Nooyi does not fit the stereotype of the CEO of one of the world's largest companies. A former member of an all-girl rock band, non-Western, and female, she has overcome a complex set of barriers to reach the highest level of corporate leadership. She, however, is comfortable enough with herself to walk around the office barefoot, sing in the hallways—she is a karaoke fan—and go to a formal job interview with the button-down U.S. consulting firm, the Boston Consulting Group, and to PepsiCo board meetings wearing a sari. She believes that being genuine is a key to her success and likes to blend her cultural roots with her corporate image.

Nooyi's sharp wit and irreverence was most evident when she delivered the business school graduation speech at Columbia University in 2005 and compared the world with five major continents (with her apologies to Australia and Antarctica) to a hand, making the U.S. the middle finger for its strength, its most prominent position, and its ability to both help and offend (for a complete text of the speech see, Graduation Remarks, 2005). Although she had to clarify her statements and apologize for having offended some people, she also made a compelling case for global cooperation and diversity. She stated, "the five fingers are not the same . . . and yet the fingers work in harmony without us even thinking about them individually. . . . Our fingers—as different as they are—coexist to create a critically important whole" (Graduation Remarks, 2005). She further urged graduates to take an active part in developing cultural awareness and sensitivity, creating harmony and cooperation and developing bonds between countries: "My point is that it's not enough just to understand that the other fingers coexist. We've got to consciously and actively ensure that every one of them stands tall together, or that they bend together as needed" (Graduation Remarks, 2005).

Many celebrate Nooyi's leadership at Pepsi as a victory for diversity. PepsiCo, however, has been at the forefront of promoting diversity with actress Joann Crawford, widow of the company's president, replacing her husband on the board of directors in 1959 and Brenda Barnes heading the North American divisions for many years (before leaving in 1989 with a much publicized statement that she wanted to spend more time with her family). In the 1940s, the company was one of the first to create an all-black sales team to market to African American consumers (Cole, 2006). Nooyi's predecessor, Steven Reinemund, is recognized as a champion of diversity, who stated, "I often refer to our diversity and inclusion as a marathon. . . . The challenge comes in creating an environment in which every associate—regardless of ethnicity, sexual orientation, gender or physical ability—feels valued and want to be part of our growth" (Ortiz, 2006). Amy George, PepsiCo's vice president of global diversity and inclusion, believes that Nooyi will further reinforce the company's stance on diversity by bringing her own uniqueness to the leadership role (Ortiz, 2006).

Even before becoming CEO, while taking care of the CFO and other duties, Nooyi created programs to help women network, learn from successful role models, and to develop skills to manage their careers better. She also sponsored events to showcase and promote the company's diversity and inclusiveness. She readily acknowledges the challenges she has faced: "Being a women, immigrant, and person of color made it thrice as difficulty." She states, "So therefore, the only way out, was to work twice as hard as your male counterparts" (Indra Nooyi takes over Pepsi HQ, 2006). Her formula for success is relatively simple; she suggests that success comes from five "Cs": competence, confidence, communication skills, having a moral compass and integrity, and being the conscience for the organization (Indra Nooyi's 5-C formula, 2006). She continues to practice what she preaches. She admits at being consumed with PepsiCo; the company is her passion. Answering emails at 4 A.M. and being the last one to leave the office are typical behaviors for Nooyi, who balances a family and being CEO of a Fortune 100 company (Indra Nooyi's 5-C, 2006). And by most accounts, she does it all brilliantly.

QUESTIONS

1. What are the elements of Nooyi's leadership?
2. What role does diversity play?

Sources: Brady, D., 2007. "Indra Nooyi: Keeping cool in hot water," *Business Week,* June 11: 49; Cole, Y., 2008. "PepsiCo's diversity legacy," *Diversity Inc.* March 28. http://www.diversityinc.com/public/1627.cfm (accessed August 8, 2007); Kavilanz, P. B., 2006. "PepsiCo names first woman CEO," *CNN Money.com,* August 14. http://money.cnn.com/2006/08/14/news/companies/pepsico_ceo/ (accessed August 6, 2007); Graduation Remarks. 2005. *Business Week,* May 20. http://www.businessweek.com/bwdaily/dnflash/may2005/nf20050520_9852.htm (accessed August 6, 2007); Indra Nooyi's 5-C formula for global success. 2006. *The Times of India,* August 16. http://timesofindia.indiatimes.com/articleshow/1898674.cms (accessed August 6, 2007); India Nooyi takes over Pepsi HQ.2006. *India Times,* August 15. http://economictimes.indiatimes.com/articleshow/1893960.cms (accessed August 7, 2007); Ortiz, P., 2006. "Historic change: Indra Nooyi to be CEO of PepsiCo," *Diversity Inc.,* May. http://www.diversityinc.com/public/637.cfm (accessed August 8, 2007).

Early Theories

The Foundations of Modern Leadership

The people who get on in this world are the people who
get up and look for circumstances they want, and, if they
can't find them, make them.
—GEORGE BERNARD SHAW

A pretzel-shaped world needs a pretzel-shaped theory.
—FRED FIEDLER

After studying this chapter, you will be able to:

■ Identify the three major eras in the study of leadership and their contributions to modern
leadership.

■ Explain the methods, results, shortcomings, and contributions of the trait and behavior
approaches to leadership and identify their impact on current approaches.

■ Present the most significant early theories of leadership and their implications for current
theory and practice of leadership.

The roots of the modern study of leadership can be traced to the western industrial
revolution that took place at the end of the nineteenth century. Although many
scholars throughout history focused on leadership, the modern approach to leadership brings scientific rigor to the search for answers. Social and political sciences and
management scholars tried, sometimes more successfully than other times, to measure
leadership through a variety of means. This chapter reviews the history of modern
leadership theory and research, and outlines the early theories that are the foundations
of modern leadership.

A HISTORY OF MODERN LEADERSHIP
THEORY: THREE ERAS

During the industrial revolution, the study of leadership, much like research in other
aspects of organizations, became more rigorous. Instead of relying on intuition and a
description of common practices, researchers used scientific methods to understand and
predict leadership effectiveness by identifying and measuring leadership characteristics.

The history of the modern scientific approach to leadership can be divided into three general eras or approaches: the trait era, the behavior era, and the contingency era. Each era has made distinct contributions to our understanding of leadership and continues to influence our thinking about the process.

The Trait Era: Late 1800s to Mid-1940s

The belief that leaders are born rather than made dominated much of the late nineteenth century and the early part of the twentieth century. Thomas Carlyle's book *Heroes and Hero Worship* (1907), William James's writings (1880) about the great men of history, and Galton's study (1869) of the role of heredity were part of an era that can be characterized by a strong belief that innate qualities shape human personality and behavior. Consequently, it was commonly believed that leaders, by virtue of their birth, were endowed with special qualities that allow them to lead others. These special characteristics were presumed to push them toward leadership regardless of the context. The historical context and social structures of the period further reinforced such beliefs by providing limited opportunities for common people to become social, political, and industrial leaders. The belief in the power of personality and other innate characteristics strongly influenced leadership researchers and sent them on a massive hunt for leadership traits made possible by the advent of personality and individual characteristics testing such as IQ in the early twentieth century. The major assumption guiding hundreds of studies about leadership traits was that if certain traits distinguish between leaders and followers, then existing political, industrial, and religious leaders should possess them (for a thorough review of the literature, see Bass, 1990a). Based on this assumption, researchers identified and observed existing leaders and followers and collected detailed demographic and personality information about them.

More than 40 years of study provided little evidence to justify the assertion that leaders are born and that leadership can be explained through one or more traits. Some traits do emerge as important. For instance, much evidence indicates that, on the average, leaders are more sociable, more aggressive, and more lively than other group members. In addition, leaders generally are original and popular and have a sense of humor. Which of the traits are most relevant, however, seems to depend on the requirements of the situation. In other words, being social, aggressive, lively, original, and popular or having any other combination of traits does not guarantee that a person will become a leader, let alone an effective one.

> **More than 40 years of study provided little evidence to justify the assertion that leaders are born and that leadership can be explained through either one or a collection of traits. Some traits do emerge as important. Which of the traits are most relevant, however, seems to depend on the requirements of the situation.**

Because of weak and inconsistent findings, the commonly shared belief among many researchers in the late 1930s and early 1940s was that although traits play a role in determining leadership ability and effectiveness, the role is minimal and that leadership should be viewed as a group phenomenon that cannot be studied outside a given situation (Ackerson, 1942; Bird, 1940; Jenkins, 1947; Newstetter, Feldstein, and Newcomb, 1938; Stogdill, 1948). More recent studies in the 1960s and 1970s reinforced these findings by showing that factors such as intelligence (Bray and Grant, 1966) or assertiveness (Rychlak, 1963) are related to leadership effectiveness, but they alone cannot account for much of a leader's effectiveness.

Recent views of the role of traits and other individual characteristics, such as skills, refined our understanding of the role of individual characteristics in leadership (for an example and review, see Mumford et al., 2000a, b). Current interest in emotional intelligence has also yielded new research on the leader's individual characteristics (e.g., Humphrey, 2002). These characteristics are discussed in more detail in Chapter 4. The leader's personality, by limiting the leader's behavioral range or by making it more or less difficult to learn certain behaviors or undertake some actions, plays a key role in his or her effectiveness. The leader's personality, however, is by no means the only or even the dominant factor in effective leadership.

The Behavior Era: Mid-1940s to Early 1970s

Because the trait approach did not yield the expected results and as the need for identifying and training leaders came to the forefront during World War II, researchers turned to behaviors, rather than traits, as the source of leader effectiveness. The move to observable behaviors was triggered in part by the dominance of behaviorist theories during this period, particularly in the United States and Great Britain. Instead of identifying who would be an effective leader, the behavior approach emphasizes what an effective leader does. Focusing on behaviors provides several advantages over a trait approach:

➤ Behaviors can be observed more objectively than traits.

➤ Behaviors can be measured more precisely and more accurately than traits.

➤ As opposed to traits, which are either innate or develop early in life, behaviors can be taught.

These factors provided a clear benefit to the military and various other organizations with a practical interest in leadership. Instead of identifying leaders who had particular personality traits, they could focus on training people to perform effective leadership behaviors. The early work of Lewin and his associates (Lewin and Lippit, 1938; Lewin, Lippit, and White, 1939) concerning democratic, autocratic, and laissez-faire leadership laid the foundation for the behavior approach to leadership. Democratic leaders were defined as those who consult their followers and allow them to participate in decision making, autocratic leaders as those who make decisions alone, and laissez-faire leaders as those who provide no direction and do not become involved with their followers. Although the three types of leadership style were clearly defined, the research failed to establish which style would be most effective or which situational factors would lead to the use of one or another style. Furthermore, each of the styles had different effects on subordinates. For example, laissez-faire leadership, which involved providing information but little guidance or evaluation, led to frustrated and disorganized groups that, in turn, produced low-quality work. On the other hand, autocratic leadership caused followers to become submissive, whereas groups led by democratic leaders were relaxed and became cohesive.

Armed with the results of Lewin's work and other studies, different groups of researchers set out to identify leader behaviors (e.g., Hemphill and Coons, 1957). Among the best-known behavioral approaches to leadership are the Ohio State Leadership Studies. A number of researchers developed a list of almost 2,000 leadership behaviors (Hemphill and Coons, 1957). After subsequent analyses (Fleishman, 1953;

Halpin and Winer, 1957), a condensed list yielded several central leadership behaviors. Among them, task- and relationship-related behaviors were established as primary leadership behaviors. The Ohio State studies led to the development of the Leader Behavior Description Questionnaire (LBDQ), which continues to be used today.

Although the Ohio State research, along with other studies (e.g., Bowers and Seashore, 1966), identified a number of leader behaviors, the links between those behaviors and leadership effectiveness were not clearly established. After many years of research, it is still not obvious which behaviors are most effective. It is consistently agreed, though, that considerate, supportive, people-oriented behaviors are associated with follower satisfaction, loyalty, and trust whereas structuring behaviors are more closely related to job performance (for a recent review, see Judge, Piccolo, and Ilies, 2004). Evidence, although somewhat weak, shows that effective leadership requires both consideration and structuring behaviors (Fleishman and Harris, 1962; House and Filley, 1971). These findings, however, have failed to receive overwhelming support. Furthermore, the leadership dimensions of initiation of structure and consideration do not describe leader behavior adequately for cultures other than the United States that might be less individualistic and hold up different ideals of leadership (Ayman and Chemers, 1983; Chemers, 1969; Misumi and Peterson, 1985).

Similar to the trait approach, the behavior approach to leadership, by concentrating only on behaviors and disregarding powerful situational elements, provides a simplistic view of a highly complex process and, therefore, fails to provide a thorough understanding of the leadership phenomenon.

The Contingency Era: Early 1960s to Present

Even before the behavior approach's lack of success in explaining and predicting leadership effectiveness became evident, a number of researchers were calling for a more comprehensive approach to understanding leadership (Stogdill, 1948). Specifically, researchers recommended that situational factors, such as the task and type of work group, be taken into consideration. It, however, was not until the 1960s that this recommendation was applied. In the 1960s, spearheaded by Fred Fiedler, whose Contingency Model of leadership is discussed later in this chapter, leadership research moved from simplistic models based solely on the leader to more complex models that take a contingency point of view. Other models such as the Path-Goal Theory and the Normative Decision Model, also presented in this chapter, soon followed. The primary assumption of the contingency view is that the personality, style, or behavior of effective leaders depends on the requirements of the situation in which the leaders find themselves. Additionally, this approach suggests that there is no one best way to lead, that the situation and the various relevant contextual factors determine which style or behavior is most effective, that people can learn to become good leaders, that leadership makes a difference in the effectiveness of groups and organizations, and that personal and situational characteristics affect leadership effectiveness.

Although the contingency approach to leadership continues to be well accepted, the most recent approach to leadership focuses on the relationship between leaders and followers and on various aspects of charismatic and visionary leadership. Some researchers have labeled this approach the neo-charismatic school (Antonakis, Cianciolo, and Sternberg, 2004). We will present this most recent view of leadership in detail in Chapter 6.

EARLY THEORIES

An effective leader must know how to use available resources and build a relationship with follower to achieve goals (Chemers, 1993). The early leadership theories of leadership addressed these two challenges in a variety of ways.

Leadership effectiveness is a function of the match between the leader's style and the leadership situation. If the leader's style matches the situation, the leader will be effective; otherwise, the leader will not be effective.

Fiedler's Contingency Model

Fred Fiedler was the first researcher to propose a contingency view of leadership. His Contingency Model is the oldest and most highly researched contingency approach to leadership (Fiedler, 1967). Fiedler's basic premise is that leadership effectiveness is a function of the match between the leader's style and the leadership situation. If the leader's style matches the situation, the leader will be effective; otherwise, the leader will not be effective. Fiedler considers how the leader uses available resources to make the group effective.

Leader Style

To determine a leader's style, Fiedler uses the least-preferred coworker (LPC) scale, a measure that determines what motivation the leader has: task motivation or relationship motivation. Fiedler's research shows that people's perceptions and descriptions of their least-preferred coworker provide insight into their basic goals and priorities toward either accomplishing a task or maintaining relationships (see Self-Assessment 3-1). According to Fiedler, people with low LPC scores—those who give a low rating to their least-preferred coworker (describing the person as incompetent, cold, untrustworthy, and quarrelsome)—are task motivated. They draw their self-esteem mostly from accomplishing their task well (Chemers and Skrzypek, 1972; Fiedler, 1967; Fiedler and Chemers, 1984; Rice, 1978a, b). When the task-motivated leaders or their groups fail, they tend to be harsh in judging their subordinates and are often highly punitive (Rice, 1978a, b). When the task is going well, however, the task-motivated leader is comfortable with details and with monitoring routine events (Fiedler and Chemers, 1984; Table 3-1).

Table 3-1   Differences Between Task- and Relationship-Motivated Individuals.

Task-Motivated (Low LPC)	Relationship-Motivated (High LPC)
• Draws self-esteem from completion of task	• Draws self-esteem from interpersonal relationships
• Focuses on the task first	• Focuses on people first
• Can be hard with failing employees	• Likes to please others
• Considers competence of coworkers to be key trait	• Considers loyalty of coworkers to be key trait
• Enjoys details	• Gets bored with details

People who have high LPC scores rate their least-preferred coworker relatively positively (describing that person as loyal, sincere, warm, and accepting); they are relationship motivated and draw their self-esteem from having good relationships with others. For them, the least-preferred coworker is often someone who has been disloyal and unsupportive rather than incompetent (Rice, 1978a, b). Relationship-motivated persons are easily bored with details (Fiedler, 1978; Fiedler and Chemers, 1984) and focus on social interactions (Rice, 1978a, b; see Table 3-1). The task-motivated person's focus on tasks and the relationship-motivated person's concern for relationships are most obvious in times of crisis when the person is under pressure.

Brady W. Dougan—the new 47-year-old CEO of Credit Suisse Group, a major global bank, and its youngest CEO to date—is detailed oriented and task motivated (Anderson, 2007). He gets to work around 5 A.M. and is known to work out twice a day while he trains for marathons. He recently spent two months practicing to dance with a Broadway star during a charity event (Anderson, 2007). Marissa Peterson, executive vice president of worldwide operations of Sun Microsystems, is also task motivated. Her strength is in clearly outlining what role every one of her 2000-strong staff plays. Her focus is on "developing the strategy for achieving my operation's goals and then laying out that vision for my team" (Overholt, 2002: 125). Peterson sticks to a strict routine in managing her daily and weekly activities. Contrast these task-motivated leaders with Mort Meyerson, chairman of Perot Systems, a computer firm based in Dallas, Texas, and Darlene Ryan, founder and CEO of PharmaFab, a pharmaceuticals manufacturer also located in Texas. Meyerson believes, "Most companies are still dominated by numbers, information, and analysis. That makes it much harder to tap into intuition, feelings, and nonlinear thinking—the skills that leaders will need to succeed in the future. If you work with the whole person, and their whole mind, you will reach a better place—for them and the company" (Meyerson, 1997: 99). Darlene Ryan takes a similar approach. She runs her company like a family; she encourages dissent and delegates and is a consensus builder. She is a great listener and is able to take her time when facing tough decisions (Black, 2004).

Individuals who fall in the middle of the scale have been labeled socio-independent. They tend to be less concerned with other people's opinions and may not actively seek leadership roles. Depending on how close their score is to the high or the low end of the scale, they might belong to either the task-motivated or relationship-motivated group (Fiedler and Chemers, 1984). Some research suggests that middle LPCs may be more effective than either high or low LPCs across all situations (Kennedy, 1982). A potential middle LPC is Colin Powel. Even though he has been in many leadership positions, he has shied away from the presidency, and he has proven himself an outstanding follower to several presidents.

Despite some problems with the validity of the LPC scale, it has received strong support from researchers and practitioners and has even translated well to other cultures for use in leadership research and training (Ayman and Chemers, 1983, 1991). A key premise of the LPC concept is that because it is an indicator of primary motivation, leadership style is stable. Leaders, then, cannot simply change their style to match the situation.

Situational Control

Fiedler uses three factors to describe a leadership situation. In order of importance, they are (1) the relationship between the leader and the followers, (2) the amount of structure of the task, and (3) the position power of the leader. The three elements combine to define the amount of control the leader has over the situation (see Self-Assessment 3-2).

According to Fiedler, the most important element of any leadership situation is the quality of the relationship and the cohesion between the leader and the followers and among the followers (Fiedler, 1978). Good leader–member relations (LMR) mean that the group is cohesive and supportive, providing leaders with a high degree of control to implement what they want. When the group is divided or has little respect or support for the leader, the leader's control is low.

Task structure (TS) is the second element of a leadership situation. It refers to the degree of clarity of a task. A highly structured task has clear goals and procedures, few paths to the correct solution, and one or few correct solutions and can be evaluated easily (Fiedler and Chemers, 1974). The degree of task structure affects the leader's control. Whereas the leader has considerable control when doing a structured task, an unstructured task provides little sense of control. One factor that moderates task structure is the leader's experience level (Fiedler and Chemers, 1984). On the one hand, if leaders have experience with a task, they will perceive the task as more structured. On the other hand, not having experience will make any task appear to be unstructured.

The third and least influential element of the leadership situation is the leader's position power (PP), which refers to the leader's official power and influence over subordinates to hire, fire, reward, or punish. The leader with a high amount of formal power feels more in control than one who has little power.

The combination of LMR, TS, and PP yields the amount of situational control (Sit Con) the leader has over the situation. At one end of the continuum, good leader–member relations, a highly structured task, and high position power provide the leader with high control over the situation where the leader's influence is well accepted. In the middle of the continuum are situations in which either the leader and the followers do not get along or the task is unstructured. In such situations, the leader does not have full control over the situation and the leadership environment is more difficult. At the other end of the situational control continuum, the leader–member relations are poor, the task is unstructured, and the leader has little power. Such a situation is chaotic and unlikely to continue for a long period of time in an organization. Clearly, this crisis environment does not provide the leader with a sense of control or any ease of leadership (see Self-Assessment 3-2 for Sit Con).

Predictions of the Contingency Model

At the core of the Contingency Model is the concept of match. If the leader's style matches the situation, the group will be effective. Because Fiedler suggests that the leader's style is constant, a leader's effectiveness changes as the situation changes. The Contingency Model predicts that low-LPC, task-motivated leaders will be effective in high- and low-situational control, whereas high-LPC, relationship-motivated leaders will be effective in moderate-situational control. Figure 3-1 presents the predictions of the model.

In high-control situations (left side of the graph in Figure 3-1), task-motivated, low-LPC leaders feel at ease. The leader's basic source of self-esteem—getting the task done—is not threatened, so the leader can relax, take care of details, and help the

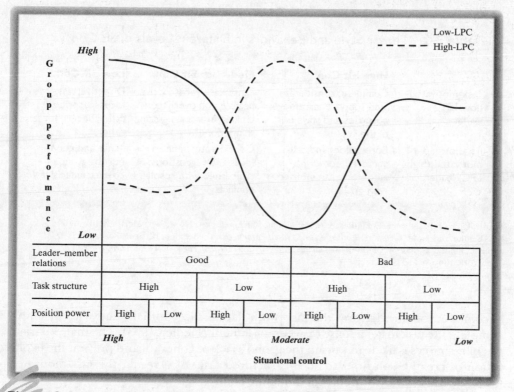

Figure 3-1 (legend): Low-LPC (solid line), High-LPC (dashed line). Group performance axis ranges from High to Low. Situational control axis ranges from High to Moderate to Low.

Leader–member relations	Good				Bad			
Task structure	High		Low		High		Low	
Position power	High	Low	High	Low	High	Low	High	Low

Figure 3-1   Fiedler's Contingency Model.

followers perform. The same high-control situation leads to a different effect on relationship-motivated, high-LPC leaders. They are likely to be bored and feel either that there is nothing to do or that nobody needs them. Because the group is cohesive and the task is clear, the leader is needed mainly to get the group the resources it needs, take care of details, and remove obstacles—all activities that are not appealing to high LPCs, who might, therefore, start being overly controlling and interfere with the group's performance to demonstrate that they are needed (Chemers, 1997; Fiedler and Garcia, 1987a). See Table 3-2 for a summary of the leaders' behaviors in each situation.

Moderate-situational control (the middle of graph in Figure 3-1) stems from lack of cohesiveness or lack of task structure. In either case, the situation is ambiguous or uncertain, and task completion is in jeopardy. The relationship-motivated, high-LPC leader's skills at interpersonal relationships and participation are well suited for the situation. This type of leader seeks out followers' participation and focuses on resolving task and relationship conflicts. The high-LPC leader uses the group as a resource to accomplish the task. The same elements that make moderate control attractive to relationship-motivated leaders make the situation threatening to the task-oriented, low-LPC leader. The lack of group support, the ambiguity of the task, or both make the low LPCs feel that the task might not be completed. The task-oriented leader

Table 3-2   Leader Style and Behaviors in Different Levels of Sit Con.

	High Sit Con	Moderate Sit Con	Low Sit Con
Task-motivated (low-LPC) leader	Confident; considerate and supportive; removes obstacles and stays out of the way	Tense; task-focused; overbearing and overly controlling; insists on getting things done	Directive; task-focused; serious; little concern for others
Relationship-motivated (high-LPC) leader	Bored; aloof and self-centered; somewhat autocratic; can interfere with group	Considerate; open to ideas and suggestions; concerned with resolving conflicts	Tense and nervous; hurt by group's conflict; indecisive

Sources: Partially based on F. E. Fiedler, *A Theory of Leadership Effectiveness* (New York: McGraw-Hill, 1967); F. E. Fiedler and M. M. Chemers, *Leadership and Effective Management* (Glenview, IL: Scott-Foresman, 1974); and F. E. Fiedler and M. M. Chemers, *Improving Leadership Effectiveness: The Leader Match Concept*, 2nd ed. (New York: John Wiley, 1984).

becomes autocratic, ignores the task and relationship conflicts, and tries to simply complete the task to get a sense of accomplishment (Fiedler, 1993). The inappropriate use of resources is likely to worsen the group's lack of cohesion and prevent the exploration of creative solutions to an unstructured task. As a result, the task-motivated leader's group performs poorly in moderate control.

Consider several of the recent U.S. presidents. Former presidents Richard Nixon and Jimmy Carter were task-motivated leaders. Both were highly intelligent, focused on the task, and able to analyze large amounts of detail. Both needed to stay in control, held uncompromising views and approaches to issues, and could be harsh toward failing subordinates. They performed well in high control. Nixon experienced considerable success in foreign policy, where he was respected, the task was clear, and he held power tightly. As his legitimate power and popularity decreased—leading to moderate control—he became controlling, punitive, and ineffective. Carter's effectiveness followed a similar pattern, although he never faced a high-control situation, a factor that might explain his overall poor effectiveness ratings as president. Almost immediately after being elected, he found himself in moderate control with poor relations with the U.S. Congress and an unstructured task exacerbated by his limited experience in foreign policy. His single-minded focus on human rights and his inability to compromise made him ineffective.

At the other end of the continuum are former presidents Ronald Reagan and Bill Clinton, both high LPCs who focused on interpersonal relations, were bored with details, and demonstrated an apparently unending ability to compromise, a desire to please others, and the ability to perform and put on a show for their public. Both enjoyed working with people and were popular with crowds. Reagan was well liked but faced an unstructured task with moderate power. Clinton faced a novel and unstructured situation but continued to enjoy unprecedented support of the electorate. Both these relationship-motivated presidents were in moderate control where, by many accounts, they performed well.

As a situation becomes chaotic and reaches a crisis point with no group cohesion, no task structure, and no strong position power (the right side of the graph in Figure 3-1), the task-motivated, low-LPC leaders' need to complete the task pushes them to take over and make autocratic decisions without much concern for followers. As a result, although performance is not high and followers might not be satisfied, groups with a low-LPC leader get some work done. For the relationship-motivated, high-LPC leader, the low Sit Con environment is a nightmare. The group's lack of cohesion is further fueled by its inability to perform the task and makes efforts at reconciliation close to impossible. The high-LPC leader's efforts to gain support from the group, therefore, fall on deaf ears. In an attempt to protect their self-esteem, high-LPC leaders withdraw, leaving their group to fend for itself and causing low performance. The data for the socio-independent leaders are less clear. Fiedler (1978) suggests that they generally perform better in high-control situations, although more research is needed to predict and explain their performance.

Evaluation and Application

Although a large number of studies have supported the Contingency Model over the past 40 years, several researchers have voiced strong criticisms regarding the meaning and validity of the LPC scale (Schriesheim and Kerr, 1974), the predictive value of the model (Schriesheim, Tepper, and Tetrault, 1994; Vecchio, 1983), and the lack of research about the middle-LPC leaders (Kennedy, 1982) have come under attack. Forty years of research have addressed the majority, although not all, of the concerns. As a result, the Contingency Model continues to emerge as one of the most reliable and predictive models of leadership, with a number of research studies and meta-analyses supporting the hypotheses of the model (see Ayman, Chemers, and Fiedler, 1995; Chemers, 1997; Peters, Hartke, and Pohlmann, 1985; Strube and Garcia, 1981).

Applying What You Learn
Putting the Contingency Model to Work

Fiedler's contingency model suggests that instead of focusing on changing their style, leaders should learn to understand and manage the situations in which they lead. Chances, however, are that most of the leadership training programs you may attend will focus on changing the leaders' style to adapt to different situations. Here's how you can take advantage of those training programs while following the contingency model's recommendations:

• Remember that learning will take place when you challenge yourself to undertake and master behaviors that do not come easily and therefore may be outside your comfort zone or primary motivation area.

• Regardless of your style, you can always learn new behaviors and expand your current range.

• All training, by design or default, will expose you to many new leadership situations. Take the opportunity to practice analyzing them to ascertain situational control.

• Do not expect miracles or even quick changes. Increasing your effectiveness as a leader is a long journey.

Importantly, a person's LPC is not the only or the strongest determinant of a leader's actions and beliefs. Although the focus has been on the description of stereotypical task-motivated and relationship-motivated leaders, a person's behavior is determined by many other internal and external factors. It would, therefore, be inappropriate to carry the task or relationship orientation considerably beyond its use in the Contingency Model. It is a reliable predictor of leadership effectiveness within the model but not necessarily beyond it.

The Contingency Model has several practical implications for managers:

➤ Leaders must understand their style and the situation to predict how effective they will be.

➤ Leaders should focus on changing the situation to match their style instead of trying to change how they act.

➤ A good relationship with followers is important to a leader's ability to lead, and it can compensate for lack of power.

➤ Leaders can compensate for ambiguity of a task by getting training and experience.

Fiedler's focus on changing the situation rather than the leader is unique among leadership theories. Interestingly, Marcus Buckingham, well-known leadership consultant, has recently suggested that leaders should focus on developing their strengths rather than trying to compensate for their weaknesses, advice that is consistent with Fiedler's approach (Buckingham, 2005). As opposed to Fiedler, the Normative Decision Model considered next, along with many other leadership models, assumes that the leader can change styles depending on the situation.

The Normative Decision Model

Should a leader make decisions alone or involve followers? What factors can help a leader determine how to make decisions? Consider the case of Junki Yoshida, the Japanese-born, 58-year-old martial artist and founder and owner of Yoshida Group enterprises. In 2005 he was voted as one of the 100 most respected Japanese in the world by the Japanese edition of *Newsweek* magazine. His company includes Mr. Yoshida Original Gourmet sauces and marinades and is comprised of 18 highly diverse companies that include Jones Golf bags, OIA Global Logistics, and a graphic design company (Yoshida Group, 2007). When he starts a new venture, Yoshida plays an active role in every aspect and stays close to every decision. Once the business takes off, however, he delegates to carefully selected specialists and lets them make many of the decisions. The way he makes decisions about his businesses changes as each business matures (Brant, 2004). The Normative Decision Model (also referred to as the Vroom–Yetton model), developed by researchers Victor Vroom, Philip Yetton, and Arthur Jago, addresses such situations and prescribes when the leader needs to involve followers in decision making (Vroom and Jago, 1988, 2007; Vroom and Yetton, 1973). It is called *normative* because it recommends that leaders adopt certain styles based on the prescriptions of the model. Like Fiedler, Vroom and his associates recommend matching the leader and the situational requirements. They, however, differ on several points. The Normative Decision Model is limited to decision making rather than general leadership and it assumes that leaders can adopt different decision-making styles as needed.

The model relies on two well-established group dynamic principles: first are the research findings that groups are wasteful and inefficient, and second, that participation in decision making leads to commitment. The model recommends that leaders adjust their decision style depending on the degree to which the quality of the decision is important and the likelihood that employees will accept the decision.

The Normative Decision Model recommends that leaders adjust their decision style depending on the degree to which the quality of the decision is important and the likelihood that employees will accept the decision.

Leader's Decision Styles

The Normative Decision Model identifies four decision methods available to leaders (Vroom and Jago, 1988). The first method is autocratic (A), in which the leader makes a decision with little or no involvement from followers. The second decision method is consultation (C), which means that the leader consults with followers yet retains the final decision-making authority. The third decision method is group (G). Here, the leader relies on consensus building to solve a problem. The final method involves total delegation (D) of decision making to one employee. The decision styles and their subcategories are summarized in Table 3-3.

A leader must decide which style to use depending on the situation that the leader and the group face and on whether the problem involves a group or one individual.

Table 3-3   Decision Styles in the Normative Decision Model.

Decision Style	AI	AII	CI	CII	GI	GII	DI
Description	Unassisted decision	Ask for specific information but make decisions alone	Ask for specific information and ideas from each group member	Ask for information and ideas from whole group	Ask for one person's help; mutual exchange based on expertise	Group shares information and ideas and reaches consensus	Other person analyzes problem makes decision
Who makes the decision	Leader	Leader	Leader	Leader with considerable group input	Leader and one other person	Group with leader input	Other person
Type of Problem	Group and individual	Group and individual	Group and individual	Group	Individual	Group	Individual

Key: A = Autocratic, C = Consultative, G = Group

Sources: V. H. Vroom and A. G. Jago, *The New Leadership: Managing Participation in Organizations* (Upper Saddle River, NJ: Prentice Hall, 1988); and V. H. Vroom and P. W. Yetton, *Leadership and Decision Making* (Pittsburgh: University of Pittsburgh Press, 1973).

Individual problems affect only one person, whereas group problems can affect a group or individual. For example, deciding on raises for individual employees is an individual problem, whereas scheduling vacations is a group problem. Similarly, deciding on which employees should receive training or undertake overseas assignment is an individual problem, whereas moving a business to another state or cutting down a city service is a group problem. The distinction between the two is not always clear; individual problems can affect others, and group problems can have an impact on individuals.

Contingency Factors and Predictions of the Model

The two central contingency factors for the Normative Decision Model are the quality of the decision and the need for acceptance and commitment by followers. Other contingency factors to consider are whether the leader has enough relevant information to make a sound decision, whether the problem is structured and clear, the likelihood that followers will accept the leader's decision, whether the employees agree with the organizational goals, whether employees are cohesive, and whether they have enough information to make a decision alone. Table 3-4 presents the eight contingency factors.

The Normative Decision Model is a decision tree, as shown in Figure 3-2. Leaders ask series of questions listed in Table 3-4; the questions relate to the contingency factors and should be asked sequentially. By responding "yes" or "no" to each question, managers can determine which decision style(s) is most appropriate for the problem they face. Figure 3-2 presents the most widely used Normative Decision Model and is labeled "time efficient," based on the assumption that consultation and participation

Table 3-4   Contingency Factors in the Normative Decision Model.

Contingency Factor	Question to Ask
Quality requirement (QR)	How important is the quality of the decision?
Commitment requirement (CR)	How important is employee commitment to the implementation of the decision?
Leader information (LI)	Does the leader have enough information to make a high-quality decision?
Structure of the problem (ST)	Is the problem clear and well structured?
Commitment probability (CP)	How likely is employee commitment to the solution if the leader makes the decision alone?
Goal congruence (GC)	Do employees agree with and support organizational goals?
Employee conflict (CO)	Is there conflict among employees over solution?
Subordinate information (SI)	Do employees have enough information to make a high-quality decision?

Sources: V. H. Vroom and A. G. Jago, *The New Leadership: Managing Participation in Organizations* (Upper Saddle River, NJ: Prentice Hall, 1988); and V. H. Vroom and P. W. Yetton, *Leadership and Decision Making* (Pittsburgh: University of Pittsburgh Press, 1973).

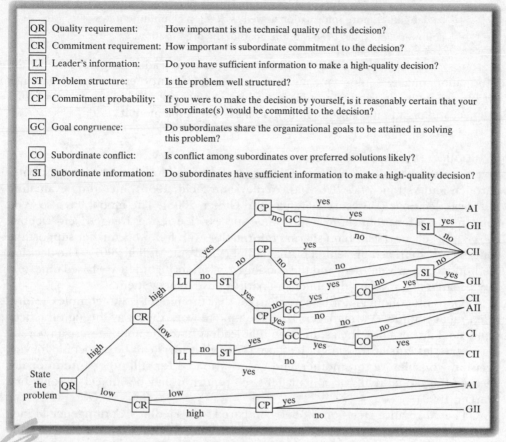

Figure 3-2   Normative Decision Model.

Source: Adapted and reprinted from *Leadership and Decision-Making* by Victor H. Vroom and Philip W. Yetton, by permission of the University of Pittsburgh Press. Copyright © 1973 by University of Pittsburgh Press.

require time and are not efficient (Vroom and Jago, 1988). Thus, whenever appropriate, the model leans toward more autocratic decision making. A second version of the model, labeled "time investment," focuses on the development of followers at the expense of efficiency. This version recommends more participative decision making whenever possible.

An autocratic decision-making style is appropriate in the following situations:

➤ When the leader has sufficient information to make a decision
➤ When the quality of the decision is not essential
➤ When employees do not agree with each other
➤ When employees do not agree with the goals of the organization

A consultative style of decision making is appropriate in the following situations:

➤ The leader has sufficient information, but the employees demand participation to implement the decision.

➤ The leader has insufficient information, and employee consultation will help the leader gather more information as well as develop commitment.

➤ Followers generally agree with the goals of the organization.

A group-oriented decision style should be used when the leader does not have all the information, quality is important, and employee commitment is essential. Delegation is used to assign the decision to a single individual who has the needed information, competence, and organizational commitment to make and implement it.

Evaluation and Application

Several research studies support the Normative Decision Model in a variety of settings (Crouch and Yetton, 1987; Tjosvold, Wedley, and Field, 1986), including evaluating historical decisions (Duncan, LaFrance, and Ginter, 2003). The model has also been applied in not-for-profit settings with some success (Lawrence, Deagen, and Debbie, 2001), and recent research on sharing information with followers further support the contingency approach presented by the model (Vidal and Möller, 2007). The decision methods are clearly defined, and the contingency factors included are based on extensive research about group dynamics and participative management.

Some practitioners and theorists argue that the model is too complex to provide practical value. Few managers have the time to work their way through the decision tree. Furthermore, the assumption that leaders have the ability to use any of the decision styles equally well might be flawed. Not all leaders can be autocratic for one decision, consultative for another, and group oriented for still others. Additionally, because the model relies on a manager's self-report, it may be subject to some bias (Parker, 1999).

The Normative Decision Model, compared with Fiedler's Contingency Model, takes a narrower focus on leadership decision making. Within that limited focus, the model works well and can be a helpful tool for leaders. The model suggests several practical implications:

➤ Leaders must understand the situation and understand how and when to use the different decision methods.

➤ Participation is not always desirable as a leadership style.

➤ Leaders must pay particular attention to their followers' needs and reactions when making a decision.

In addition to Fiedler's and Vroom and Yetton's theories that focus on how leaders use their resources, three other contingency models hinge on how leaders manage their relationships with followers.

Path-Goal Theory

The Path-Goal Theory of leadership, developed in the early 1970s, proposes that the leader's role is to clear the paths subordinates use to accomplish goals (House, 1971; House and Dessler, 1974). By doing so, leaders allow subordinates to fulfill their needs, and, as a result, leaders reach their own goals as well. The concept of exchange between leaders and subordinates, whether it is an implicit or explicit contract, is at the core of this model. The leader and followers establish a relationship that revolves around the exchange of guidance or support for productivity and satisfaction.

The Framework

The major conceptual basis for the Path-Goal Theory is the expectancy model of motivation (Vroom, 1964). Expectancy theory describes how individuals make rational choices about their behavior, based on their perceptions of the degree to which their effort and performance can lead to outcomes they value. The key to motivation, then, is to remove the various obstacles that weaken the linkages between effort and performance and between performance and outcomes. The nature of the task and follower characteristics determine which leadership behavior contributes to subordinate satisfaction. If the task is new and unclear, the followers are likely to waste their efforts owing to lack of knowledge and experience. They might feel frustrated and unmotivated, so the leader must provide instructions and training, thereby removing obstacles to followers' performance and allowing them to do their job. If a task is routine and subordinates performed it successfully a number of times, however, they might face an element of boredom, which would require the leader must show consideration, empathy, and understanding toward subordinates.

Behaviors the leader uses to motivate employees further depend on the employees themselves (Griffin, 1979; Stinson and Johnson, 1975). Some employees need guidance and clear instructions; others expect to be challenged and seek autonomy to do their own problem solving. The followers' need for autonomy and other personal characteristics, such as locus of control, are factors that the leader needs to consider before selecting an appropriate behavior. For example, a follower who likes challenges and needs autonomy will not need or want the leader to be directive even during an unstructured task. For that employee, leader directiveness can be irrelevant or even detrimental because it might reduce satisfaction.

Evaluation and Application

Despite several supportive research studies (e.g., House and Mitchell), the empirical support for the Path-Goal Theory remains mixed (Downey, Sheridan, and Slocum, 1975; Szilagyi and Sims, 1974). The model is generally under-researched, although researchers have proposed several new potential applications (Elkins and Keller, 2003). Notwithstanding contradictory findings, the Path-Goal Theory contributes to our understanding of leadership by once more focusing attention on the behavior of providing guidance and support to followers. It adds to resource utilization models, such as Fiedler's Contingency Model, by including followers' perceptions of the task and the role of the leader in removing blocks to task accomplishment. The Path-Goal Theory's use of employee satisfaction as a criterion for leadership effectiveness broadens our view of leadership. The model's suggestion that not all behaviors will be effective with all subordinates points to the importance of an employee's need for challenge and desire to be autonomous as a determinant of a leader's behavior. Interestingly, the role of the leader in the Path-Goal Theory is that of obstacle remover, which is similar to the role ascribed to team leaders (see Chapter 8).

The next theory reviews a leadership model that focuses on how leaders interpret their followers' actions and use that information as the basis for their relationship with them.

Leading Change   Jim Goodnight of SAS

"Employees don't leave companies, they leave managers" (Lauchlan, 2007). The statement summarizes the importance Jim Goodnight places on leadership and managing people well. He cofounded SAS, the world's largest privately held software company, and with John Sall, continues to fully own the company so that the two can think long-term and do what it takes to take care of their employees and their customers. With a 98 percent customer renewal rate, negligible turnover, and global sales of $1.34 billion, they are doing something right (Bisoux, 2004). Goodnight is the public face of the company and deserves much credit for that success. SAS has kept its workforce happy by giving its employees challenging work, letting them enjoy at 35-hour work week, free on-site day care, health care, an extensive fitness center, car detailing, and discounts to country club memberships; and free M&M's one day a week. Although the candy costs the company $45,000 a year, Goodnight believes it is a small price to show appreciation for his employees and is an indicator of the organization's friendly culture (Bisoux, 2004).

Goodnight believes that when the company removes day-to-day challenges, people can focus on their jobs. He tells his managers, "If you treat people like they make a difference, then they will make a difference" (Lauchlan, 2007). For him, it is about giving people a chance to prove themselves. Valuing employees is as important to him as keeping his customers happy. Goodnight states, "I simply wanted to create a company where I would want to work. Over the years, I've learned how employee loyalty leads to customer loyalty, increased innovation, and higher-quality software" (Faiola, 2006). He considers his employees and his customers the building blocks of the success of his organization (Goodnight, 2005). During his speech after being named as the year's top executive in 2005, Goodnight echoed this theme: "I simply facilitate a creative environment where people can create great software and foster long-term relationships with our customers" (Stevie, 2004). While he stays involved in the daily operations, he has the opportunity to stay close to both employees and customers and hear first-hand about ideas and challenges SAS may face. His formula for success is simple: "Keep you customers happy. Value your employees . . . while you may not grow your profits every quarter, you will grow your business over time" (Bisoux, 2004: 20).

Sources: Bisoux, T., 2004. "Corporate counter culture," *BizEd*, November–December: 16–20; Faiola, A. M., 2006. *Inc,* June, *xx.*; Goodnight, J., 2005. "Software 2005: Building blocks for success," http://www.sandhill.com/conferences/sw2005_proceedings/goodnight.pdf (accessed July 8, 2007); Lauchlan, S., 2007. "Interview with Jim Goodnight," *MyCustomer.com,* May 22. http://www.mycustomer.com/cgi-bin/item.cgi?id=133019&d=101&h=817&f=816 (accessed July 8, 2007); Stevie Award. 2004. http://www.crm2day.com/news/crm/EpluuFlFFpWCyCGeTT.php (accessed July 8, 2007).

ATTRIBUTIONAL MODELS

A component of the exchange between leaders and followers is the way the leader perceives and interprets followers' behaviors and uses these interpretations to make decisions about future actions. For example, when an employee fails to contact a key potential client and, as a result, loses that client to a competitor, the manager will attempt to understand the cause of the error to decide what needs to be done. Whether the manager perceives the cause to be the employee's laziness or lack of concern for the job or whether the problem was caused by the manager's failure to communicate the importance of the client will determine future actions. In the first case, the employee is to blame, and a reprimand or more serious disciplinary action might be appropriate. In the second case, because the manager shares the blame, he or she is not likely to reprimand the employee.

A number of research studies focused on understanding the processes described in the preceding example (Green and Mitchell, 1979; Mitchell and Wood, 1980; Offermann, Schroyer, and Green, 1998). These processes are called *attribution* and focus on explaining the way we interpret the cause of others' behaviors and our own (Jones and Davis, 1965; Kelley, 1967). Our interpretations depend on many factors, including our analysis of the situation and national culture. Two factors come into play in leadership situations. First, the leader must determine whether the cause of the error is internal to the employee (e.g., lack of ability or effort) or external to the employee (e.g., task difficulty, lack of training or support, bad luck, etc.). Second, the leader must decide on a corrective course of action. The degree to which the employee's actions impact goal accomplishment and productivity (i.e., the seriousness of the consequences) provides further information to determine subsequent action. The employee is much more likely to be blamed and held responsible for the following types of errors:

- ➤ When the consequences are severe (e.g., the loss of an important client or the anger of a major constituent)
- ➤ When the employee has a mediocre track record on similar and different types of tasks and other employees are successful under similar circumstances
- ➤ When the employee shows defensiveness in responding to the manager's inquiry
- ➤ When the manager's success depends on the employee's good performance

One factor that can further impact how leaders make attributions is national culture. Consider the following example. A Canadian expatriate manager working in Jordan seeks the advice of his Jordanian assistant before he makes a decision on the purchase of new equipment from a local manufacturer. The Jordanian assistant appears noncommittal and provides no concrete answers but seems to suggest that a certain manufacturer would be better than the other. The Canadian manager orders from that manufacturer. The decision turns out to be costly and disastrous. The Canadian manager interprets his assistant's behavior as uncooperative, indicating a lack of initiative, or even as incompetent and disloyal. The Jordanian assistant is puzzled by his leader's lack of confidence and inability to lead. Leaders, after all, are supposed to have the answers.

This scenario illustrates typical misattributions that occur when people interpret behaviors across cultures. The leader in this case is interpreting his subordinate's response from his own cultural framework. The Canadian culture is low power distance; therefore, when a leader does not have all the information, it is acceptable and desirable to request feedback from a subordinate. A subordinate who refuses to help appears to be incompetent or disloyal. On the other hand, the Jordanian assistant also is interpreting behavior within his own cultural context, which includes high power distance and a strong paternalistic tradition. To him, a leader who does not have solutions and must ask for his employees' help is incompetent and weak.

The potential for bias and misinterpretation is greatly increased when individuals from one culture interpret and make attributions about the behavior of individuals from a different culture. Even within the same cultural context, however, attributions are subject to considerable biases.

Evaluation and Application

The attributional model of leadership is based on well-established psychological principles whose application to leadership situations is supported by research. It, however, is not a broad model of leadership and is concerned with only a particular aspect of the relationship between leaders and followers—namely, how a leader interprets followers' behaviors and actions and how such interpretations affect the leader's interactions. Despite their limited scope, the propositions and findings of attributional models offer many applications to leadership situations. In particular, because interpretation and evaluation of followers' actions is a central part of leadership activities, understanding these processes can be helpful to leaders.

Because the interpretation and evaluation of followers' actions is a central part of leadership activities, the propositions and findings of attributional models offer many helpful applications in understanding and managing these processes.

The next model considers situations in which leadership is not needed.

Applying What You Learn
Avoiding Biases

Research on social perception, attribution theory, and attributional models of leadership indicate that what we perceive is often more important than objective reality. It is, therefore, essential that leaders and followers carefully manage perception, and consider the following points:

- Be aware of your biases; this awareness allows you to get as close to an objective evaluation and judgment as possible.

- Depend on objective, reliable measures of performance when available.

- Keep notes about your own work and reactions, as well as the work and reactions of your followers; for most of us, our memory is not as good as we think it is.

- Actively seek all sides of an issue; listen to your followers to hear their side of events. Every situation always involves more than one perspective and explanation.

- Do reality checks not only with your close associates but also with others whom you respect but who might not be close to you or to the problem you encountered.

Substitutes for Leadership

In some situations, a relationship between a leader and the followers is not needed to satisfy the followers' needs. Various aspects of the work environment provide enough resources and support to allow subordinates to achieve their goals without having to refer to their leader. For example, an experienced team of pharmaceutical salespeople, who spend a considerable amount of their time on the road and who have control over their commissions, are not likely to rely much on their manager. Their job provides them with challenges, and their experience allows them to make many decisions on their own. The office is not accessible, and they often rely on other salespeople for help and information. Similarly, skilled emergency room nurses and technicians do not rely on a leader or manager to take care of their patients. In such circumstances, various situational factors replace the leader's functions of providing structure, guidelines, and support to subordinates.

Such situations led to the development of the Substitutes for Leadership Model (SLM) (Kerr and Jermier, 1978). SLM proposes that various organizational, task, and employee characteristics can provide substitutes for the traditional leadership behaviors of consideration and initiation of structure (Table 3-5). In general, if information about the task and its requirement is clear and available to the subordinates through various means such as their own experience, their team, or through the organization, they are not likely to need the leader's structuring behaviors. Similarly, when support and empathy are not needed or are available through other sources such as coworkers, the subordinates will not seek the leader's consideration behaviors.

Table 3-5   Leadership Substitutes and Neutralizers.

Substitutes or Neutralizers	Consideration	Structuring
Follower Characteristics		
1. Experience and training		Substitute
2. Professionalism	Substitute	Substitute
3. Lack of value for goals	Neutralizer	Neutralizer
Task Characteristics		
1. Unambiguous tasks		
2. Direct feedback from task		Substitute
3. Challenging task	Substitute	Substitute
Organizational Characteristics		
1. Cohesive team		Substitute
2. Leader's lack of power	Substitute	Neutralizer
3. Standardization and formalization	Neutralizer	Substitute
4. Organizational rigidity		Neutralizer
5. Physical distance between leaders and followers	Neutralizer	Neutralizer

Source: Based on S. Kerr and J. M. Jermier, "Substitutes for leadership: Their meaning and measurement," *Organizational Behavior and Human Performance,* 22 (1978): 375–403.

In addition to substituting for leadership, some situations can neutralize the effect of the leader. Most notably, the leader's lack of power to deliver outcomes to followers and an organization's rigid culture can prevent a leader's consideration and structuring behaviors from affecting subordinates. For example, a subordinate whose manager is in another state or is powerless to deliver on promises and reward or a subordinate who does not value the rewards provided by the manager is not likely to be affected by the leader's behaviors (see Table 3-5). The situation neutralizes the leader.

Consider how Ricardo Semler (featured in Leading Change in Chapter 5), president of the Brazilian firm Semco, author and proponent of open-book management, set up his company so that it runs with few managers (Leading by Omission, 2005). Workers are trained carefully; provided with considerable information, including detailed financial data and salary information; and left to set their own hours, evaluate and vote for their managers, and make most of the decisions. The workers' training and experience allows the company to function with few senior managers. The structure, training, and teamwork at Semco act as substitutes for leadership.

Evaluation and Application

The SLM has not been tested extensively and needs considerable clarification regarding the nature of the various substitutes and neutralizers and the situations to which they might apply. Because of inconsistent results, some researchers suggest that it suffers from methodological problems (Villa et al., 2003), and the few studies performed in non-U.S. cultural settings failed to yield support for the model (Farh, Podsakoff, and Cheng, 1987). Like the next model we will discuss, the leader–member exchange, however, the SLM is intuitively appealing and addresses processes not taken into account by other leadership models. In particular, it questions the need for leadership in certain situations and points to the difficulty of being an effective leader when many neutralizers are present (Howell et al., 1990). Furthermore, the model provides considerable potential for application. Depending on the culture, strategy, and goals of an organization and on a specific leader's personality, the leader might want to set up or remove leadership substitutes. For some control-oriented leaders or in organizations with traditional structures and hierarchies in place, the presence of substitutes could be perceived as a loss of control and authority.

Given the flattening of many organizations and the push toward empowerment and use of teams, judicious use of substitutes can free up the leader for other activities, such as strategic planning, and still allow the organization to achieve its objectives. The use of information technology tools that make information widely available and support work structures, such as telecommuting and outsourcing, further reduces the need for leadership in some situations (Howell, 1997). Consider the case of one of the oldest and fifth largest breweries in the United States. Despite its 175-year-old history, D.G. Yuengling & Son uses a modern, relatively flat structure that focuses on not becoming bureaucratic. Respect for the individual and a positive work environment are part of its core values (Yuengling, 2007). The company offers relatively high-paying jobs in an area where jobs are scare and has developed a loyal following (Rubinkan, 2007). Like many other family operations, however, employees and managers found themselves relying too much on the owner, Dick Yuengling. Yuengling recognizes the need to set up substitutes for his hands-on leadership: "You've got to get people in the proper place" (Kurtz, 2004: 71). The company's chief operating officer, David Cainelli, along with Jennifer Yuengling, set up the structures that would allow for decision making to be decentralized and delegated to people closest to the products and markets (Kurtz, 2004).

Autonomous and self-managed teams provide an application of the SLM. The goal of such teams is to function without supervision. The team becomes a substitute for leadership. Extensive technical and team-building training, selection of team members with a professional orientation, intrinsically satisfying tasks for which team members are given considerable autonomy, and direct feedback can be used as substitutes for leadership structuring behaviors. Similarly, a cohesive team replaces the leader's supportive behaviors. The factors identified as substitutes can be used as a guide in setting up such autonomous work teams. One final implication of the SLM is leadership training. Based on this model, leadership training might need to focus on teaching the leader to change the situation as much as it focuses on teaching effective leadership behaviors. Leaders can be taught how to set up substitutes and avoid neutralizers. Such a recommendation is similar to those based on Fiedler's Contingency Model discussed earlier in this chapter.

The next model we consider focuses on the dyadic relationship between leaders and followers.

Leader–Member Exchange

Many of us experience leadership, either as leaders or followers, as a personal relationship between a leader or a subordinate rather than a group phenomenon. We interact daily with our managers and forge an individual relationship with them. As leaders, we do not experience the same relationship with all of our followers. Each dyadic relationship is different. A leader establishes a one-on-one relationship with each follower (Figure 3-3), and each relationship varies greatly in terms of the quality of the exchange. These concepts are at the core of the Leader–Member Exchange (LMX) model, which was called the Vertical Dyad Linkage Model in its earlier versions (Dansereau, Graen, and Haga, 1975; Graen and Shiemann, 1978). LMX model focuses on the unique, relationship-based exchange between a leader and followers (Graen and Uhl-Bien, 1995).

In each exchange, the leader and follower establish a role for the follower. Those followers with a high-quality relationship are in the in-group. High-quality LMX involves mutual respect, anticipation of deepening trust, and expectations of continued and growing professional relationships and obligations. In-group followers enjoy their leader's attention, support, and confidence, and receive challenging and interesting assignments. The leader might overlook their errors (Duarte, Goodson, and Klich, 1994) or attribute them to factors outside of the followers' control. In exchange for the in-group status, the followers' role is to work hard, be loyal, and support the leader. They are likely to work beyond their formally prescribed job duties (Liden and Graen, 1980) and increase their commitment to their goals (Klein and Kim, 1998).

For the members of the in-group, such high-quality exchange often becomes a self-fulfilling prophecy and leads to high performance, high satisfaction, and low stress. Studies extend the impact of a positive LMX to safety communication, commitment, and reduction of accidents (Hofmann and Morgeson, 1999). Other studies found that a positive LMX is related to higher frequency of communication, which in turn, leads to

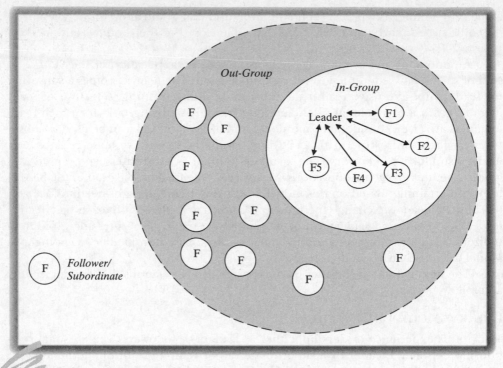

Figure 3-3   Leader–Member Exchange Model.

more favorable job performance ratings (Kacmar, Witt, Zivnuska, and Gully, 2003) and may lead to higher outputs in research and development teams (Elkins and Keller, 2003). Conceptual extensions of the model suggest that the positive work relationship might even extend to social networks, whereby leaders sponsor members of their in-group into various social networks (Sparrowe and Liden, 1997). Research indicates that a positive exchange with a leader plays a role in the extent to which employees feel the organization supports them (Wayne, Shore, and Liden, 1997).

The followers in the out-group face a different situation. The leader might perceive them as less motivated or less competent, interact with them less, provide them with few opportunities to perform, and promote them less often (Wakabayashi et al., 1988). Their role tends to be limited to that defined by formal job descriptions, with little or no expectation of high performance, commitment, or loyalty. They often have to find ways of compensating for the low-quality relationship they have with their leader (Kacmar, Zivnuska, and White, 2007). Regardless of whether the leader's perception and expectations are accurate and fair, members of the out-group are likely to live up, or down, to them. As a result, out-group members who have a low-quality LMX will perform poorly and experience more stress. They also file for grievances more often (Cleyman, Jex, and Love, 1993) and are more likely to take retaliatory actions against the organization (Townsend, Phillips, and Elkins, 2000).

The relationship between the leader and each follower forms early. The LMX model suggests that development of the leader–follower relationship takes place in

Table 3-6   Stages of Relationship Development Between Leaders and Their Followers.

Stage	Description
Testing and assessment	No relationship is yet formed. Leaders consider followers who do not yet belong to a group in terms of objective and subjective criteria for inclusion in either in-group or out-group. Followers' potential, ability, skills, and other psychological factors, such as loyalty, may be tested. Group assignments are made. The relationship with out-group followers does not progress beyond this stage.
Development of trust	This stage only exists for in-group members. Leader provides in-group followers with challenges and opportunities to perform that reinforce development of trust. In return, followers perform and demonstrate their loyalty to the leader.
Creation of emotional bond	In-group followers with a well-established relationship may move to this stage where the relationship and the bond between them become strong and emotional. Followers are highly committed to leader's vision.

Source: Partially based on information in Graen and Uhl-Bien, "The transformation of work group professionals into self-managing and partially self-designing contributors: Toward a theory of leadership-making," *Journal of Management Systems* 3, no. 3 (1991): 33–48.

stages summarized in Table 3-6. Additionally, leaders create positive relationships with three types of followers: those who are competent and show relevant skills, those whom they can trust, and those who are willing to assume more responsibility. Some research further suggests that followers can create a positive LMX by seeking feedback about their performance as long as the supervisor attributes the behavior to work rather than a desire to make a positive impression (Lam, Juan, and Snape, 2007). Culture can also play a key role in how in-group membership is assigned and which of these three factors is given more weight. In achievement-oriented cultures, such as the United States and Germany, individuals are evaluated based on their performance and achievement rather than on their past or their membership in certain castes (Trompenaars, 1994). Therefore, it is expected that leaders select their in-group members based on competence, performance, and commitment to the organization rather than based on a personal relationship. Anything else would be called favoritism and nepotism. As a result, formal human resource policies and procedures, as well as day-to-day personnel practices, in such cultures focus on fairness, equal opportunity, and on hiring those who are most qualified for the jobs based on their personal competence.

In ascriptive cultures, such as many in the Middle East or France, a higher-quality exchange may depend more on the leader's ability to trust followers, which is likely to be based on issues such as social class and birth (Trompenaars, 1994). The concepts of nepotism and inappropriate favoritism to one's in-group do not apply readily in ascriptive and collectivist cultures, where loyalty to one's village, clan, or family is the primary concern. In such cultures, managers hire those they know directly or who

In achievement-oriented cultures, such as the United States and Germany, individuals are evaluated based on their performance and achievement rather than on their past or their membership in certain castes. In ascriptive cultures, such as many in the Middle East or France, a higher-quality exchange may depend more on the leader's ability to trust followers, which is likely to be based on issues such as social class and birth.

are recommended by others they know. Skills and competence are secondary to such personal recommendations. In Hong Kong, for example, leaders are obligated to take care of their own people first (Adler, 1991). Malaysians place a strong emphasis on loyalty and harmony in the work group (Kennedy, 2002). In many Middle Eastern countries, including Arab and non-Arab countries, such as Afghanistan and Iran, leaders surround themselves with family and clan members who can be trusted and who are loyal. Doing otherwise would be disloyal to ones' community and even foolish. In such cultures, a wise leader does not allow strangers into the in-group, no matter how competent and qualified they are. Outsiders are hired to help, but access to the in-group is based on community factors. Recent studies further suggest that organizational culture may also impact the quality of the LMX, with better relationships in team-oriented cultures (Erdogan, Linden, and Kramer, 2006).

Evaluation and Application

Interest in LMX theory continues to be strong with many recent extensions and testing of its component (e.g., Chattopadhyay, Tluchowska, and George, 2004; Lam et al., 2007). Several areas require further clarification. Specifically, researchers question the adequacy of the theory, the multiple measures, and the methods used to test the concepts (for a detailed review, see Schriesheim, Castro, and Cogliser, 1999). Additionally, despite continued research, the factors that lead to the development of an in-group versus an out-group relationship need more attention. Some research suggests that similarity in regard to personality plays a key role early in the relationship (Dose, 1999; Murphy and Ensher, 1999), whereas performance matters more as time goes on (Bauer and Greene, 1996). More research needs to be conducted in other areas as well, including identifying factors that affect the development of the LMX, assessing the desirability of having the two groups or the conditions under which subordinates move from one group to the other, and exploring the cultural factors that are likely to affect the decision on who belongs to the in-group. The research on the impact of gender similarity on the development of LMX, for example, produced mixed results and requires further clarification (see McAllister, 1995; Tsui and O'Reilly, 1989). The results of at least one study in Mexico, however, show gender similarity to be related to lower absenteeism, particularly with female leaders (Pelled and Xin, 1997) and higher trust (Pelled and Xin, 2000).

From a practitioner and application point of view, the LMX model is appealing. Anyone who has been part of an organization has experienced the feeling of being part of either the in-group or the out-group. Many have seen the departure of a well-liked manager, who is replaced with someone who has his own team. The quick movement from in-group to out-group is felt acutely. The concept of in-group and out-group also can be perceived as violating the norm of equality (Scandura, 1999), which is highly valued in many Western cultures, including the United States. As leaders, most of us can identify our in-group (see Self-Assessment 3-3). Our in-group members are the people we trust. They are our right-hand assistants. We can give them any assignment with confidence. They will get the job done without us having to check up on them. We also know the members of our out-group. Toward some, we feel neutral; others we dislike and may try to get transferred. In both cases, those individuals do not get many chances to interact with us, and they are not provided with many opportunities to demonstrate their competence on visible and key projects.

The development of an individual exchange with others is a natural part of any interaction. Such a situation can be highly positive for an organization, allowing for the identification of competent individuals and ensuring that they achieve organizational goals. The creation of in-groups and out-groups, however, can also be highly detrimental, leading to feelings and accusations of unfair treatment (Scandura, 1999). Alan Canton, president of Adams-Blake Co., a software company in California, faced considerable obstacles in the development of a new software when three of the five-member team assigned to the task formed a friendship—a clique—and decided to exclude the other two members (Rich, 2005). Canton addressed the problem head-on to get rid of the unproductive in-group/out-group that formed. The key issue is the basis upon which such relationships are formed. Researchers suggest that personal compatibility and employee ability are the basis for selection (Graen and Cashman, 1975). Unfortunately, organizational reality does not always match theory. Most of us can identify, or were part of, LMX relationships based on either positive or negative personal feelings, stereotypes, or interpersonal conflicts. Many highly competent and qualified employees are excluded from a leader's in-group based on personal dislike or organizational politics. After all, leaders are subject to human error just like the rest of us.

Abuse of power (discussed in Chapter 5) and membership of some top management teams (discussed in Chapter 7) are examples of the potential negative effects of in-groups. Being able to work with people you trust and agree with and who share your vision for the organization sounds like an ideal situation for any leader, who would then not face unnecessary arguments and delays. Decisions would be made quickly and efficiently, and goals would be achieved. This ideal situation is exactly what many top-level executives attempt to set up when they select their top management team and the members of their board of directors. They pick people they trust and can work with. Executives rarely consciously and willingly pick members with whom they have major conflicts and differences. The goal is to create a workable team—a team made up of in-group members.

An example of the importance of being part of a team is the now-classic case of Michael Ovitz, who was hired to be Disney's president and fired 14 months later, receiving a $140-million severance package for his short tenure. During the trial of a lawsuit filed by a Disney shareholder against CEO Michael Eisner for wasting company resources by hiring and then firing Michael Ovitz, Ovitz testified that from the first day, he was left out of decisions and undercut by the Disney management team who did not report to him (Holson, 2004a). Eisner, for his part, testified that he had to spend too much time managing Ovitz (considered one of the most powerful and successful wheeler-dealers in Hollywood when he headed the Creative Artists Agency before coming to Disney): "Every day I was trying to manage Michael Ovitz. I did little else" (Holson, 2004b: C1). Eisner further accused Ovitz of "un-Disney-like" behavior and of not fitting in with the rest of management team. Eisner cited an example of Ovitz taking a limousine instead of a bus with other executives and states that Ovitz "was a little elitist for the egalitarian cast members" (Holson, 2004b: C12). Although the Ovitz–Eisner case is much more complex than an LMX relationship, the poor relationship and the fact that Ovitz either did not fit in or was not allowed to be part of the in-group clearly played a role in his firing from Disney, a factor that, in turn, was central to the shareholder lawsuit.

Research on friendship patterns and attraction to others indicates that people tend to associate with those who are like them, have similar backgrounds, and share their values and beliefs. To counteract this potential bias, Maggie Widerotter of Wink Communication makes a point of taking time to look for employees she does not see on a regular basis. She takes time to get out of her office and go on a "lion hunt" (McCauley, 2000: 114). She says, "That gives me a chance to connect with employees who I don't usually talk to. . . . I always walk away from the experience having learned something: I have a renewed understanding of what we're doing at my company" (114).

Without a conscious effort to seek out new people, the in-group for most leaders includes people who are like them, with similar backgrounds and views. This homogeneity in top management teams and board membership caught the blame recently for many of the problems in U.S. businesses. Industrial giants such as Ford, AT&T, and IBM suffered from the lack of initiative and creativity of their top management teams. The members worked well together and disregarded input from outsiders. As a result, they failed to foresee the problems and full consequences of their decisions or inaction. The same pursuit of homogeneity is also seen as a weakness in President George W. Bush's inner circle and administration and its decision making on highly complex issues such as the war in Iraq or the firing of U.S. attorneys. The ease, comfort, and efficiency of working with a cohesive in-group are usually because of the similarity of its members. These advantages, however, are sometimes offset by a lack of creativity and limited decision making. In an ideal case, no in-group or out-group should exist. All of a leader's subordinates should have equal access to the leader and to projects and resources. Those who do not perform well should be helped or moved out of the group altogether. Reality, however, is different, and avoiding the creation of in-groups and out-groups is difficult.

One of the key issues then becomes how members are selected to be in each group. For the individual relationship to be productive, leaders should follow some general principles in creating in-groups and out-groups and in selecting their membership. It is important to note that these guidelines apply mostly to achievement-oriented rather than ascriptive cultures:

> ➤ Pick in-group members based on competence and contribution to the organization.
> ➤ Periodically evaluate your criteria for in-group and out-group membership.
> ➤ Assign tasks to persons with the most applicable skills regardless of group membership.
> ➤ Set clear, performance-related guidelines for in-group membership.
> ➤ Avoid highly differentiated in-groups and out-groups.
> ➤ Keep membership fluid to allow movement in and out of the groups.
> ➤ Maintain different in-groups for different activities.

The concept of exchange in the leadership interaction and the importance of the relationship between leaders and their followers are expanded and developed further in a more recent model of leadership, Transactional-Transformational Leadership, covered in more detail in Chapter 6.

SUMMARY AND CONCLUSION

The scientific approach to understanding leadership that started at about the time of the industrial revolution added rigor and attempts at precise measurement to other already-existing views about leadership. The first modern approaches focused on the identification of traits that would distinguish leaders and followers. Although certain traits were found to be associated with leadership, no simple sets of traits consistently predicted who would be an effective leader. Because of inconclusive results, researchers turned their attention to leadership behaviors. The two major categories of initiation of structure and consideration were established as the central leadership behaviors. The switch from simple traits to simple behaviors still did not account for the complex leadership process and, therefore, did not allow researchers to make strong predictions about leadership effectiveness.

The early theories that are the foundation of modern leadership theory address either the way leaders use resources or the relationship between the leader and the follower. Normative Decision Model and Fiedler's Contingency Model consider how the leader uses resources that are available and propose that the leader's style must be matched to the situation to achieve effectiveness. Whereas the Contingency Model assumes that the leader's style (LPC) is determined by internal traits and therefore difficult to change, the Normative Decision Model relies on decision-making styles that are assumed to be learnable. The two also differ on the criteria they use for leadership effectiveness. The Contingency model looks at group performance; the Normative Decision Model focuses on decision quality. Perhaps their most interesting contribution to leadership application and training is that both models involve a series of well-defined variables that can be used to improve leadership effectiveness.

The relationship-based theories focus on the relationship between the leader and the follower. The Path-Goal Theory proposes that the leader's main function is to remove obstacles in the subordinates' path to allow them to perform their jobs and to be motivated and satisfied. The attributional models consider the way in which a leader interprets performance information about followers. The Substitutes for Leadership Model (SLM) explores situations in which a relationship between the leader and subordinates is not needed and is replaced by individual, group, and organizational factors. Finally, the Leader–Member Exchange (LMX) Model focuses on the dyadic relationship between a leader and each follower and proposes the concept of in-groups and out-groups as the defining element of that relationship.

All the models use a contingency view of leadership, and in all of them, the leader's behavior or style depends on the requirements of the situation. Although the concept of task and relationship orientation continues to be dominant, several of the models consider other factors, thereby expanding our views of leadership. The structure and routine of the task continue to be key situational factors, although other variables such as follower independence and maturity are also introduced.

The contingency models of leadership presented here are the foundation of current theory in leadership and continue to dominate the field of leadership. The

Table 3-7   Comparison of the Early Contingency Models of Leadership.

	Leader Characteristic	Follower Characteristic	Task	Other Factors	Effectiveness Criteria
Fiedler's model	LPC based on motivation; not changeable	Group cohesion	Task structure	Position power	Group performance
Normative Decision Model	Decision-making style; can be changed	Group cohesion	Available information	Agreement with goals Time	Quality of the decision
Path-Goal theory	Leader behavior; can be changed	Individual follower need to grow	Clarity and routineness of task		Follower satisfaction and motivation
Substitutes	Leader behavior; can be changed	Group cohesion	Clarity of task; availability of information	Organization culture, structure, and processes	Need for leader
LMX					Quality of relationship with follower

models differ in the factors they use to describe the leader's style or behavior and elements of the leadership situation that are considered (Table 3-7).

For each model, however, whether in resource utilization or in exchange and relationship development models, the focus is on the match between the leader and the situation. The extensive research about the various contingency models, although not always consistent and clear, led to the broad acceptance and establishment of the concept of contingency in leadership. Clearly, no one best way to lead exists. Effective leadership is a combination of and match between the leader and the leadership situation.

LEADERSHIP CHALLENGE: THE IN-GROUP APPLICANT

You are an expatriate manager sent to work in the Indian operation of your company. As you get settled in, one of your first decisions is to hire an assistant manager. Your efficient office manager, who has been extremely helpful to you already and has been with the company for many years, quickly suggests one of his relatives, who, he tells you, would be perfect for the job. According to him, his cousin just graduated from a top business school and, most importantly, is trustworthy, loyal, and eager to work and learn. Your office manager tells you that his cousin will be coming shortly to introduce himself. He tells you that you don't have to be inconvenienced any further and won't need to waste your time and risk having an unreliable stranger become your assistant.

1. How do you interpret and explain your office manager's actions?
2. Will you hire the "cousin"?
3. What factors do you need to consider before making your decision?

REVIEW AND DISCUSSION QUESTIONS

1. What are the similarities and differences between the trait and behavior approaches to leadership?
2. What are the major assumptions of the contingency approach to leadership?
3. Define the leadership and situational factors included in Fiedler's Contingency Model. What are the primary predictions of the model?
4. After assessing your own style, interview several people with whom you worked to determine whether their perceptions match your score based on the LPC.
5. Provide examples for the situations in which each of the major decision styles of the Normative Decision Model would be appropriate.
6. Provide examples of how the Path-Goal Theory of leadership can be used to improve leadership effectiveness.
7. How can leaders' knowledge of attributional processes increase their leadership effectiveness?
8. How does the LMX Model differ from all the other contingency theories of leadership?
9. What are positive and negative impacts of substitutes on leaders and organizations? Provide examples.
10. How can leaders use the LMX Model in improving their effectiveness?
11. Compare and contrast the contingency models of leadership. How do they each contribute to our understanding of leadership?

EXERCISE 3.1:   THE TOY FACTORY

The goal of this exercise is for each group to produce as many high-quality toy wolves as possible. Your instructor will assign you to a group, designate the leader, and provide you with a list of materials needed for making the toy wolves. Your team leader will give you instructions on how to make the toys. After a 15-minute production run, each group's productivity will be measured.

The Toy Factory Worksheet

1. How would you describe your team leader's style of leadership? Provide several specific behavioral examples.

2. How did you react to your leader's style? How satisfied were you?

3. What improvement suggestions (if any) could you offer your leader?

EXERCISE 3-2: USING THE NORMATIVE DECISION MODEL

This exercise is based on the concepts and principles presented in the Normative Decision Model of leadership. Use the contingency factors presented in Table 3-4 to analyze each case. Figure 3-2 along with Table 3-3 provides a guide to the appropriate decision styles for each case.

Case 1: Centralizing Purchasing

You are the western regional manager in charge of purchasing for a group of hospitals and clinics. Your territory includes eight western states. You recently joined the group but you brought with you nearly 10 years of experience in purchasing with one of the company's major competitors. One of your major achievements in the previous job was the implementation of a highly efficient companywide purchasing system. The health group oversees more than 30 associated health clinics and hospitals in your region alone. Each center operates somewhat independently without much control from the regional purchasing manager. Several of the clinics are cooperating under informal arrangements that allow them to get better prices from suppliers. The purchasing managers from the larger hospitals in your region, on the other hand, have almost no contact with one another or you. As a result, they are often competing for suppliers and fail to achieve economies of scale that would allow them to save considerable costs on their various purchases. In other cases, the managers rely on totally different suppliers and manage to obtain advantageous contracts.

With the pressure to cut health-care costs, the health group's board of directors and the group's president identified purchasing as one area where savings need to be achieved. You are charged with centralizing purchasing, and you are expected to reduce the costs of purchasing by at least 15 percent within a year.

You still need to meet many of the purchasing managers who are supposed to report to you. Your appointment was announced through a memo from the group's president. The memo also mentioned the need to cut costs in all areas and indicated the need to focus on purchasing as first step. The purchasing managers you did meet or contact were civil but not overly friendly. With only six months to show the first results, you need to start planning and implementing changes as soon as possible.

Analysis and Recommendation
Using the problem requirements, decision rules, and leadership styles of the Normative Decision Model, indicate which decision style(s) would be most appropriate.

1. What type of problem is it: group or individual?

2. Contingency Factors:
   Is there a quality requirement?
   Does the leader have enough information to make a high-quality decision?
   Is the problem clear and structured?
   Is employee acceptance of the decision needed for its implementation?
   Will subordinates accept the decision if the leader makes it by himself or herself?
   Do subordinates share the organization's goals for the problem?

Is there conflict among subordinates (are they cohesive) regarding the problem?

3. What are acceptable decision styles? Why?

4. What are unacceptable decision styles? Why?

Case 2: Selecting the Interns

You are the manager of the public relations and advertising department of a large electronics plant. Through your contacts with a local university, you made arrangements for your department to hire several interns in public relations and marketing every summer. Your company supports the idea, because ties with universities are important to you. The interns provide support to your department and work directly with your assistant and report to him. They spend most of their time observing various activities and helping where needed. The interns hired over the past years were all excellent and helpful. Your assistant enjoys working with them and even helped several of them find jobs after they graduated, some within your company.

This year, you received more than twenty applications, but your funding only allows you to hire two. You need to decide which two to hire.

Analysis and Recommendation

Using the problem requirements, decision rules, and leadership styles of the Normative Decision Model, indicate which decision style(s) would be most appropriate.

1. What type of problem is it: group or individual?

2. Contingency factors:
   Is there a quality requirement?
   Does the leader have enough information to make a high-quality decision?
   Is the problem clear and structured?
   Is employee acceptance of the decision needed for its implementation?
   Will subordinates accept the decision if the leader makes it by himself or herself?
   Do subordinates share the organization's goals for the problem?
   Is there conflict among subordinates (are they cohesive) regarding the problem?

3. What are acceptable decision styles? Why?

4. What are unacceptable decision styles? Why?

Case 3: Moving to a New Location

You are the manager of a medium-sized city in the Midwest. Through a number of exchanges between the state, local cities, and several businesses, the city recently acquired a building that could house several departments. The building is within one-half mile of

(*Continued*)

other major municipal offices. Although the building is newer than most of the other city buildings and offers larger offices, it is relatively sterile and does not have the charm of many of the older buildings. You inspected the building and also just received the report from the space allocation committee that is working on the problem of overcrowding of several departments. You identified five departments that could move to the new location. After the initial disruption caused by the move, neither the departments' employees nor their constituents would be affected by the move.

Because of the demand for office space, you must make the decision in the next two days. You are aware of the considerable disagreement among the various departments' employees as to which building is a better location and who would be less negatively affected by the move. Everyone agrees that overcrowding is a problem.

Analysis and Recommendation
Using the problem requirements, decision rules, and leadership styles of the Normative Decision Model, indicate which decision style(s) would be most appropriate.

1. What type of problem is it: group or individual?

2. Contingency factors:

    Is there a quality requirement?
    Does the leader have enough information to make a high-quality decision?
    Is the problem clear and structured?
    Is employee acceptance of the decision needed for its implementation?
    Will subordinates accept the decision if the leader makes it by himself or herself?
    Do subordinates share the organization's goals for the problem?
    Is there conflict among subordinates (are they cohesive) regarding the problem?

3. What are acceptable decision styles? Why?

4. What are unacceptable decision styles? Why?

SELF-ASSESSMENT 3-1: DETERMINING YOUR LPC

To fill out this scale, think of a person with whom you have had difficulty working. That person may be someone you work with now or someone you knew in the past. He or she does not have to be the person you like the least well, but should be the person with whom you experienced the most difficulty. Rate this person on the following scale.

				Score
Pleasant	8 7 6 5 4 3 2 1	Unpleasant		_____
Friendly	8 7 6 5 4 3 2 1	Unfriendly		_____
Rejecting	1 2 3 4 5 6 7 8	Accepting		_____
Tense	1 2 3 4 5 6 7 8	Relaxed		_____
Distant	1 2 3 4 5 6 7 8	Close		_____
Cold	1 2 3 4 5 6 7 8	Warm		_____
Supportive	8 7 6 5 4 3 2 1	Hostile		_____
Boring	1 2 3 4 5 6 7 8	Interesting		_____
Quarrelsome	1 2 3 4 5 6 7 8	Harmonious		_____
Gloomy	1 2 3 4 5 6 7 8	Cheerful		_____
Open	8 7 6 5 4 3 2 1	Guarded		_____
Backbiting	1 2 3 4 5 6 7 8	Loyal		_____
Untrustworthy	1 2 3 4 5 6 7 8	Trustworthy		_____
Considerate	8 7 6 5 4 3 2 1	Inconsiderate		_____
Nasty	1 2 3 4 5 6 7 8	Nice		_____
Agreeable	8 7 6 5 4 3 2 1	Disagreeable		_____
Insincere	1 2 3 4 5 6 7 8	Sincere		_____
Kind	8 7 6 5 4 3 2 1	Unkind		_____
		Total		_____

Scoring Key: A score of 64 or below indicates that you are task-motivated or low-LPC. A score of 73 or higher indicates that you are relationship-motivated or high-LPC. If your score falls between 65 and 72, you will need to determine for yourself in which category you belong.

Source: F. E. Fiedler and M. M. Chemers, *Improving Leadership Effectiveness: The Leaders Match Concept,* 2nd ed. (New York: Wiley, 1984). Adapted with permission.

SELF-ASSESSMENT 3-2:   ASSESSING A LEADERSHIP SITUATION

This assessment is based on Fiedler's Contingency Model and is designed to allow you to assess a situation you faced as a leader. To complete the questions in each category, think of a current or past situation at work, in sports, or in social or church events where you were the formal or informal leader of a group of people. You were either successful or not so successful. Rate the situation by circling one of the alternatives for each of the following questions; use the same situation to answer all the questions. You will evaluate your effectiveness, relationship with your followers, the structure of the task, and the power you had.

Self-Rating of Effectiveness

1. Considering the situation and task, how effective were you as a leader?

3	2	1
Very effective	Moderately effective	Not at all effective

2. How effective was your group in completing its task?

3	2	1
Very effective	Moderately effective	Not at all effective

3. How would you rate the overall performance of your group?

4	3	2	1
Very high performance	Moderately high performance	Somewhat low performance	Poor performance

Now add up the score of the three questions. The maximum score is 10; minimum is 3. A high performance score would indicate effectiveness. A score between 7 and 10 indicates high performance; a score between 6 and 4 is moderate performance; score of 3 indicates poor performance.

Leader–Member Relations Scale (LMR)

Write the number that best represents your response to each item using the following scale:

1 = Strongly agree
2 = Agree
3 = Neither agree nor disagree
4 = Disagree
5 = Strongly disagree.

_____ 1.   The people I supervise have trouble getting along with each other.
_____ 2.   My subordinates are reliable and trustworthy.
_____ 3.   A friendly atmosphere exists among the people I supervise.
_____ 4.   My subordinates always cooperate with me in getting the job done.
_____ 5.   Friction is present between my subordinates and myself.
_____ 6.   My subordinates give me a good deal of help and support in getting the job done.

_____ 7. The people I supervise work well together in getting the job done.

_____ 8. I experience good relations with the people I supervise.

Scoring: Add up your scores for all 8 questions.

Total LMR score: _____

Task Structure Rating Scale—Part I (TS Part I)

Write the number that best describes your group's task using the following scale:

                    0 = Seldom true
                    1 = Sometimes true
                    2 = Usually true.

Goal Clarity

_____ 1. A blueprint, picture, model, or detailed description of the finished product or service is available.

_____ 2. A person is available to advise and give a description of the finished product or service, or how the job should be done.

Goal-Path Multiplicity

_____ 3. A step-by-step procedure or a standard operating procedure indicates in detail the process that is to be followed.

_____ 4. A specific way to subdivide the task into separate parts or steps is provided.

_____ 5. Some ways for performing this task are clearly recognized as better than others.

Solution Specificity

_____ 6. It is obvious when the task is finished and the correct solution is found.

_____ 7. A book, manual, or job description indicates the best solution or the best outcome for the task.

Availability of Feedback

_____ 8. A generally agreed understanding is established about the standards the particular product or service must meet to be considered acceptable.

_____ 9 The evaluation of this task is generally made on some quantitative basis.

_____10 The leader and the group can find out how well the task was accomplished in enough time to improve future performance.

Scoring: Add up your scores for all 10 questions.

*Total TS (Part I) score:*_____

Task Structure Rating Scale—Part II (TS Part II)

Only complete if your score on TS Part I is higher than 6.

(Continued)

Training and experience adjustment (circle a number for each of the following questions)

1. Compared to others in this or similar positions, how much training have you had?

3	2	1	0
No training at all	Very little training	A moderate amount of training	A great deal of training

2. Compared to others in this or similar positions, how much experience do you have?

6	4	2	0
No experience at all	Very little experience	A moderate amount of experience	A great deal of experience

Scoring: Add the numbers you circled for the two questions.

Total TS (Part II):   _____

Total from TS—Part I: _____

Subtract Total from TS—Part II _____

Total TS score: _____

Position Power Rating Scale (PP)

Circle the number that best describes your answer.

1. As the leader, I can directly or by recommendation administer rewards and punishments to my subordinates.

2	1	0
Can act directly or can recommend with high effectiveness	Can recommend but with mixed results	Cannot recommend

2. As the leader, I can directly or by recommendation affect the promotion, demotion, hiring, or firing of my subordinates.

2	1	0
Can act directly or can recommend with high effectiveness	Can recommend but with mixed results	Cannot recommend

3. As the leader, I have the knowledge necessary to assign tasks to subordinates and instruct them in task completion.

2	1	0
Yes, I have knowledge	Sometimes or in some aspects	No, I do not have knowledge

4. As the leader, it is my job to evaluate the performance of my subordinates.

2	1	0
Yes, I can evaluate	Sometimes or in some aspects	No, I cannot evaluate

5. As the leader, I have some official title of authority given by the organization (e.g., supervisor, department head, team leader).

    2   0
   Yes   No

Scoring: Add your scores for the five PP questions.
Total PP score: _____

Situation Control Score (Sit Con)

Add up the scores of the LMR, TS, and PP scales. Using the ranges provided, evaluate the situational control you have as the leader in the situation you described.

$$\frac{}{\text{LMR}} + \frac{}{\text{TS}} + \frac{}{\text{PP}} = \frac{}{\text{Sit Con}}$$

Total score: _____

Total Score	51–70	31–50	10–30
Amount of Sit Con	High control	Moderate control	Low control

Source: F. E. Fiedler and M. M. Chemers, *Improving Leadership Effectiveness: The Leaders Match Concept,* 2nd ed. (New York: Wiley, 1984). Adapted and used with permission.

Evaluation and Discussion

Self-Assessment 3-1 provided you with your LPC score; Self-Assessment 3-2 helped you assess the situational control you have as a leader. Fiedler's Contingency Model suggests that if you are a low-LPC task-motivated leader, you and your group will perform best in high and low situational control. If you are a high-LPC relationship-motivated leader, you and your group will perform best in moderate-situational control. If the leader is "in match," the group will perform best.

1. Were you "in match" with the situation you described?

2. To what extent did your level of effectiveness match Fiedler's predictions? Why or why not?

SELF-ASSESSMENT 3-3:   IDENTIFYING YOUR IN-GROUP AND OUT-GROUP

This exercise is designed to help you identify the members of your in-group and out-group and your own behavior toward members of each group.

Step 1: Identify the Members
Make a list of the subordinates (or team members) whom you **trust**. Select people who work for you (or with you) whom you like and respect, people who enjoy your confidence.

Make a list of the subordinates (or team members) that you **do not trust**. Select people who work for you (or with you) whom you do not like or respect.

Step 2: Membership Factors
What are the commonalties among the group members for each group? What are the factors that caused them to be in each group? Consider behaviors, personalities, and demographic factors, as well as any other relevant factors.

Step 3: How did You Treat Them?
Describe your own behavior as a leader toward each group and its members:

Leader Behaviors	In-Group	Out-Group
Amount of at-work interaction		
Type of interaction		
Type of assignments given		
How was feedback provided		
Amount of out-of-work		
Performance expectations		
Other factors: List		

Step 4: Self-Evaluation

1. What does it take for a person to move from your in-group to your out group?

2. How does having two groups affect your group or department and the organization?

3. To what extent is group membership based on organizational versus personal factors?

4. What are the implications for you as a leader?

Leadership in Action: The Caring Dictator

By any measure, Jack Hartnett, the president of Texas-based D.L. Rogers Corp., is a successful man. D.L. Rogers owns 54 franchises of the Sonic roller-skating nostalgic hamburger chain, which generate $44 million in revenues for the company. Hartnett's restaurants make 18 percent more than the national average, and turnover is incredibly low for the fast-food industry, with a supervisor's average tenure at 12.4 years. He knows what he wants, how to keep his employees, and how to run his business for high profit.

In a management world where everyone will tell you that you need to be soft, participative, open to ideas, and empower employees, Jack Hartnett appears to be an anachronism. He runs his business on the Sinatra principle: "My Way!" He tolerates little deviation from what he wants, his instructions, and his training. He is absolutely sure he knows the best way, and more than one employee is scared of disagreeing with him. He likes keeping people a little off balance and a little queasy so they will work harder to avoid his wrath. Hartnett even has his own Eight Commandments, and he will fire those who break any one of them twice. The last Hartnett commandment is "I will only tell you one time."

Hartnett restaurants run like clockwork. He does the top-level hiring himself and is reputed to spend as long as 10 grueling hours with prospective managers and their spouses. He wants to know about their personal lives and their financial health and looks for right responses and any signs of reticence to answer questions. Hartnett says, "I want them to understand this is not a job to me. This is a lifetime of working together. I want partners who are going to die with

me" (Ballon, 1998: 67). If you are one of the selected few, you are expected to be loyal and obedient. Once a quarter, you can also expect a Hartnett "lock-in" meeting, where Jack will take you away along with other supervisors to a secret location with no chance of escape. You can expect to be blindfolded, put through survival exercises, and sleep in tents before you go to a luxury resort to discuss business.

For all their trouble and unquestioning obedience and loyalty, D.L. Rogers' employees and supervisors find a home, a family, a community, and a place to grow. If you have problems with your husband, like Sharon, the wife of one of the D.L. Rogers' supervisors, you can call Jack. He will listen to you, chew your spouse out, and send him home for a while. Hartnett says, "I don't want you to come to work unhappy, pissed off, upset, or mad about anything, because I don't think you can be totally focused on making money if you're worried" (Ballon, 1998: 63). He pays his employees considerably above national averages, plays golf with them, and gets involved with their personal lives. Hartnett wants to create a bond that lasts. A few years ago, he spent $200,000 to take 254 managers and their families to Cancun, Mexico, for four days. They got training on better time management and marketing techniques, and on how to be a better spouse.

Hartnett also likes to have fun. Practical jokes, including gluing supervisors' shoes to the floor, are common. But he also works hard. Eighty-hour weeks are common, and he starts his days earlier than most. He is not above taking on the most menial jobs in the restaurants and is willing to show the way, no matter what. His presence, his energy, and his unbending confidence in "his way" make converts. Hartnett has created an organization that is consistent and that simplifies everybody's life.

Source: Based on M. Ballon, "Extreme managing," *Inc,* July 1998, 60–72.

QUESTIONS

1. How would you describe Jack Hartnett's leadership style?
2. Why is he successful? Would you work for him?

C h a p t e r   4

Individual Differences and Traits

He who knows about others may be learned
But he who knows himself is more intelligent.
—LAO TSU

After studying this chapter, you will be able to:

■ Explain the role of individual difference characteristics in leadership.

■ Describe the difference between the past and current approaches to leadership traits.

■ Discuss the role demographic characteristics play in leadership.

■ Identify the impact of values on leadership.

■ Present the relationship between emotional intelligence and leadership.

■ Highlight the role of the "Big Five" and other personality traits that are relevant in leadership.

■ Understand cross-cultural differences in individual difference characteristics.

Even a quick reading of the history and mythology of any civilization makes it evident that leaders are considered special. Their physical characteristics are described in detail, their personalities dissected, and their actions celebrated. Long lists of traits and personal exploits are provided. The detailed information about and analyses of leaders focus our attention on the person. It represents a common belief that leaders possess something out of the ordinary—something within them that makes them worthy of our attention. Many believe that good leaders have natural, inborn characteristics that set them apart from others. Most of us can produce a list of personal characteristics of effective leaders. Leaders are courageous; they show initiative and integrity; they are intelligent, perceptive, goal-directed, and so forth. As discussed in Chapter 3, however, research findings do not clearly support many popular lay theories about personal characteristics of leaders. The results of hundreds of studies do not yield a specific profile for leaders. Traits alone do not identify and define leaders. Certain characteristics are related to leadership, if not directly linked to leadership effectiveness.

In recent years, the interest in understanding the individual characteristics and personalities of leaders has reemerged with many studies linking personality and other stable individual characteristics to leadership (for a review, see Zaccaro, 2007). Many new case studies of and interviews with successful business leaders have refocused attention on the role of individual style, demographic background, personality traits, skills, and other individual characteristics in understanding leadership. For example, Warren Bennis (1992), through numerous interviews and observations, highlights leaders' charisma and personal style and their effects on organizations. Other examples of the continued focus on individual traits are theories of charismatic leadership (Conger, 1991), transformational leadership (Bass, 1985), and the work of Kouzes and Posner (1993, 1999) about credibility as the heart of leadership. The major difference between earlier approaches during the Trait Era and the recent ones is the researchers' more complex approach. The search is not simply for one individual trait or a combination of traits. Instead, modern theorists consider the complex interaction among traits, behaviors, and situational characteristics, such as expectations of followers. Within this framework, it is important to understand the role that several personal characteristics may play in determining leadership style and behavior.

This chapter discusses the role of individual characteristics in leadership by considering demographic characteristics, values, abilities, skills, and several personality traits. These individual characteristics do not determine how effective a leader will be. They, however, do impact the way leaders think, behave, and approach problems and their interaction with others. No single individual characteristic is a direct measure of leadership style, but each can allow a better understanding of a person's basic approach and preferences.

ELEMENTS OF INDIVIDUAL DIFFERENCE CHARACTERISTICS

What makes every person unique is a combination of many factors, including demographic, physical, psychological, and behavioral differences. They are at the core of who we are. Figure 4-1 shows a framework for understanding individual differences and their complex components. Heredity and environment are the two determinants of individual characteristics. The interactionist view suggests that these two determinants interact to influence the development of those characteristics. This view is widely accepted, although experts debate the relative influence of each factor. Heredity consists of an individual's gene pool, gender, race, and ethnic background, and it creates an early, and some suggest indelible, influence on personality (Keller et al., 1992). Although genetic studies establish a link between heredity and some personality traits, research also shows that the environment strongly affects us. Influences include physical location, family, culture, religion, education, and friends.

To understand individual differences, we must consider the interaction between heredity and the environment. Environmental and social conditions can reinforce genetic patterns to influence a leader's personality, as can cultural factors, the educational system, and parental upbringing. For instance, in the United States, the genetic traits typically associated with being male are further reinforced by social norms that encourage boys to be competitive and aggressive. Similarly, although female babies tend to develop language skills earlier than males, parents who speak more to their girls and schools that expect girls to be proficient in language further reinforce their

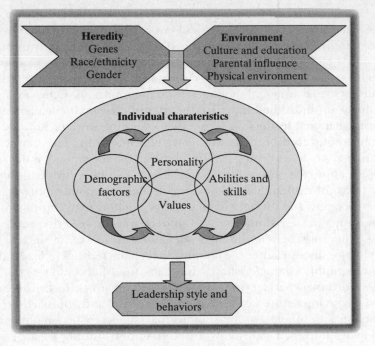

Figure 4-1   Individual Differences Framework.

verbal skills. These genetic and environmental influences interact and are reflected later in life in leadership styles and behaviors.

As shown in Figure 4-1, four major individual difference characteristics can affect leadership style: demographic factors, values, abilities and skills, and personality. Demographic factors such as age and ethnic background are individual difference characteristics that may impact individual behavior and to some extent leadership style. Values are stable, long-lasting beliefs and preferences about what is worthwhile and desirable (Rokeach, 1973). Values are closely related to personality. Personality refers to a person's character and temperament, whereas values are principles that a person believes. Like personality traits, values guide a leader's behavior and are influenced by a combination of biological and environmental factors (Zaccaro, 2007). For example, leaders who hold the value "honesty is the best policy" will attempt to behave fairly and honorably and show integrity in their words and actions. Like personality, values are shaped early in life and are resistant to change. Values also are influenced heavily by one's culture.

Two related individual differences—abilities and skills—play a role in leadership. Ability, or aptitude, is a natural talent for doing something mental or physical. This category includes things such as intelligence. A skill is an acquired talent that a person develops related to a specific task. Whereas ability is somewhat stable over time, skills change with training and experience and from one task to another. You cannot train leaders to develop an ability or aptitude, but you can train them in new leadership skills. Organizations, therefore, recruit and hire leaders with certain abilities and aptitudes and then train them to acquire needed skills. Finally, personality is a stable set of physical and psychological characteristics that makes each person unique. It is made up of a number of personality traits and is the product of interacting biological and environmental factors. Although personality is stable and tends to stay the same over time and across situations, it is not rigid and can evolve gradually over the long term. Furthermore, personality consists of a set of characteristics rather than one or two traits. This set develops over time and makes the individual unique (McCrae, 1993).

Multiple Perspectives and the Impact of the Situation

Although individual characteristics are, by definition, stable, this stability does not mean that leaders cannot behave in ways that are different from their personality. A useful approach is to consider a variety of individual difference factors that explain certain aspects of a person's behavior rather than focus on any one trait. Ideally, to understand who people are and what makes them unique, one would consider all possible aspects of personality, values, attitudes, demographic factors, abilities, and skills as well as the various situations a person faces (Avolio, 2007). Such an integrative perspective can provide broad insight into a person. Note that even when considering multiple perspectives, individual difference characteristics do not dictate our behaviors.

> **Ideally, to understand who people are and what makes them unique, one would consider all possible aspects of personality, values, attitudes, demographic factors, abilities, and skills as well as the various situations a person faces. Such an integrative perspective can provide a broad insight into a person.**

When situations provide little guidance and are loosely structured, a person's individual characteristics can have a strong impact (Barrick and Mount, 1993; Mischel, 1973; Weiss and Adler, 1984). When the situation provides strong behavioral cues—cues that signal what behaviors and actions are expected and appropriate—however, most people behave according to those cues regardless of their personality traits or other individual characteristics. For example, a highly mechanistic and bureaucratic organization with a strong culture that provides detailed, clear rules of behavior will not encourage its managers to express their individuality. In contrast, a loosely structured, organic organization that provides autonomy will allow leaders the latitude to experiment and show their individual differences.

Individual Characteristics Provide a Range

Although individual characteristics tend to be stable, that stability does not mean that people cannot behave in ways that are inconsistent with their personality, values, and attitudes. Instead, each characteristic provides a behavioral zone of comfort as presented in Figure 4-2. The zone of comfort includes a range of behaviors that come naturally and feel comfortable to perform because they reflect individual characteristics. Behaving outside of that zone is difficult, takes practice, and in some cases might not be possible. Although we are at ease in our behavioral comfort zone, we learn and grow by moving to our zones of discomfort. The behaviors outside of the comfort zone challenge us and push us to our limits. Therefore, although it is difficult to do so, an effective learning tool is to move outside of the comfort zone. The remainder of the chapter presents individual difference variables with the potential to affect leadership or that can help in understanding leadership styles, ending with consideration of several personality traits.

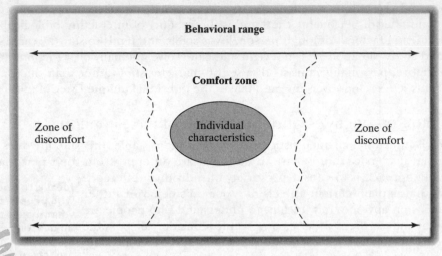

Figure 4-2   Individual Characteristics and Behaviors.

Traits Revisited: A Fresh Look at Leaders' Individual Characteristics and Leader Behaviors

Although strong evidence of a consistent relationship between specific traits and leadership effectiveness is lacking, interest in understanding the personal characteristics of leaders continues. In 1974, a thorough review of traits (Stogdill, 1974) together with other findings reestablished the validity of the trait approach, reviving research on the topic. In general, activity level and stamina, socioeconomic class, education, and intelligence, along with a variety of other traits, appear to characterize leaders, and especially effective leaders. The role of situational characteristics, however, is also recognized as giving way to the situational and contingency approaches to leadership.

Kirkpatrick and Locke (1991) have proposed a modern approach to understanding the role of traits in leadership: several key traits alone are not enough to make a leader, but they are a precondition for effective leadership. Kirkpatrick and Locke list a number of traits that facilitate a leader's acquisition of needed leadership skills. The key traits are as follows:

➤ Drive, which includes motivation and energy
➤ Desire and motivation to lead
➤ Honesty and integrity
➤ Self-confidence
➤ Intelligence
➤ Knowledge of the business

Some of the traits, namely intelligence and drive, cannot be acquired through training. Others, such as knowledge of the industry and self-confidence, can be acquired with time and appropriate experience. The trait of honesty is a simple choice. Studies of managers and leaders in other cultures found similar traits present in successful leaders. For example, successful Russian business leaders are characterized by "hard-driving ambition, boundless energy, and keen ability" (Puffer, 1994: 41). Chinese business leaders value hard work and an impeccable reputation for integrity. Being hard-driving to the point of being a workaholic is not an uncommon trait in U.S. business executives either. Surveys indicate that 60 percent of people in high-earning jobs work more than 50 hours a week; 35 percent more than 60 hours a week (Armour, 2007).

Consider how many business executives demonstrate the traits that Kirkpatrick and Locke propose. Lisa Harper, CEO of Gymboree Corp., remembers the time when she took over the company with the task of turning it around: "I was passionate about the people, the product, and the customer . . ." (Canabou, 2003a: 58). Keith Blackwell, cofounder and CEO of Bristol Technology, believes that you demonstrate leadership when you "are extremely clear about the future and who is going to get you there" (60). Small business owners succeed because of their extreme confidence in their own abilities (Wellner, 2004). Steve Jobs of Apple and Fumio Mitarai of Canon are famous for their drive, energy, intelligence, and self-confidence, as are other business leaders, such as Heidi Miller, executive vice president of JP Morgan Chase Treasury and Security Services, and Herb Kelleher, the famous founder of Southwest Airlines. Goran Lindahl, the former chief executive of the Swiss-Swedish engineering group ABB, was driven almost to the point of obsession to keep his company's stock prices high (Tomlinson, 2000). Other leaders develop knowledge of their business. Meg Whitman, CEO of eBay, makes a point of traveling coach instead of taking the corporate jet. She likes to wear an eBay T-shirt so that she can talk to people about their experience with her company and gather information (Dillon, 2004). Emilio Azcarraga Jean, chair of Grupo Televisa SA, the largest Spanish-language media company in the world, learned all the details of the family business when he took over for his ailing father (Kroll and Fass, 2007). Through his intense drive and motivation, he refocused his organization's culture from loyalty to performance to gain ground in the U.S. market.

Interestingly, integrity, or lack of it, is cited as a key factor in leadership. Many anecdotes about bad leadership contain elements of lack of trust, dishonesty, and unwillingness to be held accountable on the part of the leaders. The corporate scandals of the early 2000s increased and renewed the focus on the importance of transparency and honesty (Pagano and Pagano, 2004). The GLOBE researchers have found that integrity is one of few culturally universal leadership characteristics (House et al., 2004), although other studies found cultural differences in managers' willingness to justify ethically suspect behaviors (Cullen, Parboteeah, and Hoegl, 2004; Garibaldi de Hilal, 2006). Followers all over the world complain bitterly when leaders abuse their trust, lie to them, or mislead them. The scandal at the Italian food manufacturer Parmalat provides a striking example of blatant dishonesty. Calisto Tanzi, the company's chief executive, Fausto Tonna, its chief financial officer, and other top executives, falsified accounts and embezzled millions of Euros, leading to the company's bankruptcy and public outrage. Goran Lindahl, mentioned earlier for his almost obsessive focus, was also severely criticized for taking large retirement packages while the company reported losses.

Just as some traits are necessary for leadership, they can be detrimental when carried to an extreme (Kirkpatrick and Locke, 1991). A leader with too much drive might refuse to delegate tasks, and a desire for too much power can work against a leader's effectiveness (Bennis and Nanus, 1985). For example, Michael Eisner, the president of Disney, was not able to hold on to several talented executives because of his need for control and inability to delegate, which stemmed in part from his drive and motivation to lead. These characteristics were blamed for the high turnover on top. Eisner's tight hold on power also caused bitter disputes with several board members, triggered investor law suits, and was one of the factors that led to Eisner's resignation (Holson, 2004a). His replacement Bob Iger is known to be understated, calm, diplomatic, and collaborative, all characteristics that Eisner lacked (Steptoe, 2007). Small business owners who are highly driven face similar challenges when it comes to delegation. For example, Andrew Nadel, owner of Pride Products, a promotional and corporate gift company, does everything from calling customers to assembling new office chairs himself, even though he employs a staff to take care of many of these tasks (Wellner, 2004).

The current approach to understanding the role of leadership traits suggests that, as many of us believe, leaders are indeed gifted in at least some areas. Those gifts and talents alone, however, are not enough. Experience, correct choices, and exposure to the right situations are the keys to allowing those gifts to bloom.

THE DEMOGRAPHIC CHARACTERISTICS OF LEADERS

One approach to understanding the personal characteristics of leaders is to look at their demographic characteristics. Several research projects considering the demographic characteristics of who has and gets power in the United States have yielded consistent results (e.g., Mayo and Nohria, 2006). Kurtz, Boone, and Fleenor conducted one such comprehensive survey of nearly 800 U.S. executives in 1989 with interesting information about CEOs' demographic backgrounds. All were male. The majority of executives in their sample were firstborns in two-parent, middle-class families living in the rust belt. Close to 90 percent were married, with a median age of 58, and many considered themselves to be religious. Eighty percent were right-handed; they were taller and smoked less than the general population, and tended to exercise a fair amount. The CEOs were considerably more educated than the general population, with 47 percent having graduate degrees. The majority studied in public universities, and many paid for their own education, at least to some extent.

The most striking result of this extensive survey is the homogeneity of the executives, in spite of some differences among industries. Researchers Mayo and Nohria found similar results and conclude that although education opens the door for diverse people to reach leadership positions and although there has been progress in the number of women and people of diverse nationalities in leadership positions, the leadership path is still primarily influenced by birthplace, nationality, religion, education, social class, gender, and race (Mayo and Nohria, 2006). Other studies further show progress at least in some areas. For example, a U.S. government study indicates that in 2002, women owned 28.2 percent of nonfarm firms (Lowrey, 2006). Reports from the Center for Women's Business Research further indicate that women own part or all of 46 percent of privately held businesses (Franklin, 2003).

Even though women and minorities have made their way up many organizations in the United States and other countries, as we discussed in Chapter 2, formal organizational leadership is still heavily dominated by males. Despite some changes, the top executives in the United States and also in many other parts of the world are still a homogeneous group. The homogeneity in demographic background does not necessarily lead to similar approaches in managing a business and leading followers. It is also unlikely, however, to lead to high diversity of thought and approaches to management. Although homogeneity can be a strength if unity of purpose is needed, it can be a weakness where creativity is required. Many studies (e.g., Hackman, 1990; Nahavandi and Aranda, 1994) propose that lack of support from top management is a key obstacle in the implementation of innovative management approaches. With the current state of flux of public and private organizations, the need for diverse and innovative approaches is strong. Given the homogeneity of current business leaders in the United States and around the world, it is not surprising that such innovation is sometimes lacking. The homogeneity of executives might be one of the factors that indicate the need to further diversify business leadership.

VALUES

Values are long-lasting beliefs about what is worthwhile and desirable. They are personal judgments about what is right and wrong, good and bad. Understanding values is important for leaders because they affect how leaders lead. This section examines value systems, investigates how culture affects values, and considers the interplay between values and ethics.

Value System and Culture

The ways in which a person organizes and prioritizes values is that person's value system (see Self-Assessment 4-1). For instance, for one person family may be a central value and a top priority when compared with other issues, such as faith, career, and social relationships. Other people might value their career more than their family or put their faith and spirituality above all else. Each of us has a personal value system around which we prioritize what we value most. Some people are aware of their values and their priorities, whereas others are unclear about their own priorities and become cognizant of them only when conflicts arise. Each individual's value system is unique, although members of one family or culture might share certain key values. Many factors influence what an individuals' values are. Particularly, researchers have found consistent gender and cultural differences in values (e.g., Golob and Bartlett, 2007; Schwartz, 2005). For example, surveys of political attitudes in the United States consistently reveal what some people call the gender gap, a difference in the value system of men and women. In the United States, many women place a higher value on family and social issues, whereas men focus more on economic problems. In the 2004 U.S. presidential elections, although the gender gap narrowed, women still placed a high value on security. These value differences were reflected in how they voted. In addition to gender-based differences, many generational and culture-based value systems differences also exist. The cultural dimensions presented in Chapter 2 include cultural values. For example, individualism is typically highly valued in industrialized Western countries, whereas collectivism is a dominant value in many Eastern cultures. Leaders must understand their own values and those of their followers and how they influence styles and behaviors.

Cultural values indicate what a cultural group considers important, worthwhile, and desirable. We share the values of our culture. The cultural values form the basis for a leader's individual value system. Clearly, not everyone holds the same values (Bigoness and Blakely, 1996). For example, certain values—fairness, honesty, frugality, compassion, and humility—are universal. In contrast, the value of individual dignity—which refers to placing focus on the uniqueness, self-control, and self-governance of individuals—is more prevalent in individualistic than in collectivistic cultures (Anderson, 1997). The GLOBE research, presented in Chapter 2, indicates that not all cultures value the same traits in their leaders and that many characteristics are culturally contingent (House et al., 2004).

In general, the Euro-American cultures within the United States, as well as many other Western cultures, value individuality. As a result, leaders from these cultures rate personal achievement and recognition highly, and organizations target individuals for rewards and recognition. Displays of individuality are welcomed, as evidenced by the respect many people have for entrepreneurs. By contrast, collectivist cultures place a higher value on the community and a lower value on the individual. For instance, the Japanese value and reward conformity to the group. Parents teach children not to stand out or draw attention to themselves. The Japanese proverb "the nail that stands out will be hammered down" reflects the value system of many Japanese, who believe that they should sacrifice the self for the good of the collective. Leaders are similarly valued for their conformity to the social order as much as their uniqueness.

Several Native American cultures, such as the Navajos, have comparable cultural values. Navajos, who are a horizontal collectivistic culture, devalue individualism and standing out in one's community and, indeed, consider such behavior inappropriate. They appreciate leaders primarily for their contribution to their community. Hofstede's other cultural values of avoidance of uncertainty, power distance, and masculinity further influence an individual's value systems. When a culture emphasizes low power distance—such as in Sweden, which is individualistic but horizontal—leaders are likely to be cooperative and avoid status symbols and hierarchy. When the culture is masculine, individuals are likely to emphasize honor and self-reliance. The concept of high and low context can further affect values. In high context cultures, such as Mexico, bending the truth to preserve relationships or protect feelings is much more accepted than in low-context cultures, such as Germany or the United States.

Generational Differences

In addition to national cultural differences, theorists debate the effects of age, ethnic, and other group cultural differences on value systems. Research suggests that many people from the older generation in the United States believe that the younger generation does not work hard and lacks respect for leaders; the younger groups think the older generation's value system is stale and useless. Table 4-1 presents some value differences based on age. Different generations often hold different views of what effectiveness and efficiency mean. Older generations consider loyalty, regular work hours, and consistent attendance to be primary. They are often less optimistic and less confident about their future (Tyson, 2002). Generation Xers and Millennials hop from one job to another, work odd shifts, rely on technology, work late into the night, and may not consider the traditional 8-hour work day appropriate. They have an optimistic view of their future and are bolder, an approach that was reflected, for example, in their

Table 4-1   Generation-Based Value Differences in the United States.

Generation	Key Social and Historical Influences	Dominant Value System
GI generation, 60+ (born 1940s or before)	Raised by Depression era parent in post-depression period or around WW II	Hard word; frugality; patriotism; Protestant work ethic; respect for authority
Baby boomers, 45–60 (born between late 1940s and 1960s)	Raised by WW II parents; grew up during Korean and Vietnam wars; Kennedy assassination; moon landing; rock & roll and Woodstock; cold war energy crisis	Non-conformity; idealism; self-focus; distrust of establishment; happiness and peace; optimism; involvement
Baby Busters, 35–45 (born between the 1960s and 1970s)	Raised by the early hippies; post Vietnam era; Watergate	The Yuppies; "me" generation; ambitious; material comfort; success driven; stressed out
Generation Xers, 25–35 (born between 1970s and 1980s)	Peaceful era; fall of communism; Iran hostage crisis; recession and economic changes; Bill Clinton; Aids; MTV	Enjoyment of life; jaded; latch-key kids; single-parent family; desire for autonomy and flexibility; self-reliance; spirituality; diversity; balance work and personal life
Millennials or Nexters under 25 (born after the mid-1980s)	A lot of parental focus; Oklahoma bombings; 9/11 World Trade Center attack; school shootings; globalization; George W. Bush; Internet and media; tech savvy	Flexibility; choice; socially conscious; meaningful experiences and work; diversity; achievement; tolerance and openness

Sources: Partially based on N.A. Hira, "You raised them, now manage them," Fortune, May 28 2007, 38–43; M. E. Massey, "The past: What you are is where you were when" (videorecording) (Schaumberg, IL: Video Publishing House, 1986); D .J. Cherrington, S. J. Condies, and J. L. England, "Age and work values," *Academy of Management Journal,* September 1979, 617–623.

initially more positive view of the Iraq war in 2002 (Tyson, 2002). Technology provides another divide where younger workers often are impatient with older workers' perceived lack of expertise in technology. Some, however, believe that while the Millennials may need a lot of attention, they are also high performing. Describing the values and behaviors of that generation, generational researcher Bruce Tulgan suggests, "They walk in with more information in their heads, more information at their fingertips—and, sure, they have high expectations, but they have the highest expectations first and foremost for themselves" (Hira, 2007).

A survey of 66,000 people around the world by the Pew Research Center for the People and the Press indicates that generational value differences are prevalent particularly in Western Europe, but almost nonexistent in Asia, Africa, and the Middle East (Pew Global Attitudes Project, 2004). Older people in the United States and Western Europe express more national pride and are worried about globalization more so than younger generations in those countries. The older generations also demonstrate a stronger sense of cultural superiority, whereas the younger generations feel less tied to their national cultural identity.

Each individual develops a different value system that shapes attitudes and behaviors. Value systems, in turn, affect ethical behavior in organizations, a factor with critical implications for leaders.

Values and Ethics

One value related to leadership is ethics. Ethics are a person's concept of right and wrong. Two general views of ethics are the relativist and universalist views. Individuals with a relativist view of ethics believe that what is right or wrong depends on the situation or the culture (Donaldson, 1994). An index collected by Transparency International, an organization that uses a complex set of data to monitor corruption around the world, shows distinct national differences in ethical behaviors. In their 2006 index, Haiti, Myanmar, Iraq, Guinea, and Sudan were ranked as some of the most corrupt nations; Finland, Iceland, New Zealand, Denmark, and Singapore were ranked as the least corrupt (Transparency International, 2006). The United States ranked 22 out of 163, behind most Western countries and Canada. To illustrate, businesspeople in many places consider gifts, bribes, or kickbacks acceptable behavior in contract negotiations, although these activities are unethical and illegal based on U.S. values and laws. A person with a relativist view of ethics would take a "when in Rome, do as the Romans do" approach. That is, a U.S. manager who learns that it is generally accepted to bribe officials in Thailand to secure a contract would consider bribing a Thai official acceptable and ethical behavior. Note that it is rarely possible for managers of U.S.-based companies to adopt a relativist view of ethics in business situations simply because U.S. laws forbid any form of bribery anywhere in the world. In contrast, a person with a universalist view of ethics believes that all activities should be judged by the same standards, regardless of the situation or culture. For example, a U.S. oil company manager would appoint a female manager to its Saudi operations, based on U.S. laws of equal opportunity and the principles of cultural diversity, despite the religious and cultural problems it might create.

The value and ethical issues facing leaders are highly complex. Global and cross-cultural issues further add to the complexity. For example, research by Triandis and his associates (Triandis et al., 2001) indicates that collectivism tends to be related to greater use of deception in negotiation, as well as higher levels of guilt after using deception. Particularly, Koreans and Japanese feel considerable guilt and shame after using deception. Furthermore, based on what a culture values, individuals within that culture might lie for different reasons, such as protecting their privacy in the case of the United States or benefiting family members in the case of Samoans (Aune and Waters, 1994). Other research, comparing United States and Hong Kong Chinese, shows cross-cultural differences in attitudes toward breach of contract (Kickul, Lester, and Belgio, 2004). United States employees responded more negatively to breaches of intrinsic contracts (e.g., autonomy) by displaying lower levels of job satisfaction and commitment. The Hong Kong Chinese are less accepting than U.S. workers of violations of extrinsic contract violations (e.g., salary or job training), but more tolerant of violations of intrinsic contract. The researchers attribute the differences to the Chinese Confucian value to preserve harmony as compared with the U.S. value of individual success. Still other research shows that different factors motivate managers in different cultures (Mathur, Zhang, and Meelankavil, 2001), and factors that determine commitment to work depend to some extent on cultural values (Andolšek and Štebe, 2004), suggesting a strong link between culture and values.

Because of complex cross-cultural and individual differences in values, handling ethical and value-driven issues will continue to be a major part of every manager's job. Chapter 6 will review several new approaches to leadership that consider values to be at the core of leadership.

ABILITIES AND SKILLS

Much of the early research in leadership characteristics focused on establishing leadership abilities. Although leaders clearly must have some abilities, competencies, and skills, these characteristics do not have high correlations to leadership effectiveness (for a review of the early research, see Bass, 1990a). Intelligence in its various forms and technical, interpersonal, and cognitive skills have received particular attention.

Intelligence

Intelligence is one of the most often used characteristics to describe leaders and is often included in discussions of leadership (Sternberg, 2007). It is clear that the complex task of leading requires a person with cognitive ability to remember, collect, and integrate information, analyze problems, develop solutions, and evaluate alternatives, all of which are related to traditional definitions of intelligence. For most people, intelligence is a factor in leadership; however, actual link between intelligence and effectiveness is far from clear (Rubin, Bartels, and Bommer, 2002). Correlations vary and many studies suggest that the link is relatively weak (for a review of past research, see Bass, 1990a). To date, only one leadership theory, the Cognitive Resource Model (Fiedler and Garcia, 1987a, b), has used intelligence explicitly as a factor. Reviews of the link between general intelligence and leadership indicate that it is an important aspect of leadership (Cornwell, 1983; Lord, De Vader, and Alliger, 1986). The relationship, however, may be moderated by many factors. For example, when being competent is important, leaders who are more intelligent might do better, but in situations that require interpersonal skills, general intelligence might not be sufficient. The level of leadership also may be a factor. Particularly, intuition may be especially important for leaders at upper organizational levels. Furthermore, some early research shows that a curvilinear relationship may exist between intelligence and leadership (Ghiselli, 1963). Those individuals with either low or high scores are less likely to be effective and successful leaders. Both, for different reasons, might experience difficulty communicating with their followers and motivating them to achieve the task.

Consider Scott Rudin, producer of hit movies such as *Notes on a Scandal, Failure to Launch, Stepford Wives,* and *Clueless.* Some of the people who work with him consider Rudin to be "one of the smartest and most clever and witty guys I have ever met" (Carvell, 1998: 201). He is bright and creative, and many admire his work, but his intelligence and creativity are not enough and not his only well-known qualities. Rudin is famous for his fiery outburst, throwing phones and office supplies, outrageous demands, and on-the-spot firing and re-hiring of assistants—by some accounts 250 in a 5-year period (Kelly and Marr, 2005). As one of Rudin's ex-assistants states, "I think the people that work there—most of them hate him. Nobody likes him. Everybody's miserable" (Carvell, 1998: 201). Rudin simply suggests, "The thin-skinned guys don't like it. The thick skinned people . . . understand that I am working as hard as them" (Kelly and Marr, 2005). Even his mentor, Edgar Scherick, referred to his protégé as "Scott Rude." As this example illustrates, being intelligent is not sufficient for being an effective leader. Many other characteristics play important roles. In Rudin's case, his high level of intelligence and creativity are not matched by his ability to relate to others.

Practical and Emotional Intelligence

In the past few years, other perspectives have been added to the concept of intelligence. Instead of primarily focusing on memory and analytical skills, several researchers have suggested that being able to work well with others or having the skills needed to succeed in life are important components of intelligence. Researcher Robert Sternberg and his colleagues introduced the concept of practical intelligence to address the types of skills and attributes that people use to solve everyday challenges they may face (Headlund et al., 2003; Sternberg, 2002a; Sternberg et al., 2000). People with this type of intelligence either change their behavior to adapt to the environment, manipulate the environment, or find a new environment (Sternberg, 2007). Sternberg further proposes a model of leadership, WICS, that integrates, wisdom, intelligence, and creativity in a systems approach putting intelligence at the center of leadership traits (Sternberg, 2003). Although the concept has received some attention, research about its link to leadership is still scarce (for an example, see Hedlund et al., 2003).

Peter Salovey and John Mayer (1990) coined the term emotional intelligence (EI; or EQ for emotional quotient) to describe the social and interpersonal aspect of intelligence. Whereas intelligence generally is defined in terms of mental and cognitive abilities, some argue that the ability to relate interpersonally contributes another type of intelligence (see Goleman, 1995, 2004). The ability to interact well with followers, satisfy their emotional needs, and motivate and inspire them is another key to effective leadership. Table 4-2 summarizes the five elements of EI/EQ.

Individuals with high EI/EQ are in touch with their emotions and demonstrate self-management in their ability to control their moods and feelings productively and

Table 4-2   Components of Emotional Intelligence.

Component	Description
Self-awareness	Being aware of and in touch with your own feelings and emotions
Self-regulation	Being able to manage various emotions and moods without denying or suppressing them
Self-motivation	Being able to remain positive and optimistic
Empathy for others	Being able to read others' emotions accurately and putting yourself in their place
Interpersonal and social skills	Having the skills to build and maintain positive relationships with others

Source: Based on D. Goleman, "What makes a leader?" *Harvard Business Review*, 82, no. 1 (2004): 82–91; and D. Goleman, R. E. Boyatzis, and A. McKee, *Primal Leadership: Realizing the Power of Emotional Intelligence* (Boston: Harvard Business School Press, 2002).

in staying motivated and focused even when facing obstacles. They can calm themselves when angry and stay balanced. They also are able to read others' emotions, feel empathy for them, and put themselves in their place. The last component of EI/EQ is having the ability to develop productive and positive interpersonal relationships through understanding, conflict resolution, and negotiation (Goleman, 1998; see Self-Assessment 4-2). Goleman suggests that EI/EQ is important in leadership because of the increased use of teams, globalization, and the need to retain talented followers (Goleman, 1998). As a result, in the past few years, researchers have considered the link between EI/EQ and leadership (for a review, see Humphrey, 2002). Many have explored the relationship between EI/EQ and transformational leadership; that topic is covered in Chapter 6. Some studies show that EI is related positively to attitude toward change (Vakola, Tsausis, and Nikolaou, 2004). Others have focused on the role empathy plays in leadership, suggesting that it is a good predictor of leadership emergence in teams (Wolff, Pescosolido, and Druskat, 2003). Although it may be obvious that the leader's ability to understand followers is a component of relationship-orientation and consideration behaviors (Kellett, Humphrey, and Sleeth, 2002), empathy also plays a role in the leader's task-orientated behaviors (Wolff et al., 2003). Specifically, leaders who show empathy are better able to guide their followers around challenging tasks because they can recognize patterns and coordinate group activities.

A leader's ability to self-regulate and manage his or her emotions, another component of EI, also affects followers. Research by Newcomb and Ashkanasy (2002) indicates that how a leader delivers a message can be more important than the content of the message. When subjects in their study used positive facial expressions, they were rated higher than when they used negative expressions, which led to the suggestion that leadership is an emotional process where a key leadership role is the management of emotions. Furthermore, research in psychology about how people experience emotion (e.g., Gohm, 2003) links it to the abilities to regulate mood and to make judgments, once more emphasizing the potentially strong role emotions can play in leadership.

The ability to interact well with followers, satisfy their emotional needs, and motivate and inspire them is another key to effective leadership.

Psychologist Daniel Goleman states, "The rules for work are changing, and we're all being judged by a new yardstick—not just how smart we are and what technical skills we have, which employers see as givens, but increasingly by how well we handle ourselves and one another" (Fisher, 1998: 293). Although competence and cognitive ability—namely, traditional intelligence—might be keys for success when working alone, leadership requires successful interaction with others and the ability to motivate them to accomplish goals. Therefore, EI/EQ is a central factor in several leadership processes, particularly in the development of charismatic and transformational leadership, where the emotional bond between leaders and followers is imperative. Being able to empathize with followers can further allow a leader to develop followers and create a consensus. Some researchers suggest that emotional intelligence contributes to effective leadership because an emotionally intelligent leader focuses on followers, on inspiring them, and on developing enthusiasm (George, 2007). Whereas leaders with a high IQ lead with their head, leaders with a high EI/EQ lead with their heart and address their followers' emotional needs.

Ken Chenault, CEO of American Express (AmEx), one of only a few African American leaders of Fortune 500 companies in the United States, is able to win his

Applying What You Learn
Developing Your EQ

Awareness and development of EI/EQ elements can be a useful tool for self-development. Here are some areas to work on:

- Learn about your strengths and weaknesses by taking self-assessments, engaging in honest reflection, and seeking and listening to feedback.

- Keep a journal to track your feelings and behaviors.

- Seek the help of a friend, coworker, or mentor to provide you with feedback.

- Admit your mistakes and learn from them.

- Work on controlling your temper and your moods; stay composed, positive, and tactful when facing difficult situations.

- Stay true to your word and your commitments; integrity is a choice. Walk the talk.

- Set challenging goals and be willing to work hard to achieve them.

- Build relationships with others and develop your network.

- Practice active listening and pay attention to those around you; be concerned about their well-being and their feelings.

employees' trust and build cohesion partly through his empathy and ability to express his emotions. He is described as understated, modest, and unassuming, with quiet warmth and a style that makes people want to be on his team (Schwartz, 2001). He believes that although the rational aspects of leadership are essential, values are what make a leader. He states, "what I have seen in companies throughout my career is that if you are not clear on who you are, on what it is you stand for, and if you don't have strong values, you are going to run your career off a cliff" (*Knowledge@Wharton*, 2005). After AmEx was driven out of its Manhattan headquarters by the September 11 terrorist attacks, Chenault moved into a cramped windowless office with standard issue furniture. While addressing the AmEx employees during a company town-hall meeting after September 11, he openly expressed his emotions, embraced grief-stricken employees, and stated, "I represent the best company and the best people in the world. In fact, you are my strength, and I love you" (Byrne and Timmons, 2001). Tom Ryder, who competed with Chenault for the top AmEx job, said, "If you work around him, you feel like you'd do anything for the guy" (Schwartz, 2001: 62). For Chenault, integrity, courage, being a team player, and developing people are foundations for becoming a leader; all are elements of emotional intelligence.

Because of the potential of EI/EQ to address an important aspect of leadership, many organizations are finding that developing their managers' EI can lead to higher performance. Danny Myers, who owns several highly successful restaurants in New York City, including the Union Square Café and Gramercy Tavern, and who has written a book about delivering first-class service (Meyer, 2006), believes that the secret of his success is that he has surrounded himself with people who have higher EQs than IQs. He looks for people who have natural warmth, optimism, intelligence, and curiosity. Similarly, business education that, for many years, emphasized analytical and numbers-oriented skills is shifting some attention to developing interpersonal skills. Well-respected MBA programs at University of Pennsylvania's Wharton Business School, the University of Chicago, and Berkeley's Hass Business School are stressing teamwork and teaching listening skills mostly in response to employers' need to hire people who have such skills (Fisher, 2007).

Creativity

A leader's ability to be creative is ever more important, given the uncertainty that many businesses face. Creativity—also known as divergent thinking or lateral thinking— is the ability to combine or link ideas in new ways to generate novel and useful alternatives (Sternberg, 2007). Lateral thinking focuses on moving away from the linear approach advocated by rational decision making (De Bono, 1992). Donna Kacmar, principal architect at Architects Works Inc. in Houston, Texas, sees creativity as "new possibilities for what might be considered dumb or mundane problems" (Underwood, 2004: 44). Patrick Le Quément, French car maker Renault's chief designer, is credited with many of the company's cutting-edge and highly unusual designs. He believes that being original is the key to his creativity, stating "it's worth alienating most of your customers if you can make the rest love you" (Wylie, 2004a: 90). Because creativity is a complex process, leading creative efforts also is a highly complex activity.

Creativity is a necessary component of leadership because leaders are often expected to develop new ideas and directions that others will follow. Creative leaders listen intently to all sources, especially to bad news, in order to know where the next problem is emerging. They value subjective as well as objective information. They turn facts, perceptions, gut feelings, and intuitions into reality by making bold and informed decisions. Other factors found to be important are modeling creative and unconventional behaviors, delegation, monitoring the process, and showing followers how their work affects the organization (Basadur, 2004). Creative leaders must not only be creative, but also have considerable technical expertise to lead their followers through the challenges of creative decision making (Mumford and Licuanan, 2004). Creative leaders typically share four characteristics (Sternberg and Lubart, 1995):

1. *Perseverance in the face of obstacles and self-confidence.* Creative individuals persevere more in the face of problems and have strong beliefs in the correctness of their ideas.
2. *Willingness to take risks.* Creative individuals take moderate to high risks rather than extreme risks that have a strong chance of failing.
3. *Willingness to grow and openness to experience.* Creative individuals are open to experiences and are willing to try new methods.
4. *Tolerance of ambiguity.* Creative individuals tolerate lack of structure and not having clear answers.

As this list suggests, creative leaders tend to be confident in the paths they select and are willing to take risks when others give up. They also focus on learning and are willing to live with uncertainty to reach their goals. As with any other characteristic, the organizational setting can have a great impact on allowing creativity to flourish (Zhou and George, 2001). Some suggest that creative people make a decision to be creative when facing challenging problems (Sternberg, 2002b). Interestingly, some research suggests a link between a leader's EI and the ability to encourage followers to be creative (Zhou and George, 2003). Because creativity is an emotional process, managing emotions well can play a positive role in the creativity process. Teresa Amabile, head of the Entrepreneurial Management Unit at Harvard Business School, believes that creativity is not just the domain of creative people, but requires experience, talent, and motivation to push through problems. She also suggests that people are least creative when they feel time pressure, fear, or intense competitive pressures (Breen, 2004).

Skills

The research on leadership skills is considerably clearer and more conclusive than that on leadership abilities. Leadership skills are divided into three categories: technical, interpersonal, and conceptual (Table 4-3).

As leaders and managers move up in their organization, they rely less on technical skills and increasingly on interpersonal and conceptual skills. Company CEOs, school principals, or hospital administrators do not need to be able to perform various jobs in detail. They, however, should be able to negotiate successfully and effectively and manage various interpersonal relationships inside and outside the organization. Furthermore, top executives more than lower-level leaders and managers need to read and analyze their internal and external environments and make strategic decisions that require considerable problem-solving skills.

The impact of ability and skills on leadership depends to a great extent on the situation. Situational factors, such as the type of organization, level of leadership, ability and needs of followers, and type of task at hand, all influence what abilities and skills leaders will need to be effective. Additionally, although skills can be learned and can affect a leader's behavior, research suggests that a lag time occurs between learning skills and translating them into actual behavior (Hirst et al., 2004.)

RELEVANT PERSONALITY TRAITS

Although a review of early trait research, summarized in Chapter 3, indicates that no specific traits can predict who will become a leader or which leader will be effective, traits do play a role in leadership in several ways (for a review, see Zaccaro, 2007).

➤ First, as discussed in Chapter 3, researchers have identified some traits that are consistently associated with leadership.

➤ Second, a leader's personality influences his or her preferences, style, and behavior.

➤ Third, personality may affect the ease with which a leader learns skills and is able to implement them.

Table 4-3 Leadership Skills.

Skills Category	Description
Technical skills	Knowledge of the job processes, methods, tools, and techniques
Interpersonal skills	Knowledge of interpersonal relationships including communication, conflict management, negotiation, and team building
Conceptual skills	Knowledge of problem solving, logical thinking, decision making, creativity, and reasoning in general

➤ Fourth, being aware of key personality traits shown to affect work-related behaviors can help leaders develop their self-awareness and aid them in their learning and development.

➤ Finally, traits can be strong predictors of leadership when considered in an integrated system that includes several individual difference characteristics and situational and contextual variables.

The next section presents seven personality traits with implications for leadership.

The Big Five Personality Dimensions

Over time, psychologists and organizational behavior researchers have condensed countless personality traits into a list of five major personality dimensions, known as the *Big Five* (Barrick and Mount, 1991; Digman, 1990; Norman, 1963). Research shows that these five dimensions are consistent components of personality not only in the United States, but in several other cultures as well (Paunonen, 2003; Schmitt et al., 2007). Table 4-4 summarizes the key elements of the Big Five personality dimensions.

The Big Five dimensions allow the grouping of many different traits into a meaningful taxonomy for studying individual differences. These five dimensions are relatively independent, with several implications for management. A number of the Big Five personality dimensions have links to work-related behaviors such as career success (Judge et al., 1999; Seibert and Kraimer, 2001) and the performance of managers who work abroad (Caligiuri, 2000). None, however, alone strongly predicts performance or leadership effectiveness, even though some links to work involvement have been established (Bozionelos, 2004). Of the five dimensions, *conscientiousness* is the most strongly correlated to job performance. This connection makes sense: individuals who are dependable, organized, and hard working tend to perform better in their job (Barrick and Mount, 1991; Frink and Ferris, 1999; Hayes, Roehm, and Catellano, 1994). Most

Table 4-4   Big Five Personality Dimensions.

Personality Dimensions	Description
Conscientiousness	Degree to which a person is dependable, responsible, organized, and plans ahead
Extraversion/ Introversion	Degree to which a person is sociable, talkative, assertive, active, and ambitious
Openness to experience	Degree to which a person is imaginative, broad-minded, curious, and seeks new experiences
Emotional stability	Degree to which a person is anxious, depressed, angry, and insecure
Agreeableness	Degree to which a person is courteous, likable, good-natured, and flexible

Sources: Based on descriptions provided by W. T. Norman, "Toward an adequate taxonomy of personality attributes: Replicated factor structure in peer nomination personality ratings," *Journal of Abnormal and Social Psychology* 66 (1963): 547–583; J. M. Digman, "Personality structure: Emergence of the five-factor model," *Annual Review of Psychology* 41 (1990): 417–440; and M. R. Barrick and M. Mount, "The five big personality dimensions and job performance: A meta-analysis," *Personnel Psychology* 44, no. 1 (1991): 1–76.

managers would agree that a good employee is dependable, shows up on time, finishes work by deadlines, and is willing to work hard. For instance, Andy Grove, former CEO of Intel and management guru, used to make a list of which of his employees showed up on time. He believes that dependable employees perform better.

Extraversion is the Big Five dimension with the second-highest correlation to job-related behaviors and is particularly important in jobs that rely on social interaction, such as management or sales. It is much less essential for employees working on an assembly line or as computer programmers (Hayes, Roehm, and Catellano, 1994). Unlike conscientiousness, which can apply to all job levels or occupations, extroversion is not an essential trait for every job, and individuals can succeed without being extroverted. In fact, one of the United States' most-admired business leaders, Lew Platt, previous CEO of Hewlett-Packard, is not an extravert. "Lew Platt isn't a loud, extroverted guy, but he is . . . in his own quiet, blushing way getting his colleagues not only to understand but to agree " (Stewart, 1998a: 82). Alan Wurtzel, the man who is often credited with the success of Circuit City, the electronics store, and its extraordinary performance compared with others in its industry, is described as hardworking, self-effacing, and quiet; more "plow horse than show horse" (Collins, 2001: 33).

Openness to experience can help performance in some instances, but not in others. For example, being open to new experiences can help employees and managers perform well in training because they will be motivated to explore fresh ideas and to learn (Goldstein, 1986), and it might help them be more successful in overseas assignments (Ones and Viswesvaran, 1999). Ken Chenault, CEO of AmEx, believes that being open to change and able to adapt to it are the most important characteristic today's leaders need to have. He states, "It's not the strongest or the most intelligent who survive, but those most adaptive to change" (Chester, 2005). Le Quément of Renault is a risk taker who is always looking for new ideas (Wylie, 2004). Bill Gates, CEO of Microsoft, is legendary for his intelligence and his thirst for new ideas. After his travel to India in 1997, he observed, "Even though 80 percent of what you hear from customers is the same all over the world, you always learn something you can apply to our business elsewhere" (Schlender, 1997: 81). But the same eagerness to explore new ideas and ways of doing things can be an impediment to performance on jobs that require careful attention to existing processes and procedures.

As one would expect, *emotional stability* also is related to job behaviors and performance. At the extreme, individuals who are neurotic are not likely to be able to function in organizations. Some degree of anxiety and worrying, however, can help people perform well because it spurs them to excel. Andy Grove's book *Only the Paranoid Survive: How to Exploit the Crisis That Challenges Every Company and Career* is an indication of the sense of anxiety he instills at Intel to make sure employees perform and the organization excels. Finally, although *agreeableness* is a highly desirable personality trait in social situations, it generally is not associated with an individual's work-related behaviors or performance. Furthermore, some recent research suggests that leaders who are higher on emotional stability, extraversion, and agreeableness, while low on conscientiousness have followers with higher job satisfaction and job commitment (Smith and Canger, 2004).

The most important managerial implication of the Big Five dimensions is that despite the reliability and robustness of the Big Five as measures of personality, no single trait is linked strongly to how well a leader or manager will perform in all types and levels of jobs. The links to leadership that do exist are relatively weak, and even a broad

Leading Change   Steve Bennett "Thinks Smart and Moves Fast"

Intuit Corp. is known for its user-friendly software, such as Quicken and Turbo Tax, which help many loyal customers save much time and money. When the company itself needed help in 1999, it turned to Steve Bennett, a 23-year General Electric veteran, with a strong background in finance. Even though Bennett knew little about the business, he was hired to bring a new business model, new perspectives, and to shake up the young, but well-entrenched company culture. Bennett prides himself on "seeing things the way they are, not the way you want them to be" (Palmer, 2004: 17). What Bennett saw was Intuit's democratic, employee-centered culture with flexible schedules that allowed for considerable autonomy, an organization that had been consistently rated as one of the best places to work (Shinn, 2007). But, when Bennett took the leadership, the company still ran like a small start-up despite significant growth and its founder Scott Cook believed it was not achieving its potential.

Bennett took the change head-on and told employees at his first meeting that the company was underperforming and needed a shake up. As he learned about the company, he quickly moved to refocus attention on performance, violating many dearly held Intuit operational values such as "Speak, listen, and respond" (Tischler, 2002). He refused to meet with the 200 employees who requested to see him as soon as he was appointed and reorganized the company taking out layers to focus on the customer and develop new products for small businesses. Bennett believes the managers should not meddle with their employees' business. He states that Inuit needs "facilitative leadership, not someone who is an expert in software" (Shin, 2007: 22). For him, the leader's job is to "conduct the orchestra, not to play all the instruments" (Tischler, 2002: 108). One of Bennett's strengths is his ability to focus on important priorities and not spend time on trivial matters. Managing his time is one of his own priorities to make sure he has opportunities to play golf.

Although Intuit's long-time employees were quite shocked by the new CEO's methods and directions, the shake-up paid off, allowing the company to enter new markets through growth and acquisitions and turn itself around. As company performance improved, Bennett was able to relax and take part in "Speak, listen, and respond," by wandering around the office. In spite of the changes, the company maintained its relaxed feel (Tischler, 2002).

Sources: Intuit: Executive profile. 2007. http://www.intuit.com/about_intuit/executives/steve_bennett.jhtml (accessed July 20, 2007); Palmer, J., 2004. "Intuitively clear," *Baron's*, February 24: 17; Tischler, L., 2002. "Sudden impact," *Fast Company*, September: 106–118; Shin, S., 2007. "Think smart, Move fast," *BizEd*, May/June: 2024.

personality measure such as the Big Five alone cannot account for success or failure in the complex leadership process.

Other Individual Personality Traits

Another approach to understanding the role of traits in leadership is to take into consideration personality traits that may affect the way a person leads. As is the case with the Big Five dimensions, many of the traits fit into the framework and categories proposed by Kirkpatrick and Locke (1991) discussed earlier in this chapter. We consider six such traits that impact leadership style.

Locus of Control

The concept of locus of control, introduced by Rotter in 1966, is an indicator of an individual's sense of control over the environment and external events. People with a high internal locus of control (i.e., a high score on the scale; see Self-Assessment 4-3) believe that many of the events around them are a result of their actions. They feel a sense of control over their lives. They attribute their successes and failures to their own efforts. Because of this attribution, individuals with an internal locus of control are more proactive and take more risks (Anderson, Hellreigel, and Slocum, 1977). As such, they demonstrate the motivation, energy, and self-confidence proposed by Kirkpatrick and Locke (1991) to be central leadership traits. Research indicates that internals are less anxious, set harder goals, and are less conforming to authority than externals (for a review of the literature, see Spector, 1982). In addition, internals make greater efforts to achieve their goals and tend to be more task oriented than externals and are more proactive when managing stress (Nonis and Hoyt, 2004). They also tend to be more ethical in their decision making and harsher on bribery (Cherry and Fraedrich, 2000) and more open to globalization (Spears, Parker, and McDonald, 2004). Some research also indicates that internal leaders of not-for-profit organizations are more successful than externals at generating funding commitments from their members (Adeyemi-Bello, 2003).

Individuals with an external locus of control attribute the events in their lives to forces external to them—to factors such as luck, other powerful people, or a deep religious faith. They attribute their success to luck and interpersonal skills rather than to their intelligence and ability (Sightler and Wilson, 2001). In other words, they do not generally perceive a high degree of control over their lives. Therefore, they are more reactive to events and less able to rebound from stressful situations. They rely on others' judgments and conform to authority more readily than internals (Spector, 1982). As leaders, externally controlled individuals are likely to use more coercive power, a factor that stems from projecting their own sense of lack of control onto others. Because they do not feel they control events and because they tend to be reactive, they believe others will do the same and overcontrol their followers to compensate for how they perceive others.

Several studies have explored the link between leadership and locus of control. Some findings indicate that internals are more likely to emerge as group leaders and that groups led by internals perform better than those headed by externals (Anderson and Schneier, 1978). Other research has looked at the effect of locus of control on CEOs' behaviors and choices of strategy for their organizations. The results indicate that internally controlled CEOs select risky and innovative strategies for their firms to a higher degree than do externals (Miller and Droge, 1986; Miller, Kets de Vries, and Toulouse, 1982). They also tend to be more proactive and future oriented as indicated by the findings that internals are more entrepreneurial (Hansemark, 2003).

Although research is limited, the pattern of results is highly consistent. A clear difference is evident between the behavior and decision-making patterns of internally and externally controlled individuals. Such patterns are not the only determinant of a leader's behavior, but they potentially affect a leader's actions.

Type A

Beginning in the late 1960s, researchers have focused on the concept of the Type A behavior pattern as a risk factor for coronary disease (Glass, 1983; Rosenman and Friedman, 1974). Psychologists and management researchers are also interested in the Type A personality (Baron, 1989). Generally, Type As are described as trying to do more in less and less time. As compared with Type Bs, they are involved in a whirlwind of activity. At the heart of the Type A construct is the need for control (Smith and Rhodewalt, 1986; Strube and Werner, 1985). As opposed to Type Bs, who tend to have less need for control, Type A individuals show a high need for control, which manifests itself in four general characteristics (Figure 4-3).

The first Type A characteristic, time urgency, leads Type A individuals to be concerned with time. Being in a hurry, impatience with delays, and worries about time are

Figure 4-3   Type A Characteristics and Behaviors.

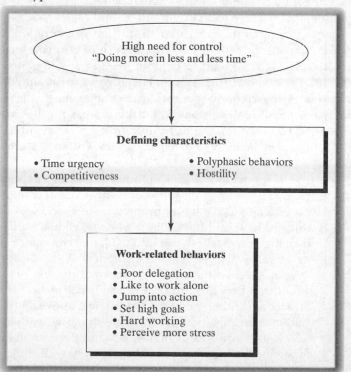

aspects of time urgency. The second Type A characteristic is competitiveness. Type A individuals are generally highly competitive in work, social, and sport situations. They measure their outcomes against others and keep track of their performance; getting ahead and winning are major concerns. The third characteristic, polyphasic behaviors, involves doing several things at once. Although everyone is likely to undertake several activities when pressured, Type As often do so even when not required to by work or other deadlines. For example, they might make a list of specific activities to undertake during a vacation. The last Type A characteristic is hostility. It is the only characteristic still found by researchers to be tied to coronary problems and other health problems (Alspach, 2004). It is manifested in explosive speech; diffused anger; intolerance for delays or mistakes; and a generally fiery, aggressive (Baron, Neuman, and Geddes, 1999), and sometimes malicious style of interaction (Strube et al., 1984).

These four sets of characteristics are triggered by the Type A's need for control and are aimed at providing the Type A with a sense of control over the environment (see Self-Assessment 4-4). Interestingly, although the Type A and locus of control concepts use the construct of control as a key defining element, the two scales are not related. Internally controlled individuals feel they control their lives; Type As need an increasing amount of control over events even when they exhibit internal locus of control. Type A characteristics are neither bad nor good. Type As and Type Bs possess certain traits and behaviors that can either be helpful or provide obstacles to being effective leaders; situational requirements are the key.

The relationship of Type A to leadership has not been extensively studied, but a number of findings that link Type A behavior to work-related behaviors provide interesting insights. The results of one study suggest that being Type A affects the way CEOs approach organizational strategy (Nahavandi, Mizzi, and Malekzadeh, 1992). Type A executives see more threats in the environment of their organizations and set challenging strategies that still provide them with a sense of control. Furthermore, as compared with Type Bs, Type As tend to be poor delegators and generally prefer to work alone (Miller, Lack, and Asroff, 1985). They like to maintain control over all aspects of their work. The lack of delegation can be damaging to a leader and often is considered a major pitfall of management. Furthermore, with the increasing focus on cooperation, use of teams, and empowerment as a leadership style, the inability to delegate can present an obstacle to successful leadership.

> Type As tend to set high performance goals and have high expectations for themselves and those around them. Such high expectations lead to faster promotions at lower organizational levels. When taken in a leadership context, such high expectations can lead to high performance and high quality, as well as to overload and burnout when carried to an extreme.

Type As tend to set high performance goals and have high expectations for themselves and those around them. Such high expectations lead to faster promotions at lower organizational levels (Stewart-Belle and Lust, 1999). When taken in a leadership context, such high expectations can lead to high performance and high quality, as well as to overload and burnout when carried to an extreme. Type As, besides having high expectations, do not recognize and admit that they are tired. They are hard workers who might not understand other people's less-intense approach to work. Scott Rudin, the Hollywood producer we discussed earlier, is at work at 6:30 A.M. and works at high-speed until late hours of the night, expecting his assistants to be there with him all along. Avery Baker, senior vice president of marketing at Tommy Hilfiger, and her boyfriend Tony Kruz, managing director at Capital Alliance Partners, are both in high-pressure jobs they love that require long hours and extensive travel (each log 400,000 and 300,000 miles a year respectively; Tischler, 2005). Both sleep only a few hours a night as they hop around the globe, not seeing each other for weeks at a time. Gerard Mestrallet, the CEO of the French utilities company Suez Lyonnaise des Eaux, is obsessed with his company's performance so much so that he interrupts interviews to check on stock prices (Tomlinson, 2000). Carlos Ghosn, CEO of Nissan Motors, recently cut back from a 16-hour day to a 14-hour day stating, "I'm saving energy that I need for the future . . . I'm conscious that what's important is to be able to last" (Alderman, 2005: C8).

One manifestation of the hard-driving Type A behavior in U.S. business is the how little vacation time people take. Gian Lombardo, who together with his wife manufactures luxury luggage, hardly ever takes a vacation or enjoys those he takes. During his last one, he spent all his time in his hotel room on his BlackBerry (his wife calls it Pearl, his mistress). He admits that he is a "total nutcase" (Conlin, 2007). Tom DeMarco, a high-tech consultant, suggests that many companies believe that they are "effective only to the extent that all their workers are totally and eternally busy" (Anders, 2001: 28). Such an approach pushes employees and managers to take on many Type A characteristics.

As is the case with locus of control, the Type A construct is linked directly to leadership in only a few studies. The consistency of the findings that Type As like to maintain control, are active and hard working, and tend to be impatient with delays and with their coworkers, however, allows us to consider the potential implications for leadership. These behaviors are similar to the high energy and motivation that Kirkpatrick and Locke (1991) propose as central leadership traits. Type A leaders are likely to be intense and demanding, set high performance standards, and be intolerant of delays and excuses. They also might find it difficult to delegate tasks or work in a team environment. Some recent research suggests that Type As and Bs both prefer working in teams made up of others similar to them (Keinan and Koren, 2002). Other research indicates that Type As and Bs may be effective in different types of jobs (Rastogi and Dave, 2004). Yet, although some Type A characteristics appear to define effective leaders (such as drive, ambition, and energy), others, such as impatience with delays and a tendency to jump into action, are characteristics that do not serve leaders well. One recent study found that Type personality is related to depression and lower individual performance over time (Watson, 2006).

Self-Monitoring

When observing some leaders, we can identify their style and even personality traits easily. They seem to be an open book, and their behavior is consistent in many different situations. For example, Herb Kelleher, founder of Southwest Airlines, has a forceful but open style in all settings, whether he is dealing with the Southwest employees or stockholders or presenting at a business conference. Similarly, it was never hard for anyone to read Michael Eisner, the former CEO of Disney; he was highly aggressive and demanding in all settings. Other leaders are harder to read, or their behaviors appear to change from one situation to another.

One reason it might be easy to read some people and establish their style but difficult to do so for others is self-monitoring. Developed by Snyder (1974), the self-monitoring scale identifies the degree to which people are capable of reading and using the cues from their environment to determine their behavior. High self-monitors (SMs)—individuals who score high on the scale (see Self-Assessment 4-5)—are able to read environmental and social cues regarding what is appropriate behavior and use those cues to adjust their behaviors. They can present themselves and manage impressions (Turnley and Bolino, 2001) and are able to mirror and mimic others' behaviors better than low SMs (Estow, Jamieson, and Yates, 2007). Studies also find that high SMs are particularly good at getting along with others and even may be more likely to emerge as leaders because of their ability to get ahead (Day and Schleicher, 2006) and that they may be more adaptive and innovative (Hutchinson and Skinner, 2007). Low SMs either do not read the cues or do not use them to change their behavior. For high SMs, behavior is likely to be the result of a perception of the environment and is therefore likely to change depending on the situation. Low SMs' behaviors are more internally determined and are likely to appear constant across different situations. This internal focus also seems to make them more accurate decision makers regarding performance ratings and personnel decisions (Jawahar, 2001).

Many leadership theories rely on the assumptions that leaders (1) have the ability to evaluate various situations and (2) can change their behaviors to match the requirements of the situation. In that context, being a high SM might become a key leadership trait. Being a high SM should help a leader better perceive and analyze a situation. Furthermore, given SMs' higher ability to adjust their behaviors, it is reasonable to suggest that, at least in situations that are ambiguous and difficult to read, they might be more effective leaders. Some studies support these ideas (e.g., Dobbins et al., 1990). Researchers have found that high SMs emerge as leaders more frequently than do low SMs, leading to the hypothesis that self-monitoring is a key variable in leadership and job performance (Day, Schleicher, Unckless, and Hiller, 2002). The concept has also been linked to transformational leadership behaviors (discussed in Chapter 6). Interesting findings also have emerged regarding the link between Type A and self-monitoring, as well as the role that gender might play in self-monitoring.

Several studies looked at the impact of gender, self-monitoring, and Type A on conflict management and leadership in organizations (Baron, 1989; Becker, Ayman, and Korabik, 1994; Dobbins et al., 1990). The studies indicated the following results:

- ➤ High SMs emerge as leaders more often than do low self-monitors.
- ➤ Men emerge as leaders more often than do women.
- ➤ Type As are in conflict more often than are Type Bs, particularly when dealing with their subordinates.
- ➤ High SMs resolve conflicts cooperatively when dealing with their subordinates and their supervisors.
- ➤ Women generally report lower levels of conflict with both their subordinates and their supervisors.
- ➤ High self-monitoring women are especially sensitive to various organizational cues and seem to perceive more conflict.

Overall, self-monitoring presents interesting potential applications to leadership, many of which remain unexplored (for a discussion of the potential impact of self-monitoring on leadership, see Bedeian and Day, 2004). Little doubt remains, however, that being a high SM can be a useful characteristic in helping leaders adjust their behaviors and perhaps even in learning new skills. High SMs may be better able to cope with cross-cultural experiences because such situations are ambiguous and require the ability to interpret environmental cues. Similarly, the changing leadership roles are making leadership situations considerably less routine and more uncertain than they were 20 years ago. Modern leaders must deal with diverse cultures and followers' demands for participation and autonomy, and they also need to understand an increasingly complex global environment. Self-monitoring might be a key characteristic in these new tasks.

Myers-Briggs Type Indicator

Although the research about its robustness is contradictory, the Myers-Briggs Type Indicator (MBTI) is one of the most widely used personality tests in organizations for leadership training and team building (Hammonds, 2001). Its primary use has been to help teams and work groups understand and capitalize on the individual approaches to decision making and in leadership development, in spite of some reservation from leadership scholars (Michael, 2003). As an aid to decision making and team building, the MBTI enjoys tremendous popularity. The scale classifies individuals along four bipolar dimensions that are combined to provide a profile for each person. The first two major dimensions, sensing/intuition and thinking/feeling, relate to information gathering and information interpretation (Figure 4-4). The other two are perception/judgmental (P/J) and extrovert/introvert (E/I; see Self-Assessment 4.6).

People with different styles approach problem solving and decision making differently. Some studies link MBTI to behaviors such as time urgency, academic problems, and even the selection of functional areas. For example, most scientists are sensation thinkers (STs) or intuitive thinkers (NTs), whereas research and development managers tend to be either sensation feelers (SFs) or intuitive feelers (NFs; for a review of behaviors related to MBTI, see Furnham and Stringfield, 1993). People with different dominant styles prefer a certain type of information, follow a different time orientation, and generally approach problems in different ways. The MBTI is used as a leadership training tool in several major leadership training programs, most notably in the Center of Creative Leadership (Conger, 1992). The assumption is that individuals with different MBTI styles are likely to approach their tasks and their groups differently. For example, a sensing-thinker (ST) leader is likely to require his or her group to seek out and provide facts and figures, and concrete alternatives and solutions. Because the feeling (F) dimension is secondary for that leader, focus on interpersonal issues is likely to be absent or not a primary factor, which might hinder resolution of interpersonal conflict in some situations. An intuitive-feeler (NF) leader will take little interest in the group's factual analysis and is likely to prefer to hear about possibilities and creative alternatives to problems.

Cross-cultural studies point to national differences regarding the MBTI. For example, Chinese managers are higher in introversion, sensing, thinking, and judgment than their European counterparts (Furnham and Stringfield, 1993). The Chinese management profile appears to be ISTJ (introverted–sensor–thinker–judgmental) as compared with the Europeans' ESTJ (extroverted–sensor–thinker–judgmental). For European and Chinese groups, managers' extroversion is linked to better performance and higher satisfaction. Studies also apply the MBTI to executive leadership

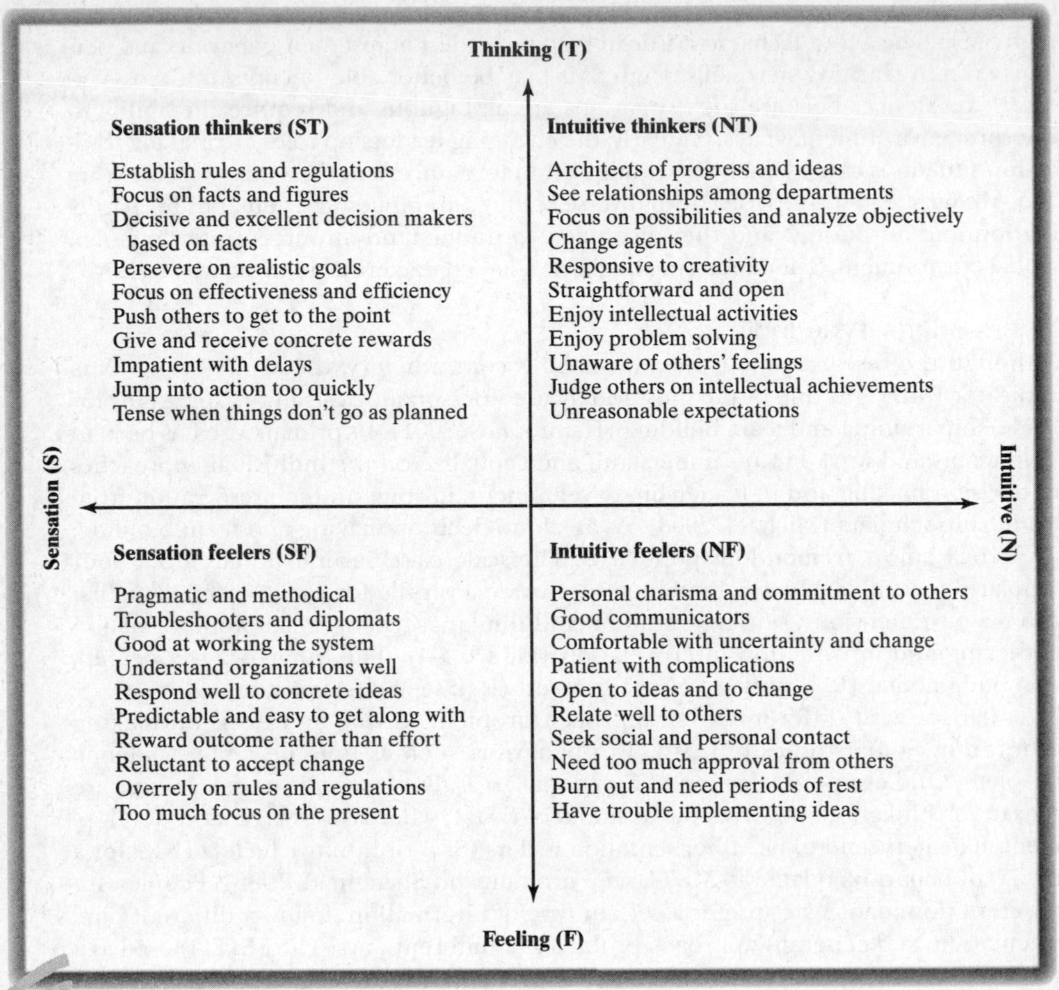

Thinking (T)

Sensation thinkers (ST)

Establish rules and regulations
Focus on facts and figures
Decisive and excellent decision makers
   based on facts
Persevere on realistic goals
Focus on effectiveness and efficiency
Push others to get to the point
Give and receive concrete rewards
Impatient with delays
Jump into action too quickly
Tense when things don't go as planned

Intuitive thinkers (NT)

Architects of progress and ideas
See relationships among departments
Focus on possibilities and analyze objectively
Change agents
Responsive to creativity
Straightforward and open
Enjoy intellectual activities
Enjoy problem solving
Unaware of others' feelings
Judge others on intellectual achievements
Unreasonable expectations

Sensation (S) ← → Intuitive (N)

Sensation feelers (SF)

Pragmatic and methodical
Troubleshooters and diplomats
Good at working the system
Understand organizations well
Respond well to concrete ideas
Predictable and easy to get along with
Reward outcome rather than effort
Reluctant to accept change
Overrely on rules and regulations
Too much focus on the present

Intuitive feelers (NF)

Personal charisma and commitment to others
Good communicators
Comfortable with uncertainty and change
Patient with complications
Open to ideas and to change
Relate well to others
Seek social and personal contact
Need too much approval from others
Burn out and need periods of rest
Have trouble implementing ideas

Feeling (F)

Figure 4-4   Four MBTI Categories.

(Haley and Stumpf, 1989; Henderson and Nutt, 1980; Nutt, 1986, 1988). In general, the findings show that STs are risk averse, whereas SFs tolerate risk better. The MBTI seems particularly applicable to upper-echelon research because the strategic domain is to a great extent a decision-making environment in which the CEO and top management team analyze the environment and make decisions regarding the best strategies to take advantage of that environment (see Chapter 7 for further discussion of the role of CEOs).

    Overall, the MBTI provides a useful tool for understanding the way individuals think and make decisions. Given that how individuals think and how they make decisions are imperative to leadership, knowledge of their MBTI score and its related behavioral correlates can help people understand their own actions as leaders and help them prepare for areas that might be difficult to undertake. For example, the MBTI score can be the basis for the selection of leadership training and development. An NF leader, for instance, is less likely to need training on interpersonal relations than an ST leader. The NF's lack of interest in facts and figures and logical problem solving, however, can become a major impediment when making a presentation to an ST-dominated board of directors. In such a situation, training NF leaders in logical problem solving might help them become more effective with some of their constituents (see Self-Assessment 4-6).

Machiavellian Personality

Do you believe that the end justifies the means? Are you skilled at manipulating others to get what you want? Are you a ruthless, skilled negotiator? Is gaining and retaining power your major concern? If you answer positively to these questions, chances are you have some elements of a Machiavellian personality (see Self-Assessment 4-7). The concept of the Machiavellian personality, developed by Christie and Geis (1970), is based loosely on Niccolo Machiavelli's work *The Prince.* The Machiavelli (Mach) scale measures an individual's willingness to put self-interests and his or her preferences above the interests of the group and the ability to influence and manipulate others for personal gain (Jaffe, Nebenzahl, and Gotesdyner, 1989; Panitz, 1989).

Individuals with a high score on the scale are comfortable using various means to achieve their personal goals. A high Mach views human nature cynically, shows few scruples, and is willing to step outside the bounds of formal authority. These individuals might lack the honesty and integrity that are requirements of effective leadership. They are also more flexible in the type of behavior they use to influence others, relying on emotional appeals rather than logic and rational argument (Allen, 1990; Reimers and Barbuto, 2002). On the other end of the scale, low Machs tend to be overly naive and trusting. Although research has not established clear linkages to leadership, it can be assumed that high Machs' political and manipulation skills allow them to be successful if not effective leaders (Luthans, 1989). Their aim is to promote themselves rather than support their followers. Low Machs, on the other hand, might not demonstrate enough political savvy and therefore might be unable to provide their group with the necessary resources and visibility.

Neither the high Machs nor low Machs are likely to be effective leaders. High Machs are too focused on their personal goals; low Machs are not skilled at the legitimate influence tactics essential for effective leadership. In general, individuals who are medium Machs tend to be the most effective leaders. Such people are good negotiators and savvy about manipulation of others to reach goals, but they do not abuse their power, and they focus on achieving organizational rather than personal goals. Medium Machs are the ones who are capable of being successful and effective.

As can be expected from a concept that relates to perception and use of power, cross-cultural differences exist with regard to Mach scores. For example, Hong Kong and People's Republic of China (PRC) managers score higher on the Mach scale than do their U.S. counterparts. It appears that the Chinese are more willing to use social power to accomplish their goals (Ralston et al., 1993a, b). This finding fits with the concept of high power distance, where authority is broad and respected.

Our popular press is full of examples of ruthless leaders from the private and public sectors, who wheel and deal their way to achieving their goals with considerable disregard for their subordinates. Some are admired for what they can achieve; others are simply feared. Several publications prepare regular lists of these tough bosses. In many cases, as long as the bottom line is healthy and key constituents, such as the board of directors or stockholders, are satisfied, the means used by these leaders are tolerated.

Narcissism

We have all worked with people who have an exaggerated need to be the center of attention, an oversized sense of self-importance, and a limited ability to think about others. It is difficult enough to deal with such people as colleagues, but working with them as supervisors and leaders is another challenge altogether. We call them selfish or self-absorbed; however, such behaviors are part of the concept of narcissism, which when occurring to an extreme and in a pervasive manner, has been identified as the Narcissistic Personality Disorder (NPD; American Psychiatric Association, 2000). Some of the characteristics of narcissism are

➤ A grandiose sense of self-importance and exaggeration of one's achievements and talents
➤ Preoccupation with power and success
➤ Arrogance
➤ Indifference to others and self-absorption
➤ Inability to tolerate criticism and a fragile self-esteem
➤ Desire to be the center of attention at all times
➤ Sense of entitlement
➤ Exploiting others without guilt to achieve goals
➤ Lack of empathy for others and inability to understand others' feelings
➤ Trouble building meaningful relationships

Although these characteristics when all present in excess can be the basis of a psychological disorder, narcissism has also been used to describe a range of "normal" behaviors (Emons, 1987; Morf and Rhodewalt, 2001; Raskin and Hall, 1979) with possible links to and implications for leadership (Popper, 2002; Rosenthal and Pittinsky, 2006). Many narcissistic traits are related to characteristics of leaders including desire to have power and influence over others and be in a leadership position (see Self-Assessment 4-8). Several aspects of the construct are part of a healthy and confident self-esteem, whereas others may be related to less-productive aspects of personality. The concept has further been linked to Machiavellianism and a subclinical form of psychopathy (Paulhus and Williams, 2002).

Well-known tyrants of history, such as Hitler and Stalin, exhibit strong narcissistic tendencies. So do other historical, social, and business leaders including Michael Eisner and Scott Rudin, discussed earlier in this chapter, and leaders such as Alexander Hamilton, Steve Jobs of Apple, and many U.S. and world leaders, including presidents Carter, Clinton, and G.W. Bush (Rosenthal and Pittinsky, 2006). Destructive narcissistic leaders self-promote, deceive and manipulate others, respond poorly to criticism and feedback, and blame others for their failures (Delbecq, 2001; Rosenthal and Pittinsky, 2006). Their apparent high degree of self-confidence and certainty about their decisions are likely to lead to poor decisions and lapses in ethics and personal conduct related to their exaggerated sense of self and entitlement. Several researchers have linked the narcissistic arrogance to a deep sense of inferiority (e.g., Zeiger-Hill, 2006) that such leaders are able to mask with self-promotion and constant attention grabbing. One of the most negative aspects of narcissism, when it comes to leadership, is the lack of empathy for others, which when combined with paranoia and a sense of entitlement can lead to dire consequences (Judge, LePine, and Rich, 2006).

Positive narcissistic leaders may have an exaggerated sense of self and entitlement, but they use their self-confidence, power, and influence to achieve goals, much the same way a moderate Machiavellian would. They can therefore be a positive force for their group and their organization.

Positive narcissistic leaders may have an exaggerated sense of self and entitlement, but they use their self-confidence, power, and influence to achieve goals, much the same way a moderate Machiavellian would. They can therefore be a positive force for their group and their organization. Research about narcissism and its links to other personality traits and leadership is relatively new. Much of link to leadership has been established in the area of charismatic and transformational leadership, a topic we discuss in Chapter 6.

Each of the preceding individual characteristics and traits plays a role in how leaders interact with others or make decisions. Any one trait alone, or even a combination, cannot explain or predict leadership effectiveness. These characteristics can be useful tools for self-awareness and understanding and as guides to leadership development. Certain characteristics, though, have been found to be detrimental to effective leadership.

Applying What You Learn
Dealing with Abusive Bosses

Many of us have been faced with supervisors and bosses who appear to have strong narcissistic characteristics. Here are some suggestions in dealing with them. These do not all work and different ones work depending on the situation and the person you are dealing with:

- Keep your cool; do not react with an emotional response; remain professional even if the boss is not. You can't control his or her behavior; but you can control your reaction.

- Make sure you clearly understand and are able to describe the type of behavior you are facing (e.g., too much criticism, inaccurate feedback, yelling, etc.).

- Document everything! Keep careful notes of incidents.

- Make sure that your work and behavior are impeccable and beyond reproach.

- Do not get defensive; respond with level-headed comments without taking the abuse.

- Seek help from HR if that is available, especially if there are legal ramifications (e.g., discrimination, sexual harassment, or other ethical or legal violations).

- Maintain good working relationships and a strong network at work.

- Go up the chain of command as a last resort; provide facts and evidence—not just emotional reactions.

- Plan an exit strategy; look for another position.

- Unless the situation is dangerous, don't make a quick decision about leaving; carefully plan for contingencies and eventual exit.

- Only you can determine when it's too much; with planning, you can leave on your own terms.

CHARACTERISTICS OF LEADERS WHO FAIL

Another way to learn about leaders' individual characteristics is to evaluate leaders who are not successful and who derail. Do they share some common characteristics? Are they any different from those who succeed? The Center for Creative Leadership conducted research tracking leaders who derail (McCall and Lombardo, 1983), and many anecdotal accounts report characteristics of leaders who do not succeed (Hymowitz, 1988; Nelton, 1997). A book by Barbara Kellerman, the director of the Center for Public Leadership at Harvard University, suggests that we can learn as much from bad leaders as we can from good ones (Kellerman, 2004). Excessive greed and corruption, incompetence, rigidity, isolation from others, and lack of caring for others are some of the characteristics of bad leaders. The following are the primary reasons for derailment:

➤ An abrasive, intimidating style
➤ Coldness and arrogance
➤ Untrustworthiness
➤ Self-centeredness and overly political actions
➤ Poor communication
➤ Poor performance
➤ Inability to delegate

As the list indicates, lack of people skills and the inability to manage relationships are central causes of failure. Leaders who are good with followers and other constituents face a better chance of success. Pam Alexander, the CEO of Ogilvy Public Relations Worldwide, a public relations firm that concentrates on building relationships, states, "To build trust, invest in your relationships constantly. Don't sweat the ROI; help people, whether or not they can return the favor. Connect them to appropriate opportunities whenever you can" (Canabou and Overholt, 2001: 98–102). More and more, leaders who rule with an iron fist, exercise power without accountability, and are unwilling or unable to allow followers to contribute and develop are rated poorly (Joyce, 2005). Other key contributors to leadership failure are organizational factors, unrelated to the leader's style and personality. Organizational climates that tolerate or even encourage unethical behavior (e.g., Enron), board of directors who fail to take action in time (e.g., Disney), and employees who are scared or prevented from taking action all allow the negative characteristics of leaders to affect the whole organization. Alan Greenspan, the chairman of the U.S. Federal Reserve, recently observed, "It is not that humans have become any more greedy than in generations past. It is that avenues to express greed have grown so enormously" (Pink, 2002: 44).

USING INDIVIDUAL CHARACTERISTICS

The various individual characteristics presented in this chapter do not allow us to develop a clear leadership profile. We still do not know what traits make an effective leader, although we recognize some indications about undesirable characteristics. The different characteristics are generally independent from one another. In other words, an individual might have an internal locus of control, be a Type B, NF, moderate Mach, positive narcissist, and high SM. Although certain combinations are intuitively more likely to occur, the scales are not statistically correlated. Research in the area is minimal, and it is reasonable to assume that some combinations of traits make certain traits and behaviors more salient and dominant. For example, a low SM Type A who also happens to be an ST with internal locus of control is likely to have a highly proactive and aggressive style in many situations. On the other hand, a high SM Type B with high scores on the feeling dimension of the MBTI is likely to come across as low key, interpersonally oriented, and socially sensitive, especially if the person believes that the situation requires such behavior.

Despite the validity of the constructs presented, it is important to limit the use of the scales to the purpose for which they were developed until further research evidence allows for broader application. The scales are all good self-awareness and self-development tools. The issue of self-awareness, through various means, has become an important part of leadership training and development (for a detailed presentation, see Chapter 10). The first step to leadership effectiveness is being aware of one's strengths, weaknesses, and personality characteristics. These characteristics explain in part why learning certain new behaviors is harder for some people than for others; they are not selection tools and should not be used for promotional or other job-related decisions. Several organizations, ranging from Dell to General Electric to Bristol-Myers and Hewlett-Packard, however, require candidates for top leadership positions to undergo hours of psychological testing, spending upwards of $5000 for each evaluation (Daniels, 2001). These companies claim that the results of such tests help them pick leaders who fit well with their culture.

The self-awareness trends in the business sector are leading to the use of 360-degree feedback, which allows managers to receive feedback about their behaviors, style, and performance not only from their bosses but also from their peers and subordinates. Although the results are sometimes painful, they are a helpful step in overcoming weaknesses. Another self-awareness tool gaining popularity with companies such as AT&T and PepsiCo is the use of meditation and self-reflection as a means of increasing self-awareness and managing stress (Sherman, 1994). These individual tools often are combined with seminars such as Covey's Seven Habits of Highly Effective People, where the focus is on self-mastery and positive thinking. In times of change and with increasing pressure on leaders to be flexible, to be creative, and to deliver high performance, the push toward better self-knowledge allows for necessary self-development. Although it used to be assumed that leaders needed little training, the current trend brings continuous improvement down to the individual level.

SUMMARY AND CONCLUSION

This chapter presents the current thinking on the role of traits in leadership effectiveness and identifies several individual differences and personality characteristics that impact a leader's style and approach. Although these individual differences do not dictate behavior, they establish a zone of comfort for certain behaviors and actions. Values are long-lasting beliefs about what is worthwhile. They are strongly influenced by culture and are one of the determinants of ethical conduct. Intelligence is one of the abilities that most affects leadership. Although being intelligent is related to leadership to some extent, it is not a sufficient factor to predict effectiveness. On the other hand, research suggests that the concept of emotional intelligence, which focuses on interpersonal rather than cognitive abilities, may link to leadership emergence effectiveness. Creativity is another ability that might be important in leadership effectiveness, especially in situations that require novel approaches.

One of the most reliable sets of personality traits is called the Big Five. Although the conscientiousness and extraversion dimensions in the Big Five show some links to work-related behavior, the traits are not linked directly to leadership. Several other individual traits do link to leadership. Locus of control is an indicator of the degree to which individuals perceive that they have control over the events around them. Individuals with internal control are found to be more proactive, more satisfied with their work, and less coercive. Type A behavior also deals with issues of control but focuses on the need for control as demonstrated through a person's time urgency, competitiveness, polyphasic behaviors, and hostility. The Type A's need for control makes it difficult to delegate tasks and pushes the individual toward short-term focus and selection of strategies that maximize control. Another relevant personality characteristic, self-monitoring, is the degree to which individuals read and use situational cues to adjust their behavior. High self-monitors possess a degree of flexibility that might be helpful in leadership situations.

One of the most-used personality variables assessments is the MBTI, which focuses primarily on the way a person gathers information and uses it to make decisions. The various MBTI types approach situations differently and focus on different factors as leaders. Machiavellianism focuses on the use of social power to achieve goals. High Machs are adept at manipulating others to achieve their personal goals. The concept is related to the last personality trait we discuss, narcissism. With a grandiose and exaggerated sense of self and low concern for others, those with high narcissistic characteristics have the potential for being highly destructive leaders, although some of the traits associated with the construct are part of leadership.

All of the concepts discussed in this chapter allow for better self-understanding and awareness. Although none is a measure of leadership style, they all relate to many leadership behaviors, such as delegation and decision making. The measures are well validated, but they are not meant to be used for selection or promotion decisions. Interestingly, cross-cultural research indicates many differences on the scales in terms of gender and national cultures. These differences point to the potential role of culture in an individual's personality characteristics.

LEADERSHIP CHALLENGE: USING PSYCHOLOGICAL TESTING

Organizations are relying increasingly on psychological tests to select, evaluate, promote, and develop their employees and managers. Although many of the tests are reliable and valid, many others are not. Additionally, tests developed in one culture do not always apply or have predictive validity in other cultures. However, such tests do provide a seemingly quick and efficient way to get to know people better.

As a department manager, you are faced with the selection of a new team of 10 members to run the marketing research and advertising campaign for a new product. The ideal employee profile includes intelligence, creativity, assertiveness, competitiveness, ability to persuade others and negotiate well, and ability to work with a team. Your human resources department conducted extensive testing of 50 inside and outside applicants for the new team. As you review the candidates' files, you notice that the majority of candidates who fit the profile best are young, Caucasian males, while women and minorities tend to have low scores, particularly on assertiveness and competitiveness.

1. How much weight do you give the psychological tests? What factors do you need to consider?
2. Who do you select for the team?

REVIEW AND DISCUSSION QUESTIONS

1. What is the impact of individual characteristics on behavior?
2. How do values affect behaviors, and what impact does culture have on our value system?
3. How do emotional intelligence and general intelligence impact leadership?
4. What role does productivity play in leadership? Can a leader be effective with only average creativity?
5. Describe the seven personality traits and their implications for leadership.
6. In your opinion (or based on your experience), do certain characteristics and traits lead to a greater impact than others on a person's leadership style? Explain your answer.
7. What are the limitations of the personality approach presented in this chapter, and how should the information about personal characteristics be used in leadership?
8. After completing the personality self-assessment surveys at the end of this chapter, consider your personal profile. What is the impact of this profile on your leadership style?

EXERCISE 4-1: YOUR IDEAL ORGANIZATION

This exercise is designed to help understand the way different individuals perceive and define organizations.

Part I: Individual Description

Think of working in the organization of your dreams. What would it look like? How would it be organized? How would people interact? Your assignment in this part of the exercise is to provide a description of your ideal organization. In doing so, consider the following organizational characteristics and elements.

1. What industry would it be?

2. What is the mission of your ideal organization?

3. What is the culture? What are the basic assumptions? What are the behavioral norms? Who are the heroes? How do people interact?

4. How would people be organized? What is the structure? Consider issues of centralization, hierarchy, formalization, specialization, span of control, departmentation, and so on.

5. What is the role of the leader? What is the role of followers?

6. Describe the physical location, office spaces, office decor, and so on.

7. Consider issues such as dress code, work schedules, and others that you think are important in describing your ideal organization.

Part II: Group Work

Your instructor will assign you to a group and provide you with further instructions.

SELF-ASSESSMENT 4-1:   VALUE SYSTEMS

Rank the values in each of the two categories from 1 (most important to you) to 5 (least important to you).

Rank	Instrumental Values	Rank	Terminal Values
2	Ambition and hard work	1	Contribution and a sense of accomplishment
1	Honesty and integrity	2	Happiness
4	Love and affection	7	Leisurely life
6	Obedience and duty	3	Wisdom and maturity
3	Independence and self-sufficiency	4	Individual dignity
5	Humility	6	Justice and fairness
7	Doing good to others (Golden rule)	5	Spiritual salvation

Scoring Key: The values that you rank highest in each group are the ones that are most important to you. Consider whether your actions, career choices, and so forth are consistent with your values.

Source: Based on C. Anderson, "Values-based management," *Academy of Management Executive* 11, no. 4 (1997): 25–46; M. Rokeach, *Beliefs, Attitudes, and Values* (San Francisco: Jossey-Bass, 1968).

SELF-ASSESSMENT 4-2:   EMOTIONAL INTELLIGENCE

Indicate whether each of the following statements is true or false for you.

Self-Awareness

_T_ 1. I am aware of how I feel and why.

_T_ 2. I understand how my feelings affect my behavior and my performance.

_T_ 3. I have a good idea of my personal strengths and weaknesses.

_T_ 4. I analyze things that happen to me and reflect on what happened.

_T_ 5. I am open to feedback from others.

_T_ 6. I look for opportunities to learn more about myself.

_T_ 7. I put my mistakes in perspective.

_T_ 8. I maintain a sense of humor and can laugh about my mistakes.

Managing Emotions and Self-Regulation

_T_ 9. I can stay calm in times of crisis.

_F_ 10. I think clearly and stay focused when under pressure.

_T_ 11. I show integrity in all my actions.

_T_ 12. People can depend on my word.

_T_ 13. I readily admit my mistakes.

_F_ 14. I confront the unethical actions of others.

_T_ 15. I stand for what I believe in.

_T_ 16. I handle change well and stay the course.

_T_ 17. I can be flexible when facing obstacles.

Self-Motivation

_F_ 18. I set challenging goals.

_T_ 19. I take reasonable and measured risks to achieve my goals.

_T_ 20. I am results oriented.

_T_ 21. I look for information on how to achieve my goals and improve my performance.

_F_ 22. I go above and beyond what is simply required of me.

_F_ 23. I am always looking for opportunities to do new things.

_T_ 24. I maintain a positive attitude even when I face obstacles and setbacks.

_T_ 25. I focus on success rather than failure.

_F_ 26. I don't take failure personally or blame myself too much.

Empathy for Others

_T_ 27. I pay attention to how others feel and react.

_T_ 28. I can see someone else's point of view, even when I don't agree with them.

_T_ 29. I am sensitive to other people.

_T_ 30. I offer feedback and try to help others achieve their goals.

_T_ 31. I recognize and reward others for their accomplishments.

_F_ 32. I am available to coach and mentor people.

_T_ 33. I respect people from varied backgrounds.

_T_ 34. I relate well to people who are different from me.

_T_ 35. I challenge intolerance, bias, and discrimination in others.

Social Skills

F 36. I am skilled at persuading others.

T 37. I can communicate clearly and effectively.

T 38. I am a good listener.

F 39. I can accept bad as well as good news.

F 40. I can share my vision with others and inspire them to follow my lead.

T 41. I lead by example.

T 42. I challenge the status quo when necessary.

T 43. I can handle difficult people tactfully.

T 44. I encourage open and professional discussions when there are disagreements.

T 45. I look for win-win solutions.

T 46. I build and maintain relationships with others.

T 47. I help maintain a positive climate at work.

T 48. I model team qualities such as respect, helpfulness, and cooperation.

T 49. I encourage participation from everyone when I work in teams.

T 50. I understand political forces that operate in organizations.

Scoring Key: For each of the 50 items, give yourself a 1 if you marked "true" and 0 if you marked "false." Consider your total for each of the subscales and your overall total score:

Self-awareness: _____8_____ out of 8

Managing emotions
and self-regulation: _____8_____ out of 9

Self-motivation: _____5_____ out of 9

Empathy for others: _____8_____ out of 9

Social skills: _____12_____ out of 15

Overall total: _____41_____ out of 50

Those with higher scores in each category, and overall, demonstrate more of the characteristics associated with high emotional intelligence.

Source: Based on information in D. Goleman, *Working with Emotional Intelligence* (New York: Bantam Books, 1998); MOSAIC competencies for professional and administrative occupations (U.S. Office of Personnel Management); Richard H. Rosier (ed.), *The Competency Model Handbook*, Volumes One and Two (Boston, MA: Linkage, 1994 and 1995).

SELF-ASSESSMENT 4-3:   LOCUS OF CONTROL

Read the following statements and indicate whether you agree with Choice A or Choice B.

	A	**B**		
1.	Making a lot of money is largely a matter of getting the right breaks.	Promotions are earned through hard work and persistence.	*B*	*l*
2.	I have noticed a direct connection between how hard I study and the grade I get.	Many times the reactions of teachers seem haphazard to me.	*A*	*l*
3.	The number of divorces indicates that more and more people are not trying to make their marriages work.	Marriage is largely a gamble.	*B*	
4.	It is silly to think that one can really change another person's basic attitudes.	When I am right I can convince others.	*A*	
5.	Getting promoted is really a matter of being a little luckier than the next person.	In our society a person's future earning power depends on his or her ability.	*B*	
6.	If one knows how to deal with people, he or she is really quite easily led.	I have little influence over the way other people behave.	*A*	*l*
7.	The grades I make are the results of my own efforts; luck has little or nothing to do with it.	Sometimes I feel I have little to do with the grades I get.	*A*	*l*
8.	People like me can change the course of world affairs if we make ourselves heard.	It is only wishful thinking to believe that one can readily influence what happens in our society at large.	*A*	*l*
9.	A great deal that happens to me is probably a matter of chance.	I am the master of my fate.	*B*	*l*
10.	Getting along with people is a skill that must be practiced.	It is almost impossible to figure out how to please some people.	*A*	*l*

Scoring Key: Give yourself 1 point for each of the following selections: 1B, 2A, 3A, 4B, 6A, 7A, 8A, 9B, and 10A. Scores are interpreted as follows:

8–10 = High internal locus of control	5 = Mixed
6–7 = Moderate internal locus of control	3–4 = Moderate external locus of control
	1–2 = High external locus of control

Source: Adapted with permission from Julian B. Rotter, "External Control and Internal Control," *Psychology Today*, June 1971: 42. Copyright 1971 by the American Psychological Association.

SELF-ASSESSMENT 4-4: TYPE A BEHAVIOR PATTERN

Indicate whether each of the following items is true or false for you.

_T_ 1. I am always in a hurry.

_T_ 2. I have list of things I have to achieve on a daily or weekly basis.

_T_ 3. I tend to take one problem or task at a time, finish, then move to the next one.

_T_ 4. I tend to take a break or quit when I get tired.

_T_ 5. I am always doing several things at once both at work and in my personal life.

_F_ 6. People who know me would describe my temper as hot and fiery.

_F_ 7. I enjoy competitive activities.

_T_ 8. I tend to be relaxed and easy going.

_T_ 9. Many things are more important to me than my job.

_F_ 10. I really enjoy winning both at work and at play.

_T_ 11. I tend to rush people along or finish their sentences for them when they are taking too long.

_F_ 12. I enjoy "doing nothing" and just hanging out.

Scoring Key: Type A individuals tend to answer questions 1, 2, 5, 6, 7, and 10 as true and questions 3, 4, 8, 9, and 12 as false. Type B individuals tend to answer in the reverse (1, 2, 5 as false and 3, 4 as true and so forth).

SELF-ASSESSMENT 4-5:   SELF-MONITORING

Indicate the degree to which you think the following statements are true or false, by writing the appropriate number. For example, if a statement is always true, you should write 5 next to that statement.

> 5 = Certainly always true
> 4 = Generally true
> 3 = Somewhat true, but with exceptions
> 2 = Somewhat false, but with exceptions
> 1 = Generally false
> 0 = Certainly always false

_5_ 1. In social situations, I have the ability to alter my behavior if I feel that something else is called for.

_3_ 2. I am often able to read people's true emotions correctly through their eyes.

_4_ 3. I have the ability to control the way I come across to people, depending on the impression I wish to give them.

_4_ 4. In conversations, I am sensitive to even the slightest change in the facial expression of the person I'm conversing with.

_3_ 5. My powers of intuition are quite good when it comes to understanding others' emotions and motives.

_3_ 6. I can usually tell when others consider a joke in bad taste, even though they may laugh convincingly.

_1_ 7. I feel that the image I am portraying isn't working, I can readily change it to something that does.

_1_ 8. I can usually tell when I've said something inappropriate by reading the listener's eyes.

_1_ 9. I have trouble changing my behavior to suit different people and different situations.

_4_ 10. I have found that I can adjust my behavior to meet the requirements of any situation I find myself in.

_4_ 11. If someone is lying to me, I usually know it at once from the person's manner or expression.

_1_ 12. Even when it might be to my advantage, I have difficulty putting up a good front.

_4_ 13. Once I know what the situation calls for, it's easy for me to regulate my actions accordingly.

Scoring Key: To obtain your score, add up the numbers written, except reverse the scores for questions 9 and 12. On 9 and 12, 5 becomes 0, 4 becomes 1, and so forth. High self-monitors are defined as those with score of approximately 53 or higher.

Source: R. D. Lennox and R. N. Wolfe, "Revision of the self-monitoring scale," *Journal of Personality and Social Psychology*, June 1984: 1361. Copyright by the American Psychological Association. Reprinted with permission.

SELF-ASSESSMENT 4-6: MBTI

The goal of this exercise is to identify your cognitive style. There are no right or wrong answers. Please respond to the following 16 items. After you complete all items, use the scoring key to identify your style.

Part I. Circle the Response That Comes Closest to How You Usually Feel or Act

1. Are you more careful about:
   A. People's feelings
   B. Their rights

2. Do you usually get along better with:
   A. Imaginative people
   B. Realistic people

3. Which of these two is the higher compliment:
   A. A person has real feeling
   B. A person is consistently reasonable

4. In doing something with many other people, does it appeal more to you:
   A. To do it in the accepted way
   B. To invent a way of your own

5. Do you get more annoyed at
   A. Fancy theory
   B. People who don't like theories

6. It is higher praise to call someone
   A. A person of vision
   B. A person of common sense

7. Do you more often let:
   A. Your heart rule your head
   B. You head rule your heart

8. Do you think it is worse:
   A. To show too much warmth
   B. To be unsympathetic

9. If you were a teacher, would you rather teach:
   A. Courses involving theory
   B. Fact courses

Part II. In Each of the Following Pairs, Circle A or B Next to the Word That Appeals to You More

10. A. Compassion   B. Foresight

11. A. Justice   B. Mercy

12. A. Production   B. Design

13. A. Gentle   B. Firm

14. A. Uncritical   B. Literal

15. A. Literal   B. Figurative

16. A. Imaginative   B. Matter of fact

Scoring Key: To categorize your responses to the questionnaire, count one point for each response on the following four scales and total the number of points recorded in each column.

Sensation		Intuition		Thinking		Feeling	
2B.	_____	2A.	_____	1B.	_____	1A.	___/___
4A	_____	4B.	___/___	3B.	_____	3A.	___/___
5A.	_____	5B.	___/___	7B.	_____	7A.	___/___
6B.	_____	6A.	___/___	8A.	_____	8B.	___/___
9B.	_____	9A.	___/___	10B.	_____	10A.	___/___
12A.	_____	12B.	___/___	11A.	_____	11B.	___/___
15A.	___/___	15B.	_____	13B.	_____	13A.	___/___
16B.	_____	16A.	___/___	14B.	_____	14A.	___/___
Totals:	___/___		___6___		_____		___8___

Part III. Identify Your Style

If your intuition score is equal to or greater than sensation score, select intuition. If sensation is greater than intuition, select sensation. Select feeling if feeling is greater than thinking. Select thinking if thinking is greater than feeling. When thinking equals feeling, you should select feeling if a male and thinking if a female.

My style is (Circle the two dimensions based on the preceding instructions.)

Sensation **or** Intuition   Thinking **or** Feeling

Source: J. W. Slocum, Jr., and D. Hellreigel, "A look at how managers' minds work," *Business Horizons,* July–August 1983: 58–68. Used with permission.

Part IV. Interpret Your Style

The MBTI is an indicator of the way people gather and use information. Each of the four styles views problem solving, decision making, use of information, time, and general view of how things should be done differently. Each style has strengths and weaknesses, with no one style being the best. The MBTI is used extensively in a number of organizations as part of team building to allow team members to assess their strengths and weaknesses.

SELF-ASSESSMENT 4-7: MACHIAVELLIANISM

For each statement, circle the number that most closely resembles your attitude.

Statements	Disagree			Agree	
	A lot	**A little**	**Neutral**	**A little**	**A lot**
The best way to handle people is to tell them what they want to hear.	(1)	2	3	4	5
When you ask someone to do something for you, it is best to give the real reason for wanting it rather than giving reasons that might carry more weight.	1	2	3	4	(5)
Anyone who completely trusts anyone else is asking for trouble.	(1)	2	3	4	5
It is hard to get ahead without cutting corners here and there.	(1)	2	3	4	5
It is safest to assume that all people have a vicious streak and that it will come out when they are given a chance.	(1)	2	3	4	5
One should take action only when it is morally right.	1	(2)	3	4	5
Most people are basically good and kind.	1	2	3	(4)	5
There is no excuse for lying to someone else.	(1)	2	3	4	5
Most people more easily forget the death of their father than the loss of their property.	(1)	2	3	4	5
Generally speaking, people won't work hard unless they're forced to do so.	(1)	2	3	4	5

Scoring Key: To obtain your Mach score, add the number you circled on questions 1, 3, 4, 5, 9, and 10. For the other four questions, reverse the numbers you circled: 5 becomes 1, 4 becomes 2, and so forth. Total your 10 numbers to find your score. The higher your score, the more Machiavellian you are. Among a random sample of American adults, the average Mach score was 25.

Source: R. Christie and F. L. Geis, *Studies in Machiavellianism* (New York: Academic Press, 1970). Copyright Academic Press. Reprinted with permission.

SELF-ASSESSMENT 4-8:   NARCISSISM

For each of the following statements, indicate the degree to which you think each describes you by writing the appropriate number. For example, if a statement fits you well and sounds a lot like you, you would write 4.

> 1 = Does not sound like me at all/does not fit me at all
>
> 2 = Does not sound like me
>
> 3 = Sounds like me
>
> 4 = Sounds a lot like me/fits me very well

___2___ 1. I see myself as a good leader.

___2___ 2. I know that I am good because everyone tells me so.

___2___ 3. I can usually talk my way out of anything.

___2___ 4. Everybody likes to hear my stories.

___2___ 5. I expect a great from other people.

___3___ 6. I am assertive.

___3___ 7. I like to display my body.

___2___ 8. I find it easy to manipulate other people to get what I want.

___3___ 9. I don't need anyone to help me to get things done.

___3___ 10. I insist on getting on the respect I deserve.

___2___ 11. I like having authority over other people.

___2___ 12. I enjoy showing off.

___2___ 13. I can read people like a book.

___3___ 14. I always know what I am doing.

___2___ 15. I will not be satisfied until I get all that I deserve.

___2___ 16. People always seem to recognize my authority.

___2___ 17. I enjoy being the center of attention.

___2___ 18. I can make anybody believe anything.

___2___ 19. I seem to be better at most things than other people.

___2___ 20. I get upset when people don't notice me or recognize my accomplishments.

___2___ 21. I enjoy being in charge and telling people what to do.

___3___ 22. I like to be complimented.

___2___ 23. I can get my way in most situations.

___3___ 24. I think I am a special person.

___2___ 25. I deserve more than the average person, because I am better than most people.

___2___ 26. I have a natural talent for leadership.

___3___ 27. I like to look at myself in the mirror.

___2___ 28. I know how to get others to do what I want.

___2___ 29. The world would be a better place if I was in charge.

___3___ 30. I am going to be a great person.

(Continued)

Scoring Key:

Desire for power and leadership (L): add up scores for items: 1, 6, 11, 16, 21, and 26:
Total: __16__

Need for admiration and self-admiration (SA): add up scores for items: 2, 7, 12, 17, 22, and 27.
Total: __15__

Exploitiveness (EX): add up scores for items: 3, 8, 13, 18, 23, and 28.
Total: __12__

Arrogance and a Sense of superiority (A): add up scores for items: 4, 9, 14, 19, 24, and 29.
Total: __15__

Sense of Entitlement (ET): add up scores for items: 5, 10, 15, 20, 25, and 30.
Total: __15__

Add up the total for the five subscales: __73__ (120 highest possible score).

Interpreting Your Score

The five subscales are the key factors in narcissism. The highest possible total in each subscale is 24, with highest possible total score of 120. The higher your scores, the more narcissistic characteristics you have. Some degree of narcissism is associated with healthy self-esteem and effective leadership.

Sources: Based on Emmons, 1987; Raskin and Terry, 1988, Rosenthal and Pittinsky, 2006.

Leadership in Action: Pernille Spiers-Lopez Assembles a Winning Team at IKEA

"Leadership is about me. It's about what I stand for and my values. . . . It is about being in front of everybody and taking steps that others can't always see" (Pernille Spiers-Lopez, 2004). Effective leadership starts with self-examination, states Spears-Lopez, president of IKEA North America. This philosophy leads to clear priorities in her life: her family comes first. "I am very aware of the necessary give-and-take between the importance of my work and of my life at home. . . . I have no illusions about obtaining a complete balance. Ultimately there isn't one" (Marcus, 2007). She was forced to clarify her values in 1999 after she was taken to the emergency room with what first appeared to be a heart attack, but turned out to be an extreme stress reaction. She recalls, "I was going and going and going. . . . I said to myself, 'so this is success'" (Mendels, 2005). Since then she takes time for yoga and meditation, and she has worked on clarifying her values, which has not only helped her to chart the course for her own career, but has also guided her goals and strategies as a leader.

IKEA, the Danish furniture maker, achieved success with customers wherever it opened stores in 31 countries in Europe, Asia, and North America. In North America, the company's success is partly because of the leadership of Pernille Spiers-Lopez since February 2001, when she was appointed president of IKEA North America. Since joining the company, first in human resource management, Spiers-Lopez has made nurturing coworkers, as employees are called, one of her major goals. In addition to flexible and creative work hours,

partner's health benefits, full benefits for part-time workers, a generous maternity leave policy, and a family-friendly environment, IKEA is mindful of providing its employees with opportunities to spend quality time with family and friends. Spiers-Lopez believes that "if an employee's personal life is in disarray, it can affect their productivity at work" (Fleury, 2004). So the company does its best to help employees balance their work and life and create an egalitarian workplace both in terms of philosophy and actual physical space. Describing the new IKEA headquarters in Pennsylvania Spiers-Lopez states, "We wanted a workplace that embraces our 'we are all equal' organization, to be able to live like a family and share our core beliefs; a home that caters to conversation, open ideas and collaboration" (Van Allen, 2007). She further believes, "We empower our coworkers and respect people's personal lives. . . . This has a tremendous influence on job productivity, growth, and development, which ultimately benefits our customers" (Fleury, 2004).

Her efforts have paid off, not only in providing excellent customer service and high sales but also in attracting and maintaining coworkers, who are essential in delivering those results. In October 2004, IKEA was named as one of *Working Mother* magazine's 100 best companies for working mothers, and Spiers-Lopez was singled out for the Family Champion Award (Fleury, 2004). During Spiers-Lopez's tenure, staff turnover dropped from 77 to 36 percent (Meisler, 2004). With more than 8000 workers in 11 states in the United States alone, sales

(Continued)

Leadership in Action: (*Continued*)

exceeded $2.5 billion in 2006 (Van Allen, 2007). Spiers-Lopez has also influenced IKEA's overall corporate culture. With close to a majority of employees being female, almost half of the company's 75 top earners are also female; the board of IKEA North America has gone from one female member to five (Mieser, 2004).

Spiers-Lopez's focus on employees stems from her personal values and drive. In her mid-forties, she is married to Jason Lopez, a high school principal, and they have two teenagers. Everyday she faces the struggles of balancing her life and career and addressing her personal and career goals. One of her mentors, Ulf Caap, says that she often carries heavier loads than she should and that "she has the guts and fire to go where few people ever go" (Binzen, 2004). While she strives to maintain the balance in her own life, she is driven to deliver results beyond her own expectations. Her husband and staff remind her to keep her balance and take breaks. They make fun of her being tireless and pushing herself and others too hard (Meiser, 2004). Interestingly, Spiers-Lopez does not like to make too many plans for the future. "We live in complexity and ambiguity, and I have to be comfortable with that. I think leadership today is really about enjoying change."

QUESTIONS

1. What are Spiers-Lopez's key individual characteristics?
2. What are the factors that contribute to her effectiveness?

Sources: Binzen, P., 2004. "IKEA boss assembles happy staffs," *Philadelphia Inquirer*, September 29; Fleury, M., 2004. *Working Mother* magazine award winner. http://www.suite101.com/print_article. cfm/3684/110941 (accessed December 10, 2004); Marcus, M., 2007. "Finding the balance: Pernille Spiers-Lopez," *Forbes*, March 19. http://www.forbes.com/2007/03/19/spiers-lopez-balance-lead-careers-worklife07-cx_mlm_0319spierslopez.html (accessed July 20, 2007); Meisler, A., 2004. "Success, Scandinavian style," *Workforce Management*, August: 26–32; Women's Leadership Exchange. Pernille Spiers-Lopez President, IKEA North America. http://www.womensleadershipexchange. com/index.php?pagename=la&sectionkey=17#66; Mendels, P., 2005. "When work hits home," *All Business*, March 1. http://www.allbusiness.com/human-resources/employee-development-leadership/ 366999-1.html (accessed July 11, 2007); Van Allen, P., 2007. "IKEA tenets part of the its HQ." *Philadelphia Business Journal*, January 19. http://www.bizjournals.com/philadelphia/stories/ 2007/01/22/story5.html (accessed July 11, 2007).

Part I:
Building Blocks

Power and Leadership

Nearly all men can stand adversity, but if you want to test
a man's character, give him power.
—ABRAHAM LINCOLN

Power tends to corrupt, and absolute power corrupts absolutely.
—LORD ACTON

After studying this chapter, you will be able to:

▪ Define power and its key role in leadership.

▪ Understand the cross-cultural differences in the definitions and use of power.

▪ Identify the individual and organizational sources of power available to leaders and describe their consequences for followers and organizations.

▪ Understand the role of power in the leadership and effectiveness of teams.

▪ Identify the power sources available to top executives.

▪ Explain the sources of power corruption and present ways to prevent its occurrence.

▪ Trace the changes in use of power, the development of empowerment, and explain their consequences for leadership.

Power and leadership are inseparable. An integral part of the study of leadership is the understanding of power and how leaders use it. Power is essential to effective leadership. Leaders need power to get things done. Without it, they cannot guide their followers to achieve their goals. We expect great things from our leaders and provide them with wide latitude and power to accomplish goals. Using their power, department heads, CEOs, and city mayors can order the layoffs of thousands. They make decisions that result in considerable financial and social impact on a wide range of stakeholders. In many countries and states, employment-at-will laws allow managers to fire employees without much reason or notice. All societies shower their leaders with great privilege. In addition to high salaries and other financial incentives (some of the highest in the world in the case of U.S. business executives), organizations provide their leaders with many benefits, such as company cars and planes, luxurious offices, generous expense accounts, and access to subsidized or free housing, just to name a few.

By and large, we willingly give our leaders power and privileges, even in a culture such as the United States, where power distance is relatively low. We understand that leaders need power to get things done, but in recent years, the new management philosophies such as teaming and empowerment are leading organizations to question the need for centralized and concentrated power. As a result, we are changing the way we view power and how leaders use it. Additionally, research concerning the potential of power to corrupt indicates the need to consider and use power with caution.

This chapter examines the various approaches to power and their implications for leadership. It presents the sources of power for individuals and groups and discusses the potential detriments of excessive and concentrated power. Finally, the chapter analyzes current views of power in organizations in light of cultural differences and the changes in our management philosophies and organizational structures.

POWER IN ORGANIZATIONS: DEFINITION AND CONSEQUENCES

The terms *power, influence,* and *authority* are often used interchangeably. In its most basic form, power is the ability of one person to influence others or exercise control over them. It also implies some degree of effectiveness. Influence is the power to affect or sway the course of an action. The two terms are therefore almost synonymous, although influence refers to changing the course of an action or opinion. Clearly, both power and influence are not exclusive to leaders and managers. Individuals at all levels inside an organization, as well as outsiders to an organization—namely, customers or suppliers—can influence the behavior and attitudes of others; they have power. Authority, on the other hand, is the power vested in a particular position, such as that of a CEO or hospital manager. Therefore, even though people at all levels of an organization may have power to influence others, only those holding formal positions have authority.

Consequences of Using Power

The reaction to the use of power depends to a great extent on the source and manner in which leaders use it. The three most typical reactions to use of power and attempts at influencing others are commitment, compliance, and resistance. Commitment happens when followers welcome the influence process and accept it as reasonable and legitimate. Consider the employees at Zingerman's Community of Business (ZCoB), a group of seven food-related businesses built around a delicatessen and a highly successful human resource training company, headquartered in Ann Arbor, Michigan. In 2007 the company was named one of the world's most democratic workplaces (WorldBlu, 2007). The founders, Ari Weinzweig and Paul Saginaw, pride themselves on being close to their community and customers, offering exceptional quality and building strong employee team spirit (Burlingham, 2003). In growing their business, they look for people who work with passion and take ownership. Weinzweig explains, "We wanted people who had vision of their own. Otherwise whatever we did would be mediocre" (Burlingham, 2003: 70). Todd Wickstrom, one of ZCoB's managing partners who gave up his own business to join the company, says, "I would have come in as a dishwasher to be in this environment. Working here has never felt like a job to me. I'm constantly learning about managing, about food, and about myself" (66).

Another potential reaction to power is compliance. In this case, although followers accept the influence process and go along with the request, they do not feel any personal acceptance or deep commitment to carry out the order. Subordinates go along with their boss simply because they are supposed to. An example would be the imposition of unpopular new rules by a school administrator. Because of the administrator's authority, the faculty and staff are required to implement the rules. They, however, do so without any personal commitment; they simply comply.

The third possible reaction to power is resistance. The target in this case does not agree with the attempt at influence and either actively or passively resists it. Examples of resistance to a leader's authority abound in our institutions. The most dramatic ones occur in the labor–management disputes, when employees who typically either accept or comply with management's requests refuse to do so and take overt or covert action against management. The 2004–2005 National Hockey League players' strike in the United States represents such overt action. Another labor dispute occurred between the U.S. men's soccer team, which ranked 11th in the world and was a strong contender for the 2006 World Cup, and the U.S. Soccer Federation. The players asked for a doubling of their salary to bring it up to the level of other players in the world; the federation threatened to hire replacement players. The dispute put in jeopardy the United States' chances of playing in Germany in 2006 (Seigel, 2005). Recent strikes by grocery workers in several parts of the United States are other illustrations of the resistance to power.

As a general rule, a leader's power increases when employees are personally committed and accept the leader's ideas and decisions as is the case in ZCoB. Based on Fiedler' Contigency Theory we reviewed in Chapter 3, power based on simple compliance, does not increase the leader's power. Similarly, some research shows that managers who lead with a firm hand may actually encourage deviant behaviors in their employees (Litzky, Eddleston, and Kidder, 2006). In spite of much evidence supporting this assertion, leaders may come to rely excessively on compliance, which, as you will read in this chapter, sometimes leads to dire consequences. In understanding the sources of power, it is important to evaluate individual factors and organizational elements. Power can be drawn from what a person does or is and from the structure of an organization.

Distribution of Power

Traditional organizations typically concentrate power in a few positions. Authority is vested in formal titles, and nonmanagers are given limited power to make decisions. Their role is primarily implementing the leaders' decisions. Despite the vast amount of publicity about the use of empowerment and teams and their potential benefits, not many organizations around the world rely on such methods. Democracy is even less common in business and other types of organizations than it is in political systems despite research support regarding its benefits (Harrison and Freeman, 2004). Interestingly, even before empowerment and teaming became a business trend in the late 1980s, research about the effect of the distribution of power in organizations suggested that concentrated power can be detrimental to organizational performance (Tannenbaum and Cooke, 1974). The more equal the power distribution is throughout the organization, the higher the performance of the organization. This research further reinforces the need to distribute power as evenly as possible within organizations.

One factor to consider in power distribution is culture. Perceptions of power and egalitarianism vary widely across cultures and even across genders. For example, employees in the United States respond well to managers they like, but Bulgarian

A leader's power increases when employees feel personal commitment and acceptance of the leader's ideas and decisions. Leaders, however, may come to rely excessively on simple compliance, which sometimes leads to dire consequences.

employees follow directions when their managers are vested with legitimate power or authority (Rahim et al., 2000). Other research suggests that because of cultural factors, such as paternalism, delegation and power sharing may not be as effective in some Middle Eastern cultures (Pellegrini and Scandura, 2006). Based on research by Hofstede (1997, 2001) and others regarding different cultural values in management, the United States tends to be a low to medium power distance culture. The differential of power between the highest and lowest levels of the organization is not great (although the salary differential is one of the highest in the world). The low power distance allows employees in the United States, and in other low power distance cultures such as Australia, to call their bosses by their first name, interact with them freely, and express their disagreement with them. In such cultures, employees do not expect their managers and leaders to know all the answers and accept the fact that leaders, too, can make mistakes (Adler, 1991; Laurent, 1983). Low power distance further facilitates the implementation of participative management and other power-sharing management techniques.

In cultures with high power distance, employees have limited expectations for participation in decision making and assume leaders to be somewhat infallible (e.g., Pelligrini and Scandura, 2006). For example, many Chinese business leaders who operate from a variety of locations around the Pacific Rim work within highly authoritarian-oriented, family-controlled organizations (Kraar, 1994). These leaders make decisions without questions or challenges from followers. Even though their approach is contrary to current U.S. thinking about management and leadership, their organizations are successful despite continued reliance on hierarchical structures. Their structure and power distribution fit their culture. The Chinese value order, hierarchy, and a clear delineation of power. Their organizations function in accordance with those cultural values. Likewise, the French, Italians, and Germans expect their managers to provide answers to subordinates' questions and problems (Laurent, 1983). The Eiffel Tower model of organizational culture, used by the French as presented by Trompenaars, for example, concentrates power at the top of the organization. French managers report discomfort at not knowing who their boss is. They also place less emphasis on delegation of responsibility (Harris, Moran, and Moran, 2004). The need for a clear hierarchy is likely to make it more difficult for the French than for Swedes or North Americans to function in a leaderless, self-managed, team environment.

In other countries such as Japan and Indonesia, people value clear hierarchy and authority. Mexican workers may be less comfortable with taking responsibility for problem solving (Randolph and Sashkin, 2002). The Mexican culture—with a family type of organization culture, its strong paternalistic tradition, and the presence of the machismo principle—expects leaders to be strong, decisive, and powerful. Leaders, like powerful fathers, must provide answers, support the family, and discipline members who stray (Teagarden, Butler, and Von Glinow, 1992). Workers feel they owe their loyalty to their boss or "patron" (Harris et al., 2004). In higher power distance cultures, power bases are stable, upward mobility is limited, and few people have access to resources (House et al., 2004). The combination of the culture's power distance and its tolerance for uncertainty determines part of the power structure of an organization. The higher the power distance is and the lower the tolerance for uncertainty is, the more likely leaders are to hold a high degree of power that subordinates expect them to use. In such cultures, the implementation of power sharing is likely to face more obstacles than in cultures where subordinates do not rely heavily on their supervisor.

The following section considers the sources of power for leaders.

SOURCES OF POWER

Alan Greenspan, who was the chairman of the U.S. Federal Reserve (Fed) from 1987 to 2006, an unprecedented 19 years, was considered one of the most powerful executives in the United States (Bligh and Hess, 2007). As chairman, Greenspan was able to set policies to sustain low to moderate economic growth, assuring that the U.S. economy expanded but did not overheat, thereby avoiding high inflation. In a 1996 survey of 1000 CEOs of the largest U.S. companies, 96 percent wanted him to be reappointed as the leader of the Fed (Walsh, 1996). Greenspan held considerable power with which to chart the course of the U.S. and world economies. He is a well-known economist, a consummate relationship builder, and described as low key and down to earth. He stated once that he learned to "mumble with great incoherence" (Church, 1997). Greenspan held no executive power, could not implement a single decision, and employed only a small staff. Nevertheless, he was powerful and had considerable authority. He was able to convince the U.S. president, the Congress, other members of the Fed board, and the financial markets that his policies were devoid of politics and in the best interests of the United States. Where did Greenspan get his power? He relied on individual and organizational sources of power.

Sources of Power Related to Individuals

One of the most widely used approaches to understanding the sources of power comes from the research by French and Raven (1968). These researchers propose five sources of power vested in the individual: legitimate power, reward power, coercive power, expert power, and referent power (see Table 5-1 for a summary).

Table 5-1   French and Raven's Sources of Individual Power.

Legitimate power	Based on a person holding a formal position. Others comply because they accept the legitimacy of the position of the power holder.
Reward power	Based on a person's access to rewards. Others comply because they want the rewards the power holder can offer.
Coercive power	Based on a person's ability to punish. Others comply because they fear punishment.
Expert power	Based on a person's expertise, competence, and information in a certain area. Others comply because they believe in the power holder's knowledge and competence.
Referent power	Based on a person's attractiveness to and friendship with others. Others comply because they respect and like the power holder.

Sources and Consequences

The first three sources of individual power—legitimate, reward, and coercive—are position powers. Although they are vested in individuals, the individuals' access to them depends on the position they hold. In the case of legitimate power, most managerial or even supervisory titles in any organization provide the ability to influence others. When a legitimate authority source asks them to, subordinates comply with requests and implement decisions (Yukl and Falbe, 1991). Alan Greenspan holds considerable legitimate power, although his power to reward and punish is limited. In most cases, offering rewards or threatening punishment is another way managers can further convince reluctant subordinates. Managers and executives generally hold all three of these sources of power.

All three of these sources of individual power depend on the organization that grants them, not the person who holds them. Once the access to title, rewards, or punishment is taken away by the organization, a leader or individual relying on such sources loses power. Because the source of power is related to the individual's position, followers are most likely to react by complying or resisting, as illustrated in Figure 5-1. Generally, the harsher the source of power that is used, the less willing subordinates will be to comply.

The last two sources of individual power—expert and referent—are based on the person rather than the organization. Access to these two sources of power does not depend solely on the organization. In the case of expert power, people may influence others because of special expertise, knowledge, information, or skills that others need.

Figure 5-1   Potential Reactions to Individual Sources of Power.

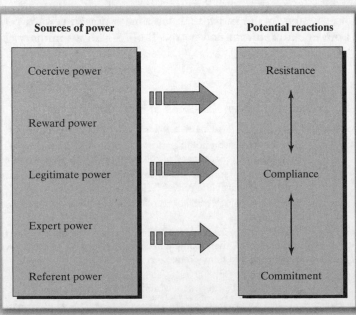

People listen to the experts, follow their advice, and accept their recommendations. Alan Greenspan provides an excellent example of expert power. His knowledge, expertise, and an established record of success were the bases of his power. Although Greenspan also held legitimate power, in many other cases those with expert power might not hold official titles or have any legitimate power. People, however, will bypass their manager and their organization's formal hierarchy and structure to seek help from those with the expertise they need. For example, a department's computer expert has power even if she is young and relatively inexperienced.

Referent power operates in much the same way. Individuals with referent power can influence others because they are liked and respected. As with expert power, this power does not depend on the position or the organization. The person's power stems from being a role model for others. Greenspan was well liked for his ability to work with others. Employees at ZCoB respect Weinzweig and Saginaw for their vision and leadership style. The respect and friendship come on top of other considerable sources of power. In the cases of expert and referent power, followers welcome the influence process and in many cases seek it. As a result, they generally respond with commitment and acceptance. The use of expert and referent power also is related to higher follower satisfaction and performance (Yukl and Falbe, 1991).

Using Individual Sources of Power

Although power and influence are closely related, some research indicates that the two can be treated as separate concepts. A leader with power might not be able to influence subordinates' behaviors, or influence can occur without a specific source of power. Several researchers, most notably Kipnis and his colleagues (Kipnis, Schmidt, and Wilkinson, 1980) and Yukl along with several others (e.g., Yukl and Falbe, 1990, 1991), identified various influence tactics. The result of their work is the classification of influence tactics into nine categories (Table 5-2). Each tactic relies on one or more of the sources of power related to the individual. Each is appropriate in different situations and carries the potential for leading to commitment on the part of the person being influenced. For example, personal appeal relies on referent power and tends to be appropriate when used with colleagues; it is not likely to lead to a high degree of commitment. Inspirational appeal, which also relies on referent power, leads to high commitment. Rational persuasion relies on expert power and is appropriate to use when trying to influence superiors. The commitment tends to be moderate.

Although leaders must rely on all sources of power to guide and influence their followers and others in their organization, they often have to adjust how they use power throughout their career. J. P. Kotter, a well-respected writer on issues of leadership and managerial power, suggests that in the early stages of a manager's career, the manager must develop an adequate base of power (Kotter, 1985). A manager can be effective by relying on the various bases of personal power. In particular, young leaders must develop a broad network of interpersonal relationships and establish credibility through information and expertise. Other means involve becoming visible by volunteering for challenging and high-visibility projects.

The demonstration of competence and skills is central to the development of power in the early stages of a leader's career. In mid-career, most successful leaders already possess some degree of legitimacy through formal titles, along with other status symbols that demonstrate their power. Their early efforts are likely to establish their

Table 5-2 Using Power: Influence Tactics and Their Consequences.

Influence Tactic	Power Source	Appropriate to Use With . . .	Effectiveness and Commitment
Rational persuasion	Expert and access to information	Supervisors	Moderate
Inspirational appeal	Referent	Subordinates and colleagues	High
Consultation	All	Subordinates and colleagues	High
Ingratiation	Referent	All levels	Moderate
Personal appeal	Referent	Colleagues	Moderate
Exchange	Reward and information	Subordinates and colleagues	Moderate
Coalition building	All	Subordinates and colleagues	Low
Legitimate tactics	Legitimate	Subordinates and colleagues	Low
Pressure	Coercive	Subordinates	Low

credibility and competence within a well-developed network of loyal subordinates, peers, and bosses (Kotter, 1985). Therefore, leaders in mid-career stage already hold considerable power. The challenge at this point is to use the accumulated power wisely and ethically to achieve organizational goals and personal benefits.

Finally, leaders during the late-career stage must learn to let go of power gracefully. By the time they reach retirement age, successful leaders in thriving U.S. public and private organizations enjoy considerable power and influence. To use power well at this career stage, a leader needs to plan for its orderly transmission to others while simultaneously finding new personal sources of power and fulfillment.

Sources of Power Related to Organizational Structure

The differences between organizational and individual sources of power are not always obvious. The structure of an organization provides sources of power to individuals and groups over and above those listed in Table 5-1. Although individuals can also rely on organizational sources of power, these sources are particularly important for teams. Aside from the expertise of their members, teams have access to power in organizations mainly because of their control of strategic contingencies.

The concept of strategic contingencies was originally developed to understand the distribution of power across departments (Hickson et al., 1971; Salancik and Pfeffer, 1977b); however, it also applies directly to teams. Strategic contingencies suggest that individuals, teams, or departments gain power based on their ability to address issues that are instrumental to reaching organizational goals. For example, if a team removes obstacles for others and helps them achieve goals, its leader and members will accumulate power. Mervyn's, a California-based retailer, uses special teams that rush into stores in response to management requests to solve critical problems quickly. These teams, called SWAT after the police fast-response units, consist of highly trained members with broad expertise who can deal with crises that could affect the organization (Carbonara, 1998). Because of their ability to deal with many problems, these teams are highly regarded and hold considerable power. Table 5-3 summarizes the four strategic contingencies that are the basis of organizational sources of power.

Individuals, teams, or departments gain power based on their ability to address issues that are instrumental to reaching organizational goals.

Coping with Uncertainty

The first source of power for teams is their ability to help others cope with uncertainty. With the increased competition and constant changes in the political and economic environments facing many institutions, having information about the changes and alternatives for dealing with them is essential to performance. For example, the leader and members of a cross-functional team designed to provide an organization with market information regarding future products and competitors will gain considerable influence by virtue of the fact that others need that information. The team's product or service reduces uncertainty. A case in point is governmental liaison teams and lobbyists in the United States in a time of change in the health industry. These groups acquire particular power because they help others within the organization reduce or manage the uncertainty they face.

Teams and their leaders can reduce uncertainty through three interrelated methods. First, through market research, polls, contact with key constituents, focus groups, or reliance on external experts, they obtain information that others need. The second method—uncertainty prevention—focuses on the prediction of upcoming changes.

Table 5-3   Organizational Sources of Power: Strategic Contingencies.

Coping with uncertainty	Power based on the ability to reduce uncertainty for others. This power can be achieved by obtaining information others need, making predictions and engaging in forecasting, or by preventing the effect of change on others. Others comply because the power holder helps them achieve their goals by reducing uncertainty.
Centrality	Power based on being central to how the organization achieves its mission and goals. Others comply because what the power holder provides is key to organizational activities.
Dependency	Power based on others depending on power holder to get their work done. Others comply because they cannot accomplish their goal without the power holder's help.
Substitutability	Power based on providing a unique and irreplaceable service or product to others. Others comply because they cannot find elsewhere what the power holder provides.

Source: Based on Hickson et al., "A strategic contingencies theory of intra-organizational power," *Administrative Science Quarterly* 16 (1971): 216–229.

For example, a team might research and predict the moves of competitors. Public university administrators rely on their legislative liaison team to predict the mood of the legislature regarding funding of universities. Third, a team reduces uncertainty for others through absorption. In this situation, the team takes certain steps to prevent the change from affecting other teams or departments. The university administrator with information about the legislative mood might try to forestall budget cuts through lobbying. If the cuts happen anyway, various groups within the university might undertake less painful internal budget-reduction mechanisms, such as nonreplacement of retiring employees, thereby preventing more drastic measures from being imposed by outside sources and absorbing uncertainty. Through the use of these three methods, a team and its leader can reduce uncertainty for others and thus acquire power.

Centrality

Another organizational source of power is the centrality to the production or service delivery process. This factor relates to how a team's activities contribute to the mission and goals of the organization. Teams closest to the customer, for example, will gain power. Members of an executive team who work closely with the CEO of the organization also will gain power via their access to the CEO. For example, the librarian team at Highsmith reports directly to the company's executives—a factor that gives its members further power (Buchanan, 1999). Another case in point is the management of diversity in organizations. As was presented in Chapter 2, one of the recommendations for the successful implementation of diversity plans in organizations involves making diversity central to the organization and to the organization's leaders. The most successful programs put the individuals and teams in charge of diversity planning and implementation in strategic positions within organizations, reporting directly to the CEO.

Dependence and Substitutability

A final structural source of power available to teams and their leaders closely resembles the reward and expert power of individuals. This source of power depends on the extent to which others need a team's expertise. If employees depend on a team to provide them with information and resources, the team's power will increase. The larger the number of departments and individuals who depend on the team, the greater the team's power will be. In addition, if the tasks performed by the team are unique and not easily provided by others in the organization and if no substitutes are available, the dependence on the team and its power increases. If the team's collective expertise is duplicated in others and its function can be performed easily by another individual or group, however, the team will lack the influence necessary to obtain needed resources and implement its ideas. For example, despite the widespread use of personal computers and information technology tools, many individuals still require considerable assistance to use technology effectively. This factor allows information technology departments to gain power and obtain resources.

Interestingly, the major complaint from teams in many organizations is their lack of power to obtain resources or implement their ideas (Nahavandi and Aranda, 1994). In the new organizational structures, team leaders often do not have any of the formal powers traditionally assigned to managers. In the best of cases, team members respect their leader because of personal relationships or expertise. These individual sources of power, however, do not translate to power in the organization. As a result, many team

Applying What You Learn
Using Power Effectively

Judicious use of power can contribute greatly to a leader's effectiveness. Consider the following guidelines for developing and using power:

- Be willing to disclose information about yourself and admit your weaknesses instead of covering them up. This openness will help you establish a personal connection with others.

- Develop your competencies and expertise. Expert power is one of the most "powerful" sources; no one can take it away from you, and it leads to commitment from others.

- Develop good working relationships with a broad base of people inside and outside of your organization. These professional and personal friendships provide you with a wide base of influence.

- Be generous with handing out rewards when you have access to them. Not only are rewards a source of power, but your generosity will help you build other relationships that will outlast your access to rewards.

- Apply coercive power with great care. As others comply with you out of fear, giving you short-term compliance, you will lose their long-term commitment.

- Make those around you feel powerful. The more power you give away and share with others, the more powerful you will become.

leaders express anger and frustration at their lack of ability to get things done. Recommendations on how to make teams more effective often include making them central to the mission of the organization, assigning them to meaningful tasks, and providing them with access to decision makers (Katzenbach and Smith, 1993; Nahavandi and Aranda, 1994).

Special Power Sources of Top Executives

Top executives of our institutions hold tremendous power. One obvious source of power is the legitimacy of their position. A number of symbols establish and reinforce that legitimacy: They have separate executive offices, pictures of past executives hang in public hallways, they eat in separate dining facilities, and they are able to maintain privacy and distance from other employees (Hardy, 1985; Pfeffer, 1981). Many use their powers to benefit their organizations. Dipak Jain, the dean of the Kellogg School of Management, has found that "the way to manage your peers—past and future—is through a culture of inclusiveness" (Canabou, 2003b). John Wood, one of the Microsoft alumni and millionaires, is the founder of Room to Read, a not-for-profit group that builds schools and libraries in poor countries. He uses his contacts and power to achieve his goal of helping 10 million children become literate by 2010 (Canabou, 2002). Along with the sources of power we discussed earlier, top executives have four other sources of power:

➤ *Distribution of resources:* Top managers, either alone or in consultation with a top management team, are responsible for the distribution of resources throughout the organization. This access to resources is a key source of power.

➤ *Control of decision criteria*: A unique power source available to executives is the control of decision criteria (Nahavandi and Malekzadeh, 1993a; Pettigrew, 1973). By setting the mission, overall strategy, and operational goals of organizations, top executives limit other managers' and employees' actions. For example, if a city mayor runs his or her campaign on the platform of fighting crime and improving education, the city's actions and decisions during that mayor's term will be influenced by that platform. Crime reduction will be one of the major criteria used to evaluate alternatives and make decisions. For instance, funding requests for increased police training or for building a neighborhood park will be evaluated based on the crime-fighting and education values of the proposals. If the requests address the decision criteria set by the mayor, they stand a better chance of passage, relying on the mayor's weight behind them. If they do not, such proposals might not even be brought up for consideration.

➤ *Centrality in organization*: Another source of executive power is a top manager's centrality to the organizational structure and information flow (Astley and Sachdeva, 1984). Whether the organization is a traditional hierarchical pyramid or a web, CEOs are strategically placed for access to information and resources. Indeed, new top managers often bring with them a group of trusted colleagues who are placed in strategic locations throughout the organization to ensure their access to information.

➤ *Access*: Top executives' access to all levels of the organization assists in building alliances that further enhance their power. The most obvious example is the change in personnel in Washington with the election of a new president. Similar personnel changes occur on different scales in all organizations when a new leader is selected. University presidents bring with them several top assistants and create new positions to accommodate them. Other members of the top university administration are slowly replaced with those selected by the new leader. In the private sector, the changes designed to put key people in place are even more drastic and obvious. At General Electric, the selection of Immelt (see Leading Change in Chapter 9) to succeed Jack Welch as CEO led to the turnover of several top management team members who were contenders for the position. Whether new leaders force out several individuals to make room for their own team or whether the individuals leave on their own, the outcome of the personnel shuffle is to allow new leaders access to trustworthy people and information.

In addition to their considerable power, top executives are often not accountable for their actions. This lack of accountability can lead to abuse and corruption, the topics considered next.

THE DARK SIDE OF POWER: CORRUPTION

Power allows leaders to influence others and help their team, department, or organization achieve its goals; power is essential to effective leadership. The very nature of leading, whether it is a business organization or a social movement, may require disregard for norms and possible consequences of violating them (Magee et al., 2005). Behaving outside of the norms may be the only way leaders can implement change, but such disregard can also carry a negative side as evidenced by the situation at Enron, Tyco, and, as some would suggest, the G.W. Bush administration. These examples illustrate how leaders can defy social convention, established tradition, and even the law. Lord John Brown left British Petroleum in disgrace in 2007 partly because his own behavior did not follow the principles that he loudly proclaimed guide his company's actions (Sonnenfeld, 2007). Conrad Black, CEO of Hollinger International, a newspaper company, billed $2400 in handbags and the tab for his servants to his company, earning him the title of "kleptocrat" (Chandler, 2004). The outlandish compensation of Richard Grasso, described at the end of this chapter, is another illustration of the excessive powers of top executives. The old adage "power corrupts" continues to be true. Power changes people. Some research indicates that when they become leaders, people may start thinking of themselves, their work, and others differently, and as a result, change their behavior as well (for a review, see Magee et al., 2005).

The privilege associated with power and leadership has come under scrutiny as being at best unnecessary and at worst dysfunctional (Block, 1993). Interestingly, people often have a love–hate relationship with power (Cronin, 1984). Particularly, in the United States, framers of the Constitution were particularly wary about concentrating power in the hands of one person or one group (Cronin, 1987). Power without accountability is blamed for many excesses, ranging from poor decision making and financial waste to fraud to sexual harassment. Unchecked power is blamed for two of Europe's biggest financial scandals: the Paris-based Credit Lyonnais in the 1990s and the Parmalat case in 2003. Calisto Tanzi, Parmalat's CEO, was accused of falsifying records and embezzling millions of euros. He fled Italy then returned to arrogantly and shamelessly admit his involvement, whereas his closest associate Fausto Tonna wished journalists and their families "a slow and painful death" (Wylie, 2004b: 34). Similarly, in Enron's, WorldCom's, and Tyco's cases in the United States, all the legal requirements and checks and balances did not prevent executives from abusing their power and avoiding accountability for a period of time. The list of managers and top executives who were fired in 2004 includes many who either acted illegally and unethically or were too arrogant to correct their mistakes (BW: "The fallen managers," 2005).

One of the consequences of power, be it legitimate or excessive and abusive, is to change how individuals view themselves and increase the distance between leaders and followers. Power also can remove leaders from the inner workings of their organizations. Such separation and distance can cause leaders to become uninformed and unrealistic and can lead to unethical decision making. The power abusers may become more concerned with maintaining their power than with developing followers and achieving organizational goals. The following sections consider the causes, consequences, and solutions to abuse of power.

> One of the consequences of power, be it legitimate or excessive and abusive, is to change how individuals view themselves and increase the distance between leaders and followers. Power also can remove leaders from the inner workings of their organizations. Such separation and distance can cause leaders to become uninformed and unrealistic and can lead to unethical decision making.

Causes and Processes

The causes of power corruption stem from personal characteristics of the leaders and from organizational factors (see Table 5-4 for a summary).

Leader Characteristics

The leadership characteristics that may affect corruption closely relate to the narcissistic and Machiavellian personality traits we reviewed in Chapter 4. Several researchers (e.g., Brown, 1998; Delbecq, 2001; Kets de Vries, 1993) have identified individual

Table 5-4 Causes of Corruption.

Leaders' Individual Characteristics	Organizational Factors
• Inflated view of self; arrogant and controlling	• Organizational culture
• Rigid and inflexible	• Hiring practices based on personal relationships rather than objective performance
• Sense of entitlement	
• Willing to use and exploit others	• Short-term oriented reward system focused on limited criteria
• Lack empathy for others; uncaring	
• Disinhibition, viciousness and ruthlessness	• Centralized organizational structure
• Overly concerned with power	• High uncertainty and chaos
	• Highly unequal power distribution

Sources: N. Brown, *The Destructive Narcissistic Pattern* (Westport: Praeger, 1998); A. Delbecq, " 'Evil' manifested in destructive individual behavior: A senior leadership challenge," *Journal of Management Inquiry* 10 (2001): 221–226; and M. F. R. Kets de Vries, *Leaders, Fools, and Imposters: Essays on the Psychology of Leadership* (San Francisco: Jossey-Bass, 1993).

characteristics of leaders that make them likely to abuse power. These managers are called "evil" (Delbecq, 2001) or destructive narcissists (Brown, 1998). Often bright, but with an inflated view of themselves, they are highly controlling, rigid, power hungry, and ruthless. They work well with supervisors and impress them, but they are uncaring and vicious with their subordinates. Their sense of entitlement and their belief that they deserve special treatment (Lubin, 2002) allow them to easily abuse their power and their followers. Such behavior can bring devastation to their organization by terrifying their colleagues through ruthless and assured retribution and destruction of trust and collegiality. Their world is divided into those who agree with them and the rest, whom they view with excessive suspicion and even paranoia. Those who are on their side are supported, at least temporarily; those who are not are denigrated, ridiculed, and eventually moved out.

Unfortunately, these types of managers are often able to climb the corporate ladder because others see their self-confidence as evidence of ability (Lubin, 2002). Once in power, they maintain their power by surrounding themselves with weak followers, ruthlessly attacking those who disagree with them and managing their superiors so that they can continue their quest for power. Classic cases of evil, or destructive, narcissistic leaders include Al Dunlap (nicknamed "Chainsaw Al"), who ruthlessly cut jobs and abused followers in one job after another until he was fired as CEO of Sunbeam Corp. Philip Agee is another case. As CEO of Morrison Knudson (MK), he not only abused and fired employees based on personal animosity, but is also accused of using company funds for his personal gain. When he was finally fired after much manipulation of board members, the company employees cheered in the parking lot (Lubin, 2002).

Other research about changes that happen to people when they gain access to power focuses on the experience of power and its psychological effects rather than on personality of the individuals (Magee et al., 2005). For example, some studies by Galinski and his colleagues suggest that having power makes people more action oriented (2003).

Others found that males who are already likely to sexually harass others are more likely to do so when given power. A Review by Magee and his colleagues (2005) provides evidence that those who are given power lose their ability to empathize with others and to see others' perspectives and that they are more likely to take credit for their followers' success. Similarly, members of majority groups with more power are more likely to negatively stereotype those in the minority (Keltner and Robinson, 1996).

Whether related to the personality of the power holder or because of general psychological impact of having power, there is a tendency for those who have power to behave differently than those who do not.

Organizational Factors

A person's individual characteristics may make him or her more willing to abuse power, but a person can only do so when the organization allows it. The most important determinant of power abuse is the culture of an organization. What is tolerated, accepted, encouraged, and rewarded determines whether a destructive leader can survive. Hiring practices, the characteristics and style of upper management, and the focus on short-term financial performance all contribute to allowing a destructive leader to last and even flourish. The more centralized and concentrated the power and hierarchy and the more closed the communication within an organization, the less likely that power abuses will be noticed or reported, further perpetuating the abuse. Centralized structures create distance between leaders and followers, allow them to make decisions without consultation and input, and may isolate the leader from others. Closed communication networks further reinforce the isolation and prevent followers from reporting abuses of power easily. Additionally, organizations where power is concentrated in the hands of few and organizations that face uncertainty and chaos provide fertile grounds for power abuse (Hodson, Roscigno, Lopez, 2006). When power is unequal or when there is high uncertainty, rules are unclear, allowing for more abuse to take place or to go unnoticed.

Corruption Cycle

Individual leader characteristics and organizational factors combine to create a corruption cycle described in Figure 5-2. The leader's increasing power, real or perceived, to act without accountability and with impunity leads to followers' compliance. In some cases, subordinates may follow leaders because of personal commitment and acceptance of their decisions, or they might truly respect their leaders' expertise. In other cases, compliance simply comes from fear of retribution or the desire to obtain resources and rewards from the leader (Prendergast, 1993). The subordinates' continued compliance can cause leaders to believe that their actions and decisions are always correct, thus reinforcing their inflated view of themselves.

The power, the compliance, and the physical and psychological distance between leaders and followers all contribute to the development of leaders' inflated views of themselves. By virtue of the hierarchical structure of many organizations, powerholders are separated from those they lead. Based on psychological effects of power, leaders may have the tendency to devalue their subordinates. Both of these can contribute to the corruption cycle. Even though the press and public appears to value leaders such as Meg Whitman of eBay, who works in a cubicle and often takes commercial

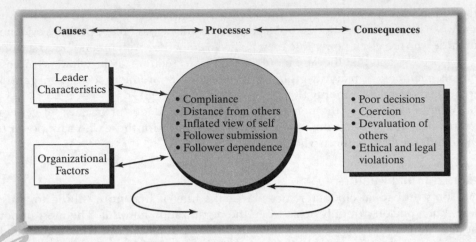

Figure 5-2 Power-Corruption Cycle.

flights instead of flying the corporate jet (Dillon, 2004), and despite changes made in many organizations, leaders still occupy offices on separate floors, park their cars in reserved areas, eat in executive dining rooms, and spend a great deal of their time with other power holders. All these symbols of power increase the legitimacy of leaders. The distance and separation can be justified based on the need to protect the leaders' valuable time and to allow them access to other powerholders with whom they need to work to make decisions. These symbols, however, can also corrupt leaders by providing them with an overly inflated view of themselves.

From fear, desire to ingratiate themselves, or simple weakness and incompetence, subordinates often submit to the leader's whim and adopt flattery as a means of influencing their leader concerning their ideas or for obtaining the personal or departmental resources that they need. Few dare argue or disagree with the leader. Even when they express disagreement, they do so in the softest, most roundabout ways, after praising the leader's ideas and painstakingly recognizing that the leaders are correct. Most of us have witnessed or even been party to such political behavior, which is considered essential to obtaining needed resources. Such flattery, however, can further feed into a potentially destructive leader's sense of self importance and entitlement reinforcing their devaluation of followers and creating a self-fulfilling prophecy.

Consider the case of Donald Carty, former CEO of American Airlines. While his company was experiencing serious financial trouble in early 2000, seeking $410-million help from the U.S. Congress, he successfully convinced union members and other employees to agree to considerable cuts in pay, benefits, and jobs worth $1.8 billion. Carty conveniently never informed union leaders that airline executives had already assigned themselves lucrative bonuses for the same period (Zellner, 2003). As the union concessions were becoming final, the executive bonuses were revealed, throwing months of painstaking negotiation off course (Meyerson, 2003). Company executives attempted to delay the required announcement of their bonuses until the unions formally approved the concessions, but miscalculated their timing. Under public outrage,

Carty recalled a few of the bonuses, but he protected most of the pension funds for executives. His deception eventually cost him his job in April 2003.

Another example of blatant abuse because of power without accountability is Richard Scrushy, former CEO of HealthSouth Corporation, a multibillion-dollar health-care company, who was famous for wielding tremendous power while in office. He intimidated his employees, going as far as sending them out of meetings if he did not like their clothing (Jones, 1998). He was ousted when accused of a $2.7-billion accounting fraud along with perjury, obstruction of justice, money laundering, and wire and securities fraud (Ryerson-Cruz, 2004). With more HealthSouth executives indicted for fraud, Scrushy's successor, Jay Grinney, CEO since 2004, states that the company was "managed from the top down" and that "those days are over" (Reyerson-Cruz, 2004).

Consequences of Corruption

The excessive power and accompanying corruption of leaders can lead to serious consequences for an organization. The first and most common consequence is poor decision making. Leaders' lack of relevant information because of their distance from others in the organization puts them in the danger of poor decision making. Employees filter information, avoid giving bad news, and hide their mistakes, providing an overly rosy picture of the organization. As a result, leaders lose touch with their organization and its customers. Because of the compliance of followers, leaders might see their followers as dependent and incapable of autonomous behavior and decisions. Leaders then come to see themselves as the source of all events in the organization and consequently might rely less on persuasion and more on coercive methods to get followers to comply. These processes are supported further by a general devaluation and denigration of followers.

Leaders come to see their subordinates as less than competent and therefore unable to function without the leader's strong guidance. This devaluation of followers carries a potential for a self-fulfilling prophecy. The leader continues to maintain total control, not allowing followers' input into decisions. The followers comply and encourage such behavior, further proving to the leader the futility of power sharing. The leader sees such compliance as evidence of subordinates' weakness and incompetence, thereby centralizing decision making even further. This self-fulfilling prophecy can become a major obstacle in the successful implementation of various organizational initiatives.

The development of a separate sense of morality based on all the other factors allows the leaders to easily fall into unethical decision making and actions. Such leaders come to believe that regular rules simply do not apply to them. Scrushy's and Carty's actions, as well as in those of many other executives who lie and steal from their company, are examples of such situations. Tyco's executives firmly believed that their outrageous salaries and bonuses were fully justified. The former CEO L. Dennis Kozlowski, currently on trial for stealing and hiding unauthorized bonuses, forgiving loans to himself, and earning $430 million by inappropriately inflating Tyco's stock, justified his behavior: "I worked my butt off and it was all based on my performance in Tyco's long-established pay-for-performance culture" (Maull, 2005: D5). Leaders who are caught in the corruption cycle become poor role models and lose their credibility and their ability to be effective in the long run. Amiable negotiation and win-win strategies to resolve conflict and disagreements are replaced with executive fiats and intolerance of diverse opinions. This negative shift, in turn, leads to further bad decisions, to follower resistance and reactance, and to followers' unwillingness to take any risks. The power-corruption cycle, if not stopped, feeds on itself and can lead to dire consequences for any organization.

Solutions

Preventing corruption requires addressing both the leadership and organizational factors. Identifying individuals with a propensity for power abuse early is one obvious solution; however, it is not always possible or feasible. There are no magic formulas that will prevent the rise of destructive managers and power abuses; the following factors can help:

➤ *Accountability.* Leaders who know that they will be held accountable for their actions are much more likely to consider the consequences of their actions and act thoughtfully. Although many mechanisms are in place to monitor the behavior of leaders in for-profit, not-for-profit, and governmental organizations, these mechanisms need be implemented to hold leaders accountable. Maintaining checks and balances in the public sector and reinforcing the power of board of governors and directors in other organizations so that they can be independent from the leader are necessary steps towards holding leaders accountable (Colvin, 2007).

➤ *Encouraging open and broad communication and feedback.* The more followers and others are able to provide feedback both to the leader and to other powerful members of the organization, the more likely it is that destructive leaders will be detected and power abuses stopped. A recent study suggests that the presence of intranets and other technology-based communication tool encourages flexible control and empowerment equalizing power in an organization (Denton, 2007). Additionally, open communication and transparency regarding financial information further increases the leader's accountability (Welch and Welch, 2007).

➤ *Involving the leader in day-to-day activities.* The closer the leader is to the day-to-day activities of followers and to the organization's customers, the less likely is leader corruption (Block, 1993; Prendergast, 1993).

➤ *Reducing the followers' dependency on the leader.* The more independent the followers are, the less likely they are to contribute—intentionally or unintentionally—to the corruption cycle. If a person's pay, promotion, and career depend entirely on the manager's subjective opinion and rating, a person is more likely to comply with that manager (Prendergast, 1993).

➤ *Using objective measures of performance.* Instituting objective measures of performance, either through precise measurement or based on direct feedback from relevant constituents, is one way to curtail the excessive power of the leader and ensure proper and accurate flow of information. The subordinate can act for the benefit of the customers with feedback from them, rather than for the benefit of the boss.

➤ *Involving outsiders in decision making.* By opening up the decision-making process to outsiders, an organization can get an objective view and prevent inbreeding. Outsiders can bring a fresh perspective that can break the corruption cycle. For example, the presence of outsiders on a company board of directors contributes to keeping executive salaries more in line with company performance (Conyon and Peck, 1998).

➤ *Changing and monitoring the organizational culture.* The most difficult and most effective solution to preventing power corruption is a change in the culture and structure of organizations (Delbecq, 2001). The change should focus on performance, productivity, and customer service rather than on satisfying the leaders.

The new CEO of American Airlines, Gerard Arpey, provides an example of the challenge of correcting power abuses by attempting to change the culture while trying to maintain the organization intact (Flint, 2006). After Carty's departure, among its other challenges, the new management desperately needed to rebuild badly eroded trust. Arpey's approach, called "working together," is simple and focuses on rebuilding the culture based on openness and participation (Cameron, 2007). He explains, "I think you will make better decisions and execute better on those decisions if you involve the people who actually do the work . . . the process of listening to each other can't help but lead to better outcomes, no matter which way you go" (Tahmincioglu, 2004). Arpey has made particular efforts to build bridges with labor groups. He states, "If you even allow yourself or your management to identify labor as the problem, you are not only wrong, you also cause everyone else to wait for the solution" (Flint, 2006: 41). He has implemented the new culture by getting to know employees and managers, instituting an open-door policy with union leaders and seeking their advice, promptly returning phone calls, turning down a raise, and agreeing to an initial $110,000 annual salary. Other culture-building mechanisms include use of innovative human resource management techniques and joint decision making through "Joint Leadership Teams" (Tahmincioglu, 2004). In spite of all these actions and the fact that the airline showed a profit in 2006, problems are not yet over. Anger over high executive pay and bonuses resurfaced in 2007, evidence of the difficulty of changing the culture of an organization (Cameron, 2007). Grinney, the new CEO of HealthSouth, is taking similar actions to open up the culture and rebuild trust. He says, "Paying up the sins of the past is a process" (BW: "The cleanup crew," 2005: 72).

Partly because of many abuses of power and partly because of philosophical and structural organization changes, the face of power is changing in many of today's organizations.

EMPOWERMENT: THE CHANGING FACE OF POWER

One of the major forces for cultural and structural changes in organizations comes from the empowerment movement. Empowerment involves sharing power with subordinates and pushing decision making and implementation power to the lowest possible level. Its goal is to increase the power and autonomy of all employees in organizations. Its roots lie in perceptions of Japanese management, the quality circle efforts of the 1970s and the quality of work life (QWL) approach (Lawler and Mohrman, 1987), and the psychological concept of self-efficacy (Bandura, 1977). The underlying theme of empowerment is the giving away to and sharing of power with those who need it to perform their job functions. Such power sharing provides people with a belief in their abilities and enhances their sense of effectiveness. Research on the distribution of power (Tannenbaum and Cooke, 1974) and anecdotal and case evidence (Bennis and Nanus, 1985; Block, 1987) strongly suggest that equal power sharing contributes to an organization's effectiveness.

Empowerment of employees can be a powerful motivational tool because it provides them with control and a sense of accomplishment. Business organizations of all sizes, organizations in the nonprofit sector as well as schools and governmental agencies have all implemented various aspects of empowerment (for examples, see Klidas, van den Berg, and Wilderom, 2007; Marshall, Talbott, and Bukovinsky, 2006; Silver,

Randolph, and Seibert, 2006). Keys to empowerment are giving employees control over how they perform their work and over their work environment and building a sense of self-efficacy or competence by providing them with opportunities to succeed. Additionally, encouraging participation in goal setting helps followers internalize the goals and builds commitment to them, an important factor in producing a feeling of empowerment (Menon, 2001). The continued emphasis on teams, flexibility, and quick response to environmental change further make empowerment an effective tool for organizations (Callanan, 2004).

When Linda Ellerbee, television reporter and CEO of Lucky Duck Productions, an award-winning television production company, learned of her cancer diagnosis, she gave up the reins of her company to her employees. Although she previously involved herself in every aspect of her company, she found out that "I had hired really good people who were good at their job, and what they needed was for me to get out of their way. The company continued to thrive in my absence. I never tried to micromanage again" (Ellerbee, 1999: 81).

Steps to Empowerment

Once managers and leaders decide to adopt and implement empowerment as a management technique, they must adjust the culture and structure of their organization. Many managers talk about empowerment, but few fully accept the concept and implement it completely. Several leadership and organizational steps must be taken to implement empowerment (Table 5-5).

The Leadership Factors

The style of leadership potentially creates considerable impact on followers' perception of being empowered and on how effective teams can be (Ozaralli, 2003; Srivastava, Bartol, and Lock, 2006). When empowering employees, the role of the leader is to provide a supportive and trusting atmosphere that encourages followers to share ideas, participate in decision making, collaborate with one another, and take risks. Allowing employees closest to the customer to make decisions is crucial. The leader can achieve empowerment through various means, such as role modeling, openness to others, and enthusiasm. Leaders who want to implement empowerment successfully must "walk the talk," be aware of their verbal and nonverbal signals, and

Table 5-5   Leadership and Organizational Factors in Empowerment.

Leadership Factors	Organizational Factors
• Creating a positive emotional atmosphere	• Decentralized structure
• Setting high performance standards	• Appropriate selection and training of leaders and employees
• Encouraging initiative and responsibility	
• Rewarding openly and personally	• Removing bureaucratic constraints
• Practicing equity and collaboration	• Rewarding empowering behaviours
• Expressing confidence in subordinates	• Careful monitoring and measurement
	• Fair and open organizational policies

believe in the empowerment process. They must encourage experimentation and tolerate mistakes. Leaders can further encourage an atmosphere of openness by increasing their informal interaction with subordinates in and out of the workplace.

High work and productivity standards, clarification of organizational missions and goals, and clear and equitable rewards for proper behaviors and proper productivity outcomes must accompany the positive atmosphere the leader creates. Empowerment does not mean a lack of performance or standards. Rather, it involves providing employees with many opportunities to set high goals, seeking out resources they need, supporting them in their decisions and actions, and rewarding them when the goals are achieved. The leader needs to convey high expectations and express confidence in the followers' ability to deliver high performance.

Roy Vagelos, CEO of Merck, a drug manufacturer, insisted on the impossible when he set out to eradicate river blindness, a disease that had long gone without a cure. The price of the project was an apparently unmanageable $200 million for a drug whose customers were unlikely to be able to afford it. Vagelos forged ahead and continued to expect that the project would succeed. His high expectations paid off when the drug was developed and distributed to reach 19 million people (Labarre, 1998).

The Organizational Factors

In addition to the leader's role in empowerment, the organization also needs to take steps to empower employees (see Table 5-5). First and foremost, the structure of the organization must encourage power sharing by breaking down formal and rigid hierarchies and by decentralizing decision making (Menon and Hartmann, 2002). It is difficult for a leader to empower employees to make decisions when the organizational structure does not recognize the empowerment. The traditional lines of authority and responsibility do not lend themselves well to the empowerment process, so before new techniques can be implemented, organizations must evaluate their structure with an eye for removing bureaucratic barriers. In many cases, the physical office space must be changed to accommodate the new way people will be working. Formal offices and cubicles indicate hierarchy and individual work, so encouraging interaction will require a different work space that promotes flexibility and cooperation. Several organizations found that changing their office layout was the key to better performance (Goldstein, 2000).

In order to empower people, the structure of the organization must encourage power sharing by breaking down formal and rigid hierarchies and by decentralizing decision making.

Another organizational step is the selection of leaders and employees who are willing to share power. The change in structure and empowerment can be difficult for leaders and followers who are not comfortable with such a process (Frey, 1993). Along with proper selection, appropriate training can introduce the new behaviors of collaboration, encouragement, participation, and openness. Washington Mutual Inc. (WaMu) is an unusual bank that prides itself on delivering superior service to regular customers. CEO Kerry Killinger wants to reinvent how people think about banking and enjoys considerable financial success in doing so (Tischler, 2003). Deanna Oppenheimer, president of WaMu's banking and financial group, attributes the success of the company to allowing branches local independence to serve their customers. She further believes that WaMu's practice of hiring employees with retail rather than banking experience and encouraging them to care about the customer, be fair and dynamic, and come up with new ideas helps the organization remain creative

Leading Change Sharing Power and Reaping Profits

"As long as we know what each member of staff agrees to deliver in a period of time, their working hours or where they work are no longer important" (Glamoran, 2006). Such a statement is typical of Ricardo Semler, CEO of Semco, a Brazilian company that produces marine and food processing equipment. He is used to being called a maverick. He actually wrote a book on the topic (Semler, 1993). One of the early proponents of open-book management, a method based on sharing financial information with employees and training them to interpret and use it to set and achieve performance goals, Semler believes in sharing information and power. He proposes that people who make far-reaching and complex decisions in their own lives every day are fully capable of managing themselves at work. He believes, "Freedom is the prime driver of performance" (Shinn, 2004: 18). He also believes that even though most people want democracy as a political system, most organizations do not run democratically. At Semco, employees not only pick the color of their uniforms and their work hours, but also vote on adopting new products and undertaking new ventures. Semler states, "At Semco, employees decide where they work and what needs to be done" (Fisher, 2005). The company has set up hammocks in offices to allow employees to relax, so that they can be more creative. Employees can also take sabbaticals and "Retire-A-Little" time, where they can take time off to do what they would do when they retire.

All the freedom and participation are coupled with high performance expectations. Employees who cannot work in the culture or who do not perform do not survive. The company has grown 900 percent under Semler's leadership, is either number one or number two in all the markets in which it competes, and has grown 27.5 percent a year for 14 years (Fisher, 2005). Semler succeeded in creating a culture where performance matters and people have freedom to do what they think is right and have the power to do it without asking their boss. He suggests that his management philosophy is not easy to implement everywhere because of two lacking elements: "One, the people in charge wanting to give up control. This tends to eliminate some 80 percent of businesspeople. Two, a profound belief that humankind will work toward its best version, given freedom; that would eliminate the other 20 percent" (Fisher, 2005). Both these elements make empowerment possible at Semco.

Sources: Colvin, G., 2001a. "The anti-control freak," *Fortune,* November 26: 60; Fisher, L. M., 2005. "Ricardo Semler won't take control," *Strategy and Business,* Winter. http://www.strategy-business.com/media/file/sb41_05408.pdf (accessed July 13, 2007); Glamorgan University international business speaker, September 2, 2006. http://news.glam.ac.uk/news/2006/sep/07/international-business-speaker-glamorgan/ (accessed June 23, 2007); Shinn, S., 2004. "The Maverick CEO," *BizEd,* January/February: 16–21.

(Tischler, 2003). A similar employee- and customer-focused approach is used by WaMu to focus on cultural diversity (Forsythe, 2005).

Setting high standards is a requirement for success of empowerment. Equally necessary, however, is the ability to monitor and measure performance and improvement. McDonald's, like many other retailers, has implemented elements of empowerment to engage and motivate employees with the belief that such programs improve morale of the frontline and the quality of service they deliver to customers. To keep track of its efforts and monitor performance, in addition to regular profit and quality measures, the company uses employee surveys and welcomes outsiders who are interested in studying its operations, thereby allowing itself to get feedback about climate and performance (Blundell, 2007).

Finally, just as leaders have to "walk the empowerment talk," so do organizations, by implementing appropriate reward structures and fair policies that allow for experimentation, initiative, making mistakes, and collaboration. Intense focus on the short-term financial outcomes can be deadly to an empowerment process that needs time to take hold. One of the ways organizations can start the process of empowerment is by recognizing and identifying the potential blocks to empowerment. Some consultants and academics even recommend that organizations and employees be encouraged to reject authority outright. Overall, empowering employees requires sharing information, creating autonomy, and holding employees accountable (Seibert, Silver, and Randolph, 2004).

Impact of Empowerment

Empowering employees is a difficult process, but it continues to be recognized as a key factor in today's new structures and a requirement for leaders (Harrison and Freeman, 2004). Leaders in large and small organizations are encouraged to give up power to their followers and rely on democratic practices. Many case examples and anecdotes illustrate that empowerment can be a motivational tool and lead to increased performance. It might even be that empowerment (or its opposite, too much control) can create a self-fulfilling prophecy (Davis, Schoorman, and Donaldson, 1997). On the one hand, the less a leader controls employees, the more likely they are to accept control and responsibility. On the other hand, increased control can cause followers to become passive and, in the extreme, can lead to corruption. The idea of self-leadership, discussed in Chapter 7, is partially based on the concept of empowerment.

There appears to be a resurgence in interest in empowerment, with many recent studies evaluating its impact, application, and effectiveness in a number of settings both in the United States and in others countries (e.g., Bording, Bartram, and Casimir, 2007; Singh, 2006). Despite the reported positive benefits of empowerment, however, research on the subject remains relatively scarce and mixed. Research conducted on the benefits for high-involvement organizations that use empowerment and employee participation to various degrees is increasing, but still includes few director empirical tests (Konrad, 2006; Lawler, Mohrman, and Ledford, 1995). Nevertheless, despite the many obstacles and difficulties and the limited empirical evidence, empowerment is a permanent feature of many organizations in the United States and many other Western countries (Randolph and Sashkin, 2002). When applied well and in culturally compatible institutions, empowerment can powerfully affect a leader's and an organization's effectiveness.

SUMMARY AND CONCLUSIONS

This chapter focuses on the link between power and leadership. A leader's power to influence others is the key to achieving goals and to being effective. In this influence process, a leader accesses a number of personal and organizational sources of power. The more leaders rely on power sources vested in themselves, the more likely it is that subordinates will be committed to the leader's decisions and actions. Reliance on organizational sources of power, such as legitimacy, reward, or punishment, at best leads to temporary employee commitment and at worst to resentment and resistance. Given the increasing use of teams in many organizations, it is also important for teams and their leaders to develop sources of power by coping with uncertainty, becoming central to their organization's mission and goals, and providing unique products or services that make them indispensable to others in their organization.

Although power is necessary in order to accomplish organizational goals, power also leads to many potential negative effects. Excessive power can cause leaders to develop inflated views of themselves due to compliance of the followers, flattery and compliments, the separation of leaders from their subordinates, and their access to too many resources without much accountability. In addition to the ethical consequences, such excessive power also can lead to poor decision making, reliance on authoritarian leadership, poor information flow, adversarial interactions, and ultimately, subordinate reactance and resistance.

The face of power is changing in many organizations. The key aspect of this change is the sharing of power to allow subordinates to participate in decision making, thereby leading to higher-quality decisions and subordinates' sense of accomplishment. This empowerment movement already includes many successes. It depends on the leader and the organization creating a positive atmosphere in which structures are decentralized and employees are encouraged to experiment and innovate; employees also must be well trained and supported. In addition, high performance standards need to be set, with rewards tied clearly and fairly to performance. Despite the bad press the abuse of power received recently, the proper application of power in organizations is essential to a leader's effectiveness. As part of the process of influencing others, power is at the core of the leadership interaction.

LEADERSHIP CHALLENGE: HOW MUCH IS ENOUGH?

Business executives, particularly in the United States, commandeer incredibly high salaries and compensation packages. The numbers are approaching and surpassing the $100-million mark, in some cases in companies that are performing poorly. A number of arguments explain the rise in compensation packages, including market forces and competition for the few talented executives. Where do you draw the line? If you were offered an outrageous compensation package to join a company that is laying off employees, declaring bankruptcy, and performing poorly overall, would you take it?

1. What factors contribute to high compensation packages?
2. What are the personal and organizational implications of your decision?

REVIEW AND DISCUSSION QUESTIONS

1. Provide examples for each personal source of power. Why are some forms of power more influential than others?
2. Provide scenarios for the appropriate use of each source of power.
3. Provide examples of how teams can use the sources of power available to them.
4. How are the team sources of power different from those available to individuals?
5. Provide examples of the use of different influence tactics.
6. What is the impact of too much power on organizations? Provide examples.
7. What are the key roles of a leader in implementing empowerment?
8. Where does the additional power to be given to subordinates come from?
9. Could empowerment lead to powerless leaders? Why, or why not?

EXERCISE 5-1:   RECOGNIZING BLOCKS
TO EMPOWERMENT

This exercise is designed to help you recognize organizational readiness for empowerment and the potential blocks to its implementation. For each question, think about the current state of your organization or department and check the appropriate box.

	Questions	Yes	No
1.	Is your organization undergoing major change and transition?	❏	❏
2.	Is your organization a start-up or new venture?	❏	❏
3.	Is your organization facing increasing competitive pressures?	❏	❏
4.	Is your organization a hierarchical bureaucracy?	❏	❏
5.	Is the predominant leadership in your organization authoritarian and top down?	❏	❏
6.	Is there a great deal of negativism, rehashing, and focus on failures?	❏	❏
7.	Are employees provided with reasons for the organization's decisions and actions?	❏	❏
8.	Are performance expectations and goals clearly stated?	❏	❏
9.	Are goals realistic and achievable?	❏	❏
10.	Are rewards clearly tied to performance or the accomplishment of organizational goals and mission?	❏	❏
11.	Are rewards based on competence and accomplishments?	❏	❏
12.	Is innovation encouraged and rewarded?	❏	❏
13.	Are there many opportunities for participation?	❏	❏
14.	Are most tasks routine and repetitive?	❏	❏
15.	Are resources generally appropriate for performing the tasks?	❏	❏
16.	Are opportunities for interaction with senior management limited?	❏	❏

Scoring: For items 1 through 6 and 14 and 16, give a score of 1 if you have marked Yes, 0 if you have checked No. For items 7 through 13 and item 15, reverse scoring giving a 0 to Yes and 1 to No.

Interpretation: The maximum possible score is 16. The closer you have rated your organization to that maximum score, the less ready it is for implementation of empowerment. An analysis of individual items can point to specific blocks to the implementation of empowerment.

SELF-ASSESSMENT 5-1:　VIEWS OF POWER

This self-assessment is designed to provide you with insight into your attitude regarding power. Indicate your opinion on each question, using the following scale:

1 = Strongly agree
2 = Somewhat agree
3 = Neither agree nor disagree
4 = Somewhat disagree
5 = Strongly disagree

_____ 1.　It is important for a leader to use all power and status symbols that the organization provides in order to be able to get his or her job done.

_____ 2.　Unfortunately, for many employees, the only thing that really works is threats and punitive actions.

_____ 3.　In order to be effective, a leader needs to have access to many resources to reward subordinates when they do their job well.

_____ 4.　Having excellent interpersonal relations with subordinates is essential to effective leadership.

_____ 5.　One of the keys to a leader's influence is access to information.

_____ 6.　Being friends with subordinates often reduces a leader's ability to influence them and control their actions.

_____ 7.　Leaders who are reluctant to punish their employees often lose their credibility.

_____ 8.　It is difficult for a leader to be effective without a formal title and position within an organization.

_____ 9.　Rewarding subordinates with raises, bonuses, and resources is the best way to obtain their cooperation.

_____10.　In order to be effective, a leader needs to become an expert in the area in which he or she is leading.

_____11.　Organizations need to ensure that a leader's formal evaluation of subordinates is actively used in making decisions about them.

_____12.　Even in most enlightened organizations, a leader's ability to punish subordinates needs to be well preserved.

_____13.　The dismantling of formal hierarchies and the removal of many of the symbols of leadership and status caused many leaders to lose their ability to influence their subordinates.

_____14.　A leader needs to take particular care to be perceived as an expert in his or her area.

_____15.　It is essential for a leader to develop subordinates' loyalty.

Scoring:　Reverse score item 6 (1 = strongly agree, 5 = strongly disagree), then add your scores on each items as follows:

Legitimate power: add items 1, 8, and 13. Total: _____

Reward power: add items 3, 9, and 11. Total: _____

Coercive power: add items 2, 7, and 12. Total: _____

Referent power: add items 4, 6, and 15. Total: _____

Expert power: add items 5, 10, and 14. Total: _____

Interpretation: Your total in each of the preceding five categories indicates your belief and attitude toward each of the personal power sources available to leaders.

Leadership in Action: The Power of Dick Grasso of the New York Stock Exchange

In May 2007 Dick Grasso won a long-fought legal battle to keep $180 million of his 2003 salary based on the ruling that the New York attorney general does not have authority over compensation in the New York Stock Exchange (NYSE; Davidson, 2007). "Grasso may be the first American CEO ever to be ousted simply for being overpaid" (Surowiecki, 2003). This statement summarizes what happened to Richard A. Grasso, former chairman of the 1500-employee $1-billion-revenue NYSE. He was fired from his job, which he was doing well, for having a salary and benefit package of $180 million. To make matters even worse for him, Elliot Spitzer, the New York state attorney general of the time, sued him to pay some of the money back. Spitzer felt that Grasso had "hoodwinked" the board into paying him too much (Davidson, 2007). His predecessors' salaries were about $2 million.

Grasso, labeled as the "CEO of capitalism" (*The Economist*, 2004), is a complex all-American success and corporate power and greed story. A working-class kid from Queens, New York, whose father abandoned him and his mother, he dropped out of college, went into the army, and started working his way up at the NYSE at the age of 22. He worked incredibly hard, learned everything there was to know about the institution, and slowly built a network of powerful relationships including becoming the protégé of exchange president John Phelan (Elkind, 2004). When Phelan retired, Grasso was passed over for the chairman position in favor of an insider with better pedigree and status. Grasso bottled up his resentment and worked even harder, became the indispensable know-it-all and

finally won the chairman's position in 1995 with a unanimous vote.

An intense, highly intelligent, and vindictive person, Grasso is described as a charmer and "king of relationship managers" (Elkind, 2004: 288). He turned the stodgy opening and closing NYSE bells into exciting public relations and marketing opportunities by inviting celebrities, professional wrestlers, and cancan dancers, and being doused with green slime for Viacom's Nickelodeon (Elkind, 2004). He took care of those in his inner circle and rewarded them handsomely. He also carefully selected and built relationships with the NYSE board members who determined his salary. Foremost among them was Ken Langone, the head of the compensation committee and a staunch Grasso supporter, who believed that one cannot pay performing CEOs enough money to stay on the job. Under Langone's leadership, Grasso's friends on the board carefully crafted a complex pay package that was equivalent to that of the biggest business CEOs, but far from that of a public regulatory agency such as the NYSE.

Grasso's dark side came out most often when running the "house of Grasso," as some people called the NYSE during his tenure. He demanded absolute loyalty, set incredibly high performance standards, scolded, intimidated, and yelled at his employees. One NYSE executive collapsed and was checked into the hospital after being scolded by Grasso (Elkind, 2004). Another former employee, describing how Grasso would use his regulatory powers to control outsiders, said, "He had the hounds after you. There was always the threat" (296). Another added,

"If you pissed him off, you're back on the streets of Queens" (296).

Grasso's performance during his time at the NYSE was, by all accounts, excellent (Surowieki, 2003). According to Langone, "In all the years I was on the board, in every evaluation, I never heard one negative comment about Dick Grasso's performance" (Elkind, 2004: 304). Although the NYSE board unanimously approved every penny Grasso received, his pay and benefits package violated many people's sense of fairness and equity in a time of corporate scandals. The salary package also hinted at what court documents suggest is an exchange of high salary for help on regulatory problems. Michael Spitzer stated, "This case demonstrates everything that can go wrong in setting executive compensation" (*The Economist*, 2004).

QUESTIONS

1. What are the sources of Dick Grasso's power?
2. What elements of power corruption are present in this case?

Sources: The people's lawyer strikes again. 2004. *The Economist*, May 26. http://www.economist.com/agenda/displayStory.cfm?story_id=2704015 (accessed December 30, 2004); Elkind, P., 2004. "The fall of the house of Grasso," *Fortune*, October 25: 284–312; Surowiecki, J., 2003. "The coup de Grasso," *The New Yorker*, October 6. http://www.newyorker.com/talk/content/?031006ta_talk_surowiecki (accessed December 30, 2004); Davidson, A., 2007. "Grasso wins round in battle over NYSE pay," National Public Radio, May 9. http://www.npr.org/templates/story/story.php?storyId=10089941 (accessed June 2, 2007).

Contemporary Concepts

Part II presents the recent views of leadership, including several approaches based on charisma and inspiration and other leadership perspectives such as upper echelon and the leadership of nonprofit organizations. After studying Part II, you will be familiar with the most current views of leadership, the importance of inspiration, and the essential role of the relationship between leaders and their followers. You will also understand the differences between upper-echelon leadership and leadership at other levels of the organization and appreciate the challenges top-level leaders face.

The management of organizations has changed considerably in the past few years. The pressure for faster decision making, increased flexibility, managing diversity, and addressing global challenges represent just few of the changes. Many consider constant change and the ability to successfully implement change to be essential in today's turbulent environment. Some have even called the current climate one of "permanent white water." To be successful and remain competitive, organizations and their leaders must be able to respond quickly to increasing environmental pressures. More than even before, the leadership of organizations matters. Followers have great expectations of their leaders, and the responsibilities we place on our leaders are increasing. The considerable upsurge in the interest in the topic of leadership is partly the result of the need and the challenge to lead organizations effectively in such complex times. The models presented here consider the type of leadership necessary to navigate organizations through change and address the deep needs followers have for leadership that goes beyond an exchange of direction or consideration for productivity and rewards.

Chapter 6 focuses on the most-current approaches to leadership. Although some of the concepts presented have ties to the relationship development approach to leadership, the fundamental difference is the relative absence of a contingency approach. Additionally, in the case of neo-charismatic and inspirational theories, the concepts address both small-group and department-level leadership and upper-echelon leadership. Chapter 7 looks at two different perspectives in leadership: the view from the top-levels of organizations and the characteristics of leading a nonprofit organization, both of which share some elements with other types of leadership we have considered, while presenting unique complexities and challenges.

New Models for Leadership

Neo-charisma, Inspiration, and the Relationship with Followers

Charisma becomes the undoing of leaders. It makes them
inflexible, convinced of their own infallibility, unable to change.
—PETER F. DRUCKER

After studying this chapter, you will be able to:

■ Describe the various leader, follower, cultural, and situational characteristics
that contribute to charismatic leadership.

■ Explain the positive and negative impacts of charismatic leadership on organizations.

■ Distinguish between transactional and transformational leadership.

■ Understand the key role of contingent rewards and the impact of management
by exception.

■ Present the elements of transformational leadership and their impact on followers
and organizations.

■ Describe the elements of value-based and spiritual leadership.

■ Identify the components of authentic leadership and the impact of this leadership
on followers and organizations.

For many people, the concept of leadership conjures up images of political or
organizational leaders who accomplish seemingly impossible feats. When asked
to name leaders, people often mention Martin Luther King Jr., Mahathma Gandhi,
and John F. Kennedy. These leaders and others like them exude confidence and
engender strong emotional responses in their followers. They change their followers,
organizations, and society and even alter the course of history. They are leaders who
have a special relationship with their followers that goes beyond setting goals, using
resources, and conducting business. The most-current approaches to leadership focus
on leaders who create special and long-lasting relationships or bonds with their followers and, through such bonds, are able to reach goals and, in some cases, achieve

extraordinary results. The concepts presented in this chapter address the different ways in which leaders establish that bond and the approach they take in engaging their followers.

The models in this chapter are part of what some researchers have called a "new paradigm for leadership" (Bryman, 1992). Although they have many differences, their common themes are inspiration, vision, and focus on the relationship between leaders and followers. Addressing the relationship with followers relates them to the exchange and relationship development models presented in Chapter 3. These models, however, go beyond the study of that relationship by highlighting inspiration and vision. Because they dominate the field of the leadership with considerable new research devoted to the concepts and because they do not rely fully on contingency approaches, they are presented separately here.

A BRIEF HISTORY OF NEO-CHARISMATIC LEADERSHIP

Although not yet old enough to have a history, the theories and research focused on charismatic, transformational, and inspirational leadership have evolved considerably since their introduction in the 1970s (for a review, see Sashkin, 2004). Such approaches are credited with bringing much-needed new life and enthusiasm to the field of leadership, which around the 1970s and 1980s was strongly criticized as irrelevant, trivial, and inconsequential (see McCall and Lombardo, 1978). Max Weber introduced the concept of charisma in the early 1920s and social historian James McGregor Burns reintroduced and refined the theory (1978) launching empirical-based investigation. Since then, researchers developed the concept of charisma for application to organizational contexts (Bass, 1985; Conger, 1989; Conger and Kanungo, 1987; House, 1977) and proposed models of leadership that focus on vision and large-scale change in organizations.

Several well-established researchers such as Bernard Bass and Robert House shifted their attention to these new models, and many of the young researchers entering the field made charismatic, transformational, visionary, and inspirational leadership their area of research. The renewed interest moved the research from purely theoretical and primarily case-oriented research to the much-needed empirical investigations of various constructs (Conger, 1999). The neo-charismatic and inspirational approaches provide several advantages over other views of leadership presented in this book:

> ➤ They allow us to look at a different aspect of leaders and their role as inspirational visionaries and builders of organizational cultures (Hunt, 1999).
> ➤ They highlight the importance of followers' emotional reactions (Chemers, 1997).
> ➤ They focus on leaders at top levels who are the subject of study in strategic leadership (covered in Chapter 7), thereby allowing for a potential integration of upper-echelon research with transformational and charismatic leadership.

Research about the models presented in this chapter continues as the concepts evolve; however, their predictions and explanations are a first step in addressing a growing need in today's organizations for understanding how leaders create and implement their vision and how they orchestrate and manage large-scale change.

CHARISMATIC LEADERSHIP: A RELATIONSHIP BETWEEN LEADERS AND FOLLOWERS

The word *charisma* means "an inspired and divine gift." Those who have the gift are divinely endowed with grace and talent. Charismatic leaders capture the imagination and inspire their followers' devotion and allegiance. We describe political and religious leaders as charismatic, but leaders in business organizations can also be gifted. Charismatic leaders are leaders who have a profound emotional effect on their followers (House, 1977). Followers see them not merely as bosses but as role models and heroes who are larger than life.

Charismatic leaders are leaders who have a profound emotional effect on their followers. Followers see them not merely as bosses but as role models and heroes who are larger than life.

Howard Charney, currently senior vice president at Cisco Systems, founder of Grand Junction Networks, a producer of digital switches based in California that was bought out by Cisco Systems, engenders strong emotional reactions in his followers. Debra Pelsma, who worked as buyer and planner at Grand Junction, describes her first meeting with Charney: "He was so optimistic, so sincere, so genuine, I decided I'd follow him anywhere" (Dillon, 1998: 92). Kathryn Gould, a venture capitalist and lead investor in the company, echoes Pelsma's feelings: "He is the kind of guy people walk through walls for" (92). Charney's view is simple: "What do people come to work for? To be successful. To be appreciated" (Dillon, 1998: 92–95). Because of his leadership skills, Charney is now in charge of selling the new vision at Cisco Systems (Moore, 2006).

Charney is a charismatic leader. He inspires followers who are devoted and loyal to him and his vision. This type of relationship involves an intense bond between leaders and their followers and goes beyond a simple exchange. Although desirable, the charismatic bond is far from typical of leadership situations. The following sections consider the three elements that are necessary for the development of charismatic leadership: leader characteristics, follower characteristics, and the leadership situation (Figure 6-1).

Figure 6-1   Requirements of Charismatic Leadership.

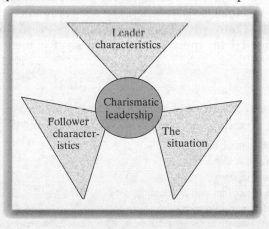

Characteristics of Charismatic Leaders

Charismatic leaders share several common personality and behavioral characteristics and traits (Table 6-1). Although many of the traits—such as self-confidence, energy, and the ability to communicate well—are related to all types of leadership, their combination is what sets apart the charismatic leaders.

One characteristic that defines charismatic leaders is their self-confidence in their own abilities and in the correctness and the moral righteousness of their beliefs and actions (Bass, 1985; Sashkin, 2004). Mahathma Gandhi's unwavering beliefs about the need for change in India and Martin Luther King Jr.'s single-minded focus on civil rights are examples of this trait. The self-confidence is accompanied by an apparent lack of internal conflict. Whereas non-charismatic leaders doubt themselves in the face of failure and criticism, charismatic leaders seem to know they are right and project that confidence. Their high level of confidence in their actions motivates their followers and creates a self-fulfilling prophecy. The more confident the leader is, the more motivated the followers are, which further emboldens the leader and encourages the followers to carry out the leader's wishes wholeheartedly. The charismatic leader's ability to express positive emotions is further linked to a positive mood in followers, which increases the attraction to the leader and his or her effectiveness (Bono and Ilies, 2006). Positive expressions, motivation, and hard work increase the chances of success, which provides proof of the leader's righteousness.

Steve Case, the highly confident founder and former CEO of America Online (AOL), made others believe in his vision of connecting everyone through the Internet. One of Case's former associates explains, "In a little company everybody's got to believe. But there needs to be somebody who believes no matter what. That was Steve. Steve believed from the first day that this was going to be a big deal" (Gunther, 1998: 71). Even though the merger of AOL with Time Warner was unsuccessful and led to a $135-billion loss, Case seemed to put all that behind him and poured his energy and money into several new ventures including one called Revolution, an organization that invests in health care and wellness (Yang, 2005), and a free health and medical information web site, RevolutionHealth. Case's advice to potential entrepreneurs is, "If you feel passionate about a particular business and have the fortitude to break down barriers and redirect when needed, you can do great things" (Edelhauser, 2007).

Many examples of the charismatic leader's self-confidence can be found also in political leaders. Fidel Castro withstood considerable pressure over the past 50 years and remains undaunted in his approach. Aung San Suu Kyi, the leader of the political

Table 6-1   Characteristics of Charismatic Leaders.

- High degree of self-confidence
- Strong conviction about ideas
- High energy and enthusiasm
- Expressiveness and excellent communication skills
- Active image building and role modeling

resistance in Burma and Nobel Peace Prize winner, who is under house arrest for many years, remains unwavering in proclaiming her agenda for democratic reform. President Gamal Abdul Nasser of Egypt galvanized Arab pride in the 1950s and 1960s, and his view of a united Arab world dominated the psyche and dreams of millions in the Middle East. Other destructive charismatic leaders used their "gift" to abuse and massacre millions; we discuss them in a later section.

Charismatic leaders generally exhibit high energy levels, along with self-confidence. They are enthusiastic about their ideas and actions, are highly expressive, and use non-verbal cues to lend dramatic support to their well-crafted verbal message. Their exceptional articulation skills that help them express their excitement and communicate the content of their ideas to their followers (Conger, 1991) are a primary tool in persuading followers to join in their vision. Martin Luther King Jr.'s considerable oratory skills provide an example, as do Hitler's and Fidel Castro's. With excellent communication skills, charismatic leaders define and frame the mission of the organization or the group in a way that makes it meaningful and relevant to followers. The process of framing puts the leader's goals in a worthwhile context that is used to draw and motivate followers (Conger, 1991; Fairhurst and Sarr, 1996). Charismatic leaders emphasize the group's history and common past, their common identity, and future hopes and common goals (Shamir, Arthur, and House, 1994). In addition, they appeal to their followers' emotion through the use of language, symbols, and imagery.

Charismatic leaders carefully craft their message and present themselves as role models to their followers. They use active impression management to support their image (Conger, 1999; Conger and Kanungo, 1998). They "walk the talk," whether it is through the self-sacrifice that they demand of their followers or the self-control they demonstrate. House and Shamir (1993) note that a large number of charismatic political leaders spent time in prison, a sacrifice that demonstrates their willingness to take risks to achieve their vision. For example, Gandhi and Nelson Mandela were imprisoned for defending their beliefs. Other charismatic leaders, such as Martin Luther King Jr., who role modeled the peaceful resistance he advocated, demonstrate through their actions what they expect of their followers. John McCain, the U.S. senator from Arizona, presidential candidate, Vietnam war hero, and prisoner of war, considers courage and self-sacrifice to be at the heart of leadership (McCain, 2004).

Hatim Tyabji, former president of VeriFone, Inc., said, "The first principle of leadership is authenticity: Watch what I do, not what I say. Leadership requires moral authority. You can't have moral authority if you behave differently from your people. If you want your people to be frugal, then don't spend money on perks designed to make your life more comfortable. (Tyabji, 1997: 98). Andrea Jung (see Leadership in Action at the end of this chapter) faced the financial problems for her company by reinventing both her company and herself. She states, "You can't ask an entire company to change and not change yourself. I have set higher expectations for myself and our people" (Jung, 2007). Bill George, the highly respected former CEO of Medtronics, considers authenticity and integrity to be the most important leadership traits: "Authenticity and courage go hand in hand. You need one to have the other" (Salter, 2004: 93). The concept plays a key role in leadership and has become the focus on a new approach to understanding leadership reviewed later in this chapter.

The process of role modeling can also be symbolic, as was the case with the well-publicized $1 salary that Lee Iaccoca accepted while receiving substantial income from stock options and other benefits or John Mackey's $1 salary for 2007 from Whole Foods (see Leadership in Action in Chapter 8). Dan Cathy, president and COO of Chick-fil-A and son of the company's founder, is passionate about customer service, and what makes him an effective leader is partly the fact that he is willing to "walk the talk." He is often found in his stores, where he introduces himself to customers with a simple "I'm Dan. I work in customer service" (McGregor, 2004: 83). He believes that "the closer top management is to the customer, the more successful an organization is likely to be" (McGregor, 2004: 84). Whether actual or symbolic, role modeling and powerful verbal messages contribute to the enhanced image of the leader. Cult leaders make use of all these behaviors to create a powerful and self-perpetuating mystique that strengthens their relationship and their hold on followers.

Charismatic leaders are masterful impression managers (Conger, 1989; House, 1977). They surround themselves with dramatic and mystical symbols that further enhance the image of the leader as a larger-than-life figure. Bass (1985) cites John F. Kennedy as a case in point. His administration carefully developed the image of Camelot, complete with Guinevere and the knights who were fighting the battle against communism. The competition to conquer space before the Russians further contributed to the mystical and heroic image of a youthful statesman struggling to pull the United States out of the stodgy Eisenhower era. The power of these symbols and their resulting emotional bonds are evidenced by the strong sense of loss after President Kennedy's assassination. Organizational leaders use equally effective symbols to maintain their image. In the case of Steve Case, founder of AOL, the mystique included being one of the gang. One AOL employee describes him in this way: "Nothing about him says media mogul—he lunches on turkey sandwiches and Sun Chips, and has the boyish good looks of an aging fraternity brother" (Gunther, 1998: 71).

Overall, the characteristics of charismatic leaders are not in dispute. The next step is describing the development of followers who are devoted to the leader.

Characteristics of Followers

Because charismatic leadership results from an interaction and relationship between a leader and followers, the followers of such leaders generally display certain characteristics. Without the leader and the follower characteristics, no charismatic relationship can form. Take away the frenzied followers and Hitler would not have been considered charismatic. The same is true for many cult leaders. Even for positive and constructive charismatic leaders such as Gandhi, followers demonstrate particular traits and behaviors (Table 6-2). First and foremost, followers hold the leader in high esteem. They are strongly devoted to him or her, and an intense emotional bond forms between the leader and the followers. These followers admire their leader; emulate the leader's behaviors and mannerisms, including talking, dressing, and acting like the leader. Consider the reaction of employees of Russ Berrie and Co. when the toymaker's founder and namesake died suddenly. Berrie had established a close family bond with his employees. He was the best man at some of their weddings and one company executive continued to visit his grave regularly because he felt a spiritual bond with the deceased leader (Marchetti, 2005). The intense emotional bond and attraction to the leader create a situation whereby followers obey without question. They have confidence in the vision and direction. Once the identification process takes place, complete internalization of the leader's values and aspirations occurs. In addition, some

Table 6-2   Characteristics of Followers of Charismatic Leaders.

- High degree of respect and esteem for the leader
- Loyalty and devotion to the leader
- Affection for the leader
- High performance expectations
- Unquestioning obedience

followers' personality traits are linked to the development of charismatic relationships. In particular, self-monitoring and self-concept might affect how the charismatic relationship develops (Weierter, 1997).

Charismatic leaders are able to connect their followers to their own vision. Researchers suggest that charismatic leaders change the followers' perception of the nature of what needs to be done. The expression of positive emotions, which indicates the leader's self-confidence, is also suggested to create a positive mood contagion (Bono and Ilies, 2006). Leaders further offer an appealing vision of the future, develop a common identity, and heighten the followers' self-esteem and sense of self-efficacy (for a review, see Conger, 1999). In addition, one of the key components of the emergence of charismatic leaders is for the followers to perceive a need for change because the current state is unacceptable and because they believe that a crisis either is imminent or already exists (Shamir, 1991; Trice and Beyer, 1993). The final element of charismatic leadership is the situation.

The Charismatic Situation

A crisis causes followers to look for new solutions. During a time of crisis, followers are ready for change. If an individual is able to capture and represent the needs and aspirations of the group, that individual is likely to become the group leader. In addition, individuals who demonstrate competence and loyalty to a group and its goals are provided with "credit" that they can spend to assume leadership roles. This idiosyncrasy credit allows certain individuals to emerge as leaders and change the direction of the group (Hollander, 1979). Because of the strong emotional impact of charismatic leaders, followers provide them with tremendous leeway (credit) to lead the group into new territory.

External Crisis and Turbulence

At the heart of the issue of charismatic leadership is how certain individuals either emerge as leaders in leaderless groups or replace an appointed leader. Many charismatic revolutionary leaders achieve their status without any formal designation. In organizations, although charismatic leaders are elected or appointed, their followers recognize them as leaders before a formal appointment, the last step in their rise to power, typically during a time of crisis. Popular political and religious leaders, such as Martin Luther King Jr. or Ronald Reagan, win the hearts and minds of their followers, who then carry them into formal positions.

Table 6-3 summarizes the external situational elements that contribute to the development of charismatic leadership. Although not all researchers believe that a

Table 6-3 Elements of Charismatic Situations.

- Sense of real or imminent crisis
- Perceived need for change
- Opportunity to articulate ideological goal
- Availability of dramatic symbols
- Opportunity to clearly articulate followers' role in managing the crisis

situation of crisis is necessary for the emergence of charismatic leadership, many suggest that a *sense* of distress or crisis is (Bass, 1985; Beyer, 1999a; Shamir and Howell, 1999). Research by Roberts and Bradley (1988) suggests that situations of crisis provide more latitude for leader initiative such that the person can demonstrate leadership abilities. Others link resilience and tolerance for ambiguity to charisma and its importance in crisis situations (Hunter, 2006), where followers believe that charismatic leaders are the only ones who can resolve the crisis. Therefore, charismatic leaders emerge in situations where a change and a new ideological vision need to be articulated and when followers are ready to be saved or more simply moved in a different direction. With an emotionally charged situation, leaders enter the field promising a new beginning, radical solutions, and a break from the unwanted values of the past (Boal and Bryson, 1987). They use dramatic symbols to illustrate their goals and point to clear and specific roles that their followers can play in resolving the crisis. As a result, followers are convinced that the charismatic leader is the only one who can help, and the leader helps followers becoming aware of how they can contribute individually.

All the historical charismatic leaders emerged in a time of crisis. Cyrus the Great of Persia united warring tribes in 1500 B.C.; Napoléon galvanized a fractured postrevolutionary France; the fascist dictators of modern Europe took power during economic and social crises; and the U.S. civil rights leaders of the 1960s rode on the wave of a cultural and civil unrest. They all brought a new vision of the future to their eager followers. In all cases, the crises and the perceived need for change set the stage for the charismatic leaders' skills.

Internal Organizational Conditions for the Emergence of Charismatic Leadership

Researchers suggest that in addition to a sense of external crisis, several internal organizational conditions also facilitate charismatic leadership (Shamir and Howell, 1999).

- ➤ *Organizational life cycle.* Charismatic leaders are more likely to emerge and be effective in the early and late stages of an organization's life cycle, when either no set direction is established or change and revival are needed.
- ➤ *Type of task and reward structure.* Complex, challenging, and ambiguous tasks that require initiative and creativity and where external rewards cannot be clearly tied to performance can be ideal situations for charismatic leaders.
- ➤ *Organizational structure and culture.* Flexible and organic structures and nonbureaucratic organizational cultures are likely to encourage charismatic leadership.

Although some evidence is available to support these propositions, empirical testing is needed before they are established fully as conditions for the emergence of charismatic leadership.

Role of Culture

As you have read throughout this book, culture strongly affects what behaviors and styles are considered appropriate and effective for leaders and limits what behaviors people learn and consider acceptable. Based on the nature and elements of charismatic leadership, it would stand to reason that cultures with a strong tradition for prophetic salvation, in particular, would be more amenable to charismatic leadership. For example, the Judeo-Christian beliefs of the coming of the savior create fertile ground for charismatic leaders to emerge and be accepted. Prophets by definition are charismatic saviors. Israel, for example, has this type of strong tradition. Another case in point is the recent rise of Islamic fundamentalism, which typically is tied to a prophetic spiritual leader, as is the case in the Sudan and Iran (Dekmejian and Wyszomirski, 1972). The case of Khomeini in Iran illustrates all the elements of a typical charismatic relationship, including leader and follower characteristics, the intense and calculated image management on the part of the leader, and the sense of crisis because of the political climate of the country in the 1970s (F. Nahavandi, 1988; H. Nahavandi, 1994).

In cultures without such prophetic traditions, few strong charismatic figures are likely to emerge. For example, in China, although periods of crisis and change have certainly occurred, it appears that the relationship between leader and followers is based more on the social hierarchy and need for order, as is prescribed in the Confucian tradition, than on the intense emotional charismatic bonds that exist in Judeo-Christian religions, which seems to be the case even for one of the few charismatic Chinese leaders, Mao Zedong. Furthermore, the development of a charismatic relationship in a culture such as Japan needs to rely on the leader's development of an image of competence and moral courage, and the securing of respect from followers (Tsurumi, 1982); by contrast, in India, charismatic leadership is associated with a religious, almost supernatural, state (Singer, 1969). In any case, even if the concept of charisma is present within a culture, its manifestations may be widely different. In some cultures, such as the United States, charisma is assertive and direct, whereas in others it may be more quiet and nonassertive (Scandura and Dorfman, 2004).

The GLOBE research, discussed in Chapter 2, has studied charismatic leadership among other leader behaviors and attributes in 60 countries (Den Hartog et al., 1999). The basic assumption of the research project is that "charismatic leadership will be universally reported as facilitating 'outstanding' leadership" (230). The researchers found that although some attributes are universally endorsed and some are universally negative, several attributes are culturally contingent (see Table 6-4 for a summary). It is important to note that although several of the behaviors associated with charismatic leadership are universally associated with effectiveness, the term *charisma* evokes mixed reactions in different cultures. In other words, being charismatic is seen as both positive and negative.

In addition to characteristics typically associated with charismatic leadership (e.g., positive and dynamic), there exist other characteristics (e.g., being a team builder and being intelligent) that are not part of charisma (see Table 6-4). Interestingly, although having a vision is universally associated with leadership, how it is expressed

Table 6-4   Cross-Cultural Attributes of Leadership.

Universally Positive	Universally Negative	Culturally Contingent
• Being encouraging, positive, and motivational	• Being a loner	• Risk taking
• Having a vision and a plan and being able to make decisions	• Being non-cooperative	• Enthusiasm
• Being dynamic	• Being ruthless and dictatorial	• How vision is communicated
• Having integrity and being trustworthy	• Non-explicit	• What constitutes good communication
• Building teams	• Irritable	• How much leader is seen as equal
• Intelligent		
• Communicator		
• Win-win problem solver		

Source: Based on information in Den Hartog et al., 1999. Culture-specific and cross-culturally generalizable implicit leadership theories: Are attributes of charismatic/transformational leadership universally endorsed? *The Leadership Quarterly* 10: 219–256.

and communicated differs greatly across cultures. For example, Chinese leaders are seen as effective if they communicate their vision in a nonaggressive and soft-spoken manner, whereas Indians prefer bold and assertive leaders (Den Hartog et al., 1999). Similarly, followers universally value communication, but the communication style (e.g., level of directness, tone of voice, etc.) that is considered desirable is highly culture specific. For example, Cambodians expressed considerable enthusiasm at the ascendance of their new king Norodom Sihamoni in October 2004, even though he lacked any political experience, because they valued his extremely modest and soft-spoken demeanor (Sullivan, 2004). Furthermore, self-sacrifice and risk taking, important components of charismatic leadership in the United States, do not contribute to outstanding leadership in all other cultures (Martinez and Dorfman, 1998).

The Dark Side of Charisma

Given the charismatic leaders' strong emotional hold on followers, they can abuse that power easily and use it toward inappropriate ends. Along with Gandhi, President Kennedy, and Dr. King, the list of charismatic leaders unfortunately includes Hitler and Jim Jones (the cult leader who convinced thousands of his followers to commit suicide). The destructive charismatic leaders resemble the positive ones in some dimensions, but several characteristics distinguish them (Bass and Steidlmeier, 1999; Conger, 1990; Howell, 1988; Howell and Avolio, 1992).

The major difference between ethical and unethical charismatic leaders is the unethical leaders' focus on personal goals rather than organizational goals. Unethical leaders use their gift and special relationship with followers to advance their personal vision and to exploit followers; they follow an internal and personal orientation, behaviors that are similar to narcissistic personality. Ethical charismatic leaders use their power to serve others, develop followers, and achieve the common vision. The unethical charismatic leader censures opposing views and engages in one-way communication, whereas the ethical one accepts criticism and remains open to communication from followers. Given the considerable power of some charismatic leaders and their extensive and intense bond with their followers, it is easy to see how the line between ethical and unethical behaviors can be blurred. Leaders who are convinced of their vision do not doubt its righteousness, and leaders who have the ability to persuade often will do so without concern for others. The characteristics of self-confidence and skillful modeling and persuasion that make a charismatic leader effective can also be the sources of highly destructive outcomes.

The major difference between ethical and unethical charismatic leaders is the unethical leaders' focus on personal goals rather than organizational goals. Unethical leaders use their gift and special relationship with followers to advance their personal vision and to exploit followers.

Distinguishing between the two types of charismatic leadership further helps explain how negative leadership can develop. Howell (1988) contrasts socialized and personalized charismatic leaders. Socialized leaders focus on satisfying their followers' goals and on developing a message that is congruent with shared values and needs and may be a factor in reducing deviance in their group (Brown and Treviño, 2006a). Personalized leaders rely on getting followers to identify and agree with their personal values and beliefs. Both examples demonstrate all the characteristics of charismatic leaders, their followers, and the situation. Personalized leadership situations, however, are more prone to abuse.

In addition to the potential for power abuse and corruption, charismatic leaders also might present other liabilities ranging from a flawed vision that is self-serving to unrealistic estimates of the environment (Conger and Kanungo, 1998). The charismatic leader's skills at impression management and influence can become a liability when leaders mislead their followers with exaggerated estimates of their own or their followers' abilities and the chances for success. Other potential liabilities of charismatic leadership include failure to manage details, failure to develop successors, creation of disruptive in- and out-groups, and engaging in disruptive and unconventional behaviors (Conger and Kanungo, 1998).

Evaluation and Application

The considerable changes in many organizations in recent years have created a sense of crisis and resulted in a perceived need for revitalization and change. Therefore, it is no coincidence that the concept of charismatic leadership dominates U.S. academic and popular views of leadership. The need to revitalize industrial, educational, health care, and governmental institutions creates one of the essential elements for charismatic leadership; many perceive that we are in a time of turbulent change, if not crisis. We make many demands on our leaders to provide us with revolutionary ideas and are often disappointed when they cannot fulfill those expectations. In fact, our expectations are so high that we are bound to be disappointed.

Researchers have developed a number of different approaches to explain charismatic leadership, ranging from an attributional perspective whereby the leader's behavior and the situation persuade followers to attribute charismatic characteristics to the leader (Conger, 1989a; Conger and Kanungo, 1987), to self-concept views that focus on explaining how charismatic leaders can influence and motivate their followers (Shamir, House, and Arthur, 1993), to psychoanalytic perspectives (Kets de Vries, 1993), and self-presentational views (Sosik, Avolio, and Jung, 2002). Much debate centers around the sociological and organizational views of charismatic leadership regarding its contents, focus, and its situational antecedents (Bass, 1999; Beyer, 1999a, b; House, 1999; Shamir, 1999). Various studies have tested the elements of the different views of charismatic leadership; the results are not always consistent (e.g., see Shamir et al., 1998). Continued research, however, provides strong support for the existence and importance of understanding charismatic relationships and how such leaders affect their followers and their organizations. For example, charismatic leaders show a positive effect on cooperation (De Cremer and van Knippenberg, 2002). They also seem to increase followers' efforts and citizenship behaviors (Sosik, 2005) and have been suggested to have a positive impact on external organizational stakeholders as well as immediate followers (Fanelli and Misangyi, 2006).

The charismatic relationship is a powerful and undeniable part of the most celebrated leadership situations in Western culture. Charismatic leaders and their followers can achieve incredible feats. Such leadership, however, is not required for an organization to be successful. Indeed, it can be destructive, as is the case of negative charismatic leadership or when a charismatic leader is wrong and drives the organization to failure. Finally, it is important to remember that charismatic leadership is not a cure-all (Bryman, 1992; Trice and Beyer, 1993). In addition, because it is difficult, if not impossible, to train someone to be a charismatic leader (Trice and Beyer, 1993), the phenomenon depends on one individual rather than on stable organizational processes that can be put in place once the leader is gone. With all its potential benefits, charismatic leadership is a double-edged sword that requires careful monitoring to avert abuse. Although charismatic leadership holds a potentially negative side as demonstrated by many destructive charismatic historical figures, transformational leadership, which is presented next, relies on charisma as one element but concentrates on the positive role of leadership in change.

TRANSACTIONAL AND TRANSFORMATIONAL LEADERSHIP

How do leaders create and sustain revolutionary change in organizations? What style of leadership is needed to motivate followers to undertake organizational transformations? Several researchers proposed transformational leadership concepts to answer these questions and to describe and explain how leaders succeed in achieving large-scale change in organizations. First developed by Burns (1978), transformational leadership theory suggests that some leaders, through their personal traits and their relationships with followers, go beyond a simple exchange of resources and productivity.

The leadership models presented in previous chapters focused on the transaction and exchange between leaders and followers. For example, in Path-Goal Theory (see Chapter 3), the leader clears obstacles in exchange for follower motivation by providing structure to the task or by being considerate. Such basic exchanges, sometimes labeled transactional leadership, are considered an essential part of leadership and leaders must understand and manage them well. To create change, however, they must supplement exchange with transformational leadership. Transformational leadership theory proposes that leaders use behaviors that are more complex than initiation of structure and consideration. Based on the observations of many leaders, it is clear that the two behavioral dimensions cannot account for the full range of behaviors ascribed to many leaders.

Transactional Leadership

Transactional leadership is based on the concept of exchange between leaders and followers. The leader provides followers with resources and rewards in exchange for motivation, productivity, and effective task accomplishment. This exchange and the concept of providing contingent rewards are at the heart of motivation, leadership, and management theory and practice. Two styles of transactional leadership are using contingent reward and Management by Exception (MBE).

Contingent Reward

Through the use of contingent reward, leaders provide followers with promised rewards when followers fulfill their agreed-upon goals. When well managed, contingent rewards are highly satisfying and beneficial to the leader, the followers, and the organization. The informal and formal performance contracts that result are highly desirable and effective in managing performance (Bass, 1985). Some research indicates that transactional leadership can provide structure and lead to positive outcomes (Walker, 2006) and that individualistic cultures may react more positively to transactional leadership than collectivistic cultures (Walumbwa, Lawler, and Avolio, 2007). Contingent rewards are part of most leadership training whereby leaders are taught to provide contingent rewards, reinforce appropriate behavior, and discourage inappropriate behavior. They are necessary components of effective leadership and management. For example, transactional leadership successfully motivated remaining employees to decontaminate and tear down the infamous Rocky Flats nuclear site in Colorado. The Environmental Protection Agency certified the nuclear weapons site "clean" in June 2007 after years of mismanagement, accidents, and extensive clean-up. Denny Ferrara, whose whole family worked at the plant, was in charge of getting employees to work themselves out of a job. He accomplished this task by setting clear goals, communicating extensively, allowing employees to provide input into how to do the work, and encouraging them with recognition and generous rewards, which in some cases topped $80,000 a year (McGregor, 2004b).

Management by Exception

Management by Exception (MBE) is a leadership style whereby the leader interacts little with followers, provides limited or no direction, and only intervenes when things go wrong. In one type of MBE, labeled "active MBE," leaders monitor follower activities and correct mistakes as they happen (Bass and Avolio, 1990a). In another type, labeled "laissez-faire," leaders are passive and indifferent toward followers and their tasks. In both cases, little positive reinforcement or encouragement is given; the leader relies almost exclusively on discipline and punishment. Some managers confuse using MBE with empowering followers. After all, it does appear that followers have freedom to do as they please, as long as they do not make a mistake. Such comparisons, however, are not warranted. Encouragement and creating a supportive and positive environment in which risk-taking is encouraged, both at the heart of empowerment, are clearly not present when a manager relies on MBE. Even though contingent reward can yield positive effects, using MBE, particularly laissez-faire, as a primary leadership style generally results in a negative impact on follower performance and satisfaction.

Despite the success of some transactional relationships in achieving performance, an exclusive focus on such exchanges and transactions with followers is blamed for low expectations of followers and minimal performance in organizations (Zaleznik, 1990). Transactional contracts do not inspire followers to aim for excellence; rather, they focus on short-term, immediate outcomes. Long-term inspiration requires transformational leadership.

Transformational Leadership

Leadership scholars and practitioners (Bass, 1985, 1990b; Bennis and Nanus, 1985; Conger and Kanungo, 1998) suggest that today's organizations need leadership that inspires followers and enables them to enact revolutionary change. For example, the

> **Transformational leadership includes three factors—charisma and inspiration, intellectual stimulation, and individual consideration— that, when combined, allow a leader to achieve large-scale change.**

health-care industry pays attention to the role of hospital administrators in guiding their organizations in uncertain times. Institutions such as Harbor Health Systems focus on clarifying each person's role in the accomplishment of the organization's mission. Pacific Presbyterian stresses strong leadership commitment to the organization's mission and goals. Leaders such as Mark Wallace of Texas Children's Hospital are celebrated for their vision, creativity, and ability to inspire followers (Lutz, 1992), all factors needed to create a new vision to deal with the dynamic and often-threatening environment that characterizes the health-care industry.

Transformational CEOs from the industrial, service, and not-for-profit sectors are also at the center of attention, and many, such as Jack Welch of GE and Andy Grove of Intel, are management gurus who provide others with extensive advice. Transformational leadership includes three factors—charisma and inspiration, intellectual stimulation, and individual consideration—that, when combined, allow a leader to achieve large-scale change (Figure 6-2).

Charisma and Inspiration

The concept of charisma is one of the three central elements of transformational leadership (Bass, 1985; Bass and Avolio, 1993). The charismatic leadership relationship creates the intense emotional bond between leaders and followers. The result is loyalty and trust in, as well as emulation of, the leader. Followers are inspired to implement the leader's vision. The strong loyalty and respect that define a charismatic relationship pave the way for undertaking major change.

Intellectual Stimulation

The second factor in transformational leadership is the leader's ability to motivate followers to solve problems by challenging them intellectually and encouraging them to come up with creative solutions. The leaders and the group question existing values and assumptions and search for new answers (Shin and Zhou, 2003). By encouraging them to look at problems in new ways requiring new solutions and by triggering controversial discussion and debate, the leader pushes followers to perform beyond

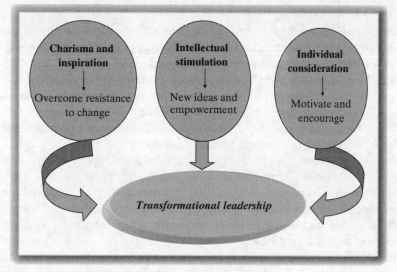

Figure 6-2   Transformational Leadership Factors.

what they previously considered possible (Boerner, Eisenbeiss, and Griesser, 2007). The charismatic bond provides support and encouragement in this endeavor and prevents followers from feeling isolated. Intellectual stimulation includes a strong empowering component, which assures followers of their abilities and capabilities, and enables them to search out new solutions. Transformational leadership has been shown to create empowerment that, in turn, increases team effectiveness (Kark, Shamir, and Chen, 2003; Ozaralli, 2003).

Individual Consideration

The last factor of transformational leadership, the development of a personal relationship with each follower, is closely related to the Leader–Member Exchange (LMX) Model presented in Chapter 6 (Howell and Hall-Merenda, 1999). The leader treats each follower differently but equitably, providing all with individual attention. As a result, followers feel special, encouraged, motivated, developed, and perform better (Dvir et al., 2002). The leader's individual consideration further allows for matching each follower's skills and abilities to the needs of the organization.

The three factors—charisma/inspiration, intellectual stimulation, and individual consideration—combine to allow the leader to undertake the necessary changes in an organization. The charismatic emotional bond overcomes the psychological and emotional resistance to change. The intellectual stimulation provides the new solutions and innovation and empowers followers. The individual relationship between the leader and follower encourages followers and provides them with additional motivation. The transactional leadership behaviors support the maintenance of the routine aspects of the organization, whereas transformational leadership allows for external adaptation. Referring back to the definition of leadership effectiveness presented in Chapter 1, we see that the transformational leadership behaviors allow for external adaptation, whereas the transactional behaviors maintain internal health.

Evaluation and Application

Transformational leadership is one of the most popular and currently heavily researched theories of leadership. The theory has moved from the development of basic concepts to the stage where the concepts are critically reviewed and various moderating variables are identified (Antonakis, Avolio, and Sivasubramaniam, 2003). Therefore, considerable research about the various aspects of transformational leadership is available, several extensions of the model have been proposed (e.g., Rafferty and Griffin, 2004), and applications to broader organizational contexts, such as the public sector, suggested (Denhardt and Campbell, 2006). Several empirical studies have tested the propositions of transformational leadership in a variety of settings (e.g., Podsakoff and MacKenzie, 1997; Shin and Zhou, 2003; Yammarino and Bass, 1990). For example, researchers find that transformational leadership can help employees accept a recent acquisition and increase job satisfaction (Nemanich and Keller, 2007). Other studies suggest that transformational leadership can impact how employees view their job particularly when the quality of the LMX is positive (Piccolo and Colquitt, 2006). Yet others extend the concept by linking personality attributes to transformational leadership. For example, one study suggests that a personality pattern characterized by high levels of pragmatism and nurturance and low levels of aggression and criticalness is associated with transformational leadership (Ross and Offerman, 1997).

Several studies consider transformational leadership theory across gender and cultures. For example, female transformational leaders form a unique relationship with each of their followers, suggesting that women favor an interpersonal-oriented style of leadership (Yammarino et al., 1997). Women leaders often exhibit concern for others, expressiveness, and cooperation (Eagly, Karau, and Makhijani, 1995), traits that are associated with transformational leadership. From a cross-cultural perspective, it appears that ideal leadership characteristics across many countries—such as Canada, South Africa, Israel, Mexico, Sweden, and Singapore—include some transformational leadership elements (Bass, 1997) and that individuals from collectivistic cultures in particular, may be most receptive to transformational leadership (Jung and Avolio, 1999; Jung, Bass, and Sosik, 1995; Walumbwa and Lawler, 2003; Walumbwa, Lawler, and Avolio, 2007).

Continued research is needed, especially in regard to the measurement of transactional and transformational behavior (Yukl, 1999) and the factors that lead to the use of transformational behavior by leaders. The only empirically derived measure, the multifactor leadership questionnaire (MLQ), does not consistently allow for separate identification of the various behaviors (Bycio, Hackett, and Allen, 1995; Keller, 1992; Seltzer and Bass, 1990; Tepper and Percy, 1994), although new research indicates that the measure offers better validity and reliability than previously thought (Antonakis et al., 2003). In addition, despite the focus on behaviors, many of the transformational behaviors include dispositional, traitlike elements and are reported to develop early in life (Bass, 1985). For example, although it might be easy to instruct a leader how to provide contingent rewards, teaching the leader to inspire and intellectually stimulate followers might not be as simple. Furthermore, even though some research links transformational leadership to emotional intelligence (e.g., Gardner and Stough, 2002), the relationship of transactional leadership characteristics with other personality traits such as the Big Five needs further research (Hautala, 2006; Lim and Ployhart, 2004). Additionally, as is the case with charismatic leadership, the tendency is to propose transformational leadership as a panacea to organizational problems. A stronger contingency approach, however, would identify various contextual organizational variables that might contribute to the effectiveness of transformational leadership (Pawar and Eastman, 1997). Some researchers further suggest that the transformational leadership theory could benefit from clarification of the difference between charismatic and transformational leadership and the mediating processes and situational variables that lead to transformational leadership (Sashkin, 2004; Yukl, 1999). As is the case with charismatic leadership, transformational leadership also involves the potential of leading to followers' excessive dependency (Kark et al., 2003) and negative and unethical behavior (Price, 2003); further research in that area would also enhance the model.

Transformational leadership concepts apply widely to organizational effectiveness and leadership training. Although charismatic leadership sometimes carries negative connotations, transformational leadership generally is perceived as positive. Research findings suggest that organizations can benefit from encouraging their leaders to be less aggressive and more nurturing (Ross and Offerman, 1997: 1084). Other recommendations for leaders based on transformational leadership models include the following:

➤ Project confidence and optimism about the goals and followers' ability.
➤ Provide a clear vision.
➤ Encourage creativity through empowerment, reward experimentation, and tolerate mistakes.
➤ Set high expectations and creating a supportive environment.
➤ Establish personal relationships with followers.

The use of transformational leadership can facilitate change in organizations. The next section considers other leadership theories that also focus on how to bring about change.

Leading Change   Sir Richard Branson and His Vision

The Virgin Group family of companies has been, for many years, a household name in much of Europe. From record stores to cell phones to airlines, Virgin is a formidable brand. No less formidable is its founder and CEO Sir Richard Branson, who built an empire by breaking all the rules and successfully taking on challenges that everyone told him would fail. Running his business from his house on the private Caribbean island of Necker, taking phone calls while resting in his hammock between tennis games, Branson considers profits to be secondary: "The bottom line has never been a reason for doing anything. It's much more the satisfaction of creating things that you're proud of and making a difference" (Deutschman, 2004: 95). Most often mentioned for his keen marketing skills and his ability to attract attention

(*Continued*)

Leading Change   (*Continued*)

through his daredevil endeavors such as hot-air balloon trips across the Atlantic, outrageous behaviors such as dressing as a bride or a pirate or being photographed nude for his biography, Branson focuses on ventures he feels passionate about and cares deeply about the culture and people in his many companies (Hawn, 2006).

Branson believes, "You can't be a good leader unless you generally like people. That is how you bring out the best in them" (*Workforce*, 2004). He believes, "it's extremely important to respond to people, and to give them encouragement if you're a leader. And if you're actually turning people down . . . take the time to do it yourself" (Branson, 2007). While recruiting managers and employees for his companies, he looks for the best so he can get the best (*Workforce*, 2004). Encouraging people through lavish praise so they can flourish, allowing them to figure out their mistakes instead of picking on them, moving employees around to help them to find a job that allows them to excel are all part of Branson's leadership philosophy. He suggests that most employees leave companies when they are frustrated because they are not heard.

Although also called a control freak for keeping a hand in all his companies (Deutschman, 2004), Sir Richard has learned to delegate and develop the people who work for him. He describes the process: "I come up with the original idea, spend the first three months immersed in the business so I know the ins and outs and then give chief executives a stake in the company and ask them to run it as if it's their own" (*Workforce*, 2004). Branson wants to make sure that whatever he builds or takes part in is something that he can be proud of. He admits, "I made and learned from lots of mistakes. In the end, the key is will power" (Hawn, 2006).

Sources: Branson, R. 2006. "How to succeed in 2007." *CNN Money.com.* http:// money.cnn.com/popups/2006/biz2/howtosucceed/4.html (accessed August 14, 2007); Deutschman, A., 2004. "The Gonzo way of branding," *Fast Company*, October: 91–96; Hawn, C. 2006. "Branson's next big bet." CNN Money.com, October 2. http:// money.cnn.com/magazines/business2/business2_archive/2006/08/01/8382250/ (accessed August 12, 2007); "The importance of being Richard Branson," *Workforce*, December 2004. www.workforce.com/archive/article/23/91/47.php (accessed January 30, 2005).

SPIRITUAL, VALUE-BASED, AND AUTHENTIC LEADERSHIP

Leadership is more than a series of behaviors and actions. For many, the leadership process is highly emotional and personal and based on fundamental values such as integrity and caring for others. Such concepts have found their way into leadership theory and research and some approaches now take into consideration values and emotions as primary aspects of leadership.

Spiritual and Value-Based Leadership

The topics of values and spirituality are increasingly finding their way into the workplace, particularly in the United States. Workplace spirituality recognizes that people often have a meaningful inner life that influences their beliefs and actions. Such approaches integrate what some consider the essence of the human existence, the body, mind, heart, and spirit (Moxley, 2000), and the search for the meaning of life and interconnectedness with others (Zinnbauer, Pargament, and Scott, 1999). Spirituality focuses on how leaders and followers tap into their basic values to transform organizations by creating a vision based on deeply held values related to making a difference, and implementing a caring and altruistic culture that supports that vision (Fry, 2003). Value-based and spiritual leaders develop their relationship with followers based on the values they share.

One such value that has particular importance to organizations is ethics. Others would be spiritual values, such as love, hope, humility, and faith. These values are considered key to leadership by some practitioners (e.g., Covey's principle-centered leadership, 1991 and Greenleaf's servant leadership, 1998), researchers (see the special issue of *The Leadership Quarter 2005*, volume 16), and leadership textbooks (e.g., Daft, 2008). Some suggest that spiritual values such as integrity, honesty, and humility are actually an inherent part of effective leadership (Fry, 2005), and research findings imply that value-based leadership practices positively impact leadership effectiveness (Reave, 2005) and are related to improved organizational learning. Although honesty and integrity are part of most conceptions of effective leadership, in the wake of business and political scandals, the call for integrity and ethics in leadership has become louder and the focus of recent research (for a review, see Brown and Treviñno, 2006b). Ethical leaders demonstrate fair, appropriate, and caring personal and social decisions and behaviors and communicate, promote, and reinforce such values and actions with followers and throughout the organization (Brown, Treviño, and Harrison, 2005).

Chris Lowney, author of *Heroic Leadership*, applies the teachings of St. Ignatius Loyola—founder of the Jesuits, one of the world's oldest and most successful religious orders—to leadership in today's organizations (2005). Lowney believes that the Jesuits' success is attributed to their focus on self-awareness (based on reflection and accounting for one's actions and goals), ingenuity (innovation, adaptation, willingness to look at new opportunities), love (support and caring), and heroism (willingness to take risks and make the best of situations). Approaches such as Lowney's and other value-based leadership are closely related to both transformational and authentic leadership through the focus on key individual characteristics of leaders regarding integrity, caring for others, and transparency.

Authentic Leadership

Authentic leaders are people who know themselves well and remain true to their values and beliefs. They have strong values and a sense of purpose that guide their decisions and actions (George, 2003). Bill George, the former CEO of Medtronics and one of the strongest proponents of authentic leadership, believes that the most effective leaders, those who have the most long-lasting impact on their

The key to authentic leadership is understanding your strengths and developing them.

followers and their organizations, are those who have a moral compass and have found their "true north" (George, 2007). For practitioners of leadership, the key to authentic leadership is understanding your strengths and developing them. Consultant Marcus Bukingham suggests, "Be authentic. To become a leader, identify where you are strongest and most confident, and then work to expand those areas. If you want to be a better leader, don't try to be all things to all people . . . you will lead best by following who you are" (Bukingham, 2005).

For practitioners of leadership, authentic leaders (George, 2003)

➤ *Understand their own purpose*: They understand themselves and their motivation and what they are looking for.

➤ *Practice solid values*: They have personal values that guide their decisions and their actions. These values develop based on their personal experiences and challenges.

➤ *Lead with their heart*: They are open with their followers and interested in them.

➤ *Connect with their followers*: By sharing themselves with followers, they establish long-lasting relationships.

➤ *Demonstrate self-discipline*: They work hard to demonstrate their values and guide their followers.

Howard Schulltz, cofounder and CEO of Starbucks, has created an organization based on what matters most to him (see Leading Change in Chapter 10). As a child, Schulltz watched his family struggle without health benefits after his father lost his job because of an injury. Those experiences left an indelible mark on Schulltz, who made taking care of employees, providing health benefits, and not leaving anyone behind the core of Starbucks' culture (Meyers, 2005). Schulltz' actions as a leader stem from his beliefs and values, which are the source of his success as a leader. Bill George (2007) cites the case of Wendy Kopp, founder of Teach For America, as another example of an authentic leader. With a strong desire to change the world and improve K-12 education, she organized conferences that included students and business leaders while she was a senior at Princeton University. Her isolated background from a middle-class family, her consideration of a teaching career, and her passion to make a difference led her to create Teach for America and lead the organization through many turbulent years before it established itself as a model for community engagement (George, 2007).

In addition to anecdotal and case examples of authentic organizational leaders, in the past few years, researchers have started exploring the concept of authenticity and are working on clarifying its various components and links to other theories (e.g., Avolio and Gardner, 2005). As in the case of spiritual leadership, the prominence of the concept of authentic leadership in research is evidenced by a recent issue of *The Leadership Quarterly* devoted to the topic (2005, issue 16).

Definition and Elements of Authentic Leadership

Researchers consider authentic leadership to be a continuum where at one end a leader is either unaware of his or her values or does not follow them and at the other end, the person is able to articulate values clearly and use them to guide his or her behavior (Figure 6-3; Avolio et al., 2004; Erickson, 1995). The roots of authentic leadership can be traced back as far as Rogers' and Maslow's concept of self-actualization and more recently to the positive psychology movement (Seligman, 2002; Seligman

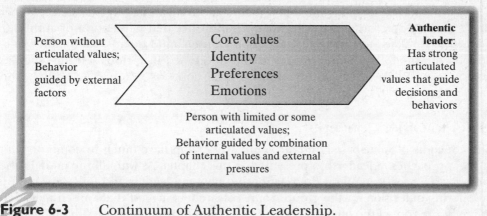

Figure 6-3   Continuum of Authentic Leadership.

and Csikszentmihalyi, 2000), the concept of positive organizational behavior (Luthans, 2002), and optimal self-esteem (Kernis, 2003). While closely related to practitioner views of authentic leadership, the research-based models offer further clarification. Specifically, the concept is considered highly complex and including traits, emotions, behaviors and attributions (Avolio and Gardner, 2005; Cooper et al., 2005). Further, authenticity is differentiated from sincerity, which involves accurate self-presentations rather than being true to oneself (Avolio and Gardner, 2005). Table 6-5 summarizes the key elements of authentic leadership.

Table 6.5   Components of Authentic Leadership.

Components	Description
Self-awareness	Being aware of and trusting one's emotions, motives, complexities, abilities, and potential inner conflicts.
Unbiased or balanced processing	Ability to consider, within reasonable limits, multiple perspectives and inputs and assess information in a balanced manner both in regards to information about the self and others.
Behaviors are true to self and motivated by personal convictions	Focused by own convictions; unencumbered by others' expectations or desire to please others; decisions and behaviors guided by personal values;
Relational authenticity or transparency	Ability to disclose and share information about self appropriately and openly to relate to others; achieving openness and truthfulness in close relationships.

Source: Based on information in Avolio, B. J., and W. L. Gardner. 2005. Authentic leadership development: Getting to the root of positive forms of leadership. *The Leadership Quarterly* 16:315–338; Kernis, M. H. 2003. Toward a conceptualization of optimal self-esteem. *Psychological Inquiry* 14:1–26.

Authentic leadership is still a new theory and remains largely untested (Cooper et al., 2005). Some early research, however, indicates that perception of authentic leadership is related to employee satisfaction (Jensen and Luthans, 2006) and extensions of the model are being proposed and developed in various settings, such as school (e.g., Begley, 2006) and other cultural contexts (Endrissat, Muller, and Kaudela-Baum, 2007).

Links to Other Concepts

The concepts of value-based and authentic leadership have much in common with other approaches to leadership presented in this chapter. As with all the models, the focus is, to a great extent, on the relationship between leaders and followers and on the sharing of a vision for the group. Some researchers suggest that authentic leadership is at the root of the other concepts (Avolio and Gardner, 2005). Although charismatic, transformational, and spiritual leaders all have to necessarily have some element of authenticity, authentic leaders do not necessarily need to be charismatic, transformational, or spiritual. Additionally, authentic leaders may lead by being task or relationship oriented or by involving and empowering followers to various degrees. Because authentic leaders are true to their own self, their behaviors, it is reasonable to assume that their actions are not guided by the situation. For charismatic and transformational leaders, the connection with followers comes from inspirational appeal, impression management, or focusing on the followers' needs. In the case of authentic leaders, a focus on followers and on attempts to win them over through arguments and rhetoric is usually absent (Avolio and Gardner, 2003). Instead, the authentic leader wins over followers by the strength of his or her own beliefs. The authentic leader does not focus on others' expectations. The essence of authentic leadership is

---

Applying What You Learn
Developing Authenticity

Being authentic may be related to self-esteem and other traits and therefore may not be something that all of us can simply implement after a few days' practice. It, however, is possible to carefully and mindfully develop more authenticity. Some practical tips include:

- Develop a clear sense of your values and beliefs; know what matters to you most and why.

- Understand how your values impact your behavior.

- Seek feedback about your behavior, strengths, and weaknesses.

- Focus on understanding and changing the sources of defensiveness regarding your own values, beliefs, emotions, and behaviors.

- Engage in open and meaningful conversations with your followers and team members regarding your values and your vision.

- Be mindful of any potential real or perceived conflicts and inconsistencies between what you say and what you do.

- Stand your ground on issues that are most important to you. You can disagree without being disagreeable!

self-awareness, knowing one's values, and remaining true to them. By knowing themselves well and being true to their own beliefs and values, authentic leaders engage their followers.

Evaluation and Application

As research topics, value-based and authentic leadership present opportunities and challenges. The concepts add considerable richness to the study of leadership by introducing and considering the role of emotions in the leadership process. Whereas most of our theories are cognitive, the concept covered in this section addresses emotional aspects of leadership. Additionally, the introduction of hope and optimism to understanding the leadership process is a significant contribution (Avolio et al., 2004). At this point in time, however, much of the information about value-based and authentic leadership theories is based either on case studies or on anecdotal accounts. Although the information is rich and provides many avenues for further study, empirical research about the topic is still scarce. Instead, the concepts are in the theoretical development and refinement phases with substantial opportunities for further contributions to the field. Among many other areas of research, the cross-cultural applications of the concepts in nonindividualistic cultures and their other cross-cultural implications should yield interesting results. Additionally, some suggest that concepts such as spirituality may be so broad to make empirical research difficult (Starck et al., 2002) thereby pointing to the need for considerable research to clarify concepts (Dent, Higgins, and Wharff, 2005).

From a practical point of view, value-based and authentic leadership have significant appeal to leaders. With the concept of spirituality playing a greater role, particularly in the United States, value-based leadership allows for approaching leadership from an angle that addresses the needs of many followers. As a root concept for leadership, authentic leadership provides general guidance for what leaders should focus on and avenues for growth.

SUMMARY AND CONCLUSIONS

This chapter focuses on recent theories of charismatic and transformational leadership and value-based and authentic leadership and their impact on leadership practice. Although the notion of charisma has been a central element of leadership for many years, recent scientific approaches allow for more-thorough descriptions of the process. In particular, current approaches view charismatic leadership as a relationship between leaders and followers, rather than as a combination of leadership traits and behaviors. For the charismatic leadership relationship to occur, leaders need certain traits and behaviors, followers must demonstrate particular traits and frames of mind, and the situation requires an element of crisis. The combination of these three factors allows for the emergence of charismatic leadership.

Charismatic leadership is one of the elements in the transformational leadership model. The model suggests that the transactional views of leadership, which focus on developing an exchange and transaction contract between leaders and followers, must be supplemented with behaviors that lead to organizational transformation. Transformational leadership provides vision, inspiration, and the intense emotions required to enact such large-scale changes in organizations. Value-based and authentic leadership concepts similarly have a focus on vision and caring for followers and consider the role emotions can play in leadership. Spiritual leadership considers how leaders and followers create organizations based on their common values and search for deep meaning. Authentic leaders build effective organizations based on self-awareness and transparent sharing of their personal values.

Charismatic, transformational, value-based, and authentic leadership concepts contribute to the demystification and understanding of leadership processes. They offer broad appeal and provide an intuitive understanding of leadership that is applicable to large-scale leadership situations. They are also responsible for a resurgence in the interest in leadership. Because of their relatively recent formation, the concepts still require much refinement and their use in training leaders needs further development, particularly with regard to identification of various situations under which change-oriented leadership might be more appropriate and more effective.

LEADERSHIP CHALLENGE: STANDING UP TO A CHARISMATIC BUT UNETHICAL LEADER

You are one of the lucky people who work with a leader who demonstrates considerable personal charisma. She holds a grand vision of the future, communicates with passion, inspires her followers, and makes them feel special. Because of prior knowledge and experience with her, however, you are one of the few people who is aware that she is disingenuous, is focused on her personal agenda and career, would not hesitate to sacrifice all her followers for her own benefit, and is ruthless with those who disagree with her. You know that it is only a matter of time before her followers suffer because of her lack of concern and extreme self-interest.

1. Should you share your concerns with other department members? With her supervisor?
2. What are the consequences of your action or inaction?
3. What course of action would you choose? Why?

REVIEW AND DISCUSSION QUESTIONS

1. What are the factors that gave rise to the development of neo-charismatic leadership theories?
2. Describe the elements of charismatic leadership.
3. What are the cultural constraints on the development of charismatic leadership?
4. Describe the elements of transactional leadership.
5. How is management by exception different from empowerment?
6. Describe the elements of transformational leadership and its role in enacting organizational change.
7. Compare and contrast value-based, spiritual, and authentic leadership concepts.
8. What are the key elements of authentic leadership?
9. What are the major shortcomings of the neo-charismatic approaches to leadership?
10. What are the major contributions of the neo-charismatic approaches to our understanding of leadership?

EXERCISE 6-1:   DO YOU KNOW A CHARISMATIC LEADER?

Identify a leader you consider to be highly effective. This person may be in your work organization or a leader in your civic, sports, educational, or religious organization.

Step 1: Describe the Leader

Rate the leader you selected on the following items using the following scale.

> 1 = Never
> 2 = Occasionally
> 3 = Often
> 4 = Always

_____ 1. The leader shows a high degree of self-confidence.

_____ 2. The leader does not show any doubt about his or her ideas.

_____ 3. The leader has a clear, well-articulated vision.

_____ 4. The leader has a high energy level.

_____ 5. The leader shows a lot of enthusiasm about the work to be done.

_____ 6. The leader is emotionally expressive.

_____ 7. The leader expresses his or her ideas well.

_____ 8. The leader is articulate.

_____ 9. The leader does all that he or she requires of followers.

_____ 10. The leader role models the desired behaviors and "walks the talk."

Scoring: Add up your scores for all 10 items. The maximum possible score is 40. The higher your leader's score, the more he or she demonstrates charismatic characteristics.
Total: _____

Step 2: Describe Followers' Reactions and Behaviors

Rate the leader's followers (including yourself) on the following items, using the following scale.

> 1 = Never
> 2 = Occasionally
> 3 = Often
> 4 = Always

_____ 1. The followers respect the leader.

_____ 2. The followers hold the leader in high esteem.

_____ 3. The followers are loyal and devoted to the leader.

_____ 4. The followers like the leader.

_____ 5. The followers believe in their own capability for exceptional performance.

_____ 6. The followers are enthusiastic about the work to be done.

_____ 7. The followers follow the leader's directions eagerly.

Scoring: Add up your rating for all seven items. The maximum possible score is 28. The higher the followers' scores, the more they demonstrate the characteristics of followers of charismatic leaders.
Total: _____

(*Continued*)

Step 3: Describe the Situation

Consider the situation that the leader and follower face in their day-to-day activities. Rate the situation on the following items using the following scale.

$$1 = \text{Never}$$
$$2 = \text{Occasionally}$$
$$3 = \text{Often}$$
$$4 = \text{Always}$$

_____ 1. Our team/organization needs to change.

_____ 2. We seem to go from crisis to crisis.

_____ 3. We could do many things better around here.

_____ 4. We do not seem to know what we are all about.

_____ 5. We have not yet explored many opportunities.

_____ 6. Many of us are not performing to our fullest potential.

Scoring: Add up your rating for all six items. The maximum possible score is 24. The higher your group's score, the more you are ready for change and face a crisis situation.
Total: _____

Step 4: Putting It All Together

Using the scores from the three previous measures, consider whether

1. Your leader has the personal characteristics of a charismatic leader.
2. The group exhibits the behaviors typically associated with charismatic leadership.
3. The group faces a crisis situation that involves a perceived need for change.

Based on these three questions, to what extent is the leader you selected charismatic?

$$1 = \text{Not at all}$$
$$2 = \text{Has some, but not all elements}$$
$$3 = \text{To a great extent}$$

Step 5: Discussion

1. What are the factors that explain your leader's effectiveness?

2. What do you foresee for the future if the situation changes?

EXERCISE 6-2:   CHARISMATIC SPEECH

One of the characteristics of charismatic leaders is their ability to articulate their ideas and vision in an inspiring manner. These articulation skills may come easier to some than to others, but they can be learned if practiced.

Two aspects go into an inspiring message: (1) proper framing of ideas to give them a powerful context, and (2) use of various rhetorical techniques to support the message.

Elements of Framing

Amplify values and beliefs.
Bring out the importance of the mission.
Clarify the need to accomplish the mission.
Focus on the efficacy of the mission.

Rhetorical Techniques

Use of metaphors, analogies, and brief stories
Gearing language to the audience
Repetition
Rhythm
Alliteration
Nonverbal message

Write a short speech that presents your goals (personal or for your team or organization). Revise and practice the message using charismatic speech methods.

Source: This exercise is based on concepts developed by Conger (1989, 1991).

SELF-ASSESSMENT 6-1: AUTHENTIC LEADERSHIP

Being an authentic leader consists of several different elements. For each of the following items indicate to what extent the statement is descriptive of you, by using the following scale:

> 1 = Strongly disagree (does not sound at all like me)
> 2 = Disagree (I rarely behave this way)
> 3 = Agree (I often behave this way)
> 4 = Strongly agree (Describes me very well)

_____ 1. I am aware of who I truly am.

_____ 2. I know what matters to me most.

_____ 3. I make my decisions based on my own principles, rather than what others think.

_____ 4. I have trouble handling my weaknesses and faults.

_____ 5. I have trouble opening up to others.

_____ 6. When I am in groups, I like to share as much information as possible with everyone.

_____ 7. Although I respect others' opinions, I tend to stick to things I believe in.

_____ 8. When I get conflicting advice, I have trouble deciding what the best course of action may be for me.

_____ 9. I am skilled at listening to and understanding many different points of view.

_____ 10. I like to hear information from all sides before I make up my mind.

_____ 11. Most people don't really know who I am.

_____ 12. I can tell when I am not being true to myself.

Scoring: Add up your rating for all 12 items. The maximum score is 48. A higher score indicates behaviors that build credibility.

Self awareness subscale: add up items 1, 2, and 12.

Total: _____

Balanced perception subscale: reverse score for item 4 (1=4, 2=3, 3=2, 1=4) and add up items 4, 9, and 10.

Total: _____

Value-based behavior subscale: reverse score for item 8 (1=4, 2=3, 3=2, 1=4) and add up items 3, 7, and 8.

Total: _____

Relational Transparency subscale: reverse score for items 5 and 11 (1=4, 2=3, 3=2, 1=4) and add up items 5, 6, and 11.

Add up the total for the four subscales.

Total: _____

Interpretation

The range for the total scale is between 12 and 48. The close you are to 48, the more elements of authentic leadership you have. Consider each of the subscales (scores range from 3 to 12) for areas where your score may be lower.

Source: This self-assessment is based on work by Kernis (2003) and Avolio and Gardner (2005).

Leadership in Action: Andrea Jung Orchestrates Avon's Makeover

Avon's history spans two centuries. The cosmetics company was global before business became global; it served and employed women before diversity became an issue; it was customer focused before the concept became an organizational mantra; and it has been successful longer than most organizations have been around. Interestingly enough, the company that almost exclusively serves women through its cosmetics did not have a female executive until 1999 when Andrea Jung was appointed CEO and chairman in 2001 (Executive Team at Avon, 2007). She faced the daunting task of moving a traditional, door-to-door sales company to the high-tech Internet world without alienating its loyal sales force—the "Avon Ladies" (Sellers, 2000b). With all its past success, Avon was getting sluggish and showing its age.

Jung undertook the makeover of Avon by pouring money into research and development, expanding the overseas markets, and focusing on jazzy marketing that included celebrities such as Salma Hayek. "Jung practically reinvented the company. She united its disconnected international operations into what she called a global 'company for women'" (Global Influentials). Her strategies paid off. Avon's sales jumped 45 percent from $5.7 billion to a projected $7.7 billion in 2004 with a 164 percent increase in stock prices (Setoodeh, 2005). The company also continues to be a responsible corporate citizen, raising millions of dollars for causes ranging from the children affected by the September 11, 2001 terrorist attack in the United States to being a corporate sponsor for "Race for the Cure." After several years of strong growth, however, the tide turned and, once more, Avon faced a turndown in 2006.

During the first five years in leadership, Yung was able to achieve impressive results through dogged determination and unwavering confidence in her strategy, which involved the slow introduction of the Internet and other retail sales and a gradual blending of new retail methods with the traditional direct sales. She strongly believes that the global force of 3.4 million independent Avon Ladies is the backbone of the company. She demonstrated her commitment to them by increasing the number of and incentives for the direct sales representatives. In meetings around the world, she involves them in the decision making rather forcing the necessary changes from the top (Menkes, 2006). Kurt Schansinger, a financial analyst at Merrill Lynch, describes Jung as having a "strong vision, high standards, deep knowledge of the business, and enough confidence to delegate key tasks" (Brady, 2001). Birdie Jarworski, an Avon representative who met Jung at a company convention, describes her as "the rock star of Avon"; she was impressed by Jung's friendliness and her dedication to the company (Chandra, 2004). Jung has the attention of her Avon Ladies, who cheered for almost two minutes at the start of her videotaped message at a recent convention. Allan Mottus, editor of a cosmetics newsletter, states that Avon "needed a person with charisma and Jung has that" (Chandra, 2004).

These attributes are mentioned often when people talk about Jung. Born into a highly educated Chinese immigrant family—her father is an architect and her mother was Canada's first female chemical engineer—Jung always was expected to succeed. She received a Princeton education, graduating magna cum laude, and speaks fluent Mandarin and Cantonese as well as some

(*Continued*)

Leadership in Action: (*Continued*)

French. When she joined Bloomingdale's, her parents did not originally approve of their daughter lowering herself to become a retailer, although her current position is winning their applause (Executive Sweet, 2005: 1). After Bloomingdale's, Jung followed her mentor Vass to I. Magnin and later to Neiman Marcus. Jung credits Vass with teaching her the art of tactful aggression, a style that matches her cultural roots (Executive Sweet, 2005: 2). She believes that she still has traces of what she calls Asian submissiveness, although she has learned to be tougher in the corporate world (Executive Sweet, 2005: 2). Jung joined Avon partly because of the corporate culture and partly because women being a quarter of the company's board of directors appealed to her. She says, "I'm very selective about the companies I work for. I started at Bloomingdale's because it was committed to developing women" (Executive Sweet, 2005: 3). As a result, she is a strong believer in mentoring and helping others succeed.

Jung states, "I have a love for this business. I have an enormous amount of passion for it. . . . I love managing people. The product is second to managing the people. And marketing to consumers is so challenging because it is evolving constantly" (Executive Sweet, 2005: 3). She also enjoys building consensus among her team and making sure everyone's voice is heard. She makes an extra effort to listen to her team members'

suggestions and ideas. When her global marketing team was having difficulty finding an appealing name for a new facial cream, she engaged everyone in the discussion. Joking about integrating everyone's ideas, she states, "It was like naming a child after your mother, your husband's mother, your grandmother, and your great aunt" (Morris, 1997: 79). Her constant smile and upbeat approach and attitude set the tone for her company and send a message of confidence and success. Discussing leadership, Jung says, "I think there is a big and significant difference between being a leader and being a manager—leaders lead from the heart. Flexibility is one of the key ingredients to being successful. If you feel like it's difficult to change, you will probably have a harder time succeeding" (Executive Sweet, 2005: 3). Facing the second big challenge of her leadership at Avon in 2006, Jung is ready: "Avon had to reinvent itself—and I had to reinvent myself along with it" (Jung, 2007). With many layoffs and a strategic redirection, her primary role continues to be communicating about Avon inside and outside the company (Byrnes, 2007).

QUESTIONS

1. What are the key elements of Andrea Jung's leadership style?
2. How closely does she match elements of charismatic and transformational leadership?

Sources: Avon Executive team at http://avoncompany.com/investor/seniormanagement/jung.html (accessed on August 12, 2007); Byrnes, N., 2007. "Avon: More than cosmetic changes," *Business Week*, April 12: 62–64; Chandra, S. 2004. "Avon's Andrea Jung Pins Hopes on China as Sales in U.S. Fade." *Bloomberg.com*, December 27. http://www.bloomberg.com/apps/news?pid=10000080&sid=aBrmvGQAml1c& refer=asia# (accessed January 31, 2005); "Executive Sweet," *Goldsea: Asian American.* http://goldsea.com/ WW/Jungandrea/jungandrea.html (accessed January 31, 2005); Global Influential. 2001. *Time.com.* www.time.com/time/2001/influentials/ybjung.html (accessed January 31, 2005); Jung, A. 2006. "How to succeed in 2007." *CNNMoney.com.* http://money.cnn.com/popups/2006/biz2/howtosucceed/40.html (accessed August 12, 2007); Menkes, J. *Executive Intelligence* (New York: Harper Collins, 2006); Morris, B., 2004. "If women ran the world it would look a lot like Avon," *Fortune*, July: 21; Sellers, P., 2000. "The 50 most powerful women in business," *Fortune*, October 16: 131–160; Setoodeh, R. "Calling Avon's Lady." *MSNBC News: Newsweek.* www.msnbc.msn.com/id/6733211/site/newsweek/ (accessed January 31, 2005).

Other Leadership Perspectives

Upper Echelon and Leadership of Nonprofits

Setting an example is not the main means of influencing another; it is the only means.
—ALBERT EINSTEIN

There are those who look at things the way they are and ask why. . . . I dream of things that never were and ask why not?
—ROBERT KENNEDY

After studying this chapter, you will be able to:

- Differentiate between micro and upper-echelon leadership.
- Describe the domain and roles of strategic leaders in the management of an organization.
- Identify the external and internal factors that impact strategic leaders' discretion.
- List the individual characteristics of strategic leaders and their impact on leadership style.
- Contrast the four strategic leadership types and discuss the role of culture and gender in strategic leadership.
- Explain the processes through which strategic leaders manage their organization.
- Review issues of executive compensation and accountability.
- Describe the characteristics and challenges of leadership in nonprofit organizations.

The press in business, public, and health sectors is replete with examples of leaders. Many publications and professional associations present yearly awards for the best leaders in their industry. The health-care industry awards a "best health care administrator award"; best and worst city mayors are ranked regularly, as are best and worst business leaders. Based on the amount of attention given to top executives, one can deduce that practitioners clearly believe that the top leader of an organization is important, but the academic interest in how leaders impact organizational elements such as culture, strategy, and structure is relatively new. With the exception of some of the leadership models discussed in Chapter 6, none of the leadership theories presented so far in this book directly addresses the role and impact of upper-echelon leaders. These issues are typically the domain of strategic management. Until recently, however, research in strategy focused more on the content and types of strategies leaders implement rather than on the leadership process itself. This chapter will clarify the differences between micro and upper-echelon (macro) strategic leadership and consider individual characteristics of strategic leaders and the processes through which they affect their organization. We will also briefly address the special characteristics and challenges leaders may face in nonprofit organizations.

DIFFERENCES BETWEEN MICRO AND UPPER-ECHELON STRATEGIC LEADERSHIP

The reviews of the role of upper-echelon leadership in organizations suggest that the practitioners' efforts at understanding executives are justified (see Finkelstein and Hambrick, 1996; Hambrick, 2007; Hambrick and Mason, 1984; Nahavandi and Malekzadeh, 1993a). Although somewhat fragmented, the research results show that the CEO has impact on the direction an organization takes and on its strategy; CEOs matter (Auden, Shackman, and Onken, 2006; Papadakis and Barwise, 2002). Many of the leadership concepts and processes presented in previous chapters operate regardless of the level of the leader. For example, the basic definition of leadership and leadership effectiveness can be transferred from small groups to upper echelons with only minor adjustments. Upper-echelon leaders are still the people who guide others in goal achievement, and their effectiveness depends on maintaining internal health and external adaptability. Therefore, the major differences between micro and macro leadership are not in the nature of the process but rather in the level and scope of leadership. We call upper-echelon leaders "strategic leaders" because they affect the whole organization. Strategic leadership is a leader's ability to anticipate events and maintain flexibility and a long-term perspective in order to guide the organization (Christensen, 1997). Table 7-1 summarizes the differences between micro and strategic leadership.

One of the first differences between micro and strategic leadership involves identifying who the leader is. In the case of micro leadership, the person leading the group, team, or department is clearly the leader. In the case of strategic leadership, the issue is often not that simple. The leader of the organization might be the president, CEO, or chief operating officer (COO), or it could be a top management team (TMT) made up of division heads and vice presidents. In some cases, the relevant strategic leadership is a governance body such as the board of directors, board of regents, or supervisors. Any of these individuals or groups might be the senior executives who make strategic choices for the organization. Research indicates that the makeup and characteristics of the TMT relate to factors such as degree of globalization (e.g., Levy, 2005; Nadkarni and Perez, 2007), the success of turnaround strategies in organizations that face

Table 7-1   Differences Between Micro and Strategic Leadership.

	Micro (Group)	Strategic (Upper Echelon)
Who is the leader?	One person heading a group, team, or department	A person heading a whole organization with a variety of titles (president, CEO, COO); Top Management Team (TMT); governance body such as board of directors
What is the scope?	Small group, team, or department	Entire organization
Where is the focus?	Internal	External
What are the effectiveness criteria?	Productivity; quality; employee satisfaction and motivation; turnover; absenteeism	Stock prices and other financial measures; stakeholder satisfaction

performance challenges (e.g., Lohrke, Bedeian, and Palmer, 2004), or corporate social responsibility (Simerly, 2003).

A second difference in leadership at the two levels is the scope of the leader's impact. Whereas most micro leaders are concerned with small groups, departments, or teams, upper-echelon leaders have jurisdiction over entire organizations that include many smaller groups and departments. Because of this broader scope, upper-echelon leaders have discretion and power over many decisions. For example, when a city mayor makes a decision, thousands, and in some cases millions, are affected. When the CEO of GM and his TMT decide to downsize, more than 300,000 employees are at risk, not to mention thousands of suppliers and the employees' families and communities. By comparison, the scope of micro leaders' decisions is limited to a smaller number of individuals.

A third difference between the two groups is their focus. The micro leaders' focus is typically internal to the organization and includes factors that affect their teams or departments. Part of their job may involve dealing with external constituents, as may be the case with a customer representative or a sales manager, or they might be under pressure to take on a more strategic view even in their small department. They, however, generally do not need an external view to perform their job. In comparison, the job of the upper-echelon leader requires almost equal attention to internal and external factors. Dealing with outside constituents, whether they are stockholders, governmental agencies and officials, or customers and clients, is central to the function of executives.

The effectiveness criteria are also different for the two groups. Although, in a general sense, they are both effective when they achieve their goals, micro leaders focus on department productivity, quality of products and services, and employee morale. Effectiveness for the upper-echelon leader is measured by overall organizational performance, stock prices, and satisfaction of outside constituents. The hospital administrator has to integrate internal productivity issues with overall performance. The CEO of a major corporation does not focus on turnover of employees as a measure of personal effectiveness. Instead, the criteria are overall return on investment and the corporation's growth.

THE DOMAIN AND IMPACT OF STRATEGIC LEADERSHIP

What is the role of senior executives? Do they simply provide direction, or do they stay involved in the day-to-day operations of their organization? The answer depends in part on the leader's style and personality. Six strategic forces depicted in Figure 7-1, are the primary domain of strategic leadership (Malekzadeh, 1995). *Culture* is defined as a common set of beliefs and assumptions shared by members of an organization (Schein, 2004). *Structure* is comprised of the basic design dimensions (centralization, formalization, integration, and span of control) that organize the human resources of an organization (Pugh et al., 1968). *Strategy* addresses how the organization will get where it wants to go—how it will achieve its goals. The *environment* includes all the outside forces that may potentially affect the organization. *Technology* is the process by which inputs are transformed into outputs, and *leadership* includes managers and supervisors at all levels.

Any strategic effort requires a balance and fit among the strategic forces. When the fit is good, the organization possesses a greater potential to be effective (Nahavandi and Malekzadeh, 1999). Consider the example of Jagged Edge Mountain Gear (JEMG), a Colorado-based company that specialized in fashionable mountaineering clothing. Twin sisters Margaret and Paula Quenemoen founded the company in 1993 based on the Asian philosophy that focused on the journey and process (Nahavandi and Malekzadeh, 1999: 108–109). JEMG's goal was to become a nationally recognized competitor in their industry. As Quenemoens state, however, "We are our own competition. We do what we

Figure 7-1   The Domain of Strategic Leaders: The Six Strategic Forces.

think is right" (Nahavandi and Malekzadeh, 1999: 108). To achieve their goal, the sisters attracted a group of passionate mountain enthusiasts who perform the many business functions while remaining dedicated to cold-weather, extreme sports. The JEMG owners, managers, and employees worked together and played together. The culture of the organization was informal and exuded the members' passion for their sports. The structure, although formally stated, remained informal, with a heavy reliance on participation and empowerment. In addition, because of the company's relative isolation in Telluride, everybody depended on information technology to stay in touch with the marketing division located in Salt Lake City and their suppliers in Massachusetts, Tennessee, and China. The Quenemoens ran JEMG successfully by creating a fit among the six strategic forces.

> **Any strategic effort requires a balance and fit among the strategic forces. When the fit is good, the organization possesses a greater potential to be effective.**

The simultaneous management of the six forces is the essence of strategic management (Malekzadeh, 1995). The upper-echelon leader's role is to balance these various factors and set the direction for the organization. Once a direction is selected, internal forces (e.g., culture, structure, and leadership) come into play once more to move the organization toward its selected path.

Role of Strategic Leaders

Strategic leaders (CEO or the TMT) are the ones in charge of setting and changing the environment, culture, strategy, structure, leadership, and technology of an organization and motivating employees to implement the decisions. Their role is to devise or formulate the vision and strategy for their organization and to implement those strategies; they play the dual role of strategy formulator and implementer (Nahavandi and Malekzadeh, 1993a). If an organization has not drafted a strategy or is looking for major changes and strategic redirection, the leaders have a vital role in formulating the direction of the organization based on their reading of the environment. If, on the other hand, the organization has a well-established, successful strategy already in place, the leaders become a key factor in implementing that strategy. The dual role of strategic leaders is depicted in Figure 7-2.

Although they play a central role in creating and maintaining major organizational elements, the top managers' influence often is moderated by a number of organizational and environmental factors. Therefore, although leaders are highly influential in many aspects of organizational decision making, many circumstances and variables limit a leader's discretion. The next section considers these factors.

Executive Discretion: Factors That Moderate the Power of Leaders

Upper-echelon leaders do not have unlimited power to impact their organization. The research about the limits of their power comes under the label of managerial or executive discretion (Finkelstein and Hambrick, 1996; Hambrick and Finkelstein, 1987) and is the subject of considerable research in strategic management for its impact on firm performance in a variety of areas (e.g., Aragon-Correa, Matias-Reche, Senise-Barrio, 2004; Bates, 2005) and CEO compensation (e.g., Cho and Shen, 2007). Table 7-2 presents the factors that moderate a leader's discretion. They are divided into external

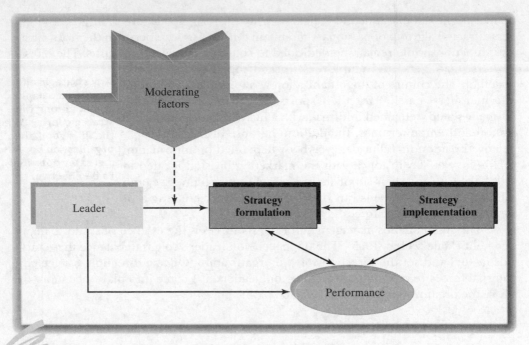

Figure 7-2   Dual Role of Upper-Echelon Leaders.

environmental and internal organizational factors. Both sets operate to limit the direct or indirect impact of senior executives on their organization.

External Environmental Factors
Several researchers suggest that the leader's role becomes more prominent when organizations face an uncertain environment (Gupta, 1988; Hall, 1977; Hambrick and Finkelstein, 1987). For example, in highly dynamic industries such as high technology,

Table 7-2   Moderators of Executive Discretion.

External Environmental Factors	Environment Uncertainty
	Type of industry
	Market growth
	Legal constraints
Internal organizational factors	Stability
	Size and structure
	Culture
	Stage of organizational development
	Presence, power, and makeup of TMT

computers, or airlines, top managers must scan and interpret their environment actively and make strategic decisions based on their interpretations. Such activities provide many opportunities for a leader to affect the organization. Charlie Feld, founder and CEO of the Feld Group, a technology and management consulting company that specializes in turnaround strategies, believes that the leader's vision and priority setting are essential to surviving a crisis (Maruca, 2001). Other external forces include market growth and legal constraints. In fast-growing markets, strategic leaders have considerable discretion to set and change the course of their organization (Haleblian and Finkelstein, 1993). Legal constraints, such as environmental laws, health and safety regulations, and international trade barriers, however, limit the discretion of leaders. In such environments, many of their decisions already are made for them, leaving less room for action.

Consider the case of utility companies that, up until a few years ago, faced a stable and calm environment. As competition increases and governments deregulate the industry, leaders of these utility companies are becoming more prominent. Similarly, the leaders of the computer industry, such as Steve Jobs (Apple), Bill Gates (Microsoft), and Michael Dell (Dell Computers), have become household names, as have leaders in many of the Internet companies, such as Margaret Whitman (eBay) and Amazon.com's Jeff Bezos.

Internal Organizational Factors

When organizations face internal uncertainty, organizational members question existing practices and decisions and rely more heavily on the leader to provide direction and guidance. In routine situations, organizational rules and regulations and a well-established culture in effect become substitutes for leadership (Kerr and Jermier, 1978). One example of a situation in which leaders are heavily relied upon would be during a threatened or actual merger. The employees are likely to seek direction from their CEO, whose every word and action will be interpreted as a signal and whose attitude toward the merger will be a role model for the employees. Professor Mike Useem, director of the Center for Leadership and Change at the University of Pennsylvania's Wharton School of Business, suggests that a leader's calm and confidence is a key factor in managing during times of crisis (Maruca, 2001). The sense of crisis provides the stage for leaders to increase their impact or to demonstrate charismatic leadership behaviors (see Chapter 8), which influence followers to a high degree.

Size and structure are the second set of internal moderators of discretion. The larger an organization is, the more likely it is that decision making is decentralized. As an organization grows, the impact of the top managers on day-to-day operations declines. In small organizations, the desires of a top manager for a certain type of culture and strategy are likely to be reflected in the actual operations of an organization. In large organizations, however, the distance between the leader and other organizational levels and departments leads to a decline in the immediate effect of the leaders. For example, the U.S. Postal Service is the largest employer in the world, with more than 650,000 employees. The postmaster's influence is diffused through numerous layers of bureaucracy and probably is not felt by local post office employees. This filtering also could be one reason it is difficult to change large organizations. Even the most charismatic, visionary leader might have trouble reaching all employees to establish a personal bond and energize them to seek and accept change.

One of the causes of internal and external uncertainty is the organization's life cycle or stage of development (Miller, 1987; Nahavandi and Malekzadeh, 1993a). When an organization is young and in its early stages of development, the impact of a leader's personality and decisions is pervasive. The personality and style of the leader/entrepreneur are reflected in all aspects of the organization. The younger an organization is, the more likely it is that its culture, strategies, and structure are a reflection of its leader's preferences. As the organization matures and grows, the leader's influence decreases and is replaced by the presence of a strong culture and a variety of well-established, successful routines. It is often at this stage that the founders of an organization leave and move on to new ventures. The leader's influence, however, becomes strong once again when the organization faces decline. The lack of success and the perceived need to revitalize the organization increase the reliance on the top managers. They once again have the opportunity to shape the organization. The case of A.G. Lafley (see Leadership in Action at the end of this chapter) at P&G illustrates this point. When Lafley become CEO in 2000, P&G faced a crisis in terms of both performance and employee morale. Lafley was the center of attention inside and outside the company as he slowly changed the culture and led the company to profitability. Lafley sees himself as a change agent who focuses on the longer-term good of the company (Jones, 2007).

Mickey Drexler, current CEO at J. Crew and former chief executive of Gap Inc., was credited with Gap's success in the late 1990s. Some even claim that he invented casual chic by allowing the average consumer to be better dressed at a reasonable cost (Gordon, 2004). He was also known for having considerable power. One former Gap employee states, "Mickey is omnipotent. There is nobody who is his equal. There is nobody who is near his equal" (Munk, 1998). Both at Gap and J. Crew, Drexler exercises considerable control and impact over his organization. He makes decisions regarding even minute details of the products and likes to communicate instantly using the public-address system (Kiviat, 2007). Because the Gap was relatively new at the time and was experiencing a revival, Drexler's influence was pervasive. Another example of the leader's impact in the early stages of an organization's life is Oprah Winfrey—the first African American and the third woman to own a television and film production studio with more than $300 million in annual revenue, runs an organization that reflects her high-energy, supportive style (Lee and Turner, 2004).

The last moderator of power and influence of top managers of an organization is the presence, power, and homogeneity of a TMT (Hambrick, 1987). As noted at the beginning of the chapter, upper-echelon leadership often involves working within a team; the presence of the team and how it interacts with the CEO has a strong impact on an organization (Peterson et al., 2003). If an organization does not have a TMT or if it is weak, the impact of its CEO is likely to be more direct. If, on the other hand, the organization is managed by a powerful TMT, such a team will moderate the power and discretion of the individual leader. For example, in 2005, Carl Vogel, the CEO of Charter Communication, a cable company, quit his job partly over frustration over the lack of support from several of the company board members (Grant, 2005). Douglas Pertz was ousted by the company's board only four months after becoming CEO because the company's shares plummeted as soon as he took over (Dash, 2007).

An interesting twist on the role and power of the TMT is the degree to which the members are similar to the leader and the diversity of the board. Much research indicates that leaders often pick board of director members and other top advisors who are similar to them. The more similar the TMT is to the leader, the greater the power of the leader (Miller, 1987). Diversity in the board can have an impact on how the company makes decisions (e.g., Jansen and Kristof-Brown, 2006). Many organizations take into account the importance of heterogeneity in the makeup of the TMT or board of directors. When Mercedes, the German automobile manufacturer, built a plant in Vance, Alabama, the heart of the Deep South, the executive leaders deliberately pieced together a diverse team of executives. It included managers with Detroit automobile experience, several who had worked for Japanese plants in North America, and four Germans (Martin, 1997). The team was designed to provide the best possible mix of experience for running a successful foreign automaker in the United States. The potential problems with a weak board or inattentive and conforming members are obvious in recent corporate scandals such as that of Dick Grasso (see Leadership in Action case in Chapter 5) or at Tyco (Bray, 2005). Because of the importance and potential power of the TMT, it has been the subject of considerable research in the past few years (for a review, see Carpenter, Geletkanycz, and Sanders, 2004). Additionally, many shareholders and stakeholders are increasingly calling for more powerful and involved board members who can closely oversee the actions of the CEO, making board memberships both riskier and more time consuming (Raghavan, 2005).

These external and internal moderating factors limit the power and discretion of strategic leaders and can prevent the leader from making a direct impact on the organization. The next section considers the key relevant, individual characteristics of upper-echelon leaders.

CHARACTERISTICS OF UPPER-ECHELON LEADERS

What impact do executives' personality and other individual characteristics have on their style and the way they run the organization? Are some characteristics or combinations of characteristics more relevant for upper-echelon leadership? Information about upper-echelon leadership characteristics is somewhat disjointed. Research about micro leadership presented throughout this book identified several important dimensions in predicting and understanding small-group leadership; the task and relationship dimensions, in particular, have dominated much of leadership theory for the past 40 to 50 years. Despite the success of those dimensions, however, they do not necessarily provide predictive value when dealing with upper-echelon leadership (Day and Lord, 1988). A number of different studies identify the individual characteristics of upper-echelon leaders.

Demographic and Personality Traits

Older CEOs are generally more risk averse (Alluto and Hrebeniak, 1975), and insider CEOs (as opposed to those who are brought in from outside) attempt to maintain the status quo and are, therefore, less likely to change the organization (Kotin and Sharaf, 1976; Pfeffer, 1983). Researchers also considered the impact of an upper manager's functional background on an organization's strategic choices (Song, 1982), and a body of research explored the various personality characteristics with a recent focus on the impact of charismatic and transformational leadership (e.g., Leban and Zulauf,

2004; Waldman, Javidan, and Varella, 2004), emotions (e.g., Kisfalvi and Pitcher, 2003), and emotional intelligence (e.g., Scott-Ladd and Chan, 2004). The concept of locus of control (see Chapter 3) is one variable that has shown links to upper-echelon decision making. Managers with internal locus of control emphasize research and development (R&D) and frequent product changes. They also tend to be more innovative than those with an external locus of control (Anderson, Hellriegel, and Slocum, 1977). Another measure is the Myers-Briggs Type Indicator (MBTI; see Chapter 3). The overall pattern of results suggests that different MBTI types perceive risk differently and, as a result, select different strategies.

Two common themes that run through the research about individual characteristics of strategic leaders are the degree to which they seek challenge and their need for control.

Most of the leader's personal characteristics studied have some impact on organizational decision making, although the effect is not always strong. Two common themes run through the research about individual characteristics of strategic leaders. They are the degree to which they seek challenge and their need for control (Nahavandi and Malekzadeh, 1993a).

Challenge Seeking

A number of researchers considered the upper-echelon leader's openness to change to be an important factor of strategic leadership. Upper-echelon management's entrepreneurship (Covin and Slevin, 1988), openness to change and innovation, futuricity (Miller and Freisen, 1982), risk taking (Khandwalla, 1976), and transformational and charismatic leadership (Tosi et al., 2004) are all part of this theme. The common thread among these constructs is the degree to which leaders seek challenge. How much is the leader willing to take risks? How much will the leader be willing to swim in uncharted waters? How much does the leader lean toward tried-and-true strategies and procedures? A more challenge-seeking person is likely to engage in risky strategies and undertake new and original endeavors (Nahavandi and Malekzadeh, 1993a). A leader who does not seek challenges will be risk averse and stick with well-established and previously proven methods. The challenge-seeking dimension is most relevant in the way a leader formulates strategy. For example, one leader might pursue a highly risky product and a design strategy that will help produce and market such a product by accepting a high level of failure risk.

Challenge-seeking executives are celebrated in the current climate of crisis in many institutions. Richard Branson's willingness to take risks (see Leading Change in Chapter 6) has been key to his success and his fame. David Rockwell, the visionary behind many of New York's trendiest restaurants, is in high demand because of his creativity and his ability to harness the energy of 90 designers who work for him (Breen, 2002). Monica Luechtefeld, the e-commerce chief of Office Depot with its annual revenue of more than $11 billion, is one of the "fearless mavericks" of e-commerce (Tischler, 2002: 124). She attributes her willingness to take on tasks that others shun to her parents' constant messages of "you can do anything" and "figure it out," an approach she passed on to her son who was raised hearing "Why not?" from her (Tischler, 2002).

Need for Control

The second theme in research about CEO characteristics is the leader's need for control, which refers to how willing the leader is to give up control. The degree of need for control is reflected in the extent of delegation and follower participation in decision making and implementation of strategy. Other indicators are the degree of centralization and formalization or encouragement and the degree of tolerance for diversity of opinion and procedures. Issues such as the degree of focus on process and interpersonal orientation (Gupta, 1984), tolerance for and encouragement of participation and openness, and what one researcher has called "organicity," which generally refers to openness and flexibility (Khandwalla, 1976), are all part of this theme.

The leader with a high need for control is likely to create an organization that is centralized, with low delegation and low focus on process (Nahavandi and Malekzadeh, 1993a, b). The culture will be tight, and focus will be on uniformity and conformity. The leader with a low need for control decentralizes the organization and delegates decision-making responsibilities. Such a leader encourages an open and adaptable culture, with a focus on the integration of diverse ideas rather than conformity to a common idea. The culture will encourage employee involvement and tolerance for diversity of thought and styles (Nahavandi and Malekzadeh, 1993a).

No apparent pattern emerges regarding how controlling the upper echelons of successful organizations are, despite the empowerment trends. In some cases, such as the CEO and TMT of Johnson & Johnson, decentralization and autonomy of various units are built into the credo of the organization and are central to the success of the company (Barrett, 2003). Similarly, A.G. Lafley, CEO of P&G (see Leadership in Action at the end of this chapter), has pushed power and control down to his managers to encourage creativity and flexibility. On the other end of the control spectrum are Mickey Drexler, CEO of J. Crew, who is well known for keeping a hand in every detail of his company, and Carly Fiorina, whose tight control was blamed for the turnover of several top Hewlett-Packard (HP) executives.

An interesting potential impact of a CEO's need for control is the implementation of cultural diversity programs in an organization. If the CEO focuses on uniform approaches and unique cultures, little room exists for cultural diversity. On the other hand, if diversity is one of the issues that the high-control CEO focuses on, the organization is likely to implement diversity programs aggressively in order to achieve the uniform goals set by the CEO. Such a situation appears to have taken place at GE, where Jack Welch pushed cultural diversity and the advancement of women as one of his personal goals. His high-control style was partly responsible for the success of such policies. Herb Stokes, the outspoken CEO of Alliance Relocation Services LLC, is equally relentless about diversity issues. He targets specific minority groups when hiring employees and will not budge until he gets his way (Hofman, 2001). Answering hints of discrimination, he states, "I'm not discriminating at all. I made a conscious decision that I wanted a diverse company, so I recruit from sources—employment agencies, placement companies—that are going to give me diverse people" (Hofman, 2001: 73).

Strategic Leadership Types

The two themes of challenge seeking and need for control impact leaders' decision making and managerial styles and the way they manage the various strategic forces (Nahavandi and Malekzadeh, 1993a, b). First, the upper-echelon leader must understand and interpret the environment of the organization. Second, as the primary decision maker, the leader selects the strategy for the organization. Third, the leader plays a crucial role in the implementation of the chosen strategy through the creation and

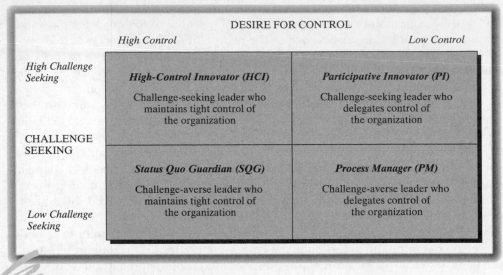

Figure 7-3   Four Strategic Leadership Types.

encouragement of a certain culture and structure and the selection of leaders and managers throughout the organization.

Challenge seeking and need for control combine to yield four strategic leadership types (Figure 7-3). Each type represents an extreme case of strategic management style, and each handles the strategic forces in a manner consistent with his or her basic tendencies and preferences. Given the pressure toward empowerment, employee participation, and the perceived need by many to be unconventional and innovative in all aspects of an organization, it might appear that some types of leaders are more desirable than others. The participative innovator (PI), in particular, could be perceived as ideal. Such an assumption, however, is inaccurate; different leadership styles fit different organizations based on their long-term strategic needs.

Strategic Leadership Types and Their Impact on Organizations

The first strategic type is the high-control innovator (HCI). The HCI leader is a challenge seeker who likes to maintain tight control over organizational functioning. This type of leader sees opportunities in the environment and is willing to use technological advancements to achieve goals. HCIs look for risky and innovative strategies at the corporate and business levels that involve navigating uncharted territories and entering new markets or new industries. (See Table 7-3 for a summary of leaders' impact on an organization and how they perceive and manage the six strategic forces.)

As opposed to the need for innovation when concerned with external factors, HCIs tend to be conservative in the management of their organization. The HCI leader has a high need for control that leads to the creation of a highly controlled culture in which adherence to common goals and procedures is encouraged and rewarded. Decision making is likely to be centralized, with the leader delegating few if any of the major decisions. The ideal organization for an HCI leader is one that is innovative

Table 7-3   The Impact of Strategic Leadership Types on the Six Strategic Forces.

Leader	Perception of Environment	Technology	Strategy	Culture	Structure	Leadership
HCI	Presence of many opportunities for growth and threats from others	Innovation and use of high-technology	High-risk; product innovation; stick to core	Strong dominant culture with few subcultures	Centralized decision making by a few people	Leaders and managers with similar styles and views
SQG	Many threats; desire to protect organization from outsiders	Little focus on innovation unless it helps control	Low risk; few innovations; focus on efficiency	Strong dominant culture; low tolerance for diversity	Centralized decision making by a few people	Leaders and managers with similar styles and views
PI	Many opportunities; tendency to open organization to outside	Encouragement of experimentation; wide use of technology	High risk; product innovation; open to new areas	Fluid main culture; many subcultures; high tolerance for diversity	Decentralized decision making to lowest levels; empowerment and participation	Leaders and managers with many diverse styles and views
PM	Threats and tendency to protect organization from outside	Moderate use of technological innovation	Low risk; few innovations; focus on efficiency	Fluid culture with focus on "no change"; tolerance for diversity	Decentralized decision making; participation	Leaders and managers with many diverse styles and views

Source: Partially based on information in Nahavandi, A., and A. R. Malekzadeh. 1993. Leader style in strategy and organizational performance: An integrative framework. *Journal of Management Studies* 30 (3): 405–425; Nahavandi, A., and A. R. Malekzadeh. 1993. *Organizational Culture in the Management of Mergers.* New York: Quorum Books.

and focused. The employees share a strong common bond and believe in "their way" of managing. Mickey Drexler, discussed previously, provides an example of an HCI. He has been described as a "visionary *and* a control freak" (Gordon, 2004). Although innovative and a risk taker in his strategies and marketing, he keeps a tight control over his organization. Drexler is described as a relentless "store walker" who picks on every detail (Kiviat, 2007). He is also known for his creativity and his ability to pick successful new trends. He states, "I like to race, run and compete. . . . I'd rather make quick mistakes than have long slow successes" (Dicocco, 2006). His COO at the Gap described him this way: "Mickey's always looking for a way to improve. He is always on the road, always talking to people in stores" (Munk, 1998: 82). Another Gap manager noted, "Nothing gets by Mickey. His attention to detail is extraordinary. He looks at threads, buttons, everything. He's difficult and very demanding. He can attack" (71). Both at the Gap and in his new leadership role at J. Crew, Drexler is known for his knowledge and control of every detail. He admits, "I spot details quickly" (Gordon, 2004).

Unlike the HCI, the status quo guardian (SQG) does not seek challenge; however, like the HCI, SQGs want to maintain control (see Figure 7-3). This type of leader needs control over the internal functioning of the organization and is risk averse. SQGs perceive their environment as threatening and tend to want to protect their organization from its impact. They do not seek new and innovative strategies, but rather stick to tried and well-tested strategies (Nahavandi and Malekzadeh, 1993b). The organization run by an SQG leader is not likely to be an industry leader in new-product development and innovation. It, however, might be known for efficiency and low cost.

The ideal organization for an SQG leader is highly focused and conservative with a tight, well-defined culture that expects employees and managers to conform to existing practices and procedures. Decision making is highly centralized, with the SQG leader keeping informed and involved in the majority of decisions. Janie and Victor Tsao, *Inc.* magazine's 2004 entrepreneurs of the year, built their $500-million, 300-person company, Linksys, on frugality, hard work, and tight control of every operation and decision (Mount, 2004). Although they develop networking products and allow employees to run their own projects, the husband-and-wife team believes that their product is neither spectacular nor involves any particular genius—just a good business plan and tight execution. One of their employees described their style: "Victor and Janie really like to see people execute" (Mount, 2004: 68). Tootsie Roll Industries Inc. is another company run by SQG leaders: Ellen Gordon, president, and her husband Melvin, chair of the board, along with four other executives, fully control all operations. Tootsie Roll is named repeatedly as one of the best-run small companies in the United States. Much of the credit for its success goes to the Gordons for their single-minded focus on their business and their benevolent, authority-oriented styles. The company managed to focus on the candy-making business for 100 years and through a number of defensive moves, warded off acquisition attempts. With a narrow strategy and tight controls, the Gordons encourage openness and feedback from employees and continue to build a strong, conservative culture.

The participative innovator is diametrically opposed to the SQG. Whereas the SQG values control and low-risk strategies, the PI seeks challenge and innovation on the outside and creates a loose, open, and participative culture and structure inside the organization. PIs view the environment as offering many opportunities and are open to outside influences that could bring change in all areas, including technology. Similar to the HCI, the PI is a challenge seeker and is likely to select strategies that are high risk. An organization run by a PI is often known for being at the cutting edge of technology, management innovation, and creativity.

The ideal organization for a PI leader is open and decentralized, with many of the decisions made at the lowest possible level, because the leader's low need for control allows for delegation of many of the decisions. The culture is loose, with much tolerance for diversity of thought and practice. The only common defining element might be tolerance of diversity—a "*vive la difference*" mentality. Employees are encouraged to create their own procedures and are given much autonomy to implement their decisions. The key to PI leadership is allowing employees and managers to develop their own structure and come up with ideas that lead to innovative products, services, and processes.

Ricardo Semler (see Leading Change in Chapter 5) is celebrated for his willingness to give up control and empower his employees while implementing innovative management strategies. Not only is Roy Wetterstrom, an entrepreneur who created several businesses, a high risk taker, but he also believes that "to make a big strategic shift, you'll need to take a breather from day-to-day stuff" (Hofman, 2000: 58) and push responsibility down the chain of command. John Chambers, CEO of Cisco Systems since 1995, often introduces himself as the "corporate overhead," serves ice cream to his employees, is open to ideas, is willing to adapt, and relies heavily on others to make decisions (Kupfer, 1998). One Cisco employee described the culture: "John has instilled a culture in which it's not a sign of weakness but a sign of strength to say, 'I can't do everything myself'" (86).

The last type of strategic leader, the process manager (PM), has the internal elements of PI leadership and the external elements of SQG leadership. The PM leader prefers conservative strategies that stick to the tried and tested. PMs are likely to shy away from risky innovation. The PM's low need for control, however, is likely to engender diversity and openness within the organization. Employees are not required to adhere to common goals and culture. As such, they have autonomy, and day-to-day operations are not highly standardized; the basic condition for decision making is not to create undue risk for the organization.

Jon Brock, who was the CEO of the world's No. 1 beer maker until 2006, is a process manager. His company InBev is part Brazilian and part Belgian with headquarters in Louvain, Belgium. It produces the famous Belgian beer Stella Artois and the Brazilian beers Skol and Brahma. Brock is informal, easygoing, and relaxed and makes it clear that he does not want to be the world's biggest brewer, just the best. His strategy focuses on efficiency and increasing profits by cutting costs. He wants to avoid hornets: "We're not going head-to-head with Budweiser, Miller, and Coors. That would be suicidal" (Tomlinson, 2004: 240).

As the former president of American Express and RJR Nabisco and CEO of IBM from 1993 to 2002, Lou Gerstner has a well-established and enviable track record as a strategic leader. He joined IBM at a time when the company was facing one of the most serious crises of its history. Gerstner is a cautious leader. While at RJR Nabisco, he opened the way for reconsideration of many internal processes. He is intelligent and has exceptional analytical skills, but he is careful about change. He strongly believes that change cannot happen unless it is balanced with stabilization (Rogers, 1994), and he is particularly skilled at letting his expectations be known. His approach is to improve existing processes slowly. He has changed some elements of IBM and is proud of the company's slow and steady progress. Some call him an incrementalist rather than a revolutionary who avoids big mistakes but is moving too slowly.

All types of successful and effective leaders can be found in organizations. The need to revitalize our organizations is likely to be the reason we are celebrating innovators. The health-care industry's award to best administrators regularly goes to innovators. The most-admired business executives are those who push their businesses through change. Many uncelebrated SQG and PM leaders, however, are managing highly effective and efficient organizations. For example, the leaders of the much-publicized Lincoln Electric Company are consistently SQGs or PMs. Their organization is a model for using financial incentives in successfully managing performance. Our current tendency to appreciate only change could make us overlook some highly effective managers and leaders.

Strategic Leadership: Culture and Gender

Given the cross-cultural differences in micro-leadership style and the importance and impact of culture on leadership behaviors, one would expect that strategic leadership also differs across cultures to some extent. Cultural values, in particular, can be expected to affect a top manager's decisions and style (Finkelstein and Hambrick, 1996).

Effect of Culture

With little empirical research conducted about the direct effect of culture on executive style, considerable anecdotal evidence suggests similarities and differences across cultures. As organizations become more global, their strategic leaders are also increasingly global, a factor that can attenuate cross-cultural differences. Consider that Lindsay Owen-Jones, who is Welsh, is the current chairman of the French cosmetics company L'Oreal. Nissan, which is owned by French car maker Renault, is run by Carlos Ghosn, who was born in Brazil from Lebanese parents and was educated in France. Swiss Nestlé is headed by Austrian Peter Brabeck-Lethmate. Other companies actively seek to build diverse and multicultural TMTs. For example, half of the senior managers at Citibank and P&G are not from the United States.

Models of cultures, such as those proposed by the GLOBE research (House et al., 2004) and Trompenaars (1994), suggest that patterns of leadership differ from one country or region to another. Particularly, the GLOBE research identified cultural clusters within the countries they researched, each with different implicit leadership theories or CLTs (culturally endorsed leadership theories; Dorfman, Hanges, and Brodbeck, 2004). For example, although most cultures value leaders who have a vision and are inspirational, Anglos, Latin Americans, Southern Asians, and Germanic and Nordic Europeans do so to a greater extent than Middle Easterners. Similarly, participation is seen as part of leadership by Anglos and Nordic Europeans, by not as much by Eastern Europeans, Southern Asians, and Middle Easterners. Columbians want leaders who are proactive and recognize accomplishment without being too proactive in terms of change (Matviuk, 2007). Middle Easterners, more than other cultural clusters, consider self-protection (including

Although most cultures value leaders who have a vision and are inspirational, Anglos, Latin Americans, Southern Asians, and Germanic and Nordic Europeans do so to a greater extent than Middle Easterners.

self-centeredness, status consciousness, and face saving) to be part of leadership (Dorfman et al., 2004). Based on the cross-cultural research and case studies, it is reasonable to suggest that upper-echelon leaders from different cultures will demonstrate different styles and approaches.

For example, being part of the cadre (French word for management) in France means having fairly distinct characteristics (Barsoux and Lawrence, 1991). In the United States, upper-echelon managers are from different social classes with many different skills and backgrounds, but the French upper-echelon leaders are much more homogeneous. In a high-power-distance culture, in which leaders are ascribed much authority and many powers, the cadre comes almost exclusively from the upper social classes. Nearly all have graduated from a few top technical universities (*Grandes Écoles*), where entry depends as much on social standing as it does on intellectual superiority. These schools have a strong military influence and continue to be male dominated. Their goal is to train highly intellectual, highly disciplined students who develop close ties and support with each other well beyond their years in school. The French cadre is, therefore, characterized by intellectual brilliance, ability to analyze and synthesize problems, and excellent communication skills. Contrary to U.S. leaders, the cadre's focus is not on practical issues or the development of interpersonal skills. Cultures with high power distance show little need to convince subordinates of the leadership's ideas (Laurent, 1983). The cadre is expected to be highly intelligent, and its decisions are not questioned.

Many of the members of French upper management have considerable experience in the public and governmental sectors. This experience allows them to forge government–business relationships that do not exist in countries such as the United States. Interestingly, graduates of the *Grandes Écoles* would not consider working for those who received regular university education. This factor perpetuates the homogeneity of the cadre, which in turn creates a group of like-minded executives who agree on many industrial and political issues. By the same token, this like-mindedness can lead to lack of innovation, as the focus on intellect at the expense of action can cause poor implementation.

Effect of Gender

Another area of interest is potential gender differences. Unfortunately, research is lacking on the topic of gender differences in strategic leadership. It is evident that many of the top-level female executives in traditional organizations succeed because their style mirrors that of their male counterparts. As Linda Hoffman, a managing partner at Coopers & Lybrand, states, "Many of the things you must do to succeed are more comfortable for men than women" (Himelstein and Forest, 1997: 68). Eileen Collins, commander of the space shuttle Discovery believes that women often try to do too much and that men are more willing to delegate (Juarez, Childress, and Hoffman, 2005), a sentiment echoed by Judith Rodin, former president of the University of Pennsylvania and president of the Rockefeller Foundation. She states, "Women moving up in their careers often feel they have to be more aggressive, be more like men. They ought to find their own voice" (Juarez, Childress, and Hoffman, 2005). Nonetheless, the more recent accounts of female executives and business owners and their focus on openness, participation, and interactive leadership provide some basis to make deductions about gender differences. It appears that the feminine style of leadership is generally low control. Meg Whitman, CEO of eBay, who has been consistently ranked among the most powerful women in business, states, "I don't actually think of myself as powerful"; instead she relies on relationship building, developing expertise and credibility, and enabling—one of her favorite words—her employees (Sellers, 2004: 161). Similarly, Parmount's Sherry Lansing is famous for her nurturing style, charm, and ability to show empathy (Sellers, 1998). Gail McGovern, president of Fidelity Investments, observes that "real power is influence. My observation is that women tend to be better in positions where they can be influential" (Sellers, 2000a: 148).

Many female leaders, however, play down the gender differences. Judith Shapiro, president of Barnard College suggests, "You need to be supportive of your people because leading is about serving. That's not a girly thing; it's what I believe a strong leader does" (Juarez et al., 2005). She attributes any gender differences to women's social experiences. CEO of the advertising company Ogilvy & Mather since 1997, Shelly Lazarus asserts, "I don't really believe that men and women manage differently. There are as many different styles and approaches among women as there are among men" (Juarez, Childress, and Hoffman, 2005). Whether they are challenge seekers or risk averse, many upper-echelon women leaders, such as those described in the research by Sally Helgesen (1995), encourage diversity of thought and employee empowerment. Their supportive style allows employees to contribute to decision making. In addition, the web structure that some women leaders are reputed to use is flat, with well-informed leaders at the center and without centralized decision making.

As is the case with micro leadership, the type of strategic leadership that is needed depends on the type of environment the organization faces, the industry to which it belongs, and the internal culture and structure that it currently has. Therefore, leaders define and influence strategic forces, and their style also needs to match existing ones. If an organization is in a highly stable industry with few competitors, the need for innovation and openness might not be as great. The appropriate focus in such circumstances would be on efficiency. For such an organization, a highly participative and innovative strategic leadership style might not be appropriate.

HOW DO EXECUTIVES AFFECT THEIR ORGANIZATION?

Regardless of the type of leadership at the top of an organization, the processes through which strategic leaders impact and influence the organization are similar. As the chief decision makers and the people in charge of providing general guidelines for implementation of the strategies, top executives influence their organizations in a variety of ways (Figure 7-4).

Direct Decisions

Leaders' decisions regarding various aspects of the organization shape the course of their organization. The choices regarding the vision and mission for an organization influence all aspects of an organization's functioning. The vision and mission affect the culture of an organization by determining the basic assumptions, what is important, what needs to be attended to first, and what is considered less valuable. Similarly, the choice of strategy is considered to be the almost-exclusive domain of top management (Gupta, 1986).

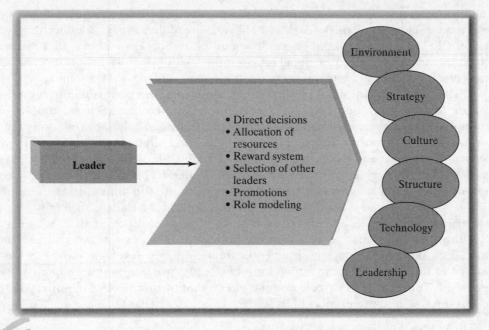

Figure 7-4   Processes Leaders Use to Impact Their Organization.

In addition to the vision, mission, culture, and strategy, the decisions to adopt a new structure, adjust an existing one, or make any changes in the formal interrelationship among employees of an organization rest primarily with top management (Miller and Droge, 1986; Nahavandi, 1993; Yasai-Ardekani, 1986, 1989). The leader can determine the structure of the organization through direct decisions on the type of structure or indirectly through the way employees share and use information. Mickey Drexler of the Gap and J. Crew does not e-mail and does not write memos. He likes to use a public-address system to communicate with people in the office and leave voice messages and communicate face to face. His employees learned to check their voice mail on a regular basis and be ready for his questions at any time (Munk, 1998). A leader who consistently communicates only through formal reporting channels sets up a different structure than one who crosses hierarchical lines and encourages others to do so, as well.

Allocation of Resources and Control over the Reward System

In addition to direct decisions, one of the most powerful effects of top managers on their organization is through the allocation of resources and the control they have over the reward system (Kerr and Slocum, 1987; Schein, 2004). A top executive is the final decision maker on allocation of resources to departments or individuals. If leaders want to encourage continued innovation and creativity, they might decide that the R&D and training departments of the organization will get the lion's share of the resources. Such allocations reinforce certain goals and actions, support a particular organizational culture and strategy, and create structures that facilitate desired outcomes and discourage undesirable ones (Kets de Vries and Miller, 1986; Miller, 1987). Consider that Jeff Bezos, CEO of Amazon.com, believes in spending resources on things that matter, which include simple and functional offices rather than luxurious furniture, creating small creative teams, and borrowing competitors' successful ideas (Deutschman, 2004).

The formal and informal reward systems also can have a powerful impact on the culture of an organization and on the behavior of its members (Schein, 2004). For example, top managers can shape the culture of their organization by rewarding conformity to unique norms and standards of behavior at the expense of diversity of behaviors and opinions (Nahavandi and Malekzadeh, 1988). This process could take place not only through encouragement of certain behaviors but also through the selection of other top managers and the promotion of those who adhere to the leader's culture. Such a process is likely to take place regardless of the leader's style of strategic leadership. For instance, an HCI will be most comfortable with other HCIs, whereas a PI will prefer other managers with a similar style in key positions. A comparable process is likely to take place on an individual employee level. Employees whose actions fit the vision, mission, and culture of the organization are more likely to be rewarded. These processes create domino effects that further lead an organization to reflect the style and preferences of its leader.

Setting the Norms and Modeling

Rewarding certain types of behaviors and decisions is an overt action on the part of the leader; modeling behaviors and setting certain decision standards and norms, however, provide more indirect ways of impacting organizations. In addition to making decisions, the top managers can set the parameters by which others make decisions. CEOs might tell their vice presidents that they will go along with their choice of a new product while also providing them with clear guidelines on which types of products are appropriate and which types of markets the organization should enter. By setting such standards, even without making a direct decision, the CEO still can be assured that the vice presidents will make the right decision.

Another subtle way in which leaders affect their organization is by the types of behavior they model (Nahavandi and Malekzadeh, 1993a; Schein, 2004). A top manager who believes that physical fitness is important might engage in vigorous exercise and invite members of the TMT to join in. Irishman Feargal Quinn, founder and president of Superquinn, a chain of supermarkets, gained a reputation as the "pope of customer service." He focuses obsessively on making sure his customers come back—an obsession that he transfers to his employees (Customer service, 2007). Similarly, A.G. Lafley of P&G reinforces the message about the importance of the customer every chance he gets. Another area in which role modeling can have a powerful impact is in ethics. Lafley considers self-sacrifice and integrity to be essential traits of leadership (Jones, 2007). Bob Moffat, IBM's senior vice president for Integrated Operations, demonstrates the need for hard work by spending 15 to 16 hours a day at the office (Fishman, 2001).

Direct decisions, allocation of resources and rewards, setting of decision norms, and modeling are some of the ways through which a leader impacts the organization. Through these various processes, leaders can make an organization the reflection of their style and preferences. They also provide strategic leaders with considerable power and influence. Such power requires some accountability, which is considered in the next section.

STRATEGIC LEADERS' ACCOUNTABILITY

Chief executive officers and TMTs around the world have considerable power and influence over people's lives. Their actions affect the economic health of countries and citizens. For this burden, CEOs are well rewarded financially and achieve considerable status. The topic of executive compensation, another governance mechanism, attracts considerable attention and criticism (e.g., Bebchuck and Fried, 2004; Dickins and Houmes, 2007). The average salary of CEOs in Standard and Poor's top 500 companies in 2006 was $14.78 million (Executive pay watch, 2007). According to the Economic Policy Institute, in 1978 CEOs were paid an average of 78 times as much as the minimum wage earner; in 2005, that difference increased to 821 times leading the average CEO to earn more before lunchtime on the very first day of work in the year than a minimum wage worker earns all year (Mischel, 2006).

Even ousted CEOs fare well. By some estimate, the cost of various severance packages in 2006 for CEOs was over $1 billion in the United States (Dash, 2007). The list includes David Edmonston, who resigned from Radio Shack after admitting lying on his resume ($1 million severance pay); Home Depot's Robert Nardelli, who received exit packages of more than $200 million, despite poor stock performance and considerable controversy and criticism; Jay Sidhum, who resigned from Sovereign Bancorp amidst cricitism ($73.56 million that includes cash and stock options, 5-year free health care, and consulting contract); William McGuire, who left United Health ($1.1 billion package is still in litigation); and Douglas Pertz, who resigned from Harman International Industries after the stocks dropped during his 4-month tenure and still earned $3.8 million in severance pay (Dash, 2007).

United States executives continue to have some of the highest compensation packages in the world (Buchanan, 2004; Taft and Singh, 2003). Japanese and European executives earn between one-half to one-tenth of comparable U.S. CEOs. These differences could be explained by considering that U.S. executives, as evidenced by a strong U.S. economy, are simply better and more effective than their counterparts all over the world; however, the issue is not that simple. Theoretically, boards of directors determine CEO compensation relative to company performance; the better the financial performance of the company, the higher the CEO's compensation. Therefore, CEO compensation can be an effective tool for motivating and controlling managers. In many cases, company leaders get fair compensation packages and perform well. The instances of lack of performance and high compensation, however, are hard to ignore. Many executives get pay raises that are considerably higher than their company's performance (Bebchuk and Fried, 2004). For example, in 2004 the share of Eli Lilly, the drug manufacturer fell by 19 percent; its CEO, Signey Taurel, got a 74-percent raise (Strauss and Hansen, 2005). After having to pull Vioxx off the market, shares of Merck slumped 30 percent, but the company board gave the CEO, Ray Gilmartin, a $1.4-million bonus and stock options valued at $19.2 million (Strauss and Hansen, 2005). While the beer maker Anheuser-Bush had lackluster performance since hiring a new CEO Patrick Stokes in 2002, his salary has increased by $1.5 million (Strauss and Hansen, 2005). Thomas Renyi took home $13 million in

Table 7-4 Factors That Affect Executive Compensation.

Firm size	The larger the firm, the higher the compensation
Industry competition	Companies often outbid one another to hire top executives
CEO power and discretion	The higher the power of the CEO, the higher the compensation package
Internationalization	Increased internationalization is related to higher executive pay
High stress and instability	CEO jobs are considered high stress, requiring high compensation

total compensation while his bank, Bank of New York, was under investigation for money-laundering charges and the overall performance was well below that of competitors (Mallello, 2005).

Based on these examples and extensive research about CEO compensation (for a recent example, see O'Reilley and Main, 2007), company performance is not the only determinant of CEO compensation. So what determines an executive's worth? Table 7-4 gives a summary of factors that affect executive compensation. One factor that seems to explain the size of executive pay in the United States is the size of the organization (for a recent study, see Geiger and Cashen, 2007): the larger the organization, the larger the CEO's compensation package, regardless of performance. Another factor seems to be the competition for hiring CEOs. As organizations outbid one another, salaries continue to increase. For example, Conseco, after firing its CEO and experiencing financial crisis, still paid former GE Capital executive Gary Wendt a $45-million cash signing bonus to forfeit his GE options and become their CEO (Colvin, 2001b).

Organizations in which top managers have more discretion also tend to have higher pay (Cho and Shen, 2007). Additionally, research shows that top management pay and company performance are more aligned when the company's board of directors is dominated by members from outside the organization (Conyon and Peck, 1998). Other research that considers the impact of internationalization found that increased internationalization is related to higher CEO pay (Sanders and Carpenter, 1998). The thought is that the high demands put on CEOs and the instability of their positions must be balanced with high salaries. These high salaries, now somewhat standard in U.S. industry, show no end in their upward trend. The result is the creation of a new, powerful U.S. managerial class and a widening of the gap between high and low levels of organizations.

The highly paid top executives have become popular heroes whose names are part of our everyday life. Based on economic and organizational theory, environmental forces will push a nonperforming leader to be replaced. Ideally, elected federal, state, and city officials who do not perform are not reelected. Similarly, the board of directors replaces a CEO who does not manage well. The principal of a school with poor academic performance of its students and a high dropout rate would be fired by the school board. These ideal situations do not seem to be common, however. Many powerful leaders are not being held accountable for their actions. They continue to hold positions of power and influence regardless of their organization's poor performance, ethical abuses, and social irresponsibility. It is not common in the United States for a company CEO or public officials to resign when they fail to live up to the promises they made. When their organizations cause major disasters or commit illegal acts, the CEOs escape unscathed. The CEO of Exxon accepted none of the responsibility for the *Valdez* fiasco. After the Bhopal disaster, with several thousand dead and hundreds of thousands injured, the CEO of Union Carbide was not replaced. Our elected officials continue to represent us poorly. It took years of mismanagement before any GM president was fired. Even then, he was replaced by a member of the inner circle that supported him.

For the benefit of organizational and social functioning and well-being, it is essential that the tremendous power, influence, and status of CEOs be accompanied by accountability and responsibility to their various constituents. Such accountability exists on paper but is hardly ever executed. The power and impact of upper-echelon leaders are undeniable. Their credibility and ability to further impact their organizations, however, can increase only with more accountability.

Leading Change   Kavita Ramdas at the Global Fund for Women

The Global Fund for Women is a San Francisco-based nonprofit organization committed to equality and social justice focused on helping women achieve full equality and participation worldwide (Global Fund for Women, 2007). The organization was founded in 1987 to raise funds to support women-led enterprises and activities that promote better health, economic, education, and social welfare for women (Social Capitalist, 2007) and has awarded over $56 million to 3371 women organizations in 165 countries (Global Fund for Women, 2007) since its creation. The organization embraces such principles as freedom and liberty for individuals, dignity for people, tolerance, education, economic independence, nonviolence, and peace. It has granted funds to causes including a Buddhist orphanage in Sri Lanka, an organization for coordination of peasant women in Bolivia, empowering women in Nepal, legal aid for women in China, and women's rights organization in Guatemala (Global Fund for Women, 2007; Patel, 2007)

The fund's current president and CEO, Kavita Ramdas, named one of the world's top 20 entrepreneurs in 2002 and holder of many other international awards, is a tireless advocate for changing women's situation in all aspects of life around the world. She suggests that there has been an undeclared
(Continued)

Leading Change   (Continued)

"war" against women around the world through increases in abuse, health crises, silence in case of abuse and neglect, and lack of resources going to support women worldwide (Now with Bill Moyers, 2004). Ramdas leads the effort to change the situation of women one person and one organization at a time, advocating for the cause she passionately represents.

Ramdas was born into a prominent secular Hindu family in Mumbai India. Her father is a retired former head of the Indian navy turned peace and antinuclear activist and her mother is highly active in social causes. Ramdas is married to a Pakistani man Zulfiqar Ahmad raised in a secular Muslim family and himself a peace advocate (Curiel, 2002), a union that has generated many concerns and comments in both India and Pakistan. At 18, Ramdas volunteered to work in a small farm in India until a village elder told her to use her education and compassion to tell the world about them (Sowing the seeds, 2006). Ramdas is educated in the United States (bachelor's degree from Mount Holyoke and masters from Princeton) and represents her organization with as much ease to U.N. officials and CEOs of major philanthropic organizations, as to villagers in all parts of the world. One of her colleagues states, "Kavita is one of the very few people who, when she enters a room, you know there's a presence. It's important in this work that we do to have that type of presence and grace—to hold people's attention" (Curiel, 2002).

Ramdas says, "For me, what I do at the Global Fund is so deeply connected to my sense of who I am and what I can give back to this world and what my responsibilities are to this world. It's a deep sense of commitment. It's not a 9–5 job" (Curiel, 2002). Ramdas' passion for what she does allows her to lead her organization to make changes to improve women's lives one step at a time.

Sources: Social capitalists: Global Fund for Women, 2007. http://www.globalfundforwomen.org/cms/ (accessed June 17, 2007); Now with Bill Moyers, 2004. http://www.pbs.org/now/politics/ramdas.html# (accessed June 17, 2007); Entrepreneurs who are changing the world, 2007. http://www.fastcompany.com/social/2007/profiles/profile17.html (accessed June 17, 2007); Curiel, J., 2002. "A woman's work," *San Francisco Chronicle,* November 10. http://www.sfgate.com/cgi-bin/article.cgi?f=/chronicle/archive/2002/11/10/CM148265.DTL&type=news (accessed June 17, 2007); Hatnell, C., 2004. "Kavita Ramdas on feminist philanthropy," *Alliance,* September. http://www.allavida.org/alliance/sep04b.html (accessed June 17, 2007); Patel, P., 2007. "Money makers: five questions for Kavita Ramdas," *Houston Chronicle,* June 12. http://www.chron.com/disp/story.mpl/business/4884490.html (accessed June 17, 2007); Empowering women. 2004. *The Common Wealth.* http://www.globalfundforwomen.org/cms/content/view/63/98/ (accessed June 17, 2007); Sowing the seeds of global change, 2006. www.mtholyoke.edu/cic/about/reasons.shtml?num=2 (accessed June 18, 2007).

UNIQUE CHALLENGES OF NONPROFIT ORGANIZATIONS

Nonprofit organizations are private organizations that cannot make a profit for its owners or members but can charge fees for services or membership. Other terms used to describe such agencies that are private, nonprofit, and with a public purpose include voluntary, not-for-profit, philanthropic, and nongovernmental organizations (NGOs; Weiss and Gantt, 2004). While many of the leadership and organizational principles that apply to business and other organizations are also relevant in nonprofit organizations, some of their distinguishing characteristics present them with unique leadership challenges. The case of Kavita Ramdas in Leading Change in this chapter provides an example of a leader of a nonprofit organization. The primary purpose of her organization is public good, and their source of funding is donations through grants, foundations, and individuals.

Characteristics of Nonprofit Organizations

Many of the characteristics that identify nonprofit organizations are related to tax-status. Other characteristics include

➤ *Operate without profit.* Although nonprofit organization charge for services or membership and many generate and use considerable sums of money, all the funds are reinvested to support the operations of the organization. Many nonprofits are highly "profitable"; however, all excess funds are reinvested to achieve their mission.

➤ *Public service mission.* The primary mission of a nonprofit organization is to serve the public good, whether it is health care (hospitals), education (schools and universities), churches, community improvement, or foundations with a broad purpose.

➤ *Governed by voluntary board of directors.* As opposed to business organizations that have paid board of directors, the governing boards of nonprofits are staffed by volunteers with a stake or interest in the mission of the organization.

➤ *Funded through contributions.* Whereas charging fees is a source of revenue for many nonprofit organizations, their primary sources of funding are contributions, grants, and donations from individuals, government agencies, and other foundations.

There are many organizations around the world that fit into the nonprofit category. Examples in the United States include the American Cancer Society, National Geographic Society, the Metropolitan Museum of Arts, Stanford University, Planned Parenthood, the Ford and Rockefeller Foundations, the National Association for the Advancement of Colored People (NAACP), and the YMCA and YWCA. Around the world, NGOs make considerable contributions to improving social, human, political, economic, and ecological conditions. Organizations such as Doctors without Border (*Médecins sans Frontières*), OXFAM, an international relief agency, the International Red Cross, and the International Wild Life Funds are just a few that encourage development and support communities in crisis around the world. These organizations survive and achieve their goals by using funds they obtain through various means. For example, physicians volunteer their time through Doctors without Borders and provide health care in remote areas of the world; OXFAM provides funds and resources to combat global poverty and social injustice.

The public-good mission of nonprofits, along with the voluntary participation of many of their employees, contributors, and other stakeholders create a particular burden on leaders of such organizations to lead through a collaborative and trust-based style.

Leadership Challenges

The leadership of nonprofit organizations involves the same principles as other organizations. Their leaders must help individuals and groups set goals and guide them in the achievement of those goals. The public-good mission of nonprofits, along with the voluntary participation of many of their employees, contributors, and other stakeholders create a particular burden on leaders of such organizations to lead through a collaborative and trust-based style. In most cases, individual donors, except for tax benefits when applicable, do not get tangible benefits from their donation, and the resources they contribute do not always stay in their community. The nonprofit is based to a great extent on the principles of altruism and self-less contribution.

As much as integrity, trustworthiness, and self-sacrifice are elements for all leadership situations, they are even more so in the nonprofit organizations. Without the profit motive, which legitimately guides business organizations and the rewarding of its leaders (e.g., top leaders being compensated with company shares), the nonprofit organizations are likely to attract leaders with a stronger focus on civic contribution. The role of leaders in nonprofit organizations is that of an intermediary (Butler and Wilson, 1990). The leader guides the organization to allocate the resources, such as donations or grants, to various receivers turning the resources that are trusted to the organization into social good (Figure 7-5). Kavita Ramdas and her Global Fund for Women distribute the resources they gather throughout the world to improve women's lives. In his commencement address at the University of Maryland, Brian Gallagher—president and CEO of the United Way, the $5-billion umbrella organization for large number of charities—emphasizes the importance of service to the community and states that his organization "improves lives by mobilizing the caring power of communities" (Gallagher, 2006: 6). Susan Berresford, president of the Ford Foundation,

Figure 7-5   Role of Leaders of Nonprofit Organizations.

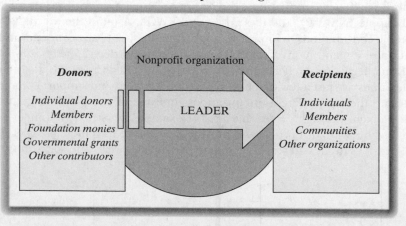

which considers itself to be a resource for innovative people and institutions world-wide, leads an organization that has as its mission to strengthen democratic values, reduce poverty, promote international cooperation, and advance human achievement (Ford Foundation Mission, 2007). The organization aims to achieve these goals by providing grants to qualified groups and organizations.

One of the major challenges that leaders of nonprofit organizations face is how to recruit, retain, and motivate employees, many of whom are volunteers, without having access to substantial monetary rewards. Even in the case of paid employees, salaries are often lower than comparable positions in business organizations. The leaders of nonprofits, therefore, require considerable skills in motivating and inspiring their followers. In many cases, followers have joined the organization because they are passionate about its mission; however, passion alone does not always lead to effectiveness. An additional factor is that the structure of many nonprofits is relatively flat with few employees and few layers of management. Effective leadership requires empowerment, use of all available resources, often by harnessing the power of teams, and participation to creatively solve problems without many resources.

According to recent studies, nonprofit organizations are facing a leadership crisis because of a significant shortfall of qualified leaders (Tierney, 2006). As more nonprofit organizations are created and step in to address growing social challenges not addressed by government or business organizations, the need for effective leadership increases. According to the Bridgespan Group's 2006 study, the total number of nonprofit organization has tripled over the past 20 years, but because of demographic shifts, retirement, and lack of active recruitment and development, the supply of potential leaders has not kept up (Tierney, 2006). One of the challenges leaders of nonprofits, therefore, face is the recruitment, retention, and development of future leaders. Such a task is much simpler in business organization where considerable resources are dedicated to recruitment and development and access to a pool of leaders from competitors is much easier.

Although many of the processes involved in leading nonprofit organizations are similar to those used in business organization, leaders of nonprofits need a particular emphasis on building relationships and trust and on the development of future leaders.

SUMMARY AND CONCLUSIONS

Many of the same processes apply to the upper levels as to the small group levels of leadership. Upper-echelon leadership, however, adds a new level of complexity to the process by focusing the leader on a whole organization rather than a small group or department and by giving the leader discretion with far-reaching influence over decisions. In addition, upper-echelon leaders focus on external constituencies as well as the internal environment and in so doing are required to lead with a team of other executives.

An integrated approach to upper-echelon leadership considers the leader to be a formulator and implementer of strategy. Therefore, in addition to considering the need to match the leader to existing strategy and other organizational elements, the integrated approach also considers the role of the leader's individual characteristics and style in the selection of various organizational elements and the implementation of decisions. The matching concept, which views the CEO primarily as an implementer of existing strategy, is also useful when selecting a leader to implement a newly charted course.

Two major themes run through the diverse research about top management characteristics. The first theme is the leader's degree of challenge seeking and preference for risk and innovation. The second is the leader's need for control over the organization. The combination of these two themes yields four types of strategic leaders: HCI, SQG, PI, and PM. These four types each exhibit different preferences for the direction and management of their organization. They exert their influence through direct decisions, allocation of resources and rewards, and the setting of norms and the modeling of desired behaviors. Through these processes, strategic leaders gain considerable power and influence. Such power is accompanied by generous compensation packages. Accountability for the actions of top executives, however, is still limited.

Although many of the processes involved in leading nonprofit organizations are similar to those used in business organization, leaders of nonprofits need a particular emphasis on building relationships and trust and on the development of future leaders. Overall, the area of strategic leadership, whether in business or nonprofit organizations, provides a different and important perspective to the study of leadership. Strategic leaders face many challenges that micro leaders do not. The study of strategic leaders is also a fertile area for integrative research linking micro and macro factors.

LEADERSHIP CHALLENGE: THE BOARD OF DIRECTORS (BOD) AND CEOs

Public corporations are led by CEOs and other upper-echelon leaders who, in turn, report to shareholders and boards of directors (BODs). Interestingly, even though the board oversees the CEOs, decides on terms of employment and salaries, and monitors their performance, the CEOs are, more often than not, the people who nominate board members. The justification is that CEOs are well placed to know what type of expertise they need on the board and should have a BOD they can work with. The relationship between BOD and CEO is a complex and interesting one.

1. What are the potential ethical and conflict-of-interest issues arising from CEO involvement in the selection of board members?
2. How can these issues be addressed?

REVIEW AND DISCUSSION QUESTIONS

1. How are current changes in organizations affecting the differences between micro and macro leadership?
2. What are the strategic forces in organizations?
3. What is the role of the upper echelon in managing the strategic forces in the formulation and implementation of strategy?
4. Provide examples for each of the moderating factors on the impact of leadership in organizations.
5. What are the major themes in various constructs used to describe upper-echelon leaders?
6. Describe each of the four strategic leadership types. Provide examples of each type.
7. How do culture and gender affect strategic leadership?
8. Describe each of the processes used by leaders to influence strategic forces in their organizations. Which of the processes is most important? Why?
9. What is the upper echelon's responsibility in organizational actions and performance?
10. What are the unique characteristics and challenges of nonprofit leadership?

EXERCISE 7-1:   UNDERSTANDING STRATEGIC FORCES

This exercise is designed to help you understand the role of leaders in managing the six strategic forces of environment, strategy, culture, structure, technology, and leadership presented in the chapter.

The Scenario

You are a member of a school board for a medium-sized middle (junior high) school in a major western city. The city has experienced tremendous growth in the past 5 years, and as a result, the student body increased by 20 percent without much change in facilities and relatively limited increases in funding. The classrooms are overcrowded, much of the equipment is old, teachers have limited resources to enrich the curriculum, and the sense of direction is unclear. During the same time period, the school slowly developed one of the poorest records for student academic performance and drop-out rate.

Earlier to the past few years, however, the school held a well-established reputation as one of the most creative and academically sound schools in the city. Traditionally, parent involvement and interest in the school varied greatly. Similarly, the faculty are diverse in their approach, tenure, and backgrounds, but the majority demonstrate dedication to their students and are committed to the improvement of the school.

Because of a number of recent threats of lawsuits from parents over equal opportunity issues, several violent incidents among the students, and the poor academic performance, the principal was asked to resign. Many parents, teachers, and board members blame her for a laissez-faire attitude and what appears to be a total lack of direction and focus. Problems and complaints were simply not addressed and no plan articulated for dealing with the changes that the school was experiencing.

After a 2-month multistate regional search and interviews with a number of finalists, the school board narrowed its search for the new principal to two candidates.

The Candidates

J.B. Davison is 55 years old, with a doctorate in education administration and B.A. and M.A. degrees in education. He previously served as principal at two other schools where he was successful in focusing on basic academic skills, traditional approaches, discipline, and encouragement of success. Before moving to school administration, he was a history and social studies teacher. The board is impressed with his clear-headedness and no-nonsense approach to education. He readily admits that he is conservative and traditional and considers himself to be a father figure to the students. He runs a tight ship and is involved in every aspect of his school.

Jerry Popovich is 40 years old. She holds M.A. and Ph.D. degrees in education administration with an undergraduate degree in computer science. She worked in the computer industry several years before teaching science and math. She worked as assistant principal in one other school and is currently the principal of an urban middle school on the West Coast. She successfully involved many business and community members in her current school. The board is impressed with her creativity and her ability to find novel approaches. She considers one of her major strengths to be the ability to involve many constituents in decision making. She describes herself as a facilitator in the education process.

(*Continued*)

Understanding Strategic Forces Worksheet: Comparing the Candidates

In helping you decide on which person to recommend, consider how each would handle and balance the six strategic management forces of environment, strategy, culture, structure, technology, and leadership.

Strategic Forces	J. B. Davison	Jerry Popovich
Environment		
Strategy		
Culture		
Structure		
Technology		
Leadership		

Discussion Items

How are the two candidates different?

What explains the differences between them?

Your Choice

Who would you recommend for the job? Why?

EXERCISE 7-2:   YOUR ORGANIZATION

This exercise is designed to illustrate the potential impact of an upper-echelon leader on the organization. Before starting this exercise, clearly define the department, team, or organization that you are rating. Your instructor may also provide you with several vignettes to use in your evaluation.

Rate your organization or team on the following items, using the following scale:

1 = Strongly disagree

2 = Somewhat disagree

3 = Neither agree nor disagree

4 = Somewhat agree

5 = Strongly agree

_____ 1. Decision making in my organization is centralized.

_____ 2. A strong, thick culture exists in my organization.

_____ 3. We are always coming up with new ways of doing things.

_____ 4. A few people make most of the important decisions.

_____ 5. The organization consists of many subgroups and cliques.

_____ 6. Our primary concern is efficiency.

_____ 7. We are known for our ability to innovate.

_____ 8. We are open to differing points of views.

_____ 9. Employees are empowered to make many decisions without checking
             with management.

_____ 10. We have not changed our course much in the past few years.

_____ 11. We take many risks.

_____ 12. Many rules and procedures are established for our tasks.

_____ 13. People are encouraged to do their own thing.

Scoring: Reverse score for items 5, 6, 8, 9, and 13 (1 = 5, 2 = 4, 3 = 3, 4 = 2, 5 = 1).

Organizational structure: Add items 1, 4, 9, and 12. Maximum score is 20. A higher score indicates a more centralized, control-oriented structure.
Total: _____

Organizational culture: Add items 2, 5, 8, and 13. Maximum score is 20. A higher score indicates a unicultural organization where diversity is not encouraged.
Total: _____

Strategy: Add items 3, 6, 7, 10, and 11. Maximum score is 25. A higher score indicates risk taking and innovation.
Total: _____

Discussion Issues
Based on your organization's score on the structure, culture, and strategy scales, what would you predict the organization leaders' strategic leadership style to be?

EXERCISE 7-3: INFLUENCE PROCESSES

This exercise is designed to help you identify the processes that upper-echelon leaders use to impact their organization and most particularly its culture. After reading each of the following scenarios, identify the processes that the leaders and TMT are using to impact the organization.

Brain Toys Executives

Stanley Wang, the CEO of Brain Toys, joined the organization a few years before the founder, J. C. Green, decided to retire. It became clear early on that Stanley was destined to rise fast. With a B.S. degree in engineering and graphic design, an MBA, and several years of experience in computer software design, he fit right in the Brain Toys culture. He was bright, witty, analytical, and competitive. J.C. took a liking to him and put him in charge of several high-visibility projects with potential for high impact and big budgets. Stanley performed every time. Within the first 2 years, Stanley won all the internal awards that Brain Toys gives its managers. Several of his peers maliciously credited Stanley's love of running rather than his technical and managerial competence as the cause of his success. Stanley ran with the boss every day before work, and they trained for many races together.

The Soft-touch Leader

Leslie Marks was proud of her accomplishment as one of the few executives in the male-dominated information technology field. As the president of Uniform Data Link, she describes herself as a "soft-touch" leader. "I just don't believe in heavy-handed leadership. People have to be able to express themselves and that is when you get the best out of them. Our best ideas come from all levels." She keeps an open door for all employees and has moved her office from the third floor to the first. She often comes to work in jeans and spends a lot of time with the engineers brainstorming on technical problems. She changed many of the evaluation and promotion procedures and asked several less-educated but highly experienced employees to work with her on important projects.

The Hospital Economist

Joseph Hadad graduated with a doctorate in economics and health-care administration from a major southwestern university and after many years of work in various health-care organizations, Hadad was named as the top administrator of a major Phoenix hospital. As an economist and a strong believer in fair pay, Hadad focused much time with the human resource managers, revamping the hospital's compensation and benefit plan. The old system based on seniority was all but dismantled and replaced with a pay-for-performance system that ties the pay of all employees, including the physicians, partially to the hospital's financial performance. The plan allows for some flexibility for 2 years, whereby employees are not penalized for poor performance, but only rewarded for good financial health. After 2 years, they shared in the good and the bad. Most of the hospital's employees complain that Hadad seemed to care about nothing else. Many also note a major change in everybody's behaviors.

Influence Process Worksheet

Influence Method	Stanley Wang	Leslie Marks	Joseph Hadad
Direct decisions			
Allocation of resources			
Reward system			
Selection and promotion of other leaders			
Role modeling			

SELF-ASSESSMENT 7-1:   WHAT IS YOUR STRATEGIC LEADERSHIP TYPE?

This exercise is a self-rating based on the four strategic leadership types presented in the chapter. You can also use the scale to rate your organizational leaders. For each of the items listed, please rate yourself using the following scale. (You can also use the items to rate a leader in your organization.)

> 0 = Never
> 1 = Sometimes
> 2 = Often
> 3 = Always

_2_ 1. I enjoy working on routine tasks.
_3_ 2. I am looking for new ways of doing things.
_1_ 3. I have trouble delegating tasks to my subordinates.
_3_ 4. I like my subordinates to share the same values and beliefs.
_1_ 5. Change makes me uncomfortable.
_3_ 6. I encourage my subordinates to participate in decision making.
_1_ 7. It is difficult for me to get things done in situations with many contrasting opinions.
_1_ 8. I enjoy working on new tasks.
_2_ 9. I feel comfortable giving power away to my subordinates.
_1_ 10. I consider myself to be a risk taker.

Scoring: Reverse scores for items 1, 5, 6, 7, and 9 (0 = 3, 1 = 2, 2 = 1, 3 = 0).

Challenge-seeking score: Add items 1, 2, 5, 8, and 10. Your score will be between 0 and 15. Transfer the score to challenge-seeking line (vertical line) on the following grid.
Total: ____8____.

Need-for-control score: Add items 3, 4, 6, 7, and 9. Your score will be between 0 and 15. Transfer the score to control line (horizontal line) on the following grid.
Total: ____10____.

What Is Your Strategic Leadership Type?
Where do your two scores intersect? For example, if you have a score of 5 on control and 10 on challenge seeking, your scores indicate that you are a participative innovator.

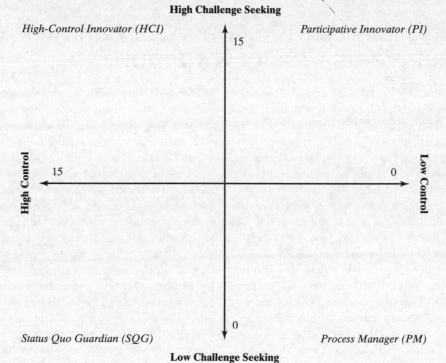

High Challenge Seeking

High-Control Innovator (HCI)   Participative Innovator (PI)

15

High Control   15   0   Low Control

0

Status Quo Guardian (SQG)   Process Manager (PM)

Low Challenge Seeking

Leadership in Action: A.G. Lafley Reinvents Procter & Gamble

The venerable consumer goods company Procter & Gamble (P&G) was founded in 1837 and is known globally for its products primarily directed at women, with brand such as Tide, Ivory, Pampers, Crest, Clairol, Cover Girl, and Pantene, just to name a few. In spite of its history and well-known brands, P&G faced turbulent times in the 1990s. Particularly, it lost market share in many areas and failed to successfully launch new products for a number of years, a problem that its previous CEO, Durk Jager and many analysts attributed to P&G's stodgy and sometimes stifling culture that "procterized" employees to fit a specific mold (Parker-Pope, 1998). With a focus on internal promotions and sets of guidelines called "Current Best Approaches" that informed employees on how to do most everything, the company was comfortably on its way to joining other disappearing business dinosaurs.

Those days are long gone. P&G is once again highly profitable and growing. Company observers and insiders agree that P&G has changed significantly: It now demonstrates energy, enthusiasm, hope, a new openness, and an outward-looking focus that were sorely lacking just a few years ago (Buckley, 2005). The man credited with much of the success is the soft-spoken and understated A.G. Lafley, who became CEO in 2000 and was named one of the best CEOs for 2006 by Harvard's Kennedy School of Government and U.S. News and World Reports (Jones, 2007). He quietly and effectively changed the culture and the performance of the company, a stark contrast to Jager, who attempted to shake up the old culture by shocking it and only survived in his position for 18 months. Often seen at the company's Cincinnati, Ohio, headquarters in an open-collar dress shirt, Lafley, a 25-year P&G veteran, changed the culture and refocused the company strategy on expanding its successful brands, growing by acquiring other successful products such

as Clairol, Germany's Wella, and the acquisition of Gillette, constantly reminding the more than 138,000 employees in 80 countries that the consumer is boss and instilling both a sense of urgency and hope for the future (Markels, 2006).

Lafley's actions that so drastically changed P&G are deceptively simple. He uses what he calls "Sesame Street language" to "make things simple because the difficulty is making sure everybody knows what the goal is and how to get there" (Markels, 2006). He consistently and patiently repeats those same messages any chance he gets. In a highly symbolic, practical, and well-publicized move, he transformed the executive offices in the top floor of the company's headquarters into a leadership training center moving the senior executives to the same floors as their staff. He created open offices, including one for himself and a couple of other executives with whom he spends most of his time, and room to bring in employees and managers from all over the world to train and meet one another. Lafley believes that the arrangement is not only symbolic of the new openness in the company and shows the importance of learning at P&G, but also conducive to collaboration, creativity, and flexibility: "I wanted an environment that would be more collaborative, more in touch, more designed to bring human beings together. . . . I wanted a place that was low tech and high touch" (*@Issue*, 2004). Other physical changes include replacing the executive conference room's rectangular table with a round one that creates a sense of equality and is more conducive to interaction (Berner, 2003).

Lafley's ability to transform P&G so quickly is even more surprising given Lafley's quiet leadership, or maybe precisely because his style seems to so well fit the family culture at the company. He states, "I'm a low-ego guy. I don't have problems putting the greater good of the company or the P&G brands way ahead of my personal aspirations or achievements" (Jones, 2007). Words such as *quiet, soft-spoken, affable, calm*, and *consensual* are often used to describe Lafley along with mentions of his sharp focus and unbending resolve. He believes in cross-functional teams, gives employees and managers room and responsibility to make decisions, and oversees them as a coach. Jeff Immelt, GE's CEO, who asked Lafley to be on his company's board, states that he is "an excellent listener. He's a sponge" (Berner, 2003). Lafley himself favors sitting back and observing people in meetings and asking questions only to get to the key issues, a process he calls "peeling the onion." Describing himself, he says, "I'm not a screamer, not a yeller. But don't get confused by my style. I am very decisive" (Berner, 2003). Regarding power, he believes, "The measure of a powerful person is that their circle of influence is greater than their circle of control" (Sellers, 2004: 162). He values leadership development and spends many Sunday evenings reviewing the performance of the company's senior executives along with P&G's head of human resources, Richard Antoine, looking for ways to help each of them become more effective (Berner, 2003) and ways of mentoring the highest potential ones to achieve their best, including many women whom he promoted to key positions. The new openness he created, his focus on people, and a strategy of emphasizing the best brands all paid off for Lafley and P&G. John Pepper, a highly popular former CEO of P&G, said, "It's now clear to me that A.G. is going to be one of the great CEOs in this company's history" (Berner, 2003).

QUESTIONS

1. What strategic forces impact P&G?
2. How would you describe Lafley's strategic leadership style?
3. What are the factors that contributed to his success at P&G?

Sources: Berner, R., 2003. "P&G: New and improved," *Business Week Online,* July 7. www.businessweek.com/magazine/content/03_27/b3840001_mz001.htm (accessed December 7, 2007); Buckley, N., 2005. "The calm reinventor," *The Business Standard,* January 31. http://www.businessstandard.com/ft/ storypage.php?&autono=179421 (accessed February 9, 2005); Jones, D., 2007. "P&G CEO wields high expectations but no whip," *USA Today,* February 19. http://www.usatoday.com/money/companics/management/2007-02-19-exec-pandg-usat_x.htm (accessed July 25, 2007); Markels, A., 2006. "Turning the tide at P&G," *U.S. New and World Reports,* October 22. http://www.usnews.com/usnews/news/articles/061022/30lafley.htm (accessed July 25, 2007); Parker-Pope, T., 1998. "New CEO preaches rebellion for P&G's cult," *The Wall Street Journal,* December 11: B1, B4; "Corporate design foundation: Procter & Gamble's A.G. Lafley on design," *@Issue: The Journal of Business and Design,* 9, no. 1 (2004). www.cdf.org/9_1_index/lafley/lafley.html (accessed February 8, 2005); Sellers, P., 2004. "eBay's secret," *Fortune,* October 18: 160–178.

Leading

Part III focuses on the practical business of leading groups and organizations including participative management and leading teams, leading change, and developing leaders. After studying Part III, you will understand the challenges of managing teams and leading individuals, teams, and organizations through change and the approaches, methods and tools available for developing leaders.

The management of organizations has changed considerably in recent years. The pressure for faster decision making, increased flexibility, managing diversity, and addressing global challenges represent just a few of the changes. To be successful and remain competitive, organizations must be able to respond quickly to increasing environmental pressures. The use of teams and increased employee involvement in decision making and implementation are central themes in organizations' attempts to remain adept in the face of these demands and remain effective. One of the biggest challenges facing leaders and organizations is how to navigate the constant change they face. The often-used cliché that "the only constant is change" has never been more accurate. The ability for leaders to guide others through what some people call the "permanent white water" environment of today's organization is crucial. Our highly dynamic organizations must also find ways to help their leaders change and develop to be ready to address the unknown challenges they will face.

Chapter 8 focuses on teams and participative management. Chapter 9 completes the discussions we started in chapter 6 regarding the change-oriented theories of leadership by considering how leaders manage change. Finally, chapter 10 explores the various ways in which leaders can improve and develop their skills and renew themselves to be able to continue being effective.

Participative Management and Leading Teams

Do you have as much sense as a goose? When geese fly in the "V" formation, the whole flock adds considerably more to its flying range than if each bird flew alone. Whenever a goose falls out of formation, it suddenly feels the drag and resistance of trying to fly alone and quickly gets back into formation to take advantage of the power of the formation. When the lead goose gets tired, it rotates back in the wing, and another goose flies point. The back geese honk from behind to encourage those up front to keep up their speed. Finally, when a goose gets sick and falls out, two geese fall out of formation with it until it is either able to fly or it is dead. They then launch on their own, or with another formation, to catch up with the group.
—ANONYMOUS

Do not wait for leaders. Do it alone, person to person.
—MOTHER TERESA

After studying this chapter, you will be able to:

■ Understand when and why participation should be used to improve leadership effectiveness.
■ Explain the role of culture in the use of participative leadership.
■ Specify the elements of effective delegation.
■ Clarify the role of leadership in self-managed teams.
■ Explain the principles of self-leadership.

Employee participation has been a central issue in leadership for many years. Almost all of our past and current models address this issue in some form. For example, Theory Y of management recommends a higher level of employee participation than Theory X does. The Theory Y manager allows employees to set the direction for their development and provides them with support, whereas the Theory X manager controls employees rather than involving them in decision making. Likewise, the initiation-of-structure construct from the behavioral approach assumes that the leader is the one who provides the structure; no mention is made of subordinate participation in the development of the structure. The consideration behaviors in the same model contain of a stronger participation component. Fiedler's task-motivated leader makes decisions alone; the relationship-motivated leader involves the group. Finally, the degree of follower participation in decision making is the pivotal concept for the Normative Decision Model.

This chapter focuses on the concept of participative management in its past and current uses in leadership. It discusses the use of participation and delegation and the challenges they present for leaders, and it considers the special characteristics of teams and the importance of self-leadership.

WHEN SHOULD PARTICIPATION AND TEAMS BE USED?

The idea of using teams rather than relying only on the individual leader to make decisions in organizations has been at the forefront of management practice for many years (for recent reviews, see Ilgen et al., 2005). Use of team and participative management occurs along a continuum. On one end, the leader retains all control and makes all decisions without any consultation or even information from the subordinates; on the other end, the leader delegates all decision making to followers and allows them the final say. Few leaders use extreme autocratic or delegation styles; rather, most rely on a style that falls somewhere in between. Similarly, few organizations are either entirely team based or make no use of teams at all. Most fall near the middle of the continuum, with a combination of teams and traditional hierarchical structures (Figure 8-1). For example, although still maintaining many elements of traditional structures, Ford Motor Company relies on teams for many tasks while maintaining a traditional centralized structure. Nancy Gioia, director of Sustainable Mobility Technology and Hybrid Vehicle Programs at the company, states, "As a director I'm very participative and hands-on when my team needs me to be. Ford's hybrid

Figure 8-1   The Continuum of Participation.

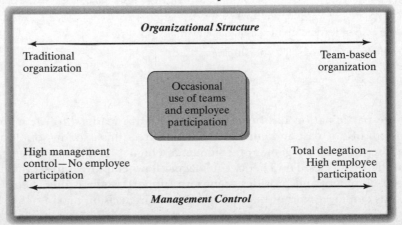

team has some of best and brightest minds around. I have complete confidence in their technical breadth and depth" (Peterson, 2005). Space X is a company at one extreme of the participation continuum. The company is trying to build faster, cheaper, and better rockets that will allow for commercial space travel. Founder and CEO Elon Musk relies on small groups of smart, motivated people to provide the creativity and innovation essential to the company. With a horizontal structure, no organizational charts, no red tape, and a culture that values teamwork and intelligence, employees are required to work together. Musk states, "I think it's really unacceptable here for anyone to bear a grudge" (Reingold, 2005: 78).

Longitudinal research about employee involvement conducted by researchers at the University of Southern California indicates that organizations can reap many benefits from employee participation and involvement initiatives, which include such methods as information sharing, group decision-making, and the use of teams, empowerment, profit sharing, and stock-option plans (Lawler, Mohrman, and Ledford, 1995). Their goal is to increase employee involvement and participation in the organization. Studies show that the adoption of such programs results in clear, positive impact on performance, profitability, competitiveness, and employee satisfaction (Lawler, Mohrman, and Ledford, 1995). Other research further suggests that using teams, participation, and engagement provide a positive impact (e.g., Forde, Slater, and Spencer, 2006) and can be used effectively in a number of business and not-for-profit organizations, such as schools (San Antonio and Gamage, 2007), health care (e.g., Mosadegh-Rad and Yarmohammadian, 2006), and urban planning (Repetti and Prélaz-Droux, 2003). Yet, others argue for using participative management and democratic systems within organizations as the only way to harness the talents of employees (Manville and Ober, 2003).

Royal Phillips Electronics, Europe's largest electronics outfit, is counting on cross-boundary cooperation and conversations and employee participation to revive the company. In his attempts to reenergize Phillips, CEO Gerard Kleisterlee gathered people who wanted to make a contribution, regardless of rank and position in the company. Kleisterlee states that "these meetings result in very clear goals and much better cooperation between the different divisions" (Wylie, 2003: 45). Genencor International, a health-care products company with 1200 employees located in Palo Alto, California, is another example of the use and benefits of employee participation. With turnover rates of 4 percent compared with the industry average of 18 percent, and growing sales, the company is an example of a successful business that relies on worker involvement and input. The employee participation started when the company built its headquarters in 1996 and offered employees the opportunity to give input into the physical design of the building. Research scientists' requests for windows in their labs as well as other employees' suggestions for a "main street" that encourages interaction were implemented with success (Haley, 2004). Employees are now regularly polled to get information about their benefit preferences and the company emphasizes a philosophy that Cynthia Edwards, the vice president for technology, believes supports employees' entire lifestyle. Based on employee suggestions, Genencor provides various commuter assistance programs, a number of on-site services such as dry cleaning and eye-glass repair, and emergency childcare. Employees get to nominate exceptionally productive colleagues for recognition and celebrate their success during Friday afternoon parties, where they have the chance to mingle and get to know one another (Haley, 2004).

The CEO until 2005, Jean-Jacques Bienaimé, believes, "If you want employees to be productive, you have to create a nurturing environment and let them be creative" (Haley, 2004: 98). Jim Sjoerdsma, the company vice president of human resources, suggests that the $700-per-employee cost for such benefits is a wise investment compared with the average $75,000 cost for recruiting and training a new employee. According to Sjoerdsma, "These programs pay for themselves" (99).

Criteria for Participation

Despite its many potential benefits, participation is not a cure-all. Its use is more appropriate in some situations than in others and should follow a contingency approach. After many years of debate and research about participative management in social sciences and management, clear criteria suggest when participative decision-making would be most appropriate (Table 8-1).

Overall, if the organization, its leaders, and its employees are ready for participative management, if the task is complex and involves no strong time pressures, and if employee commitment is important, leaders should rely on participative decision making. If time pressure is genuine or the leader, followers, or organization are not ready, however, then participation is not likely to yield many benefits. If leaders show a high need for control, are highly task oriented, and were previously successful in using an autocratic style of leadership, they are unlikely to be able to implement participation easily. Furthermore, for followers who show little need to participate or who trust their leader, participation might not be required or at least might not lead to better results than the leader making the decision alone. Additionally, some organizational cultures are more supportive of participation than others, thereby making the use

Table 8-1   Criteria for Use of Participation.

Criteria	Description
When the task is complex and multifaceted and quality is important	Complex tasks require input from people with different expertise; people with different points of view are more likely to deliver a quality decision.
When follower commitment is needed in successful implementation	Follower participation increases commitment and motivation.
When there is time	Using participation takes time; legitimate deadlines and time pressures preclude seeking extensive participation.
When the leader and followers are ready and the organizational culture is supportive	Participation can only succeed if both leader and followers agree to its benefits, are trained in how to use it, and are committed to its success. The organizational culture must encourage or at least tolerate employee participation.
When interaction between leader and followers is not restricted by the task, the structure, or the environment	Participation requires interaction between leaders and followers; such interaction is only possible if restrictions because of factors such as geographic location, structural elements, or task requirements are minimized.

of participation more or less easy. Another factor in using participation is whether the task or the structure limits its use. If followers cannot interact easily with one another and with the leader, either because of task or because of geographic restrictions, participation might not be appropriate. In some instances, legal and confidentiality requirements, such as in personnel decisions, may preclude participation.

The case of Kiwi Airlines presents a classic example of the potential pitfalls of mismanaged participation (Bryant, 1995). When Kiwi Airlines was founded in 1992, it quickly became the symbol of all that is good about participative and egalitarian leadership. Created by a group of former Eastern Airline pilots and other employees, Kiwi promised not to repeat any of Eastern's mistakes and aimed at creating a family atmosphere for all its employees. The employees were all owners with varying degrees of shares and the corresponding pride and desire for involvement, control, and commitment that come from ownership. All decisions were made with full participation. All employees, regardless of levels, pitched in to get the job done and deliver the quality service that soon earned Kiwi honors in surveys of airline quality. The airline quickly grew to more than 1000 employees with more than 60 daily flights. One of the pilot-founders and then chairman of Kiwi, Robert W. Iverson, attributed the stunning growth and success to the employees' commitment and the organization's egalitarian culture. Kiwi was truly a symbol of the benefits of participation and involvement. In 1994, the bubble burst. Kiwi's board, which included fellow founders and owners, booted Iverson out of office. This event revealed serious management and organizational deficiencies within the airline. The dark side of participation was an amazing lack of concern for management decisions. Many employee-owners failed to follow management directives if they did not agree with them. Employees demanded input in every decision, a factor that led to stagnation in decision making and an inability to act to solve problems. Iverson admitted, "One of the stupidest things I ever did was call everybody owners. An owner is somebody who thinks he can exercise gratuitous control." The case of Kiwi Airlines demonstrates the ineffective use of participation. A few managers could have handled many of the decisions more effectively and efficiently than the employees did through participation.

> **If the organization, its leaders, and its employees are ready for participative management, if the task is complex and involves no strong time pressures, and if employee commitment is important, leaders should rely on participative decision making. If time pressure is genuine or the leader, followers, or organization are not ready, however, then participation is not likely to yield many benefits.**

The Role of Culture

An important issue when considering the use of participation is national cultural values. Factors such as collectivism and power distance (Hofstede, 2001); team-oriented, participative, and autonomous leadership (House et al., 2004); and cross-cultural organizational cultures (Trompenaars, 1994) affect whether leaders can use participation successfully. The GLOBE research findings suggest that collectivistic cultures tend to emphasize cooperative team processes, compensation and promotion that take into consideration the group (Gelfand et al., 2004). Furthermore, the more the power distance, the less likely it is that teams will be empowered (Carl, Gupta, and Javidan, 2004). Other GLOBE findings suggest that a humane orientation, which includes concern for others and responsibility for their well-being, may also be a factor supporting team-oriented and participative leadership (Kabasakal and Bodur, 2004).

Japanese culture, with its strong emphasis on conformity, consensus, and collectivity at the expense of individual goals, supports the use of participative management despite its relatively high power distance. Participation in Japan is a mix of group harmony and consensus, with elements of directive leadership (Dorfman et al., 1997). In this vertical collectivistic culture, individuals are expected to sacrifice their personal goals for the good of the group. In China, establishing cooperative goals and taking care of relationships help participative leadership (Chen and Tjosvold, 2006). Mexico, which is also relatively high on collectivism, power distance, and masculinity, has a well-established tradition of autocratic leadership without a history of participative leadership (Dorfman et al., 1997). Similar cultural patterns are found in Dominicans (Montesino, 2003). In such cultural contexts, neither the leader nor the followers find participation desirable. Additionally, in the cross-cultural organizational cultures which Trompenaars labels the Eiffel Tower—France, for example—the focus is on performance through obedience and respect for legitimate authority (Trompenaars, 1994). In this environment, a leader is ascribed great authority and is expected to know much; asking for subordinate participation may be perceived as weakness and as an indicator of lack of leadership ability.

Cultures such as the United States and Australia, with relatively egalitarian power distributions and vertical individualism, pose a different challenge. The low power distance allows for participation, but the value placed on individual autonomy and individual contribution can be an obstacle to cooperation in a team environment. In horizontal individualist cultures such as Sweden, participation and team cooperation are much easier because all individuals are equal. Furthermore, appropriate team behaviors vary considerably from one culture to another (Kanter and Corn, 1993). An effective team member in Japan is above all courteous and cooperative; members avoid conflict and confrontation (Zander, 1983). In the United States, effective team members speak their mind, pull their weight by contributing equally, and participate actively, yet they expect to be recognized individually. German employees are taught early in their careers to seek technical excellence. In Afghanistan, team members are obligated to share their resources with others, making generosity an essential team behavior. In Israel, a horizontal collectivistic culture, values of hard work and contribution to the community drive kibbutz team members. The Swedes are comfortable with open arguments and will disagree publicly with one another and with their leader. Each culture expects and rewards different types of team behaviors.

These cross-cultural differences in team behavior create considerable challenges for leaders in culturally diverse teams. Success depends on accurate perceptions and careful reading of cross-cultural cues. Leaders must be flexible and patient and be willing not only to listen to others, but also to question their own assumptions. Additionally, they must keep in mind that many behavioral differences stem from individual rather than cultural sources. The only constant in the successful implementation of teams is the leader's sincere belief in the team's ability to contribute to the organization (Marsick, Turner, and Cederholm, 1989). Such belief is necessary regardless of the cultural setting.

THE ISSUE OF DELEGATION

Delegation differs from participation in a number of ways, although many managers consider it an aspect of participation. For example, many leaders define themselves as participative managers if they delegate tasks to their subordinates. Although this practice might lead to more subordinate participation in decision making, the goal of delegation is not necessarily to develop employees or create more commitment. Neither does delegation always involve power sharing with employees. The goal of delegation can be as simple as helping a leader ease an excessive workload. In its most basic form, delegation is simply handing off a task to someone else; in a more complex form, delegation can resemble participative management.

Benefits of Delegation

Delegating tasks well to subordinates is gaining importance as managerial ranks are thinned and managers see their workloads increase. Production managers find themselves with twice as many subordinates to supervise; sales managers see their territories double in current attempts to develop leaner structures. Many organizations undergoing such restructuring are testing team-based approaches. Until such techniques are well accepted and implemented, however, judicial delegation is still a basic tool for a leader's success. The potential benefits of delegation include the following:

➤ Delegation frees up the leader's time for new tasks and strategic activities.
➤ Delegation provides employees with opportunities to learn and develop.
➤ Delegation allows employees to be involved in tasks.
➤ Delegation allows observation and evaluation of employees in new tasks.
➤ Delegation increases employee motivation and satisfaction.

Aside from being a time- and stress-management tool for leaders, delegation allows subordinates to try new tasks and learn new skills, thereby potentially enriching their jobs and increasing their satisfaction and motivation. When employees perform new tasks, the leader has the opportunity to observe them and gather performance-related information that can be used for further development, evaluation, and preparation of employees for promotions. As such, delegation can be one of the tools available to leaders for succession planning in their organizations. Employees who consistently perform well on new tasks and are willing to accept more responsibility could be the future leaders of the organization. Without the opportunity to grow outside of their current job, no data are available for accurate forecasting of their performance in higher-level positions.

The final benefit of delegation is, as is the case with participation, increased employee involvement and commitment. Job enrichment and participative management research (Hackman and Oldham, 1980) indicates that employees who are interested in growth quickly feel stifled and unmotivated if they do not have the opportunity to participate in new and challenging tasks. Delegation of such tasks to them helps increase their motivation and commitment to the organization.

Guidelines for Good Delegation

As with any tool, misuse and misapplication of delegation can be disastrous. Leaders must take into account some relatively simple principles (see Table 8-2 for a summary). One of the major issues for leaders is to separate delegation from dumping. Leaders need to delegate a mix of easy, hard, pleasant, and unpleasant tasks to their subordinates. If only unpleasant, difficult, and unmanageable tasks are assigned consistently to

Table 8-2   Guidelines for Good Delegation.

Guideline	Description
Delegate, do not dump	Delegate both pleasant and unpleasant tasks; provide followers with a variety of experiences.
Clarify goals and expectations	Provide clear goals and guidelines regarding expectations and limitations.
Provide support and authority	As a task is delegated, provide necessary authority and resources such as time, training, and advice needed to complete the task.
Monitor and provide feedback	Keep track of progress and provide feedback during and after task completion at regular intervals.
Delegate to different followers	Delegate tasks to those who are most motivated to complete them as well as those who have potential but no clear track record of performance.
Create a safe environment	Encourage experimentation; tolerate honest mistakes and worthy efforts that may fail.
Develop your own coaching skills	Take workshops and training classes to assure that you have the skills to delegate.

subordinates, while leaders complete the high-profile, challenging, and interesting projects, delegation becomes dumping. One of the major complaints of subordinates regarding delegation is this exact issue. To reap the benefits of delegation, a variety of tasks should be delegated and the leaders should pay particular attention that their delegation is viewed as balanced.

Effective delegation requires more than handing off a task. Leaders must be clear about their expectations and support their followers while they perform the task. The support might include informing department members and others outside the department that the task has been delegated. Another aspect of support involves providing training and other appropriate resources that allow the subordinate to learn the needed skills. It also might require regular monitoring and clarification of reporting expectations (Foster, 2004). It is easy for an eager subordinate to make decisions that are inconsistent with the leader's goals if the leader does not properly monitor the situation.

One area that cannot and should not be delegated is personnel issues. Unless an organization or department is moving toward self-managed teams (SMTs) that have feedback and performance-evaluation responsibility, the task of performance management remains the leader's responsibility. For example, it would be inappropriate for a manager to delegate the task of disciplining a tardy employee to a subordinate or to expect the latter to monitor and manage the performance of coworkers. The situation of SMTs often changes this guideline; such changes will be discussed later in the chapter.

Leaders must choose carefully the followers to whom they delegate. The easiest choice for most managers is to delegate to the few people they know will do the job well (the in-group). Although such a position is logical and effective, at least in the short run, a leader must be aware of the in-group/out-group issues presented in Chapter 3. Therefore, leaders must select individuals who, in addition to having shown potential, are also eager and motivated to take on new tasks and have the appropriate skills for the new challenge. A follower who is competent and eager but who failed recently on one assignment might also be a good choice but could be overlooked if leaders keep relying on their few trusted in-group members. Delegation of tasks to a varied group of followers further provides leaders with a broad view of the performance capabilities and potential of their team or department. Finally, creating a climate that tolerates mistakes and encourages continued training for the leader is essential.

Why Do Leaders Fail to Delegate?

Certain circumstances justify a leader's unwillingness to delegate. In some cases, followers are not ready for delegation, are already overworked, or have such specialized jobs that they cannot be assigned new tasks. Such situations are rare, however, and the considerable benefits of delegation far outweigh many of the arguments typically presented against it (Kouzes and Posner, 1987; Miller and Toulouse, 1986). The most commonly used argument against delegation is "I will get it done better and faster myself." Table 8-3 presents the typical excuses and counterarguments for not delegating.

The excuses for not delegating tasks may be valid in the short run. By taking a long-term view that considers the leader's personal effectiveness as well as the development of followers, however, many of the excuses are no longer valid. Not only does effective delegation require effort and resources such as training, but it also allows leaders to focus on higher-level strategic issues instead of day-to-day routines. One underlying factor that might stop many leaders from delegating is their personality style, their need for control, and their fear of losing

Not only does effective delegation require effort and resources such as training, but it also allows leaders to focus on higher-level strategic issues instead of day-to-day routines.

Table 8-3   Excuses for Not Delegating.

Excuses	Counterarguments
My followers are not ready.	The leader's job is to get followers prepared to take on new tasks.
My subordinates do not have the necessary skills and knowledge.	The leader's responsibility is to train followers and prepare them for new challenges.
I feel uncomfortable asking my followers to do many of my tasks.	Only a few tasks cannot be delegated. Balancing delegation of pleasant and unpleasant tasks is appropriate.
I can do the job quicker myself.	Taking time to train followers frees up time in the long run.
Followers are too busy.	Leaders and followers must learn to manage their workload by setting priorities.
If my followers make a mistake, I am responsible.	Encouraging experimentation and tolerating mistakes are essential to learning and development.
My own manager may think I am not working hard.	Doing busy work is not an appropriate use of a leader's time. Delegation allows time to focus on strategic and higher-level activities.

it. For example, as discussed in Chapter 4, a Type A's need for control often leads to lack of delegation. Competitiveness also might lead Type A leaders to compete with their followers. Other personal needs, such as a need for power (McClelland, 1975), also might cause leaders to want to maintain power over all activities, preventing them from delegating.

Although for many years management and leadership included participation and delegation, they recently took on a new form in team-based organizations with the introduction of empowerment and concepts such as self-leadership, which are considered next.

Leading Change   Anne Sweeney of Disney-ABC Television

Anne Sweeny is quick to give her team at Disney-ABC Television credit for her success and for being considered one of the world's most powerful fifty women by *Forbes* and *Fortune* magazines. She states, "It's wonderful to be recognized, not just my accomplishments, but for my teams' accomplishments" (Bisoux, 2006: 18). Sweeney started in the entertainment business as a page with ABC and has been credited with success in creating new and unique organizations including Nickelodeon, where she became a senior vice president, and being a key player in launching the highly successful FX network. She serves as president of Disney-ABC Television since 2004 and co-chair of the Disney Media Networks. She is considered a turnaround artist and a team player and someone who hires talented people and lets them be creative (The new wave, 2005). She is credited with the revival of the network with shows such as *Desperate Housewives* and *Extreme Makeover: Home Edition* (Streisand, 2005). She has further been part of the creative and risky deal to make the networks' most popular shows available to iPod users.

Passion for innovation and ability to embrace change are characteristic of Sweeney. She has heeded her mother's advice to do what she was passionate about, considering the obstacles only those that she created for herself. Sweeney believes, "there's a lot more gratification in trying something that you haven't done and didn't know how to do" (Kantrowitz, Peterson, and Wingert, 2005). "I love the jobs that I don't know how to do. I love getting in there and figuring it out and making some good, big, noisy mistakes along the way, which is really part of the learning process (Bisoux, 2006: 22).

To run her company, she looks to people who, like herself, are able to think differently and outside the box and have passion and excitement for what they do. She is known to be a hands-off manager, who though she is an over-achiever does not grab the limelight and tends to let her people do their job with little interference (Streisand, 2005). As a mother of two, she juggles her personal life and career and talks about herself as one of the most tired person in show business rather one of the most powerful ones. Describing Sweeney, Peter Tortorici, president of MindShare Entertainment and the former head of CBS Entertainment, states, "It's hard when the world is bowing at your feet to remember who you really are besides the person who sits in that chair. Anne seems to never have lost touch with that" (Streisand, 2005). Anne Sweeney believes that her first priority is to create the environment that allows creative people to do their job (Myers, 2006).

Sources: Bisoux, T., 2006. "The change artist," *BizEd*, November–December: 18–24; Kantrowitz, B., H. Peterson, and P. Wingert. 2005. "How I got there: Anne Sweeney." *MSNBC.com: Newsweek*, October 24. http://www.msnbc.msn.com/id/9756479/site/ newsweek (accessed July 8, 2007); Streisand, B., 2005. "Learning her ABCs," *U.S. News and World Report*, September 4. http://www.usnews.com/usnews/biztech/articles/ 050912/12sweeney.htm (accessed July 8, 2007); Myers, J., 2006. "Disney's ABC's Anne Sweeney: Inspiring creativity and embracing technology," *Media Village.com*, February 13. http://www.mediavillage.com/jmlunch/2006/02/13/lam-02-13-06/#continue (accessed July 8, 2007); "The new wave," 2005. *Fast Company*, December: 50.

EVOLUTION OF PARTICIPATIVE MANAGEMENT: TEAMS AND SELF-LEADERSHIP

In many organizations that have made teams a permanent part, if not a cornerstone, of their structures, teams create a formal structure through which participation in decision making can be achieved. The use of teams in U.S. and other Western organizations was triggered to a great extent by Japan's economic success and its reliance on teams and participative management (Nahavandi and Aranda, 1994). Although teams are not uniformly successful and they often pose considerable challenges for organizations (for research about teams and their potential problems, see Allen and Hecht, 2004; Salas, Stagl, and Burke, 2004), a large number of organizations continue to use them as a technique to increase creativity, innovation, and quality.

Characteristics of Teams

While groups and teams both involve people working together toward a goal, they differ along several dimensions. Table 8-4 outlines those differences.

Rackspace, a San Antonio-based Web-hosting company, prides itself on being "fanatical" about customer service. Their goal is to "exceed expectations and make the customers say 'wow'" (Overholt, 2004: 86). To achieve this goal, David Bryce, the customer-care vice president who joined the company in 1999, reorganized employees, known as Rackers, into teams of eight. Each team, guided by a team leader, includes account managers and billing and technology specialists who are able to quickly and fully address their customers' needs without having to refer them to anyone else. Each team is its own profit center and responsible for its own performance, which is measured based on customer retention and satisfaction. Each team and its members can earn considerable bonuses if they perform well. The team approach to outstanding customer service paid off for Rackspace. The company continued to turn a profit while its competitors went bankrupt during the dot-com bust; the gift baskets that customers send their service teams to express their gratitude are just an added bonus (Overholt, 2004).

Table 8-4   Groups and Teams.

Groups	Teams
Members work on a common goal.	Members are fully committed to common goals and a mission they developed.
Members are accountable to manager.	Members are mutually accountable to one another.
Members do not have clear stable culture and conflict is frequent.	Members trust one another and team enjoys a collaborative culture.
Leadership is assigned to single person.	Members all share in leadership.
Groups may accomplish their goals.	Teams achieve synergy: $2 + 2 = 5$.

Sources: Hackman, J. R. 1900. *Groups That Work (and Those That Don't).* San Francisco, CA: Jossey-Bass; Katzenbach, J. R., and D. K. Smith. 1993. *The Wisdom of Teams: Creating the High Performance Organization.* New York: Harper Business.

As illustrated by the Rackspace example, the first distinguishing characteristic of a team is full commitment of its members to a common goal and approach that they often develop themselves. Members must agree that the team goal is worthwhile and agree on a general approach for meeting that goal. Such agreement provides the vision and motivation for team members to perform. The second characteristic is mutual accountability. To succeed as a team, members must feel and be accountable to one another and to the organization for the process and outcome of their work. Whereas group members report to the leader or their manager and are accountable to this person, team members take on responsibility and perform because of their commitment to the team.

The third characteristic of a team is a team culture based on trust and collaboration. Whereas group members share norms, team members have a shared culture. Team members are willing to compromise, cooperate, and collaborate to reach their common purpose. A collaborative climate does not mean the absence of conflict. Conflict can enhance team creativity and performance if handled constructively. Related to the team culture is shared leadership. Whereas groups have one assigned leader, teams differ by sharing leadership among all members. While this shared leadership is essential, leaders continue to play an important role in the success of teams. Particularly, leaders can help encourage a culture of collaboration (Taggar and Ellis, 2007) and help team learning by empowering members (Burke et al., 2006).

Synergy means that team members together achieve more than each individual is capable of doing. Whereas group members combine their efforts to achieve their goal, teams reach higher performance levels.

Finally, teams develop synergy. Synergy means that team members together achieve more than each individual is capable of doing. Whereas group members combine their efforts to achieve their goal, teams reach higher performance levels. As groups become teams and reach their peak level of performance potential, they may provide their organizations with benefits such as cost reduction because of less need for supervision, higher employee commitment, enhanced learning, and greater flexibility (Cordery, 2004).

Self-Managed Teams

Whereas traditional managers and leaders are expected to provide command and control, the role of leaders in teams is to facilitate processes and support team members. The leader sets the general direction and goals; the team members make all other decisions and implement them. This new role for leaders is most obvious in self-managed teams (SMTs), which are teams of employees with full managerial control over their own work (for some examples, see Barry, 1991; Spencer, 1995). Numerous organizations, such as Toyota, General Foods, and P&G, have used SMTs successfully for decades. In fact, P&G once claimed its SMTs were one of the company's trade secrets (Fisher, 1993). SMTs exhibit the following characteristics:

➤ *Power to manage their work.* SMTs can set goals, plan, staff, schedule, monitor quality, and implement decisions.

➤ *Members with different expertise and functional experience.* Team members can be from marketing, finance, production, design, and so on. Without a broad range of experience, the team cannot manage all aspects of its work.

➤ *Absence of an outside manager.* The team does not report to an outside manager. Team members manage themselves, their budget, and their task through shared leadership. Stanley Gault, once chairman of Goodyear, the largest tire manufacturer in the United States, said that "the teams at Goodyear are now telling the boss how to run things. And I must say, I'm not doing half-bad because of it" (Greenwald, 1992).

➤ *The power to implement decisions.* Team members have the power and the resources necessary to implement their decisions.

➤ *Coordination and cooperation with other teams and individuals affected by the teams' decisions.* Because each team is independent and does not formally report to a manager, the teams themselves rather than managers must coordinate their tasks and activities to assure integration.

➤ *Team leadership based on facilitation.* Leadership often rotates among members depending on each member's expertise in handling a specific situation. Instead of a leader who tells others what to do, sets goals, or monitors achievement, team leaders remove obstacles for the team and make sure that the team has the resources it needs. The primary role of the team leader is to facilitate rather than control. Facilitation means that the leader focuses on freeing the team from obstacles to allow it to reach the goals it has set.

The success of the team depends on a number of key factors. First, the members of a team have to be selected carefully for their complementary skills and expertise (for some examples of research findings, see Kang, Yang, and Rowley, 2006; Van der Vegt, Bunderson, and Oosterhof, 2006). The interdependence among the members makes creation of the "right" combination critical. The right combination depends as much on interpersonal skills as on technical skills. Second, the team members need to focus on and be committed to the team goal. For example, individuals from different functional departments such as marketing or production, although selected because of their expertise in particular areas, need to leave the department mind-set behind and focus on the task of the team. Third, the team task must be appropriately complex, as well as provided with the critical resources it needs to perform the task. Finally, the team needs enough power and authority to accomplish its task and implement its

Figure 8-2   Building Trust.

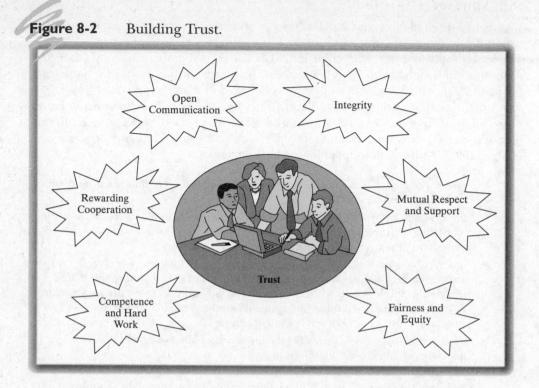

ideas. The sources of team power presented in Chapter 5 are available to the team to allow it to perform its job.

Building an effective team is a time-consuming process that requires interpersonal team-building skills and extensive technical support. The development of trust, a common vision, and the ability to work well together all depend on appropriate interpersonal skills. Trust requires a number of factors as presented in Figure 8-2. To build trust, team members must demonstrate integrity, hard work, and mutual respect. They must reward cooperation rather than competition, be fair to one another, and communicate openly. They, further, must believe that their leaders—inside and outside the team—are predictable, have their best interests at heart, and will treat them fairly (Cunningham and MacGregor, 2000).

Once the trust and goals are established, tackling complex tasks requires timely technical training. Many of these interpersonal and technical functions traditionally fall on the leader's shoulders. Leadership in teams, however, is often diffused, a factor that puts further pressure on individual team members to take on new tasks and challenges.

Helping Teams Become Effective

Several factors can help make teams effective (Hackman, 2005). Specifically, teams must be created with a real and challenging purpose in mind, be empowered to take action, and have the right amount and type of support. Even though strategies to make individuals more competent and effective will impact a team's overall ability

Applying What You Learn
Using a Sports Team Model in Management

Organizational behavior expert and Harvard professor Nancy Katz suggests that managers can learn from sports teams how to make teams more effective (Katz, 2001). Here are some guidelines based on her work:

- Encourage cooperation and competition. The first leads to cohesion; the second energizes team members to do their best.
- Provide some early wins by assigning smaller, short-term, clearer tasks. Early successes build the team's confidence and create a success spiral.

- Break out of losing streaks through positive thinking, challenging the team to succeed, and focusing team members on outside rather than internal causes for failure.
- Take time to practice; during practice the focus should be on learning and experimentation rather than success.
- Keep the membership stable to develop cohesion and give members time to learn to work together.
- Review performance, particularly mistakes and failures; analyze problems, and learn from them.

to be productive, teams often need specialized support and interventions to develop synergy. Possible team-training activities include the following (Day, Gronn, and Salas, 2004):

➤ *Team building* to clarify team goals and member roles and set patterns for acceptable interaction

➤ *Cross training* to assure that team members understand one another's tasks

➤ *Coordination training* to allow the team to work together by improving communication and coordination

➤ *Self-guided correction* to teach team members to monitor, assess, and correct their behavior in the team

➤ *Assertiveness training* to help team members express themselves appropriately when making requests, providing feedback, and other interactions among themselves

As we will discuss later in this chapter, one of the responsibilities of team leaders is to help the team get the necessary training.

Self-Leadership

One of the applications of participative management and teams is the concept of self-leadership. With the increasing use of teams in organizations, many of the traditional roles of leaders are undergoing change. As we empower individual employees and provide them with training in various areas of business, we expect them to make increasingly independent decisions. Teams are designed to complement individual employees' skills. SMTs are responsible for continuous assessment and improvement of their own product, the design of their work, and all other work processes that affect them. Leaders are elected or rotated, and individuals are pressured to accept responsibility for their decisions and actions.

These changes shift the focus of attention away from the leader to the subordinates. Charles Manz and Henry Sims first proposed a model for leadership that involves self-leadership and self-management by each team member (Manz and Sims, 2001; for a recent review, see Neck and Houghton, 2006). Self-leadership is the process of leading people to lead themselves (Manz and Neck, 2004). The concept suggests that instead of leaders who rely on fear (the "strong man"), focus on narrow exchange relationships (the "transactor"), or inspire commitment while discouraging thinking (the "visionary hero"), leaders and followers must focus on leading themselves. As a result, team members must be taught and encouraged to make their own decisions and accept responsibility to the point where they no longer need leaders. Self-leadership within teams means that all team members set goals and observe, evaluate, critique, reinforce, and reward one another and themselves. In such an environment, the need for one leader is reduced; team members set goals and decide how to achieve them. Increased use of technology, the information revolution, and the preponderance of knowledge workers all support the need for self-leadership, which involves a focus on behaviors, providing natural rewards, and engaging in constructive thought patterns (for a detailed discussion, see Manz and Neck, 2004). Specifically, self-leaders

> *Develop positive and motivating thought patterns.* Individuals and teams seek and develop environments that provide positive cues and a supportive and motivating environment.

> *Set personal goals.* Individuals and teams set their own performance goals and performance expectations.

> *Observe their behavior and self-evaluate.* Team members observe their own and other team members' behaviors and provide feedback and critique and evaluate one another's performance.

> *Self-reinforce.* Team members provide rewards and support to one another.

The role of formal leaders is, therefore, primarily to lead others to lead themselves or "to facilitate the self-leadership energy" within each subordinate (Manz and Sims, 1991: 18). Contrary to views of heroic leadership, whereby the leader is expected to provide answers to all questions and to guide, protect, and save subordinates, the concept of self-leadership suggests that leaders must get their subordinates to the point where they do not need their leader much. In effect, through the use of job-design techniques, the development of a team culture, proper performance management, and the modeling of self-leadership, the leader sets up internal and external substitutes for leadership. The right job design and the team are the external substitutes (see Chapter 3). The employees' developing skills and internal motivation serve as internal substitutes for the presence and guidance of a leader (see Exercise 7-2). Some of the strategies for the development for self-leaders include the following:

> Listen more; talk less.
> Ask questions rather than provide answers.
> Share information rather than hoard it.
> Encourage independent thinking rather than compliant followership.
> Encourage creativity rather than conformity.

Research on self-leadership continues to show support for the model (for a recent example of the link between self-leadership and entrepreneurship, see, D'Intino et al., 2007). The dimensions of self-leadership are valid and distinct from other personality variables (Houghton and Neck, 2002; Houghton et al., 2004), and some research suggests that the practice of self-leadership can be beneficial to an organization (VanSandt and Neck, 2003). Recent research also considers the applicability of the concept in other cultures (e.g., Alves et al., 2006; Neubert and Wu, 2006). The concepts provide considerable appeal for the development of leaders and to help establish workable leadership roles in organizations that rely on teams and empowerment.

> **Self-leadership suggests that team members must be taught and encouraged to make their own decisions and accept responsibility to the point where they no longer need leaders. Self-leadership within teams means that all team members set goals and observe, evaluate, critique, reinforce, and reward one another and themselves.**

In 2002 when Sam Palmisano, IBM's CEO, presented the initiative that was to jump start the venerable company, Donna Riley, the company's vice president of global talent, had to work on reinventing its leadership (Tischler, 2004). With help from outside consultants, she set out to identify the set of skills, behaviors, and competencies that IBM leaders needed to help the company survive. The leadership traits they developed included trust and personal responsibility, developing people, enabling growth, collaboration, informed judgment, and building client partnerships. "In a highly complex world, where multiple groups might need to unite to solve a client's problems, old-style command-and-control leadership doesn't work" (Tischler, 2004: 113). The leadership characteristics used by IBM to shape its future are similar to those proposed by Manz and his colleagues.

In order to be successful, participative management and self-leadership require the empowerment of employees (see Chapter 5) and the changing of an organization's culture. One of the key components of the cultural change is redefining the concepts of leadership and followership. Employees who become self-leaders do not require organizing, controlling, and monitoring from their leaders. Such redefinition requires a reconsideration of many current definitions of leadership, including the one presented in Chapter 1.

THE ROLE OF LEADERS IN A TEAM ENVIRONMENT

Are leaders becoming obsolete? What happens to leadership when all employees become self-leaders and teams fulfill the traditional functions of leaders? Many managers and organizational leaders worry that once teams are successful and they train self-leaders, they may write themselves out of a job. The answers are complex and often depend on the situation and the leader. Some leaders never feel fully comfortable in a team environment, whereas others adapt to it well or even embrace it. Leaders of the first type are likely to feel that they are losing their job and might focus efforts on regaining control. Leaders of the second type might be able to redefine their role and continue contributing to the organization.

The only certainty is that the role of the leader changes in a team environment but it does not altogether disappear. The leaders are not in charge and are not meant to command and control. Although an often-used metaphor for team leadership is an orchestra conductor, as opposed to a conductor, who is often highly directive, team leadership must be much less hands-on (Hackman, 2005). For this reason, many practitioners (e.g., Katzenbach and Smith, 1993) refer to team leaders as facilitators and coaches. Leaders are caretakers of their teams, the ones who help them achieve their goals by providing them with instructions, conflict management, encouragement when needed, and resources. Leaders/facilitators still fulfill many of the functions of traditional leaders, but they do so to a lesser extent and only when asked. They assist the teams by obtaining the resources needed to solve problems and to implement solutions, and only interfere when needed. The leader's central activities, therefore, become assessing the team's abilities and skills and helping them develop necessary skills, which often includes getting the right type of training (Figure 8-3). The team leaders also play the role of conflict and relationship manager while they continue doing real work themselves.

Another role for team leaders is to make the team aware of its boundaries. Many teams fail because they take on too much or ignore organizational realities and constraints. For example, a team of schoolteachers assigned the role of revising the social studies curriculum for fourth and fifth graders might propose changes that affect other parts of the curriculum and then be disappointed when its recommendations are not fully implemented. The role of the team leader would be to keep the team focused on its specific task or to integrate the team with others who can help it with its wider recommendations.

A recent review of leadership in teams proposes that in addition to the traditional view of leaders being considered to be an input into the team (e.g., the leader does what is needed to help the team), team leaders should also be viewed as an output or

Figure 8-3   New Roles for Leaders in a Team Environment.

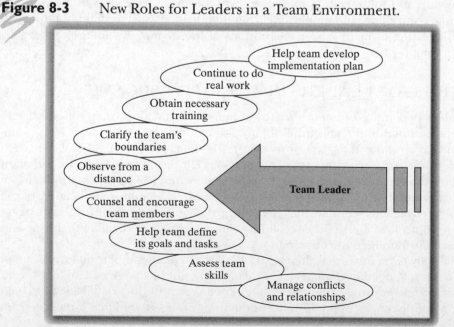

product of team processes (Day, Gronn, and Salas, 2004). Leadership is created by the team and then used as a resource or capital in accomplishing its tasks. As such, all team members share leadership as a distributed function to help the group perform. Another interesting development in the use of teams stems from the view that such structures might not be fully compatible with the Western cultural value of individualism. Some sources describe teams, although needed as a structural element, as already passé and state that the focus needs to shift to individual contributions within teams. The use of teams in the United States and many other Western industrialized nations was spurred by the West's interpretation of Japanese management style. The Japanese continue to dominate many sectors of the global economy and give much of the credit for that success to their participative, team-based decision-making and management style. It stands to reason, then, that adoption of some of the same management techniques and tools should help the Western industrialized nations regain their global economic positions. Whereas production and technological tools such as just-in-time (JIT) systems have been implemented successfully in the West, however, the people- and team-management issues have found considerably less success.

The relative failure of Japanese-style teams in the West and most notably in the United States can be blamed partially on lack of cultural fit. The collectivist Japanese culture fits well within and supports its management styles. The Western cultures by and large are considerably more individualistic, and their values often conflict with team-based approaches. Australians might have come up with a new concept: *Collaborative individualism* could be the buzzword of the future in the West (Limerick, 1990). Collaborative individuals are not limited by the boundaries of the group. They are cooperative and helpful to their team and organization while maintaining their internal motivation and conflict-tolerant skills. Based on a cultural analysis, such an approach could be much more suitable to many Western cultures, particularly those that are vertical individualists, than the Japanese search for consensus and conformity in a team (Nahavandi and Aranda, 1994). Australian researchers propose that empathy with an ability to transform organizations and to be proactive with excellent political and conflict management and networking skills, creative thinking, and maturity is at the core of the new competencies needed by future managers. Teams still exist and continue to play a key role, but individuals will be the focus for performance.

SUMMARY AND CONCLUSIONS

This chapter presents the concepts of participative management and its extension and application to the use of teams in organizations. Although many benefits can be drawn from the use of participative management, its success depends on appropriate application. Cultural and organizational factors should determine the use of participation as a management tool. A basic application of participation is the use of delegation by a leader. Delegation must be implemented carefully and judiciously to ensure fair application; leaders must consider which tasks they should and can delegate and the individuals to whom they are delegating. Thorough feedback and monitoring are also important.

Many organizations formalize the use of participation through the creation of teams. The successful implementation of SMTs and self-leadership demonstrates the role of teams in revitalizing organizations. As teams continue to be used, their nature and role change, as does the role of leadership in a team environment. Despite the need for a contingency view in the use of participative management and teams, teams provide a basic management tool in many parts of the world. More-focused attention on cultural factors along with a continued analysis of the success of participative management and teams should lead to continued evolution of the concepts.

LEADERSHIP CHALLENGE: WHO GETS THE PROJECT?

Your department includes 15 members, all of whom have been with you for at least a year. Although the department is generally cohesive and performs well, you are grooming four "stars" for promotion because you believe they are the best performers. You just landed a new account with a lot of potential, a tight deadline, and the need for considerable grooming and development. The success not only will give the person in charge of the project a lot of visibility, but also could affect your career in the company. Everyone in the department is aware of the importance of the project, and several people, including your four stars, volunteered to take it on. In particular, one of the members with the most tenure and experience (but not one of the four stars) is pushing to get the project. Given the project's importance, you want it to be handled well and without too much direction from you.

As you are about to delegate the project to your top star, you receive a call from the human resources director telling you that one of the department members filed an informal complaint against you, accusing you of favoritism. The director can't tell you the name, but wanted you to be aware of potential problems and that HR would be conducting informal fact-finding interviews.

1. Who will you assign to the project?
2. Consider the implications of your decision.

REVIEW AND DISCUSSION QUESTIONS

1. What is the role of participation in the development of leadership theory and practice?
2. How does culture affect an organization's ability to implement employee participation?
3. What organizational strategies can be used to help leaders delegate more often and more effectively?
4. Compare and contrast groups and teams. Provide an example of an effective team. What are the elements that contribute to its success?
5. What challenges do leaders face in managing teams?
6. What is the difference between delegation and implementation of self-managed teams?
7. What are the steps to leadership and self-leadership?
8. How has the role of leaders changed in team environments? What functions remain?
9. Several researchers claim that the application of Japanese-style teams is culturally inappropriate in many Western cultures. Do you agree or disagree with such assertions? Why?

EXERCISE 8-1: TO DELEGATE OR NOT TO DELEGATE?

This role play is designed to provide you with an opportunity to experience the challenges of delegation either as a leader or as a follower. Read the following situation and description of team members.

Situation

You are a team manager in the public relations and marketing department at a major resort, Sunshine Inc. Your organization specializes in all-inclusive package vacations and has a reputation for excellent customer service. As a team manager, you are responsible for the supervision and development of four account managers in the corporate area. Your team's role is sales and service to corporate clients.

Your manager, the marketing director, just handed you a new account that she inherited from another of the resort's partners. The client has been problematic in terms of payment and somewhat unreasonable demands, but it has a lot of potential. It is an entrepreneurial firm that your manager referred to as "spoiled brats." However, successful handling of this client, you are told, is important. "We don't want to lose them; in fact, we really want them to be happy! Nobody seems to have figured out how, but I'm sure you will come up with something."

You have four people in your team:

Fran Smith: Fran has been with Sunshine for 4 years. She recently obtained a bachelor's degree in marketing from a major state university. Her prior work experience was with a restaurant supplier, where she was a good performer with a lot of ambition, creativity, and motivation. You previously assigned many different tasks to her, and they were all done well. Fran is one of your in-group people and you trust her a lot. You have had many discussions about future promotions, and she has followed your advice well. Fran seemed to be in a slump for the past 3 months but has not talked to you about it and you let it go, assuming it may be a personal issue. Performance is still there, but some of the enthusiasm is gone.

Gerry Narden: Gerry has been with Sunshine for 10 years. He has an AA degree in business and got his first job as a desk clerk at the resort. Gerry has worked in many different parts of the resort and started in corporate sales only 6 months ago. He transferred in with outstanding evaluations from all his previous bosses. Gerry is the newest member of the team and has experienced some ups and downs in sales. One of them almost caused the loss of a major client. You intervened and managed to save the account. He seemed to learn from the experience and has done well in the past 2 months. You have not, however, given him any major accounts since, although he repeatedly asked for more challenge.

Terry Chan: Terry has been with your team for 5 years. Terry has a masters in communication and is a good performer. Her more than 10 years of work experience, most of which were in sales and customer relations within Sunshine, show her knack for working with "big" clients who keep coming back to her. She usually does not ask for assignments and is good at bringing her own. Terry needs little help or management from you and seems to do her own thing successfully.

(Continued)

J.P. Ricci: J.P. has been with the team for over a year. In his first job, he is a major management challenge. A bright, Ivy League graduate with a degree in hotel and restaurant management and marketing, he has considerable sales skills. J.P. wants to do things his own way. J.P.'s clients are delighted with him when he puts his heart into things, but motivation seems to be lacking sometimes. Your discussions with J.P. lead you to believe that he is bored and needs to be challenged. J.P. often talks about trying to find another job that would fit better but he really likes the sales and resort environment. J.P. seems to be in search of direction. Despite these issues, he is a good performer and delivers when it counts.

Role Play

After reading the scenario, please wait for further information from your instructor.

EXERCISE 8-1:   TO DELEGATE OR NOT TO DELEGATE?

Worksheet for Managers

1. Who would you select to manage the account? What are your reasons?

2. Plan the meeting during which you will delegate the task. What do you need to say? What areas do you need to cover? How are you addressing your employees' needs?

Worksheet for Employees

1. What do you need to do a good job?

2. Has your manager provided you with clear information about the task and expectations? What is done correctly? What is missing? Do you feel ready and motivated to take on the task?

EXERCISE 8-2: STRATEGIES FOR BECOMING A SELF-LEADER

Changing Behaviors

1. Observe yourself

   Identify specific behaviors that are related to becoming a self-leader. (List at least three.)

   Set specific goals for yourself for each behavior. (List at least three.)

   Include a time line for each goal.

   How will you measure your goals?

2. Set up opportunities for rehearsal.

   Identify settings where you can practice the new behaviors. (List at least three.)

   Identify and work with individuals who can help you rehearse.

3. Establish reminders.

   Establish reminders in your work environment to encourage the new behaviors. (List at least three.)

   List individuals who can help you. (List at least three.)

4. Set up reward and "punishments."

   List rewards that would encourage you to use self-leadership behaviors. (List at least three.) Clarify when each should be used.

   List things that would stop unwanted behaviors. (List at least three.) Clarify when each should be used.

Changing Cognitive Patterns

1. Focus on natural rewards in tasks.

   List aspects of your job that can naturally encourage self-leadership behaviors. (List at least three.)

2. Establish constructive thought patterns.

   Look for opportunities rather than obstacles.

3. Use positive mental imagery.

   Reevaluate your priorities, beliefs, and assumptions.

Source: Based on self-leadership concepts developed by Manz and Sims (1987, 1991).

SELF-ASSESSMENT 8-1:   DELEGATION SCALE

Using the following scale, indicate how much you agree with the following items.

> 1 = Strongly disagree
> 2 = Somewhat disagree
> 3 = Neither agree nor disagree
> 4 = Somewhat agree
> 5 = Strongly agree

_____ 1. I can do most jobs better and faster than my subordinates.

_____ 2. Most of my tasks cannot be delegated to my subordinates.

_____ 3. Most of my subordinates do not have the appropriate level of skills to do the tasks that I could delegate to them.

_____ 4. I feel uncomfortable delegating many of my tasks to my subordinates.

_____ 5. I am responsible for my subordinates' mistakes, so I might as well do the task myself.

_____ 6. If my subordinates do too many of my tasks, I may not be needed any longer.

_____ 7. Explaining things to subordinates and training them often take too much time.

_____ 8. My subordinates already have too much work to do; they can't handle any more.

_____ 9. If my subordinates do the tasks, I will lose touch and be out of the loop.

_____10. I need to know all the details of a task before I can delegate to my subordinates.

Scoring Key: Your total score will be between 10 and 50. The higher your score, the less inclined you are to delegate and you agree with many of the common excuses used by managers not to delegate tasks to their subordinates.

Total: _____

SELF-ASSESSMENT 8-2:   ARE YOU A TEAM LEADER?

Rate yourself on each of the following items using the scale provided here:

1 = Strongly disagree

2 = Somewhat disagree

3 = Neither agree nor disagree

4 = Somewhat agree

5 = Strongly agree

_____ 1. I enjoy helping other get their job done.

_____ 2. Managing others is a full-time job in and of itself.

_____ 3. I am good at negotiating for resources.

_____ 4. People often come to me to help them with interpersonal conflicts.

_____ 5. I tend to be uncomfortable when I am not fully involved in the task that my group is doing.

_____ 6. It is hard for me to provide people with positive feedback.

_____ 7. I understand organizational politics well.

_____ 8. I get nervous when I do not have expertise at a task that my group is performing.

_____ 9. An effective leader needs to have full involvement with his or her team's activities.

_____10. I am skilled at goal setting.

Scoring Key: Reverse score for items 2, 5, 6, 8, and 9 (e.g., 1 = 5, 5 = 1). Add your score on all items. Maximum possible score is 50. The higher the score, the more team leadership skills you have.

Total: _____

Leadership in Action: Whole Foods

"I am now 53 years old and I have reached a place in my life where I no longer want to work for money. . . . Beginning January 1, 2007, my salary will be reduced to $1, and I will no longer take any other cash compensation" (Mackey, 2007). The statement is part of a letter John Mackey, the founder and CEO of Whole Foods, wrote to his employees when the sales were below expectations and the stock prices dropped. His company and highly unique management style are a model of innovation and customer service around the world. "We're changing the experience so that people enjoy it" is how Mackey summarizes his company (Sechler, 2004: 1). With bright facilities, wide aisles, rich colorful displays, expert employees, and lots of help and information for customers, Whole Foods has changed the way many people shop for food. John Mackey started the company in 1980 in Austin, Texas, with the first organic food store; it now numbers more than 150 stores with earnings of nearly $3 billion and is making a move to become a global company with the first store opening up in the United Kingdom (Duff, 2005).

"Mackey is hardly a manager at all . . . he's an anarchist" is how a former Whole Foods executive describes the company president (Fishman, 2004: 73). The CEO, who is now in his early 50s, visits his stores in shorts and hiking boots and is equally as passionate about egalitarianism and democracy in the workplace as he is about humane treatment of animals. He interacts freely with employees and is eager to learn from them and from his customers. Wendy Steinberg, who has worked at Whole Foods since 1992, describes him as an "observer" (Fishman, 2004: 76). A vegan, who changed his vegetarian diet to exclude all animal by-products after working with a group devoted to improving living condi-

tions for farm animals, he still flies commercial airplanes, rents the cheapest cars, and is a shrewd and disciplined businessman leading his company and employees to considerable success (Fishman, 2004). Much of that success is attributed to Whole Foods' team-based culture that empowers employees and involves them in all aspects of decision making while demanding performance and customer service.

The basic decision-making power at Whole Foods rests with the teams that run each department (e.g., bakery, produce, seafood) in each store. The teams decide whom to hire, whether to retain members, what products to carry, how to allocate raises, and so forth. All teams together make more strategic decisions, such as the type of health insurance the company will offer. The National Leadership Team of the company makes the overall decision based on majority vote. Mackey says, "I don't overrule the National Leadership Team. . . . I've done it maybe once or twice in all these years" (Fishman, 2004: 74). He admits making some top-down decisions, but only when time to consult is not available.

Whole Foods has a "Declaration of Interdependence" that affirms the interdependence of all stakeholders and clearly states the goals of satisfying and delighting customers and of team-member happiness and excellence (Whole Foods philosophy, 2007). Building healthy relationships with team members, getting rid of the "us versus them" management mentality, and a deep-seated belief in employee participation are also highlighted. The core values regarding working at Whole Foods include the following (Whole Foods philosophy, 2007):

- Self-directed teams that meet to solve problems and appreciate members

- Increased communication through open-book management and "no secrets" management that allow employees access to financial data, salary and raise information, and so forth.
- Profit- and gain-sharing to provide team members incentives to perform and build the team through shared fate (nonexecutive employees hold 94 percent of the company's stock options); a salary cap that limits the salary of any team member to fourteen times the average total compensation of all full-time team members.
- Employee happiness through fun and friendship at work with liberal dress codes, ability to do volunteer work on company time, full health benefits, and emphasis on taking responsibility for successes and failures and celebration and encouragement of employees.
- Continuous learning for employees about the products they sell and the job they do.
- Promotion from within to appreciate and encourage employee talent and development and a strong equal opportunity policy.

Although the positive work culture, fun and friendship are key to the company's ongoing success, competition and focus on performance are not lost. Because individual raises are tied to their team's performance, team members want good workers on their team. Mackey, who wants his company to be based on love rather than fear, is also clearly in charge and in the forefront representing his company in the community. As he battles the animal rights groups that continue to criticize Whole Foods for being hypocritical and counterculture groups that accuse him of having become too corporate, or defending against the anti-union charges leveled at the company, Mackey responds, "We're in the business of selling whole foods, not holy foods" (Overfelt, 2003). The corporate side of the CEO became clearly evident when he had to apologize for having assumed an online alias "Rahobdeb" (an anagram of his wife's name) to bash his competitor Wild Oats Markets for years (Kesmodel, 2007; Stewart, 2007).

QUESTIONS

1. What are the elements of John Mackey's leadership?
2. What makes the teams a Whole Foods effective?

Sources: Duff, M., "The perils of the imperial reach," *DSN Retailing Today* 44, no. 1 (2005): 10; Fishman, C., 2004. "The anarchist's cookbook," *Fast Company,* July: 70–78; Kesmodel, D., 2007 "Whole Foods sets probe as CEO apologizes," *The Wall Street Journal,* July 18: A3; Mackey, J. "I no longer work for money," *Fast Company,* February, 112; Overfelt, M., 2003. "The next big thing: Whole Food Market," *Fortune,* June 2. http://www.fortune.com/fortune/print/0,15935,456063,00.html (accessed January 27, 2005); Sechler, B., 2004. "Whole Foods picks up the pace of its expansion," *Wall Street Journal,* September 29: 1; Whole Foods philosophy at http://www.wholefoodsmarket.com/company/philosophy.html (accessed August 5, 2007); Stewart, J. B., 2007. "Whole Foods chief disappoints by sowing wild oats online," *The Wall Street Journal,* July 18: D5.

C h a p t e r   9

Leading

Change

Be the change that you want to see in the world.
—MAHATMA GANDHI

When you're finished changing, you're finished.
—BENJAMIN FRANKLIN

After studying this chapter, you will be able to:

■ Define change and explain the forces for change.

■ Describe types of change and explain the change process.

■ Summarize the reasons for resistance to change and possible solutions.

■ Present the leadership practices necessary to implement change, including the importance of vision.

■ Highlight the organization characteristics that support change.

"**P**ermanent white water" and "turbulent" are some the terms used to describe the environment that today's organizations face. Their environment is changing at a rapid pace leading to the need for flexibility, innovation, and nimbleness. The effectiveness and very survival of most of our organizations depend on their ability to successfully adapt to changes in their environment while still maintaining internal health. Leading change is therefore one of the most challenging and vital responsibilities of leaders. Whether to implement new technology, update existing products or services, launch new ones, or put in place new administrative and management systems, leaders must guide their followers through change, which is more often than not perceived as painful, often resisted, and difficult to implement. Whereas managing change well is essential to the survival of the organization, some surveys indicate that many organizational leaders are not satisfied with how well their organizations can innovate and adapt to change and they fully realize that implementing change is a long-term process with many risks of failure (McGregor, 2007).

This chapter looks at the change process and the role that leaders play in leading and implementing change in their organizations.

Parts of this chapter are based on "Managing Change," in A. Nahavandi and A.R. Malekzadeh *Organizational Behavior: The Person-Organization Fit*. Upper Saddle River, NJ: Prentice Hall.

FORCES FOR CHANGE

Change is the transformation or adaptation to a new way of doings things. While related to innovation, the latter is the use of resources and skills to create an idea, product, process, or service that is new to the organization or its stakeholders. For example, when in 1992 Procter & Gamble (P&G) introduced its latest innovation, liquid detergent, to be a high-priced limited-production item, it triggered changes in the whole industry that in turn affected how P&G marketed its new product and pushed the company to change its plan and eventually mass produce liquid detergent.

Internal and External Forces

When do organizations change? What makes leaders decide to implement change? Forces for change are both external (in the environment) and internal (Figure 9-1). Changes in the environment include factors such as social trends, cultural and demographic changes, political shifts, the economy, and technological advances. For examples, in the United States and in many other parts of the world, demographic diversity related to both ethnic groups and age forces organizations to consider new ways of addressing their customers' needs. The case of Avon (Leadership in Action in Chapter 6) shows how the company had to change because, in part, demographic and social changes led many women to work outside of the home, disrupting the home-based distribution of the company's products. The CEO Andrea Jung has focused on introducing new distribution and marketing methods, changing how her employees think about the products, and getting them to accept the changes. In a similar situation, the public interest in sustainability and demand for safe products has triggered the growth of organizations such as Ecover, the Belgian-based company, which is now the world's largest producer of ecological household cleaners and product. The success of Ecover, in turn, has forced changes in other consumer-good companies. Changes in the local and global political environments compel organizations to look for innovative ways of dealing with new problems. JetBlue (Leadership in Action in Chapter 1) was one of the first airlines to install reinforced doors to their planes' cockpits in response to the terrorist attacks of 2001. To take advantage of technological tools and connect with young voters, all the

Figure 9-1   Forces for Change.

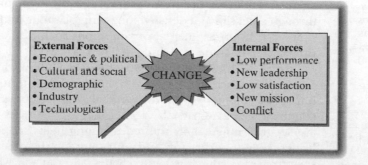

2008 U.S. presidential candidates actively use the Web to campaign pushing their political organizations to change.

The internal forces for change closely follow external forces. For example, a new service from one hospital will push others to consider changing their offerings or wide uses of new technology such as the Web lead city and state governments to expand their online services, requiring new hires, training, and new management processes. One of the most common forces for change inside organizations is the performance gap—the difference between expected and actual performance. Another potent internal force for change is new leadership at any level. Therefore, not only do leaders guide organizations through change, they are also frequently the cause of change.

Consider the forces that are pushing the U.S. Federal Bureau of Investigation (FBI) to undergo extensive changes with varying degrees of success since the 9/11 attacks on the United States. The external forces for change are global politics, considerable political pressure in the United States, public demand for security, and changing technology among others. Internally, the FBI faces a performance gap (a glaring failure by some accounts), presence of old technology, antiquated management and administrative systems, and extensive employee dissatisfaction (Brazil, 2007). Additionally, the organization's mission shifted from one of primarily solving crime and bringing criminals to justice to preventing threats to the U.S. national security before they occur. Former U.S. Attorney Dick Thornburgh states, "it's almost a total transformation of what the bureau does and how it does it. It's staggering" (Brazil, 2007). In charge of orchestrating the massive transformation is FBI Director Robert Mueller, who took leadership a week before the 9/11 attacks. The case of the FBI illustrates the many forces that push organization to change.

Culture and Change

As pressure for change increases from inside and outside of organizations, not all leaders react and respond the same way. Some perceive the pressure as a threat; others see it as an opportunity. One factor that determines the way leaders and their followers perceive pressures for change is culture, both at the national and at the organizational level. We consider the importance of organizational culture later in this chapter. From a broader perspective, national cultural values of tolerance of ambiguity and perception and use of time affect how leaders view change. In cultures such as Greece, Guatemala, Portugal, or Japan, where people do not easily tolerate uncertainty and ambiguity, pressure for change is seen as a threat and is either ignored or carefully planned and managed. A Japanese business leader is likely to manage change through extensive and detailed long-term planning and forecasting supported by governmental organizations such as the Ministry of International Trade and Industry (MITI). MITI targets certain industries for growth and supports them through various economic and political actions, thereby reducing the potential negative impact of change triggered by global competition. Similarly, in countries such as Malaysia and Thailand, with cultures that are risk averse, governmental centralized planning helps support business leaders reduce uncertainty and ambiguity. On the other end of the spectrum, in Sweden, the United States, and Canada, where change is tolerated and perceived as an opportunity, leaders deal with change by making quick changes to their organizations and implementing short-term strategies that address the immediate pressures relatively more quickly than in other cultures.

The relationship to and perception of time further affect how leaders implement change. Leaders from present-oriented cultures, where time is linear, are likely to react fairly quickly to change and focus on short-term planning. The short-term orientation leads to a state of constant change that many U.S. organizations are experiencing. For example, when, in 2000, James McNerney became the first outsider to lead the 100-year-old 3M company, he immediately announced that he would change the DNA of the company. He implemented substantial changes that deeply affected 3M and left 4 years later to lead Boeing (Hindo, 2007). Leaders from past- and future-oriented cultures are less likely to react quickly to change, taking time to plan and to consider the long-term impact of their actions.

TYPES AND PROCESS OF CHANGE

Change is stressful and usually met with some resistance as you will read in later sections of this chapter. Different types of changes, however, affect people differently and require different types of leadership. Change that is sudden and drastic is more likely to cause stress and resistance, whereas gradual and programmed change is easier to manage.

Types of Change

In some cases, leaders can carefully plan and execute change; in others, leaders and followers are caught by surprise and have to react without specific preparation. Table 9-1 summarizes the different types of changes organizations face.

Whereas many organizations try to carefully analyze their environment and internal conditions, for example through customer- and employee-satisfaction surveys or careful measures of performance, to foresee changes and to plan their course of action,

Table 9-1 Types of Change.

Type of Change	Description
Planned	Change that occurs when leaders or followers make a conscious effort to change in response to specific pressure or problem.
Unplanned	Change that occurs randomly and suddenly without the specific intention of addressing a problem.
Evolutionary	Gradual or incremental change.
Convergent	Planned evolutionary change that is the result of specific and conscious actions by leaders or follower to change the organization.
Revolutionary or frame-breaking	Change that is rapid and dramatic.

Sources: Partially based on work by Tushman, M. L., W. H. Newman, and E. Romanelli. 1986. Convergence and upheaval: Managing the unsteady pace of organizational evolution. *California Management Review*, Fall: 29–44.

many more face changes that they do not expect or are unable to foresee. Additionally, both planned and unplanned change may happen either gradually or rapidly leading to dramatic impact on the organization. In the 3M example presented earlier, James McNerney planned the changes he wanted to implement to move the organization to improved efficiency, through careful monitoring, measurement, and implementation of a process called Six Sigma, which relies on precision, consistency, and repetition (Hindo, 2007). The existing 3M culture, known worldwide for its ability to be creative and innovative, was based on experimentation and tolerance for trail and error that eventually led to innovative products and process. McNerney moved toward removing any variability from organizational processes, focusing instead on analysis, control, and efficiency. Although it was planned, the change was revolutionary and felt like a complete cultural transformation (Hindo, 2007).

The different types of change may require different actions from leaders. For example, in the case of planned and evolutionary change, a leader's ability to structure tasks may be important. When facing unplanned and revolutionary change, charismatic and transformational leadership may become more central. Additionally, based on the change process considered in the next section, the options that are available, and actions that are required from a leader may be different in each type of change. One factor that remains constant regarding the role of leadership is the need to set a vision and to help followers through the resistance that is likely to take place.

Model for Change

Understanding the course of change can help leaders plan and implement change more successfully. In the 1950s social psychologist Kurt Lewin proposed a theory of organizational change that continues to influence current thinking (Lewin, 1951). Lewin's Force Field theory proposes that organizations contain forces that drive change and forces that resist change. When the two forces are balanced, the organization maintains its status quo. When the forces for change are stronger than those that resist change, leaders can overcome inertia and implement changes. So to successfully change, leaders must either increase the forces for change or reduce the forces that resist change. Lewin further suggests that change takes place in a three-stage process presented in Figure 9-2.

Figure 9-2   Lewin's Model of Change.

Unfreezing
Preparing people
Understanding the
need for change

Changing
Implementing
actual change

Refreezing
Providing support
to assure change
becomes permanent

In the first, unfreezing state, the existing practices and behaviors are questioned and motivation to change develops. Unfreezing is likely to be easier when the forces for change, whether internal or external are strong and organizational members and leaders are aware of them. One of the major tasks of any leader is to help followers "unfreeze" and realize that there is a need for change. In the FBI example presented earlier, Director Robert Mueller has been dedicated to communicating consistently and repeatedly about the need for changing the culture and mission and the reasons why the FBI must "chart a new course" and "establish a new mission and priorities" (Brazil, 2007). Andrea Jung of Avon has likewise focused on communicating with the company's all-important sales force of "Avon Ladies" the need to change the distribution channels. In some cases, although the need for change may be obvious to some, for example to market analysts or stock holders, employees of the organization may not agree or even be aware of such a need. In the 3M case, the company's growth had slowed and the stock was performing poorly, prompting McNerney to implement drastic changes such as laying off 8000 employees (11 percent of the workforce) and putting controls on the creative inventors (Hindo, 2007). Based on all accounts, however, the employees never quite fully grasped the need for change; there had been no "unfreezing."

The second stage according to Lewin is the change itself where new practices and policies are implemented and new behaviors and skills are learned. The change can involve technology, people, products, services, or management practices and administration. The leader's role continues to be essential, supporting followers, emphasizing the importance of the change, correcting course as needed, and so forth. Most organizations focus on this stage, actually making the change without paying enough attention to either preparing the organization for the change or to the last phase, freezing. In the last phase of change, the newly learned behaviors and freshly implemented practices are encouraged and supported to become part of the employees' routine activities. The leader's role in this stage is coaching, training, and using appropriate reward systems to help solidify the changes that have been implemented.

Organizational researcher Kim Cameron believes that managing change requires fixed points. He states, "Unfortunately, when everything is changing, change becomes impossible to manage. Without a stable, unchanging reference point, direction and processes are indeterminate" (Cameron, 2006: 317). Although change is essential to survival, constant change that is not allowed to take hold is likely to be ineffective. It is important for employees to know what is not changing and to be allowed to practice the new behaviors long enough to learn them before something new is once again introduced. According to Harvard Business School professor John Kotter, a well-known authority on organizational change, leaders must also celebrate early successes and short-term progress to keep followers motivated (Brazil, 2007). In the case of the FBI, the ongoing transformation that has been taking place for the past 5 years seems to have taken a toll on morale, causing heavy turnover (Brazil, 2007). For 3M, although the implementation of the new efficiency-oriented systems lasted for 4 years and stock prices did rebound, the architect of the change, McNerney, left, and most long-time employees did not fully adopt the change. The current CEO, George Buckley, a soft-spoken company insider, has changed course to refocus on the innovation process that 3M is so famous for. He says, "Perhaps one of the mistakes that we made as a company . . . is that when you value sameness more than you value creativity, I think you potentially undermine the heart and soul of a company like 3M" (Hindo, 2007).

Lewin's model of change has four key characteristics that leaders must consider:

➤ The importance of recognizing the need for change and preparing and motivating followers to implement it.
➤ The inevitable presence of the resistance to change.
➤ The focus on people as the source for learning and change.
➤ The need to support new behaviors and allowing them to take hold.

The typical model for implementing planned change and ways of managing unplanned change are presented next.

Process of Planned Change

Planned change follows a general process outlined in Figure 9-3. The process has six steps each of which requires different types of resources and leadership skills. The first step in the process mirrors the unfreezing phase of Lewin's model. Leaders and followers must become aware of the need for change and recognize its importance to the organization's effectiveness or survival. There may be a performance gap, or employee dissatisfaction, or external pressure from customers or competitors.

The second step involves developing alternatives and ideas for change. This step can be done by organizational leaders at different levels, through small groups or teams, or even with participation of outsiders. Any process that encourages participation and input from those who are affected most by the change is likely to ease the implementation process. For example, most municipalities systematically gather input from the public about projects such as parks, freeways, or other developments. Similarly, school

Figure 9-3   The Process of Planned Change.

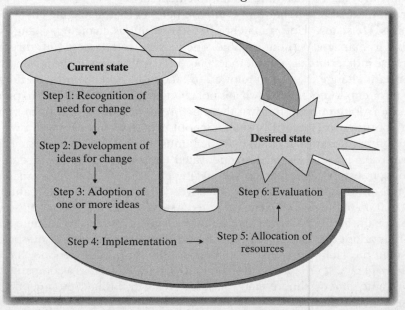

boards ask for feedback from parents when planning changes. The use of team and empowerment in organizations can be one mechanism for allowing input into the development of alternatives. Additionally, although there may not be a choice on whether or not to change, there are always many alternatives and paths to accomplish the goals; step two of the change process is an ideal opportunity to get involvement and buy-in.

The next two steps are adoption of ideas and implementation of the change plan. These two steps mirror Lewin's change phases. The fifth step is allocation of resources to support the change. Leaders have to either allocate new resources or shift current resources to help implement change and "freeze" the change. For example, FBI Director Mueller shifted some resources from fighting crime to counter-intelligence to support the new direction, and the FBI is now training its executives through additional week-long courses on leading strategic change (Brazil, 2007). The allocation of resources is a potent message from leadership that the change matters and should be taken seriously. Finally, the last step in the process is evaluation of the change process and its outcomes. The process of planned change is a continuous and dynamic loop. After change is implemented, the organization must review and evaluate its effectiveness and assess whether the objectives are met. Did the performance gap narrow or close? Are various constituencies, including employees, more satisfied? Are processes more efficient? Does the new technology work? If the goals are not achieved, the change process starts over with the recognition once again of the need to change.

The process of change either can take place in top-down manner with leaders initiating and driving the process or can be bottom-up with individuals and teams throughout the organization starting and implementing the process. A top-down change fits well with traditional, hierarchical, command-and-control organizations and tends to force rapid change. However, it also may engender more resistance. The bottom-up approach creates more involvement and participation thereby reducing resistance. Yet, the risk of such an approach is not enlisting leadership support, which is essential to the success of any change. The case study of Best Buy at the end of this chapter illustrates a bottom-up approach to change that eventually needed top management support. Another example is Toyota taking over one of the lowest performing and most hostile Chevrolet plants from General Motors in Fremont, California, in the 1980s; no one expected much success. After renaming the plant New United Motor Manufacturing Inc. or Nummi (sounds like *new me*) and keeping the same workers and the same technology, it took 3 months after the plant started to roll out cars again with almost no defects (the plant had previously averaged 40 defects per car; Deutschman, 2007). Absenteeism and costs were also down dramatically. The key to the successful change was that the workers came up with ideas on how to change things, improve quality, and cut costs (Deutschman, 2007). This bottom-up approach to change, fully supported by top management, was the magical ingredient.

Dealing with Unplanned Change

Whereas models of planned change help leaders chart the course for change, change is frequently sudden, unpredictable, and not planned. The economy changes, competitors come up with a new product, an environmental disaster happens, or unions go on strike. Managing unplanned change falls into the domain of crisis management. A crisis occurs when leaders and their organization substantially misread their environment or are caught off guard by events they could not have foreseen. Once crisis occurs, it is difficult to control. The cost to the organization, its employees, and its various stakeholders is likely to be high. Leaders can manage unplanned change to some extent by taking the following steps before a crisis develops (Mintzberg, Quinn, and Voyer, 1995; Starbuck, Greve, and Hedberg, 1978). As you will see, the steps have much in common with learning organizations, a topic we review at the end of this chapter.

➤ Avoid allowing the organization from becoming too formal, hierarchical, rigid, and inflexible.

➤ Infuse moderate amounts of unreliability, unpredictability, and spontaneity into decisions to help prevent complacency.

➤ Stay on the offensive and be proactive with introducing new strategies, products, services, or processes.

➤ Replace and rotate leaders to bring in fresh ideas, methods, and visions.

➤ Experiment often with new methods, products, processes, structures, and so forth, to help followers practice dealing with change.

Whether planned or unplanned and even with the most careful implementation, people are likely to resist change. The next section considers resistance to change, its solutions, and the role of leaders in the process.

RESISTANCE TO CHANGE AND SOLUTIONS

Change is one of the main causes of stress in our lives. Even positive changes such as receiving a promotion or getting married can create anxiety and lead to stress. Making major changes in one's life, for example changing your lifestyle after having a heart attack, has been found to be extremely difficult (Deutschman, 2007). Although people adjust to minor changes after a brief period of time, large-scale changes in life or work require long adaptation periods and much encouragement and support. Therefore, all changes, especially large-scale ones, meet with some resistance.

Causes of Resistance

Three general causes explain resistance to change: organizational factors, group factors, and individual factors. (Table 9-2 presents the causes of resistance to change.) While planning and implementing change, leaders consider all three causes. The primary organizational cause for resisting change is inertia, which is a tendency for an organization as a whole to resist change and want to maintain the status quo. Closely related to inertia are the culture and structure of the organization, which, if well established, are hard to change. Challenges faced by Ford Motor Company as it lost $12.7 billion in 2006 and as it tries to reinvent itself provide an example of inertia and the power of organizational culture, as the company is literally fighting for its life (Taylor, 2006). The company's previous CEO and now chairman of the board Bill Ford Jr. gave up his job believing that an insider could no longer fix the problems and promising that the new CEO "knows how to shake the company to its foundations" (Kiley, 2007). The current CEO, Alan Mulally, who has little experience in the car industry, is battling what some consider Ford's dysfunctional and defeatist culture. To convince employees and leaders at Ford to change, he repeats the message: "We have been going out of business for 40 years" (Kiley, 2007). Ford's complacent culture, its highly rigid structure with a hierarchical

Table 9-2 Causes of Resistance to Change.

Organizational Causes	Group Causes	Individual Causes
Inertia	Group norms	Fear of the unknown
Culture	Group cohesion	Fear of failure
Structure		Job security
Lack of rewards		Individual characteristics
Poor timing		Previous experiences

pecking order that discourages sharing ideas, and its well-established leadership-training practices that place leaders in many jobs for short periods of time, all discourage openness and cooperation and present a barrier to change.

In addition to inertia and culture and structure, organizations can provide barriers to change by not rewarding people for change or implementing change at inappropriate times, for example when the previous change has not had time to "freeze." Other causes of resistance to change are related to group norms and cohesion. Cohesive groups with strong norms present many benefits. Members stick together, work well together, and can provide a supportive environment for learning. Strong group norms, however, can also be a formidable obstacle to change (Judson, 1991). When Marc Fields, now president of Ford Americas, joined the company in 1989, he was informed of group norms in the executive suites, which included making sure to get approval from his boss before he brings up any problems at meetings (Kiley, 2007). CEO Mulally is working on changing such group norms of secrecy and hiding mistakes to encourage people to admit mistakes and share information (Fields, 2006).

> In addition to inertia and culture and structure, organizations can provide barriers to change by not rewarding people for change or implementing change at inappropriate times. Other causes of resistance to change are related to group norms and cohesion.

The final cause of resistance involves individual factors such as fear of the unknown, of failure, and of job loss. Individual characteristics can also play a key role. For example, individuals who are open to new experiences, those with internal locus of control, or high self-monitors (see Chapter 4) are more likely to be comfortable with change and able to adapt to it more quickly. Similarly, entrepreneurs who tend to be characterized by flexibility and willingness to try new ideas, are more comfortable with change. Additionally, a person's culture, particularly the degree of tolerance of ambiguity, may play a role. Finally, the person's previous experience with change may present an obstacle to change. If an individual has experienced job loss or has been through other painful organizational changes in the past, he or she is more likely to be weary of implementing change in the future.

Solutions

As we will consider in the next section, the leader of an organization can do much to initiate change, inspire followers to implement it, and reduce resistance to change through inspiration, improvisation, creativity, and motivating followers. There are also several more practical approaches to dealing with change:

➤ *Education and communication* provide information and training through a variety of means including face-to-face communication, newsletters, training sessions, and announcements. Providing information can help reduce fear of the unknown and train people for the new tasks and jobs. It can also build trust.

➤ *Participation and involvement* rely on getting input from those affected by the change to plan and implement it. Participating in the change process is one of the most effective methods of building commitment to the change.

➤ *Facilitation and support* involve active listening and supportive communication in the form of counseling and support for followers. They can be highly effective in reducing fear.

➤ *Negotiation and agreement* engage powerful parties who can block the change in discussion about planning and implementation offering incentives and trade-offs in exchange for acceptance of the change.

➤ *Manipulation and cooptation* focus employees' attention on other factors hoping to bypass resistance or get them on-board by bribing them.

➤ *Coercion* relies on threats, fear, and force to push through the resistance.

The situations to use these methods, benefits, and disadvantages of each method are presented in Table 9-3.

Leaders can prevent, manage, or reduce resistance to change by using a variety of these methods. The next section focuses on the specific role of leaders in the successful implementation of change in organizations.

LEADING CHANGE

The approaches discussed in this section focus the importance of inspiration and vision in leading organizations through change. We also consider creativity, improvisation, and the processes for changing organizational culture as a requirement to successful change.

Visionary Leadership

Providing a vision and inspiring followers are one of the most important functions of leaders during change. A clear vision provides followers with reasons for change. It further supports the actual change process helping followers keep the goal in mind and helps them stay focused during refreezing. The inspiration that a leader can provide to his or her followers sustains the followers and helps reduce the resistance to change. There is considerable diversity in the books and articles about leadership in the popular business press, but several themes emerge to define the visionary leadership essential to change:

➤ *Importance of vision.* Successful and effective leaders provide a clear vision or help followers develop a common vision. In either case, whether stemming from the leader or the followers, vision is key to effective leadership.

➤ *Empowerment and confidence in followers.* Visionary leaders emphasize empowering followers to allow them to act autonomously and independently from the leader.

CHAPTER 9 Leading Change 309

Table 9-3 Methods of Dealing with Resistance to Change.

Method	When to Use	Advantages	Disadvantages
Education and communication	When there is lack of information and fear of the unknown; in all phases of the change process	Provide facts and once persuaded, people are less likely to resist	Time-consuming when large number of people are involved
Participation and involvement	When people do not have all the information or when they have power to block implementation; in all phases of the change process	Lead to commitment and can provide richer alternatives and ideas	Time-consuming; risk of inappropriate change being implemented
Facilitation and support	When people are resisting because of factors such as fear; during the change and refreezing phases	The only option when adjustment is the cause of resistance	Time-consuming and high-risk of failure
Negotiation and agreements	When there can be winners and losers and groups and individuals have power; during the change and refreezing phases	Relatively easy to implement; only option to balance power	Can be expensive, time consuming and lead to continued and further negotiation
Manipulation	When nothing else works or other options are too expensive; during the change phase	Relatively quick and inexpensive	Can lead to mistrust and resentment
Explicit or implicit coercion	When there is no time and nothing else works; when others have power; use occasionally; during unfreezing and change	Can be fast and effective in short term to end resistance	Can lead to resentment and morale problems; only effective in the short-run

Source: Based on Kotter, J. P., and L. A. Schlesinger. 1979. Choosing strategies for change. *Harvard Business Review* March–April.

This empowerment is possible only if leaders show genuine confidence in their followers.

➤ *Flexibility and change.* The fast-changing environment requires leaders to focus on flexibility and change in their organization.

➤ *Teamwork and cooperation.* Successful leaders emphasize teamwork and, maybe more importantly, the development of shared responsibility, as well as the need for trust and cooperation between leaders and followers and among followers.

Leaders play a key role in the development and communication of the vision. Some leaders, for instance, communicate their vision and values through stories. Patrick Kelly, CEO of Physician Sales and Services (PSS), relies on his storytelling skills to remind employees what is important (Weil, 1998). Whenever he repeats one of his favorites, "PSS employees chuckle. . . . And they learn, or relearn, an important lesson: No matter how badly other people treat you, no matter how confident you get about your future, never burn your bridges" (38). Researcher Noel Tichy recommends that leaders develop

Providing and vision and inspiring followers are one of the most important functions of leaders during change. A clear vision provides followers with reasons for change. It further supports the actual change process helping followers keep the goal in mind and helps them stay focused during refreezing.

three stories. The first one, the "Who I am" story, should tell who the leader is. The second story is about "Who we are." Finally, the leader must have a "Where we are going" story (Weil, 1998). Other consultants and practitioners agree that storytelling can be one of the most powerful ways for leaders to communicate their vision to their followers. According to Harvard professor Howard Gardner, "Stories of identity convey values, build esprit de corps, create role models, and reveal how things work around here" (Stewart, 1998b: 165). For example, Howard Schulltz of Starbucks (see Leading Change in Chapter 10) is a master storyteller who relies on sharing his personal experiences as a way of explaining his vision for the company.

Similar to the ideas proposed by charismatic, transformational, value-based, and spiritual leadership (see Chapter 6), the leader's vision is vital to creating change. A motivating vision is clear and understandable, challenging, idealistic yet achievable; it appeals to emotions and is forward looking. Andrea Jung of Avon and A.G. Lafley of P&G do not rely on personal stories, but keep their message simple and repetitive to assure that their followers hear it and understand it as a priority. Having a forward-looking vision is essential for transforming organizations and enacting large-scale change. Kouzes and Posner (2007) propose one of the most clearly developed models of visionary leadership. In addition to presenting the practices of what the researchers call exemplary leadership (Figure 9-4), the model considers the followers' points of view and their expectations of leaders. Leaders have to model the way, develop and inspire a shared vision, challenge the status quo, empower and enable their followers to act, and motivate and support them (Kouzes and Posner, 1993).

Kouzes and Posner (2003a, 2007) emphasize the importance of motivation, reward, and recognition—in their words "encouraging the heart"—as key aspects of empowerment, confidence in followers, and development of trust. They specifically

Figure 9-4   Practices of Exemplary and Visionary Leadership.

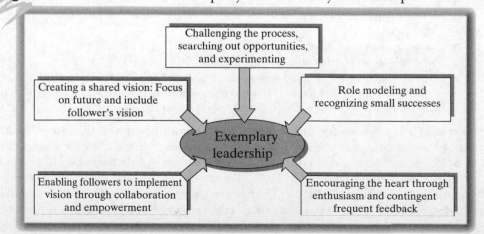

suggest that in order to truly motivate and inspire followers, the leader must do the following:

➤ Set clear standards for behavior and performance that are accepted by all followers.

➤ Expect the best from followers through a genuine belief in their abilities. This strong belief creates a self-fulfilling prophecy in followers, who will, in turn, perform better.

➤ Pay attention by being present, walking around, noticing followers, and caring about their behaviors, actions, and results.

➤ Personalize recognition not only by considering each follower's needs and preferences, but also by making them feel special in the process.

➤ Tell a story about followers, events, and performances as a way to motivate and teach.

➤ Celebrate together. Leaders must look for many opportunities to celebrate the team and the individual's success together.

➤ Role model the preceding principles to gain credibility and reinforce the message.

To be exemplary and visionary, leaders need to commit themselves to continuously questioning old beliefs and assumptions. This process leads to the creation of a new common vision. Through empowerment, encouragement, and proper role modeling, leaders can motivate followers to implement the vision. The driving force behind a leader's ability to fulfill this commitment is his or her credibility (Kouzes and Posner, 1993). By asking followers about the characteristics they admire most and expect from their leaders, Kouzes and Posner suggest that honesty, the ability to be forward looking, and the capacity to be inspiring and competent are the pillars of a leader's credibility. Leaders' ability to change followers and the organization depends on their credibility.

When Rob Waldron became CEO of JumpStart in 2002, he took over a successful organization that was sending AmeriCorps volunteers and college students to teach Head Start programs in various cities to combat the rising trend of preschoolers in low-income communities entering school without the skills needed to succeed (Overholt, 2005). With the mandate to grow the organization, Waldron admits, "This is the greatest management and leadership challenge I've ever faced. . . . I had to learn how to lead people and persuade them to a common end" (55). Waldron tackled the goals by decentralizing decision making, giving power to each center to encourage its employees to bring out their best ideas, and cutting staff at headquarters to raise everyone else's salary and attract fresh talent. His strategies paid off, and JumpStart grew 33 percent in 2003. Talking about his organization's achievement, Waldron said, "Our legacy is real social change. To have the joy of knowing your day-to-day struggles are turning into something that is life-changing. . . . I just wish everyone got to feel that way about their work" (55).

The visionary approach to leadership and change allows us to explain one of the most interesting and visible sides of leadership. It lets us talk about the leaders who everyone would agree are the real leaders—those who transform their organizations. Despite some survey-based studies, however, this approach generally lacks strong empirical research needed to establish its validity and to clarify and refine its propositions.

It is clear that visionary leadership is needed in times of crisis and that it plays an essential role in implementing change. The effect of such leadership in times when consolidation and status quo are needed, however, is not as clear. Change-oriented leadership, by definition, works in times of change; the role of such a leader when change is not the focus is not clear. Anecdotes of the disastrous effects of change-oriented leaders in times when change is not needed are common and point to the limitations of vision-ary leadership. The current discussions of visionary leaders do not address these limita-tions. Additionally, no research looks at the fate of organizations and employees who either do not buy into the leader's vision or who buy into an inappropriate vision, as may have been the case at 3M. Many historical and political examples can be found, though. The extent to which similar events would occur in organizations needs to be explored.

Despite these shortcomings, visionary leadership provides guidelines for manag-ing change. Accordingly, leaders must have passion, develop their credibility, develop and clarify their vision, share power with their followers, and—perhaps most importantly—role model all the attributes that they expect in their followers.

Leading Change   Jeff Immelt

Replacing someone who was touted as one of the best business leaders in the world and has become an icon in leadership and management is no easy feat. Jeff Immelt, who stepped in after Jack Welch to become CEO of General Electric (GE) in September of 2001, however, has taken on the task with apparent ease and comfort. He is implementing changes where many do not see an obvious need. Immelt is focusing on changing the leadership culture at GE on instituting a team culture (Nocera, 2007). He wants his company to be a role model for sustainability (McClenahen, 2005) and is reaching out to a wide range of constituencies beyond the shareholders (Murray, 2006). His soft approach and understated style are big assets to him in this process. Whereas Welch was loud, domineering, and impatient, Immelt is quiet, self-confident, and has a good dose of "people" skills. He believes the key to get-ting people onboard is that "People want to win. And if people think they've been given the capability to win and are the winner, that's how you get peo-ple in the game" (Byrne, 2005).

While much different than his predecessor, Immelt is said to be equally tireless, dedicated, intelligent, disciplined, as well as relaxed and charming (Colvin, 2005). Immelt is keenly aware of the importance of getting people onboard and the challenge in managing the change process. Discussing what university students should learn, he states, "I'd really want to re-engage peo-ple around innovation and risk-taking . . . emphasize team building. Good business is about good ideas, and good ideas come when people work together" (Bisoux, 2006: 22). At GE, everything is carefully planned and mea-sured so creating a team environment is no different. Employees are being taught team skills, managers and leaders are carefully evaluated on those skills, and those who show the best potential and performance are promoted to lead others. Through this careful process, the organization can slowly change its culture. Although innovation is Immelt's primary focus, he also considers that change needs to be focused and that people cannot take on too many initiatives at any one time. For him, the role of the leader is to keep that focus and communicate the new direction often. He states, "This is a company where we want people to make a difference. We want them to be proud of where they work" (Byrne, 2005).

Immelt's leadership is a well-thought-out process. He explains, "I always say that good leaders tend to be good students of leadership. . . . Leadership is ultimately a journey into itself" (Bisoux, 2006: 22). His low-key style and his focus on process and innovation have earned him the rank of the world's best CEOs only a few years after taking on a tough leadership challenge (Murray, 2006).

Sources: Bisoux, T., 2006. "Idea man," *BizEd*, May–June: 18-22; Byrne, J. A., 2005. "Jeff Immelt," *Fast Company*, July. http://www.fastcompany.com/magazine/96/jeff-immelt.html (accessed July 10, 2007); Colvin, G., 2005. "The bionic manager," *Fortune*, September 19. http://jcgi.pathfinder.com/fortune/fortune75/articles/0,15114,1101055,00.html (accessed July 10, 2007); McClenahen, 2005. "GE's Immelt sees green in being green," *Industry Week*, August: 13; Murray, A., 2006. "A tale of two CEOs: How public perception shapes reputation," *Wall Street Journal*, July 12: A2; Nocera, J., 2007. "Running G.E., comfortable in his skin," *The New York Times*, June 9. http://select.nytimes.com/gst/abstract.html?res=FA0B1FFC3D5B0C7A8CDDAF0894DF404482 (accessed July 10, 2007).

CREATIVITY AND IMPROVISATION

As proposed in visionary leadership, modeling the way is crucial in leading change. Leaders must show followers through their own actions how change can be implemented and how it can successful. To that end, the leader's creativity and ability to improvise become exemplary.

Creativity

Creativity, also called *diversity* or *lateral thinking*, is the ability to link or combine ideas in novel ways (see Chapter 4). Creativity for leaders and followers is a key factor in organizational ability to innovate and change (see Self-assessment 9-2). Creative people tend to be confident in the paths they select and are willing to take risks when others give up. They focus on learning and are willing to live with uncertainty to reach their goals. These traits and behaviors help when facing change. Leaders can put in place several processes to help their followers be more creative and accept change more readily:

➤ *Leadership style.* Autocratic leaders who demand obedience impede the creative process and open exchange that encourage creativity.

➤ *Flexible structure.* Less centralized and less hierarchical structures allow for free flow of ideas.

➤ *Open organizational culture.* Being creative and seeking novel solutions is more likely in a culture that values change and constructive deviance rather than tradition and conformity.

➤ *Questioning attitude.* Leaders can encourage and inspire followers to question assumptions and norms and look for novel alternatives instead of rewarding agreement and obedience.

> ➤ *Tolerating mistakes.* By encouraging experimentation, tolerating, and even rewarding some mistakes, the leader can send a strong message about the importance of taking risks.

Many decision-making tools, such as brainstorming, can be used to enhance followers' creativity. In brainstorming (or brainsailing), team members are encouraged to generate a large number of ideas and alternatives without any censorship. Another method called *cooperative exploration* requires individuals to consider a problem by taking different positions and perspectives (De Bono, 1999). Instead of looking at an issue from the typical positive and negative points of view, lateral thinking encourages people to consider a problem from neutral, emotional, optimistic, cautious, creative, and analytical perspectives. By using such techniques, leaders can encourage their followers to take broader perspectives and build a culture experimentation and creativity.

Improvisation

Closely related to creativity is improvisation. According to researchers Robert and Janet Denhardt, authors of *The Dance of Leadership,* "improvisation is a vital leadership skill, one essential to the process of emotionally connecting with and energizing others" (2006: 109). These researchers liken leadership to art, particularly dance, focusing on the intuitive nature of leadership and the need to master its rhythms. Improvisation, a term often used for artists rather than leaders, involves creation of something spontaneously and extemporaneously without specific preparation. Denhardt and Denhardt suggest that it occurs without a script and without perfect information and requires a combination of preplanned and unplanned activities and materials. Having expertise, knowledge, and perspective on the situation are also required, because without these elements, the leader is not likely to understand the leadership situation and environment enough to be able to lead. Improvisation is not "winging" a solution. It is based on deep preparation, self-knowledge, self-reflection, experience, and confidence, all also elements of authentic leadership. A musician states, "an ability to improvise . . . depends firstly on an understanding, developed from complete familiarity, of the musical context within which one improvises" (115).

Improvisation involves creation of something spontaneously and extemporaneously without specific preparation. It occurs without a script and without perfect information and requires a combination of preplanned and unplanned activities and materials. Having expertise, knowledge, and perspective on the situation are also required, because without these elements, the leader is not likely to understand the leadership situation and environment enough to be able to lead.

To be able to change their organizations, leaders themselves must be able and willing to take risks. As do artists, leaders must hone their skills, practice often, develop competence, and be willing to work with their team of followers to experiment and transform themselves and their organization.

CHANGING HOW ORGANIZATIONS APPROACH CHANGE

To implement change successfully, most organizations must change their culture in fundamental ways. Although the various methods described above all support change, the most basic and essential steps to successful change is to design organizations that are built to change (Worley and Lawler, 2006) and have cultures that are ready to change (Wall, 2005). The concept of learning organizations has been proposed to address the importance of flexibility and the ability to learn, adapt, and change continuously (Senge, 2006).

Learning Organizations

Learning organizations are organizations in which people continually expand their capacity to create, where innovation and cooperation are nurtured, and where knowledge is transferred throughout the organization. Such an organization learns and creates faster than others, and this ability becomes a major factor in its survival and success. Learning organizations do not simply manage change; their goal is to become a place where creativity, flexibility, adaptation, and learning are integral parts of the culture and everyday processes.

The elements that make up the core of learning organizations are presented in Table 9-4. In order for organizations to learn and accept change as part of their routine, the leaders and members must have a shared vision of the current and future states. Charismatic, transformational, authentic, and visionary leadership are all elements of building that vision. Then, it is essential that leaders and followers understand how the organization functions as a system both internally and within its environment and be aware of the stated and unstated assumptions that make up the culture of their organizations. Without understanding how the organization truly functions, it is hard to implement change. The vision and the knowledge of the organization and its culture allow organizational members to identify what needs to be changed and the best ways to approach the transformation. Finally, successful change requires expertise and continuous development of new skills and competencies for individuals and for teams.

Table 9-4   Core Elements of Learning Organizations.

Element	Description
Shared vision	Using cooperation and openness to build a shared vision through a common identity and a common goal of the future that leads to commitment.
System thinking	Understanding inter-relations and the invisible and visible bonds that connect people inside and outside the organization.
Mental models	Being aware of stated and unstated assumptions and mental models that guide behaviors and decisions and developing new ones based on openness and cooperation.
Personal mastery	Continually clarifying and developing personal visions and goals, and expanding skills sets and levels of proficiency.
Team learning	Developing synergy and the ability to think and work together to question assumptions and build new processes.

Sources: P.M. Senge, "*The Fifth Discipline: The Art and Practice of Learning Organizations,*" New York: Doubleday, 2006; P.M. Senge, "Leading learning organizations," *Training and Development,* 1995, 50(12), 36-37; P.M. Senge and J.D. Sterman, "System thinking and organizational learning: Acting locally and thinking globally in the organization of the future," *European Journal of Operations Research,* 1992, 59 (1), 137–140.

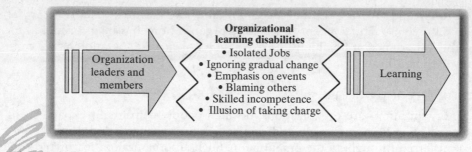

Figure 9-5   Blocks to Learning in Organizations.

Figure 9-5 presents the factors that prevent organizations from learning. These factors are organizational learning disabilities of sorts. They are patterns of thinking and behavior that members have adopted that block change. According to Senge (2006), these block or disabilities, stem from lack of system thinking that leads to looking at tasks, jobs, problems, and goals as separate and isolated from one another. Additionally, leaders that are focused on large-scale change may fail to ignore the gradual and incremental change that may be occurring and likely to lead to the same outcome. They also may focus on specific events or causes of problems without considering the context in which they may be occurring or all the system-wide factors that may be contributing to them. The focus on events results in trying to find someone or something to blame for the problems. Identifying these enemies detracts from fully considering the problems and focusing on solutions. Another organizational learning disability is skilled incompetence, which refers to relying on people with highly developed but narrow expertise who are celebrated and expected to provide answers. Because they are there to solve problems, they often cannot admit to lack of understanding or knowledge or to making mistakes. They, therefore, cannot learn and become incompetent in spite of their considerable skills. The situation becomes even more precarious if leaders are those who have skilled incompetence. Finally, another factor related to leadership is the illusion of taking charge and of one person being responsible to lead all others through the problem, instead of having shared leadership, empowerment, and cooperation.

To support their organizations in being change ready and become learning organizations, leaders can take several actions to build an open and supportive culture that will support ongoing transformation. Actions include

➤ *Openness to new ideas.* Welcoming and encouraging new ideas; this involves role modeling, tolerance for a questioning attitude, and supporting and rewarding openness.

➤ *Local solutions.* Encouraging and allowing each person, team, or department at every level of the organization to find and implement its own solutions without focusing on standardization. The local solutions can be used as learning tools by others without imposing them across the organization.

➤ *Time for learning.* Providing organizational members time and resources to learn new ideas and experiment with a focus on long-term rather than short-term results.

➤ *Appropriate leadership.* Leading organizations by inspiring a shared vision, providing guidance, support, and service rather than imposing a top-down vision and solutions.

The example of McNerney in 3M provides a case for obstacles and support for learning organizations. Based on its creativity and track record for innovation, 3M had many of the elements that encourage learning in organizations. Before McNerney taking leadership, the organization focused on local solutions, open communication among inventors, and plenty of time and tolerance for learning and experimentation. In his search for efficiency, McNerney replaced many of the elements that made 3M a learning organization with factors that blocked learning. Implementation of a one-size-fits-all Six Sigma process, focus on specific events rather than looking for system-wide causes of problems, and an imposed vision from the top rather a shared vision, all eroded the culture and 3M's ability to learn. Whereas the company continues to face challenges in maintaining its growth and profitability, the current leaders are reinstituting many of the elements that gave the company its innovative culture (Hindo, 2007).

Herman Miller, the office furniture maker, provides another example of a learning organization (Glaser, 2006; Herman Miller Culture, 2007). The company has been recognized as one of the best in its industry for its innovation and unique culture. It is known for its focus on its employees through flex-time, telecommuting, and employee learning and ownership. It works with clients to develop distinctive solutions to their unique problems (Salter, 2000b). But what makes the company truly a learning organization is the focus on curiosity and learning. Author Glaser describes the culture in her book *The DNA of Leadership:* "To encourage a wonderful sense of curiosity, leaders focus on helping Herman Miller employees experiment and take lessons from those experiments. This is such a strong part of the culture that's built into everything they do and say—it's embedded in their genetic code" (Glaser, 2006: 180).

Role of Leader in Changing Organizational Culture

Chapter 7 presented the many ways in which top-level leaders can influence their organizations (see Figure 7-4 for a summary). Additionally, Edgar Schein has identified several specific mechanisms that leaders use to shape the culture of their organization (2004). They include:

➤ *Communicate priorities.* By stating what is important, in terms of a general vision, specific issues that must be addressed, and ways in which they must be addressed, leaders make a powerful impact on their organization. For example, A.G. Lafley, CEO of P&G is relentless about repeating the simple message of paying attention to customers (see Leadership in Action in Chapter 7).

➤ *Role model.* Although what the leader says is important, even more powerful is what the leader does. Leaders must be the change they want to see. Their actions demonstrate their values and what is truly important. For example, many historical charismatic leaders including Mahatma Gandhi and Nelson Mandela have gone to prison for their beliefs. A particular opportunity to role model desired behaviors occurs during times of crisis when the focus on and the need for leadership is increased. How a leader acts when facing unplanned change, what she pays attention to, and how his priorities may change all provide authoritative guides for followers.

➤ *Allocate resources and rewards.* A more practical and equally impacting action is how the leader allocates resources and rewards. By rewarding compliance and conformity, a leader who professes that she values innovation and experimentation shows what she truly values. Similarly, by promoting individuals who demonstrate the values and mission of the organization, the leader can make a clear impact on the culture of the organization.

Applying What You Learn
Guidelines for Change

The research and practice of leading organizations through change is rich with studies and examples, all of which do not make the actual implementation of change easier. Changing people and organizations that have established a culture is a challenging task. Here are some practical pointers:

- *Communicate and explain; then repeat.* Although it may be easy to use the parental "because I say so," getting followers to understand and accept change takes communication, repetition, and clarification. You should be able to clearly explain why your followers must change and why the course of action selected is the most viable. Practice those key communications to get your message just right. You should also communicate often throughout the change process.

- *Identify people who can be change agents.* In every organization, there are opinion leaders who are respected. Winning them over and enlisting their support for the change will move implementation along much faster.

- *Involve people in the change that affects them.* You may not have a choice about the actual change, but you are more likely to have a choice about various ways to go about the change. Whenever possible get your followers involved in planning. Participation leads to commitment and reduces resistance.

- *Be supportive.* Change is painful; be understanding and supportive of your followers. Even if the need for change is accepted and there is buy-in, people will be stressed. Celebrate any success and make time for humor and relaxation as a team.

- *Don't forget those above you.* Change needs support both from the top and the bottom. As you are busy supporting your followers, don't forget to keep your supervisor informed and involved as well.

- *Role model.* Finally, nothing speaks more loudly than your actions. Monitor yourself, and make sure you do not consciously or unconsciously undermine the change effort. Be the change you want to see.

Many other mechanisms that leaders use to shape their organizations are design of the structure and processes, setting design criteria, and even selection of the physical space (Schein, 2004), several of which are discussed in Chapter 7.

SUMMARY AND CONCLUSIONS

Change has become the only constant in today's organizations. Internal and external forces pressure organizations to be flexible, adapt, and transform themselves. A leader's ability to guide and support followers through change is one of the key leadership roles and may vary depending on cultural factors such as tolerance for ambiguity and perception of time. Even though organizations would like to plan for change and implement change in gradual and incremental ways, many of them face unplanned change that is revolutionary and requires considerable transformation. Regardless of the type of change, leaders need to view change as a three-step process of unfreezing or preparing followers for change, the actual change, and refreezing, which involves providing resources and support to solidify new processes and behaviors.

Planned change often follows six steps from recognizing the need for change, to developing, adopting and implementing ideas, to allocation of resources and finally evaluation. In this process, leaders can implement the change from the top-down pushing the change faster or allow bottom-up input that helps to get commitment and reduces resistance to change. Additionally, whereas unplanned change is by definition unpredictable, leaders can prepare their followers by supporting flexibility, introducing gradual change, and experimenting with new methods. Even with careful planning and preparation, resistance to change is likely to occur because of organizational factors such as inertia and culture, group factors such as group norms, and many individual factors such as fear and individual characteristics. Leaders have many options such as education, involvement, negotiation, and even coercion to reduce resistance to change.

One of the essential roles of leaders in the change process is to develop a shared vision for the change to help support followers through the implementation phase. Other related roles for visionary leaders are challenging the process, motivating followers, role modeling, and empowerment, all of which can energize followers and establish a culture that can sustain change. Other leadership roles include role modeling and supporting creativity and improvisation. An organization that has flexible and open structures and cultures, where mistakes are tolerated and experimentation and a questioning attitude encouraged, can encourage creativity. Improvisation requires deep preparation, self-reflection, and commitment, all of which are also elements of authentic leadership.

The leader's ability to support followers through organizational change ultimately depends on having an organizational culture that is built and ready for change and continuous learning. The leader plays a critical role in creating a learning organization and in developing followers' ability to think broadly, develop personal mastery, work as a team, and develop as shared vision to assure that the organization as whole is ready to learn and change.

LEADERSHIP CHALLENGE: IMPLEMENTING UNPOPULAR CHANGE

Your supervisor has just informed you of a major restructuring in your area aimed at increasing efficiency. She is assigning you to implement the necessary changes. The plans are coming from headquarters and are not negotiable. In addition to losing a couple of positions, your department will be moved to a new less-desirable location across town and will have to share administrative support with another team. Upper management is further using the restructuring as an opportunity to implement a much-needed new web-based customer relations system.

Your team of 15 people is cohesive, and you know that letting go of two of your members will be hard on everyone. In addition, the new location is farther for all of you, and your offices will not be as nice. Although the new technology is welcome, there will be a great need for training and support before it can be fully implemented. On a personal level, you are very upset about the change. This is the second major change in as many years that you have had to implement without having a chance for input. You experience considerable stress and are worried about your team's reaction and ability to pull this through. Yet, your career depends on implementing the change.

1. How should you approach your team?
2. How much of your personal feelings should you share?
3. What are some key actions you should take?

REVIEW AND DISCUSSION QUESTIONS

1. Describe the internal and external forces for change.
2. What role does culture play in how people perceive change?
3. Describe the five different types of changes organizations face.
4. Explain Lewin's model for change and its implications for organizations.
5. Present the six steps in the process of planned change, and describe the role of leaders in each step.
6. What can leaders do to prepare their organization to deal with unplanned change?
7. Present the organizational, group, and individual causes of resistance to change.
8. Describe ways in which resistance to change can be reduced, and explain when each method can be used.
9. What is visionary leadership and how does it relate to change?
10. Compare and contrast creativity and improvisation, and explain their role in leading change.
11. What are the elements of an organizational culture that supports change, and what role do leaders play in developing that culture?

EXERCISE 9-1:   ANALYZING AND PLANNING
FOR CHANGE

This exercise is designed to provide you with the experience of defining a problem and planning for the change. It follows the model presented in Figure 9-3.

Part I: Form Teams and Select a Problem
In teams of three to five members, select a problem (organizational or personal) that one team member faces that requires change. Potential examples include the following: the sales team you supervise does not work well with the development or manufacturing department; the clerks at your agency do not have a customer-focused approach; the team you belong to in one of your classes is unfocused; the spring program committee that you lead at your child's school has been putting together boring programs for several years; the school board would like to seek more parent input in its decisions, and so on. Note that each of the problems—and any you are likely to identify—involves many different individual and organizational issues.

What problem will your group address?

Part II: Define the Problem
It is important for the team to have a clear idea about what the problem really is. As a team:

Verbally restate the problem in as many different ways as you can.

Consider all the positive and negative aspects of the problem.

Consider all the related issues.

Agree on a final description of the problem.

Part III: Plan for Change

Instead of jumping into action and proposing solutions, your team must understand the problem and the process, consider many alternatives, and evaluate them before selecting a solution.

How will you help the organization understand the need for change? What steps will you take? What data do you need?

Identify as many alternative solutions as you can without evaluating each (brainstorm)

Evaluate each solution carefully; consider the positive and negative aspects of each. Who is likely to be impacted if the solutions are implemented? Who will resist? What are the costs? Do they fully address the problem?

Select one solution; it does not have to be perfect, just based on your team's analysis. Explain why it is the best solution.

How will you implement your solution? Consider people and resources, major obstacles, potential solutions, key people to be involved, training needs, timetable, costs, how you will measure success.

Part IV: Presentation

Each team will make a brief presentation of its plan for change.

Source: Based on "Managing Change," in A. Nahavandi and A.R. Malekzadeh *Organizational Behavior: The Person–Organization Fit.* Upper Saddle River, NJ: Prentice Hall.

SELF-ASSESSMENT 9-1:   BUILDING CREDIBILITY

One of the key elements to visionary leadership is the leader's credibility. Having credibility allows a leader to undertake the necessary changes with sincerity and with followers' trust. Following are the elements of credibility. Rate yourself on each of the items using the following scale:

1 = Never

2 = Occasionally

3 = Often

4 = Always

_____ 1. I state my position clearly.

_____ 2. My coworkers and subordinates always know where I stand.

_____ 3. I listen to other people's opinions carefully and respectfully.

_____ 4. I accept disagreement from my coworkers and followers.

_____ 5. I try to integrate my point of view with that of others.

_____ 6. I encourage and practice constructive feedback.

_____ 7. I encourage and practice cooperation.

_____ 8. I build consensus out of differing views.

_____ 9. I develop my coworkers' and subordinates' skills.

_____ 10. I provide frequent positive feedback and encouragement.

_____ 11. I hold myself and others accountable for actions.

_____ 12. I practice what I preach.

Scoring Key: Add up your rating for all 12 items. The maximum score is 48. A higher score indicates behaviors that build credibility.

Total: _____

Self-analysis and Action Plan

Which items have a low score? List those areas that you need to target in order to build your credibility.

What can you do about them? Focus on clear and specific behaviors. Develop short-term and long-term goals. When will you know that you have improved? How will you measure yourself?

Source: This self-assessment is partially based on concepts developed by Kouzes and Posner (1993, 2003b).

SELF-ASSESSMENT 9-2:   CREATIVITY

Being open to change is to some extent a function of being creative. Although creativity is partly a personality trait, individuals can enhance their personal creativity in several ways. Rate each statement according to how well it applies to you by using the following scale:

1 = never

2 = some of the time

3 = always

_____ 1. My life is so hectic; I have no time to pay attention to anything new.

_____ 2. I set daily goals for myself and focus on getting them done.

_____ 3. I put considerable effort to do something well when I do it.

_____ 4. I have clear priorities about what is important to me and what is not.I look for ways to making things I enjoy more complex and challenging.

_____ 5. I know what I like and don't like in life.

_____ 6. I face problems head-on and look for solutions immediately.

_____ 7. I am disorganized and feel that my schedule is out of control.

_____ 8. I often surprise others with my unexpected actions or words.

_____ 9. My office/home is organized in a way that calms me and supports my activities.

_____ 10. I rarely follow through on things that spark my interest.

_____ 11. I keep routine things simple so that I have energy to focus on what is impor- tant.

_____ 12. I make time for relaxation and reflection.

_____ 13. I approach problems by trying to develop as many solutions as possible before I try to solve them.

_____ 14. I stop and look at unusual things, people, and events around me.

Scoring Key: Reverse score items 1, 7, 8, and 10 (1 = 3, 2 = 2, 3 = 1). Total up your score for the 15 items. The minimum is 15; the maximum is 45. A score above 30 indicates that you are undertaking many activities and managing your life in ways that enhance personal creativity. *Total:* _____

Self-Analysis and Action Plan

Which items have a low score? List those areas that you need to target in order to improve your cre- ativity.

Source: Developed based on information in M. Csikszentmihalyi, *Creativity: Flow and the Psychology of Discovery and Invention*, New York: Harper Perennial.

Leadership in Action: Best Buy Takes on Its Own Culture

The 8-to-5, five-days-a-week work week is a staple of the U.S. workplace. For most managers and corporate employees, the clock extends well beyond the 40-hour week. Being seen, getting to the office before everyone else, being the last one to leave at night, and working on weekends are all considered a badge of honor and necessary to success in corporate America. At least one U.S. company is changing these traditions with much debate and some undisputable success.

For many Best Buy employees, work is no longer a place where you go, but something that you do. The Minnesota-based electronic store has thrown out the time clock for all of its corporate employees and is considering doing the same for the store sales staff. There are no set schedules and no mandatory meetings; salaried employees spend enough time to get their work done, wherever they would like. "No one at Best Buy really knows where I am," says Steve Hance, Best Buy's employee relations manager (Kiger, 2006). He and other employees at the corporate office come and go when they want; take afternoons to go to the movies; come in late or leave early during fishing and hunting season; go home to be with their kids in the afternoon; or spend as much time as they can in their cabins in the woods; *and* produce 35 percent more than they used to before they were given the flexibility to set their own work schedule, process 13 to 18% more orders than those not in the program, and have lower turnover, reducing hiring costs (Conlin, 2006a). "It used to be

that I had to schedule my life around my work. Now I schedule my work around my life," says Hance (Kiger, 2006) This revolutionary approach to work is called Results-Only Work Environment, or ROWE.

Results-Only Work Environment focuses on evaluating employees based on meeting their goals rather than worrying about how much face time they have put in the office. The program has its own set of 13 commandments including one that states that no one needs to talk about how many hours they work (Conlin, 2006a). Meetings are considered to be "time-sucking crutches for undisciplined managers" (Conlin, 2006b), so everyone instead focuses on understanding what the goals are and actually doing the work. Implementing big changes is nothing new at Best Buy. The company has been instituting many other changes over the past few years. It stopped paying its sales force a commission in 1989, to tackle what some customers perceived as high-pressure sales (Boyle, 2006). It shifted its focus to customers and redesigned stores to address the needs of different types of customers, not just the tech junkies. It made the store more inviting to women, who influence a great majority of electronic purchasing decisions, by widening the aisles to allow baby strollers to go through easily (Fetterman, 2006). It also put much more emphasis on the "blue shirts," the sales force that the company president Brad Anderson believes makes up the core of the business (Breen, 2005). The difference between these changes and ROWE is that these changes originated from the top leadership and made their way down. The ROWE program started somewhere in middle and lower management, was intentionally kept secret from upper management, tested in a few teams; and then presented to Anderson. He did not know about the program until two years after it had been implemented in some of the corporate offices with some success.

Results-Only Work Environment is the brainchild of two HR employees, Jodi Thompson, 49, and Cali Ressler, 29, who discovered they shared views about working in cubicles and how technology and wireless access could change how people work (Conlin, 2006a). They also paid attention to the results of a 2001 survey that indicated widespread employee dissatisfaction and a perception of inability to balance work and life (Kiger, 2006). They believed that the typical flex-time solutions did not provide much benefit or flexibility and that the only solution was a radical change to how people work. Meanwhile, they heard of two department managers who were eager to implement any new methods to retain their best employees and improve morale and productivity. Thompson and Ressler suggested that they implement the first version of ROWE by focusing on how much employees produced instead of whether they showed up in the office at 6 A.M. The results were positive, and word got out about the new way to work. Those working under ROWE guarded their secret fearing a reversal from upper management. Those who didn't convinced their managers to join the program, slowly spreading word about ROWE throughout Best Buy's corporate office.

Although many employees love the program and the results have been very positive with productivity improvements and a reduction in turnover for employees who take part in ROWE, there has been some resistance. Thompson and Ressler are viewed by some as subversives who are "infecting" the company (Conlin, 2006b). More traditional managers feel threatened that they are losing control and power. Others worry about employees never being able to get away from work. Those who are in the program and the company are clearly benefiting. Steve Hance says, "It used to be that I had to schedule my life around my work. Now, I schedule my work around my life" (Kiger, 2006).

Implementing ROWE in a department is a lengthy and careful process. Each department interested in implementing the program is carefully evaluated. Employees then receive extensive training that includes role-plays about how to deal with negative comments about the program and those who participate in it and about how to implement the cultural changes necessary for ROWE to work. Giving up old habits is not easy. The primary drivers, however, are maximum accountability and flexibility (Kiger, 2006). Instead of engaging in tasks to fill up time or make a good impression on their bosses, employees focus on what matters. Ressler states, "You start looking at everything and saying, 'Is this really going to help get me to my desired outcome.' Pretty soon you've cut out 10 of those unnecessary things that use to fill up your week, and you're getting a lot more done" (Kiger, 2006). John Thompson, general manager at BestBuy.com was a late convert who finally bought into the system after seeing the data on the clear performance and morale improvements. He admits, "I was always looking to see if people were here. I should have been looking at what they were getting done" (Conlin, 2006a).

(Continued)

Leadership in Action: *(Continued)*

QUESTIONS

1. What are the internal and external forces for change at Best Buy?

2. How was change implemented?

3. What role did various leaders play in the change?

Sources: Boyle, M. 2006. "Best Buy's giant gamble." CNNMoney.com, March 29. http://money.cnn.com/magazines/fortune/fortune_archive/2006/04/03/8373034/index.htm (accessed September 3, 2007); Breen, B., 2005. "The clear leader," *Fast Company*, March: 65; Kiger, P. J., 2006. "Throwing out the rules of work," *Workforce Management*, October 7. http://www.workforce.com/section/09/feature/24/54/28 (accessed September 3, 2007); Conlin, M., 2006a. "Smashing the clock," *Business Week*, December 11. http://www.businessweek.com/magazine/content/06_50/b4013001.htm (accessed July 9, 2007); Conlin, M., 2006b. "How to kill a meeting," *Business Week*, December 11 http://www.businessweek.com/magazine/content/06_50/b4013008.htm (accessed July 10, 2007).

Developing Leaders

You must do the things you think you cannot do.
—ELEANOR ROOSEVELT

The aim of life is self-development. To realize one's nature perfectly—that is what each of us is here for.
—OSCAR WILDE

After studying this chapter, you will be able to:

- Define the elements of leader development.
- Describe the elements of learning.
- Review areas that are addressed in leader development.
- Outline criteria of an effective development program.
- Present the methods used in leader development.
- Consider the role of culture in leader development.
- Summarize the role of the person and the organization in effective leader development.

One of the fundamental premises of this book and modern leadership theory and practice is that leadership can be learned. Leaders are not born; they are made. Whereas our individual characteristics and traits may create barriers for some and make it easy for others to learn the art and practice of leadership, leadership scholars widely agree that leaders can improve and develop their leadership skills. The turbulent environment that organizations face and the need for flexibility make developing leaders and expanding their ability to lead and the skills they use in leading others even more important. It is, therefore, not surprising that organizations and individuals devote considerable resources to leader and leadership development. By some accounts, the large majority of U.S. companies with over 10,000 employees spend over $750,000 on leadership development each year (Murphy and Riggio, 2003). Developing leaders so that they are ready to address the changing needs of organizations and their stakeholders is an essential part of the effectiveness of organizations.

Questions such as how do people learn, what are key elements of developing leaders, and what are the best methods for creating long-term behavioral change are integral parts of the discussion of leader development and the focus of this chapter. We will define the concepts of leaders and leadership development, consider the necessary elements of learning, review the methods for development, and examine the role of culture. Finally, we will summarize the leadership and organizational factors that support development.

DEFINITIONS AND BASIC ELEMENTS

Development is an ongoing, dynamic, long-term change or evolution that occurs because of various learning experiences (London and Mauer, 2004). More specifically, leader development is defined as the "expansion of a person's capacity to be effective in leadership roles and processes" (McCauley and Van Velsor, 2004: 2). It focuses on the individual and involves providing leaders with the tools that they need to improve their effectiveness in the various roles they play. Leadership development, while related to leader development, is different in that it focuses on an organization's capability to get the work done through its many leaders (McCauley and Van Velsor, 2004). It is important to note the difference as they each address different levels of development. This chapter is primarily focused on leader development, although some of the methods described, when applied to the whole leadership of an organization, may affect its leadership development. Additionally, while closely related and often using similar approaches, there are some differences between managerial, leader, leadership, and executive development (London and Maurer, 2004). They differ in terms of their focus on the person or the organization and the degree to which they are customized for individual participants (Figure 10-1). For example, managerial and supervisory development primarily focuses on education and teaching participants the skills to effectively conduct their day-to-day activities and take care of their employees. The

Figure 10-1   Levels of Development.

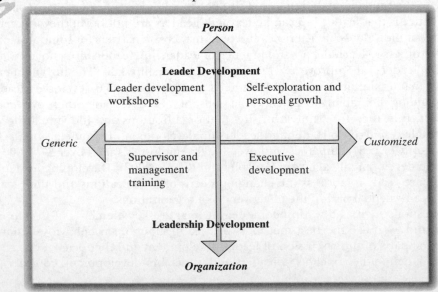

focus is on developing skills for the organization and the training programs are generic and often offered in classroom settings with many participants. Leader development focuses on developing the individual, taking a more holistic approach to increase self-awareness and provide skills. Such training may be either generic or customized. Leadership development is aimed at developing leadership ability across the organization. Finally, executive development targets developing leadership for the organization and frequently has a highly individualized nature, such as in executive coaching.

Factors in Learning

Learning involves a relatively permanent increase or change in behavior, knowledge, or skill that comes about because of some experience. In order for leaders to develop, they must learn new skills and behaviors and expand their abilities. Those changes must be relatively stable and last beyond the classroom or training setting. Whereas learning addresses the content of the change (Kegan and Lahey, 2001), development addresses the process. The two are therefore closely intertwined. Given that development and learning involve change, many of the concepts that we discussed in Chapter 9 regarding the models, processes, and resistance to change can apply to leader development as do theories of learning (e.g., Bandura, 1995). For individuals to learn and develop, they must first become aware of the need for change and accept it (unfreezing). Then after some change is implemented, it must be supported and sustained to result in the adoption and use of new behaviors, skills, or knowledge (freezing). Lasting change, which is at the heart of leader development, requires patience and persistence. As with any other change, it also is likely to be faced with resistance as the person may not be aware of the need to change, willing to make the necessary changes, or able to sustain the newly learned behaviors because of lack of practice or support. Such potential resistance must be taken into account by both the person and the organization.

Several elements make up the core of learning (McCauley, 2001). First, the person must have the willingness to learn, which requires both motivation and readiness (Figure 10-2). The motivational element is related to the unfreezing step in change. Many of us have worked with leaders who are either unaware of their areas of weakness or unwilling to invest their time in changing. Without the recognition or willingness to learn and change, no development can take place. Recent focus of some leadership development research has been on the need for leaders to conduct deep exploration to understand their motives and sensitivities and identify potential obstacles to their growth (Kaiser and Kaplan, 2006). As we will discuss later in this chapter, increasing self-awareness and personal growth form a substantial portion of most leader development programs.

In addition to motivation to learn, the person must have the ability to learn through the right combination of intelligence and personality traits. Learning may come easier to some and be more challenging for others. For example, high traditional intelligence may help one participant grasp conceptual ideas quickly, whereas another who has high emotional intelligence will quickly learn social and interpersonal skills. Third, leaders must have access to developmental experiences and have the opportunity to practice and learn. For example, employees of smaller organizations are often exposed to diverse experiences, which are an excellent source of learning. In larger companies, jobs and duties are narrower and more specialized. Large

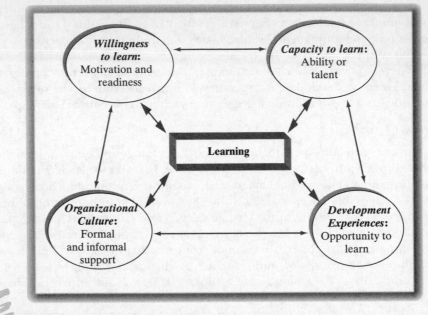

Figure 10-2   Factors in Learning.

companies, however, provide the benefit of extensive training and development resources, including educational benefits. For example, Goldman Sacks has its own university that focuses not only on leader and leadership development, but also on developing the culture of the organization (Marquez, 2007a).

Finally, the organizational culture must support and sustain learning and development. This support comes not only in the form of training programs, but also in the form of informal systems that value learning and tolerate experimentation and failure. The case study of Southwest Airlines at the end of this chapter provides an example of an organization that supports development. Mistakes are tolerated, and organizational leaders focus on developing leadership in others. Another factor in organizational support is supervision. Supervisors who support and encourage development are key to the development of leaders. Such support can be through formal assignments and training or through informal mentoring.

Learning requires consistent practice and persistence. It is interesting to note that although many of us understand the need for practice and persistence when it comes to things such as learning sports or a new language, we tend to forget the importance of practice in the even more complex skills and behaviors required to lead others. Communicating well and clearly, motivating followers, coaching them in their development and learning, and providing feedback are just some of the complex skills required to lead well. Learning any of them necessitates perseverance, making mistakes, and repetition. The CEO of L'Oreal, the giant global cosmetics company, Jean-Paul Agon states, "A career is made of great moments, difficult moments, success, challenges, joys, everything. I think each moment, good or bad is a step in a journey. There are many, many steps, and they are all important" (Shinn, 2005: 23).

Table 10-1   What Leader Development Addresses.

Area	Description
Basic knowledge	Information about content of leadership; definitions; basic concepts such as communication, feedback, contingent rewards; typically through classroom education
Personal growth	Self-awareness and understanding strengths and weaknesses; getting in touch with personal values, dreams, and aspirations
Skills development: supervisory, managerial, and interpersonal skills	How to apply knowledge; includes supervisor and managerial skills such as planning, goal setting, and monitoring, as well as conceptual skills such as problem solving and decision making, and skills related to managing interpersonal relations
Creativity	Expanding ability to think in novel and innovative ways and to think "outside the box"
Strategic issues	Developing mission; strategic planning

What Is Developed: The Content

What do leader development programs address? What are the skills, knowledge, behaviors, and so forth that are developed? Table 10-1 summarizes the typical areas that are covered by leader development. The content is broad and complex, reflecting the richness and complexity of leadership; therefore, the list is far from comprehensive. The content depends on the level of leader development such **The content of leader development programs is broad and complex, reflecting the richness and complexity of leadership.**
that basic knowledge and skills are typically aimed at supervisory and middle-level leaders whereas and strategic thinking is aimed at executives. Personal growth and self-awareness are included in most development programs with a more intense focus in top-level and executive leaders. Additionally, the content areas, while presented in separate and distinct categories, are interrelated and integrated. For example, providing feedback, which is a basic supervisory skill, is related to communication, which is part of social skills. Similarly, strategic issues such as developing a vision rely on conceptual, communication, and interpersonal skills and require creativity.

Each of the content areas can be addressed through a number of different methods and tools reviewed later in the chapter.

CRITERIA FOR EFFECTIVE DEVELOPMENT PROGRAMS

Development programs have different goals, and each program provides a number of advantages and disadvantages. Several key criteria can be used to evaluate the effectiveness of a training program (Figure 10-3). Although all are not required, satisfying more of the criteria makes a program richer and more likely to lead to long-term

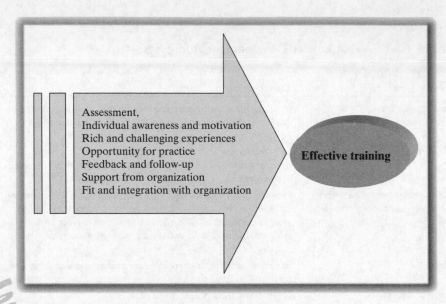

Figure 10-3   Criteria for Effective Training.

change and learning. One of the first principles of an effective development program is that it provides participants with assessment data about their current strengths, weaknesses, performance, and some information about where they stand in regard to the goals of the program and their leadership ability (McCauley and Van Velsor, 2004). The availability of information about the self can encourage participants to improve and be a guidepost for their progress throughout the program. Many organizations recognize the importance of assessment. For example, Agilent, the maker of testing tools, spends considerable resources assessing its top 100 leaders through a comprehensive program (Frauenheim, 2007). The company has hired an outside consultant to implement a high-stakes assessment program to look at the potential leadership. Leaders are evaluated based on business results, capabilities, and potential and a quarterly leadership audit completed by employees to indicate their confidence in their managers (Frauenheim, 2007).

The assessment data can help increase individual awareness, another principle of effective development programs. To learn, participants must be aware of the need for change and specific areas they should address so that they are ready to change. The awareness can result from formal data or from informal discussions with a supervisor, coworkers, a mentor, or a coach. Additionally, an effective development program exposes participants to rich experiences that challenge them to step outside their zone of comfort and pushes them to experiment with skills, behaviors, and approaches (McCauley and Van Velsor, 2004). For example, being assigned to a new task or rotating to another department or team is likely to have the potential for rich experience. Whether through a new assignment or through a specific task, or even while conducting day-to-day activities, leaders must have the opportunity to practice the behaviors or skills they have learned. One approach is to consider how artists use the studio system to integrate opportunity to practice with self-awareness and rich feedback from multiple sources (Denhardt and Denhardt, 2006). This artistic approach is gaining popularity in many areas of management (Adler, 2006). Without having the opportunity for practice, leaders cannot receive feedback about their performance, another criteria for effective development programs. As is the case with assessment, the feedback can be formal, for example when one's performance is reviewed or a 360-degree feedback is implemented, or informal through discussions with coworkers or a mentor. Anne Mulcahy, CEO of Xerox, believes that her ability to handle criticism has been essential to her success. She also suggests that the higher up leaders go, the harder it becomes to get honest and open feedback because "people around you want to please" (Kharif, 2003).

The last two criteria for effective development relate to the culture of the organization and how well it integrates its development programs with its strategic goals and with the needs of individual leaders. Supporting leaders to experiment with their new learning and providing them with training resources, opportunities for rich experiences, and feedback indicate the level of support from the organization and are a sign of the extent to which the organization as a whole supports learning. Finally, a key factor is the fit and integration of the person, the development program, and organizational goals (London and Mauer, 2004). At a very basic level, we learn and perform best when we love what we do and have passion for our work. L'Oreal's CEO, Jean-Paul Agon, recommends to students to "choose a job that is really exciting, a job that makes them want to get up from their beds every morning and feel happy about going to work" (Shinn, 2005: 23). The passion comes from a good fit between the person and the organization and the job. The same fit is essential for the effectiveness of leader development. From an organizational point of view, an effective program is based on strategic goals and support for those goals. It, therefore, has a relatively long-term focus rather than merely addressing the latest fads and trends, or what some call a "flavor-of-the-month" approach to training and development. Goldman Sachs University's managing director Carol Pledger recommends linking any training initiative to the organization's strategy and to link it to individual employees' jobs to increase the potential for effectiveness and long-term change (Marquez, 2007b).

The seven criteria discussed are key elements of development programs; although not all are required to develop leaders, without most, the program may provide at best an entertaining experience with short-term benefits, but little long-term impact, as is the case with some popular programs we consider later in this chapter. Other specific conditions that help make any method for leader development more effective include:

➤ *Clear objectives* that are tied to organizational goals, the leader's personal goals, and the current of future challenges the leader may be facing. Such objectives must be stated ahead and means of assessing them before and after the program must be available.

➤ *Using a combination of tools and methods* that provide parallel learning environments and address different learning styles or reinforce one another. For example, classroom education may be combined with an assessment center, coaching, and new assignments.

➤ *Assessment and follow-up* that measure change and support the new learning and assure that new behaviors, skills, and styles are not forgotten or not used when the development program is over. Learning takes practice and persistence, and such opportunities should be present outside of the training session.

The variety of training programs and methods available are considered next and evaluated in terms of how well they address the criteria for effective development.

METHODS OF LEADER DEVELOPMENT

There are many different approaches and methods to develop leaders, ranging from highly structured and formal programs, to classroom education, to observation and hands-on experiences. Each approach provides advantages and addresses particular aspects of leadership. Table 10-2 provides a comparison of the methods based on the criteria for effective development programs discussed above.

Self-awareness

Anne Mulcahy, CEO of Xerox, has been credited with bringing the company back from the brink of bankruptcy after it was riddled with accounting scandals and poor performance. One of her basic guidelines for good leadership is that a leader "will recognize what she does not know and be willing to learn all the time" (for Anne Mulcahy, 2001). The essential role of self-awareness in effective leadership is a theme throughout this book and in leadership practice and research (Kaiser and Kaplan, 2006; Wood and Vilkinas, 2007). Personal reflection and getting feedback from others are necessary elements of developing self-awareness, a process labeled *double-loop learning* (Argyris, 1991). Additionally, some studies show that a leader's self-awareness may be related to higher follower satisfaction and productivity (Moshavi, Brown, and Dodd, 2003).

The essential role of self-awareness in effective leadership is a key theme in leadership practice and research. Personal reflection and getting feedback from others are necessary elements of developing self-awareness.

Guidelines for increasing self awareness include:

➤ *Clarifying one's values and priorities*, a process, which is a first step in self-awareness; the person must know what is important and what factors have priority.

➤ *Seeking new experiences* that will challenge the leader to move outside of the zone of comfort and provide an opportunity to learn something about oneself; including opportunities to fail.

➤ *Seeking feedback* through formal and informal channels as often as possible from as many diverse sources as possible. For example, the feedback from a customer regarding one set of behaviors may be very different, but equally relevant, as feedback from a supervisor regarding those same behaviors.

Being able to seek and accept information about oneself may, to some extent, depend on one's personality traits. For example, the person's openness to experience, one of the Big Five Personality factors, may play a role (Chapter 4; Barrick and Mount, 1991). Other factors such as self-monitoring (Chapter 4: Snyder, 1974) may make leaders more perceptive and receptive to feedback from others and allow them to change their behaviors more easily.

Even though self-awareness is, in many ways, the cornerstone of any development program and a requirement for getting the leader to be willing to change and learn, it is not enough. Leaders must also have the tools to change. Although assessment and individual awareness are integral to a development program based on self-awareness, it does not expose the leader to rich experiences, provide opportunity for practice, or

Table 10-2 Comparison of Development Methods.

Criteria	Assessment	Individual Awareness	Rich Developmental Experience	Opportunity for Practice	Feedback on New Learning and Follow-up	Support from Organization	Fit and Integration
Self-awareness	✓	✓	—	—	?	—	—
Experience	?	✓	✓	✓	✓	✓	✓
Coaching	✓	✓	—	✓	✓	✓	✓
Mentoring	✓	✓	—	—	?	✓	✓
Feedback-intensive programs	✓	✓	—	?	—	?	?
Classroom education	?	✓	—	?	?	?	?
Outdoor challenges	—	?	—	—	—	?	?

✓ : very Likely; integral part of the method; ? : possible, depending on situation and organizational conditions; — : highly unlikely; not part of the goal of the method demonstrate support from the organization. Therefore, by itself self-awareness does not satisfy most of the criteria for an effective development program (see Table 10-2).

Experience

If self-awareness is the cornerstone of development, then experience, or developmental experience, is its core. One does not learn to lead by sitting in a classroom, reading about leaders, or observing other leaders. Transmitting information through the classroom or observation is one thing; learning to exercise judgment, understand complex systems, and act on complex information requires hands-on practice (Daloz Parks, 2005). Although information and observation may result in an increase in a cognitive understanding of what leadership is and what leaders do, they do not develop leaders. The experience of actually leading others is one of the most effective ways to develop leaders (Conger, 2004; McCall, Lombardo, and Morrison, 1988; Ohlott, 2004) and the core competencies essential to adaptability (Zaccaro and Bank, 2004). Having on-the-job experience is, in almost all organizations, essential to leadership. For example, Johnson & Johnson considers developing leaders one of the company's seven critical leadership success factors (Fulmer and Goldsmith, 2000). In many other organizations, such as small businesses or those that do not have resources to invest in formal development programs, varied job assignments and experiences are the primary development tool (Raskas and Hambrick, 1992).

For job experiences to be developmental, they need to stretch leaders and broaden their perspective by placing them in a novel and challenging situation (Ohlott, 2003). This can be achieved through increasing responsibility on a current job, a new task, working with a different or a new project team that is unfamiliar, rotating to a dissimilar job, international experiences, or even working with a difficult employee. All these experiences provide an environment where the leaders have to assess and understand a novel environment and use unfamiliar styles and behaviors. Learning from practice can further build self-confidence and a sense of self-efficacy (Bandura, 1995).

Many methods for leader development based on hands-on practice have been developed, trying to approximate experience. For example, experience can be simulated by participants' involvement in small group activities, games, role plays, or simulations, or by following up critical events with discussion and reflection (Ernst and Martin, 2007). The U.S. Army, an organization with an ongoing focus on leader and leadership development, uses a method that combines self-awareness, values development, and knowledge and experience (Campbell and Dardis, 2004). The "Be, Know, Do" (BDK) model relies on a variety of development methods. Self-awareness is achieved through clarification of core values such as loyalty, duty, respect, and personal courage and development of mental, physical, and emotional attributes. The BDK model develops knowledge and skills in specific content areas such as technical and interpersonal skills. Finally, leaders are encouraged to "do" and develop familiarity with various aspects of their jobs at the personal, organizational, and strategic levels (Campbell and Dardis, 2004).

The U.S. Army develops its leaders by integrating many of the key factors of leader development and relying on experience and practice. All other methods can be combined with experience to provide an even more complete developmental experience (Kempster, 2006). For example, coaching can occur in the context of actual performance; classroom education can become more powerful when new knowledge is tested in an actual leadership situation. Real experience, through any means, satisfies almost all the criteria for effective development (see Table 10-2). It develops individual awareness, provides a rich experience and opportunity for practice and feedback, and when used in the context of development, requires support from the organization and integrates developmental goals with organizational goals. The only potential weakness may be assessment, which can easily be built in through formal programs or use of existing organizational performance tools.

Developmental Relationships: Coaching and Mentoring

Coaching involves providing individualized and constructive feedback on someone's behavior and performance while focusing on future improvement. Mentoring provides similar individualized attention with a feedback and future orientation, but tends to be less task specific. Mentoring is a supportive long-term, formal or informal, professional relationship (McCauley and Douglas, 2004). Whereas mentoring can be informal, coaching tends to have a more structured and formal nature. Many of us have mentors and role models who provide us with advice and feedback. They are people we admire and with whom we build long-lasting relationships. Coaches are sought for specific situations and assigned by organizations. Coaching and mentoring are part of developmental relationships that can help leaders improve and grow personally and professionally. The success of all such relationships depends on establishing trust and rapport between the leader and the coach or mentor (Ting and Hart, 2004). Both coaches and mentors can be role models, demonstrating desired behaviors and thereby further enhancing learning through observation (Bandura, 1995).

Coaching

Coaching has been shown to be effective in many areas and settings (e.g., Agarwal, Angst, and Magni; 2006; Battley, 2007; Nocks, 2007) and linked to increases in leader flexibility (Jone, Rafferty, and Griffin, 2006) and expatriate success (Abbott et al., 2006). Ros Taylor, a leadership coach, states the dire need for top-level leaders to get support: "when I am brought in to coach leadership teams . . . I frequently find that they are quite literally clinging on by their fingernails. They are on the brink of committing professional suicide because they don't know who to turn to" (Cooper, 2007: 24). Because of its many potential benefits, coaching is the focus of much of the leadership development practice and is beginning to become a topic of research (e.g., Joo, 2005).

Coaching can address existing problems in a real-life setting, thereby providing opportunity for feedback and practice, as well as demonstrating support from supervisors or co-workers. Because it is focused on specific behaviors, it narrows the scope of behavior, facilitating learning. Informal coaching is part of most effective supervisors' and leaders' repertoire in supporting their followers in learning new skills. Leadership-related coaching programs are most often used in executive development where either external consultants or successful current or past company executives provide individualized coaching to leaders. Executive coaches spend substantial amount of time observing leaders, discussing behaviors, exploring options, and providing detailed feedback regarding all aspects of the leader's style, behavior, and performance. The individualized attention in the work setting can be a source of considerable development. If the coach is a person internal to the organization, the executive can further benefit from gaining a perspective on the organization. An external coach can bring fresh perspectives and approaches.

Particularly when combined with other programs—for example as a follow-up for an in-class training, used in combination with mentoring, or with assessment centers and 360-degree feedback—coaching can provide the benefits of general knowledge with specific application to day-to-day activities. Individually focused assessment takes place, there is a reasonable level of challenge, and the feedback is relevant and rich. Additionally, the experiences that are observed and discussed are those that the leader finds challenging. The resources and expenses needed for formal coaching further demonstrate the organization's commitment to the person being coached and to developing leadership overall, all factors that have the potential to make coaching a highly effective development tool. In spite of the fact that top executives get a lot of training before they are appointed to the leadership of organizations, many of them do not have the type of preparation they need to take on the complex job of upper-echelon leaders. Executive coach Ros Taylor notes, "new elected leaders are expected to run the race but have not been allowed to train for it" (Cooper, 2007: 24). Coaching can close that gap and support them in their success.

Table 10-3 presents the elements of effective coaching. As with other developmental programs, the leader's readiness is essential. Many successful executives may resist coaching because of their success or because they receive filtered and only positive feedback that makes them believe they do not need development (Battley, 2007).

As is the case with all other development programs, the success of coaching depends on integrating individual and organizational needs.

As Bill Gates stated, "Success is a lousy teacher. It seduces smart people into thinking they can't lose" (21). An important point to note is that in addition to providing support and feedback to the individual, effective coaching requires integration with wider organizational goals and systems. As is the case with all other development programs, the success of coaching depends on integrating individual and organizational needs.

Mentoring

Sara Martinez Tucker, CEO of the Hispanic Scholarship Fund, an organization that distributes more than $25 million per year in scholarship funds, joined the nonprofit

Table 10-3   Elements of Effective Coaching.

- Individual readiness and willingness to be coached
- Consideration of wider organizational context and system
- Consideration of individual goals, values, and needs
- Focus on performance and work-related issues
- Sincere caring and concern
- Advocacy for self-awareness
- Meaningful feedback
- Supportive climate

sector after working in business for many years; she believes that "Every boss is a learning opportunity—you either learn how to do things better or you learn how you never want to behave" (Shinn, 2006: 20). Throughout her career, she has learned from others who often were not similar to her. She believes that many people can be positive mentors if they understand where you are coming from. Informal and formal mentoring is a powerful leader development tool and can lead to life-long supportive relationships between a mentor and a mentee. A more experienced leader provides guidance and advice to a less experienced one. Formal mentors are assigned from within the organization, although many leaders establish mentoring relationships with individuals inside and outside their organization.

As Sara Martinez Tucker suggests, one approach to mentoring is to consider learning from those who are poor rather than good role models. Even though there is no direct mentoring relationship, there can be considerable learning from observing other leaders inside and outside your organization who behave poorly. One business writer suggests that even "antimentors" are reliable and consistent and therefore can be excellent sources of development (McFarland, 2007). Some research and anecdotal accounts suggest that formal mentoring may be less effective than informal mentoring. Because mentoring involves establishment of a personal professional relationship based on trust, forcing it through formal bureaucratic selection processes may reduce its effectiveness. A formal system, however, can be implemented to create relationships that may otherwise not develop, for example in the case of women and members of diverse groups, who often have trouble connecting with powerful mentors in traditional organizations (McCauley and Douglas, 2004).

Guidelines for establishment of productive mentoring relationships include (McCauley and Douglas, 2004):

➤ *Find many mentors* instead of looking to one person for all guidance. Different mentors can support the leader with different perspectives and expertise.

➤ *Find mentors at different levels*; although typically mentors are more senior, peers, external people, and even followers can be great source of support and developmental advice.

➤ *Informal relationships* that provide casual support can be equally helpful.

➤ *Add mentors* as roles and responsibilities change or as leaders transition to new jobs.

Though mentoring can be a great source of support, it does not have the same strong development aspects of coaching. Because of its informal and more general in nature, the advice and feedback is typically less focused and less specific and opportunity to practice with quick and direct feedback is lacking (see Table 10-2).

Feedback-Intensive Programs

One of the currently most popular methods of leader development at all levels is using intensive feedback program such as 360 degree feedback or other multisource and multimethod feedback programs (for some reviews, see Lepsinger and Lucia, 1997; Tornow and London, 1998). The programs are used in a broad range of business, governmental, and nonprofit organizations. Their goal is to assess leaders' strengths and weaknesses and to identify development needs. Assessment is based on a combination of interviews, aptitude tests, personality tests, role plays, simulations, and experiential exercises, as well as many other methods. In 360 degree and multisource feedback programs, the leaders are assessed by individuals around them, including followers, colleagues, supervisors, and in some cases, clients and other stakeholders who provide detailed feedback regarding their styles, behaviors, and performance. In most situations, the leaders' self-rating on the same dimensions are also obtained and trained facilitators consider and analyze the data from different perspectives and help the leaders interpret the information, identify areas of strengths, and recognize targets for development (Chappelow, 2004).

The formal, official, and objective nature of multisource and multimethod feedback-intensive programs helps reduce the possible discomfort leaders may experience when receiving negative feedback and neutralize some of the anxiety it typically produces. Because they can provide rich data from multiple perspectives, such programs are ideally suited for increasing individual awareness and providing a detailed evaluation of the leader. They are particularly effective when combined with coaching and mentoring (Thach, 2002); however, they do satisfy several of the criteria for development programs particularly in the areas of rich experiences, opportunity to practice new behaviors and feedback (see Table 10-2).

Table 10-4   Factors That Contribute to the Success of 360 Degree Feedback Programs.

Factor	Description
Organizational buy-in and readiness	All levels of the organization must be well informed and prepared regarding process, content, and goals of program. Top management support is particularly essential.
Confidentiality and careful administration	Maintaining anonymity of the raters and confidentiality in the process assure continued trust in the results and goals. Careful administration of surveys and handling of data are also essential.
Well-trained facilitator	Program success requires the skills of a well-trained, professional, internal or external facilitator to help interpret the information and deal with sensitive data and discomfort.
Focus on behaviors	The feedback should focus on specific behaviors that are related to job performance rather than general evaluative statements.
Clear explanation of purpose and goals	Those providing feedback and the leader receiving the feedback should be very clear on the goal of the program and how data will be used.
Separate feedback from groups	Present the leader with separate feedback from each group or source to help clarity, interpretation, and understanding.
Follow-up	The initial step of increasing leaders' self-awareness must be followed up with action plans.
Combine with other developmental programs	The feedback increases awareness but without other developmental tools, does not provide the leader with the means of changing behaviors.

Sources: Chappelow, C. T. 2004. 360-degree feedback. In *The center for creative leadership handbook of leadership development*, 2nd ed. C. D. McCauley and E. Van Velsor, 58-84. San Francisco, CA: Jossey-Bass; Lepsinger, R. and A. D. Lucia. 1997. *The art and science of 360 degree feedback.* San Francisco, CA: Jossey-Bass/Pfeiffer.

Much research has been focused on 360 degree programs. Their effectiveness depends on several factors including maturity of the organization and of its members to handle feedback openly and honestly (Reeves, 2006). Other factors that help their success are outlined in Table 10-4.

Classroom Education

By some accounts, U.S. corporations spent $20 billion on tuition assistance programs in 2005 (Meister, 2005), and the amount of money dedicated to educational programs is growing with $7500 to 10,000 for a week of instruction in many universities (Speiser, 2005). Many organizations provide their employees with some sort of educational benefit program to encourage them to develop and grow, and several have high-level executives in charge of learning, which includes leader and leadership development, or even whole "universities" dedicated to training and development (e.g., Motorola and Goldman Sachs). Even when companies are not providing support for education, however, the demand for executive education is growing (Speiser, 2007). Because of increasing development needs and the desire to integrate such programs better with organizational goals, organizations are increasingly requesting customized programs such as MBAs with specific company-focus, and other training programs designed specifically for the organization.

For example, Ingersoll-Rand, the global industrial manufacturing company, has partnered with Indiana University to offer a customized MBA program for its high-potential executives where electives address the company's strategic priorities (Meister, 2005). Other companies, such as the Home Depot, have identified specific programs that address their needs. Leslie Joyce, the company's chief learning officer states, "We decided to manage Home Depot tuition assistance programs as a strategic investment and apply the same rigor that we manage other vendor relationships" (Meister, 2005). Another example is Spectrum Health of Grand Rapids Michigan, which has partnered with universities for short-term programs to address its strategic priorities (Speiser, 2005).

Classroom education is an efficient way of conveying general information and knowledge to groups of people. It is used extensively in supervisory and mid-level management and leadership training programs. The primary goal of classroom education is to transfer knowledge. Depending on the content covered, such program may also address individual awareness, but because of the setting, the ability to provide rich developmental experiences and opportunity for practice and feedback are relatively low (see Table 10-2). The classroom experience typically includes much more than lectures and discussion. Methods such as case studies, role playing, exercises, debates, games, and simulations all are used to enrich the developmental experience (for an example, see Hess, 2007). Such methods involve practice and active involvement that enhance conceptual learning in classroom settings (Popper, 2005). The ability to practice new behaviors in the safe classroom environment, although limited, can provide a starting point for other developmental experiences.

Outdoor Challenges

A popular approach for leader and leadership development are outward challenges programs that put participants physically and mentally through increasingly difficult physical activities, such as obstacle courses, climbing, sport competitions, and games.

Leading Change   Howard Schulltz Stirs Up Starbucks

Developing employees and taking care of them is a mantra in most companies these days, but few take it as seriously and as far as Starbucks where the all employees are included in the training, skill development, and the building of a unique culture. Howard Schulltz, CEO of Starbucks, the now ubiquitous global coffee house, set out to create a different company from the moment he took charge. Motivated by a personal experience of family hardship when his father lost his job when he broke his leg, Schulltz is committed to not leaving anybody behind while pushing for constant renewal and reinvention (Myers, 2005). Schulltz believes that Starbucks "have to balance being a competitive leader with being a benevolent employer" (Meyers, 2005). With more that 13,500 stores worldwide, 150,000 employees in 39 countries, and over $7 billion annual sales, Starbuck is a well-established leader in its industry (Helm, 2007). Heath benefits, even for part-time workers, and a culture of caring are some of the ways Starbucks is committed to its employees. Although the company spends more on health care than it does on coffee, Schulltz has repeatedly stated that "we will never turn our back on this benefit for our people" (Anderson, 2006).

Highly conscious about maintaining his company's culture, in April 2007 Schulltz sent a memo to his management team that stated that the Starbucks experience has been watered down and that there was a need to go back to the roots and to maintain the "coffee *joie de vivre*" that the CEO had seen in Italian coffee bars (Helm, 2007). At the heart of the unique culture are the employees, who are trained in various programs such as the Coffee Master that teaches them the subtleties of various coffee flavors to graduate by receiving a special black apron and participating in a "cupping ceremony" where they appreciate the aroma of the coffee (Helm, 2007). The company baristas are trained to be considerate and are encouraged to be genuine (Meyers, 2005). Schulltz, who is sensitive, passionate, and a master storyteller (Meyer, 2005), seeks to build connections among people and likes to remind everyone "We're not in the business of filling bellies. We're in the business of filling souls" (Anderson, 2006).

Sources: Anderson, T. 2006. "Howard Schulltz: The star of Starbucks." *CBS News*, April 23. http://www.cbsnews.com/stories/2006/04/21/60minutes/main1532246.shtml? source=search_story (accessed September 1, 2007); Helm, B., 2007. "Saving Starbucks' soul," *Business Week*, April 9. http://www.businessweek.com/magazine/content/ 07_15/b4029070.htm?chan=search (accessed September 1, 2007); Meyers, W. 2005. "Conscience in a cup of coffee." *USnews.com*, October 31. http://www.usnews.com/ usnews/news/articles/051031/31schulltz.htm (accessed September 1, 2007);

Some suggest that sports in general, whether individual or teams, can be a good source for learning self-management, self-discipline, and teamwork (Wellner, 2007) and organizations are increasingly seeking innovative ways to both engage and entertain workshop and training participants through methods such as treasure hunts (Trucco, 2007). Many of the activities such as climbing poles, walking across rope bridges, and using trapeze are aimed at personal growth and increasing self-confidence by conquering fears and challenges. Other activities such as falling backwards to be caught by teammates or going through an obstacle course blindfolded with the help of a partner focus on building trust and cooperation among members of existing departments, teams, organizations.

Although frequently exhilarating and entertaining, the long-term impact of such programs on leader development is not well documented.

DEVELOPMENT AND CULTURE

As in all other aspects of leadership, culture impacts the process of leader development both at the national and subgroup (e.g., gender) levels. Culture impacts people's expectations of the learning context, the role of the facilitator, and what methods they prefer. For example, whereas people from the United States would comfortably and easily engage in a controversial case discussion and challenge their facilitator, many Middle Eastern or Asian participants may be more reluctant to do so. The French are taught throughout their education to question everything; so they are likely to want clear justification for the content and the methods of a program. Cultural values affect how the learning process is implemented, how feedback is provided, and the setting in which learning and development can be optimized. Leader development must therefore be considered within the cultural context (Hoppe, 2004). Table 10-5 outlines the cultural values that most impact development.

> Cultural values affect how the learning process is implemented, how feedback is provided, and the setting in which learning and development can be optimized. Leader development must therefore be considered within the cultural context.

In a high-context and collectivist culture, such as Japan or Thailand, direct feedback, which is considered essential to learning in the United States and other Western countries such as Germany, would be poorly received and may be counterproductive causing the participant to lose face. The feedback results from feedback-intensive programs will have to be carefully considered and adjusted to preserve harmony and "face" particularly in cultures that are self-protective, such as many cultures in the Middle East or Asia (GLOBE; House et al., 2004). Another cultural value to consider is the degree of individualism or collectivism. Whereas in individualistic cultures such as the United States, the focus of leader development is on the individual and on getting the most talented person ready to lead, in collectivistic cultures, leadership resides with the group. Development must therefore target the group. Another factor often related to individualism is action orientation. The U.S. approach to development and training is hands-on, providing opportunities for practice, a factor that is one of the criteria for the effectiveness of a leader development program. In other cultures, the focus may be more on conceptual and holistic understanding and theoretical development. Tolerance of ambiguity may similarly impact the content of the

Table 10-5 Cultural Values and Leader Development.

Cultural Value	Potential Impact on Leader Development
The communication context (high-low); directness	How information is communicated; how feedback is given; who provides feedback; directness of message in case of assessment and self-development
Individualism–collectivism	Focus of development on the individual leader or on the group; setting for development and training
Action-orientation	Content of development and training focused on practical matters and hands-on training or on theoretical understanding and conceptual development
Tolerance for ambiguity	Degree of exposure to new and challenging situations
Perception of time	Focus on quick and short-term results or on long-term development
Power distance and equality	Development provided to all or only individuals identified as high potential; implementation of 360 degree feedback

development program. When individuals are relatively comfortable with change, such as in the United States, development places them in increasingly novel and challenging situations. When the cultural value is to avoid uncertainty, such as in Greece, development aimed at challenging that value is likely to face resistance and be counterproductive.

Many Western cultures focus on developing their employees for the short term or generally have a shorter time frame for planning and a focus on quick results. In long-term cultures, the scope of development may be on acquiring skills and knowledge in a much longer time frame spanning over several years or even decades. It may take years to groom leaders for their positions. Finally, position power and the degree of equality in a culture may impact leader development. In more egalitarian cultures such as Denmark or Sweden, development opportunities are made available to as many people as possible and leaders may not feel comfortable being singled out (Derr, 1987). In more hierarchical and power-oriented cultures such as France, people deserving leader development are identified early through the educational system and singled out for special treatment (Barsoux and Lawrence, 1991; Belet, 2007).

The most effective development methods that are used extensively in the United States rely on intensive feedback and developmental relationships as their core. For example, the highly popular and effective method of 360 degree feedback relies on honest and direct feedback about a person's performance, style, and behavior from all levels of the organization. Interestingly, giving and receiving feedback is a highly culture-sensitive process (Hoppe, 2004). Hearing about weaknesses and mistakes directly, as is done as a result of assessment, would be highly inappropriate in some cultures, for example Thailand, where the person would be embarrassed, lose face, and perceive damage to his ability to lead effectively. Similarly, providing feedback to the leader in high power distance cultures such as Saudi Arabia or France would be uncomfortable, improper, and may be career threatening for both the leader and the followers. Even the concept of developmental relationships such as coaching and mentoring, which may be easier in collectivistic cultures, may pose some challenge when social relationships are highly prescribed and formal. Whereas a leader from a hierarchical and paternalistic culture may naturally feel a responsibility to take care of followers and develop them, such cultures may also have more rigid social structures that identify who should be developed and how negative information can be communicated. The considerable differences in cultural values and the lack of research in the applicability and generalizability of U.S. and other Western methods of leader development make their broad cross-cultural application risky. Much needs to still be done to fully incorporate culture in leader development, as the large majority of our research and reviews of practices do not consider culture (e.g., Day, Zaccaro, and Halpin, 2004).

Gender and Diversity

Other cultural factors to consider in development are how to address the need of diverse groups. Whereas all groups have the same training and development needs, one factor to consider is how to address specific needs of women and members of underrepresented groups. Some research indicates that development programs have traditionally been developed with the white and male majority of organizational leaders in mind, a factor that can negatively impact the progress of diverse groups (Morrison and Von Glinow, 1990). Moreover, the presence of diversity programs in organizations for many years sometimes leads to the false perception and belief that diversity issues have been addressed and resolved and that these programs, including those targeting leader development, are "color-blind" (Livers and Caver, 2004).

Differential opportunities for growth and limited exposure to developmental, high-visibility, high-stakes assignments and experiences, along with lack of connection to powerful and significant mentors, however, continue to be stated as key reasons for differences in advancement of men and members of diverse groups (for reviews, see Livers and Cavers 2004; Ruderman, 2004). Women and minorities may face further challenges in leader development by being assessed and compared based on norms that may not be culturally appropriate. Some studies show that women often outperform their male counterparts on the results of 360 degree feedback (Posner and Kouzes, 1993), whereas other studies show that men are rated higher on some dimensions of leadership (Eagly, Makhijani, and Klonsky, 1992).

Potential solutions to the challenges that women and members of underrepresented groups face in leader development include:

➤ *Opportunity to participate in single-identity development programs* that reinforce validation, provide role models and networking, and can make available relevant content to address specific concerns (Ruderman, 2004).

➤ *Encouraging developmental relationships* through formal and informal organizational programs to assure that women and minorities have access to powerful coaches and mentors who are both similar to and different from them (Thomas, 2001).

➤ *Developing networks* that can help women and minorities in their career development process (Ibarra, 1993).

Such measures, along with other diversity-oriented practices, several of which are presented in Chapter 2, can help address the unique challenges that women and minorities face in leader development.

EFFECTIVENESS OF DEVELOPMENT

Although highly popular and broadly implemented in many organizational settings, the effectiveness of leader development programs is not always fully evaluated and some researchers suggest that there is disconnect between the research on leadership and its application to the practice of leader and leadership development (Day, 2000). Additionally, when carefully examined, many of the existing methods and activities do not show consistent results in terms of increases in individual or organizational effectiveness. For example, although the highly trendy outward-bound experiences provide entertainment and are highly rated by participants, they do not always translate into long-term change in behavior. While some research suggests that such team activities may increase a team's cohesion, specific impact on leader effectiveness is not well documented. Even the effectiveness of the popular multisource methods have not been well established (Kluger and DeNisi, 1996).

In spite of lack of consistent research, the various methods of leader development do provide positive impact for leaders and their organization. For example, mentoring may help reduce intention to leave (Phampraha and Chansrichawala, 2007), executive coaching is showing considerable promise (e.g., Thach, 2002), and even outdoor programs show positive results in terms of development of self-concept (Marsh, Richards, and Barnes, 1987). New leadership models are increasingly calling for the inclusion of learning and development as an integral part of our understanding of leadership (e.g., Day, Zaccaro, and Halpin, 2004; Uhl-Bien, Marion, and McKelvy, 2007), and changes in the global environment and technology call for continued leader and leadership development (Avolio, 2005; Suutari, 2002).

Organizational and Personal Factors in Development

Based on the information presented in this chapter, it is clear that three factors can support leader development (Figure 10-4). First, the importance of individual leader's

Figure 10-4   Organizational and Personal Factors in Development.

commitment to learning and growth cannot be overemphasized. The leaders must be dedicated to their own development. The ability to learn and self-regulate is not something that organizations can control; therefore, the leaders' readiness for change and commitment is essential. Second, organizational commitment is equally vital. No leader can sustain new behaviors without organizational support from supervisors and coworkers. The continuing trend in flatter organizations with fewer levels of supervision has increased the need for leaders to acquire many new skills. Moreover, the use of teams puts pressure for many new behaviors (London, 2002). These and other organizational pressures must be matched with a focus on continuous learning and a culture that supports learning and change. The characteristics of learning organizations presented in Chapter 9 are some of the elements necessary to support development.

Finally, the effectiveness of development depends on integration of the program with overall organizational vision, mission, and strategic goals. It further requires a reasonable fit between the needs of individual leaders and the organizational direction. Leader development, while aimed at increasing organizational effectiveness through increasing leaders' effectiveness, must also consider the personal effectiveness of the leader. The concepts of authentic and value-based leadership (see Chapter 6) directly and indirectly address the need for such integration.

Applying What You Learn
Personal Development

In addition to formal programs, which may not be available to you, there are some steps you can take to develop your leadership.

- *Openness to new experiences.* Seek new task, projects, classes, or experiences any chance you get. Although not all may be related directly to leadership, they provide with a chance to expand your experience base.

- *Consider volunteer work.* Especially in early stages of one's career, volunteer work offers considerable "risk-free" opportunities for acquiring leadership skills. Students particularly can learn much from such experiences.

- *Seek feedback.* While working on projects, tell people you trust that you would like feedback about your behavior and performance. Not every piece of feedback you get will be helpful, but you may discern patterns in what people tell you.

- *Focus on understanding your strength.* Instead of trying to fix your weaknesses, put your energy in developing your strengths.

- *Observe leaders around you.* You can learn by observing leaders around you. Both good and bad ones can teach you plenty about effective leadership that you can put into practice.

- *Be persistent and practice.* Change and learning take time. Be patient and persistent in practicing new behaviors until they become comfortable and part of your repertoire.

SUMMARY AND CONCLUSIONS

Developing leaders so that they can continue to address the changing needs of their organizations is essential to the survival and success of organizations. Organizations can focus on developing individual managers, leaders, and executives at various levels by providing them with increased skills and knowledge, or they can focus on developing the leadership capability of the organization. The process of development is akin to change in that it requires the person to recognize and accept the need for change and have the ability to learn. It then requires the opportunity to develop through exposure to appropriate experiences. Finally, the learning must be supported by the organization to solidify and reinforce new skills and behaviors.

Proper assessment, awareness, rich experiences that provide for opportunity for practice and feedback, support from supervisors and coworkers, and fit with the organization are all factors in an effective development programs. A variety of methods are available to develop leaders. Self-awareness is at the heart of any development; leaders must know their capabilities, strengths and weaknesses, and their willingness and ability to learn. Actual leadership experiences are the most effectual method of development, whether through routine activities that are part of the job or through increasingly difficult tasks and assignments that challenge leaders to move outside of their zone of comfort. Coaching and mentoring can further enrich a leader's repertoire by providing relevant, task- and organizational-specific feedback and advice. Among other popular developmental activities are programs that rely on intensive feedback from multiple sources. Classroom education and its many different tools such as role modeling, case analysis, and games and simulations allow the leaders to increase their knowledge and practice new behaviors in a safe environment. Lastly, many other activities such as outward-bound and physical and team-building challenges address developmental needs.

Whereas the programs described in this chapter are commonly used in the United States and some other Western countries and show promising results, their applicability to other cultures is less certain. Culture must be considered when implementing any leader or leadership development program. The success and effectiveness of leader development depends first and foremost on the individual's commitment to learning and growth. Equally critical is organizational commitment to leader development. As a final point, effective leader development within organizations requires a fit and integration between the leader's individual values and needs and the vision, mission, and goals of the organization.

LEADERSHIP CHALLENGE: FINDING THE RIGHT FIT

Your supervisor has just nominated you for a lengthy and complex leadership development program that most of the top leaders of your organization have completed. It is considered to be a program for high-potential leaders and is likely to be key to a future promotion for you. Although you are flattered and the potential for a promotion and much better pay (maybe as much 50% more) is tempting, you are also concerned whether the organization is the right place for you. You value the balance between your personal life and your work and are engaged in many sustainability efforts in your community, an activity that you personally value. The organization demands considerable time from you and most evenings you do not get home before 7 or 8. You have also tried without much success to start a "green" program at the office and have brought up sustainability issues when making several decisions. Your supervisor thinks it's "cute" but has not shown any interest. Yet, you are still in the early stages of your career; the promotion would be very nice; the money even better. On the other hand, the training program will require even more time from you, time you could spend looking for other opportunities.

1. What are the factors that you should consider?
2. What would be the best decision for you? Why?

REVIEW AND DISCUSSION QUESTIONS

1. What is the difference between leader and leadership development? Why is the distinction important?
2. What are the four factors in learning? What role do they play in leader development?
3. Describe the areas that are typically addressed in developing leaders.
4. Explain the seven criteria for effective development programs. Which ones do you think are most important? Why?
5. Compare and contrast the methods of leader development described in this chapter. What advantages or disadvantages do they each provide? When should they be used?
6. What are the core and cornerstone of development? How are they related?
7. How are coaching and mentoring similar and different?
8. Describe the characteristics and benefits of feedback-intensive programs.
9. What role can classroom education play in leader development?
10. What is the role of culture in leader development? What cultural factors must be taken into account when implementing a program?
11. What are specific issues to consider when developing women and members of minority groups?
12. What are the organizational and personal factors in development?

EXERCISE 10-1:   IDENTIFYING YOUR MENTORING NEEDS AND POTENTIAL MENTORS

Mentoring is a personal professional relationship based on trust and common interests. Whereas mentors are often more senior and experienced than the people they support, many mentors can be at the same level, or even at lower organizational levels and with less experience than the mentee.

This exercise is designed to help you consider areas where you need help and identify a list of people you could approach to be your mentors.

Step I: What Do You Need?
You can identify areas where you may need development through:

➤ Either through self-exploration and careful soul-searching

➤ Looking at your most-recent performance reviews

➤ Considering the results of some assessment tools you have taken in school, or at work or

➤ Identifying patterns in informal feedback you get from family members, friends, and coworkers.

Based on your review of that information, what are the three areas that you would like to develop further expertise and competence?

Step II: Who Do You Know?
Keeping those development needs in mind, who do you know has expertise in those areas? Start with a long list; include as many people as you can think of. Bosses, instructors, and older family members are not the only ones who can help. Your peers are likely to have many areas of expertise and some less-experienced and younger members of your organization may even have specialty or skills in the areas you are interested in.

Your long list:

Your narrower list based on:

You trust them to help you:

You feel comfortable with them:

(Continued)

Part III: Creating a Mentoring Relationship

You should now write down a few names for each of the areas you would like to target. You can approach each person and ask him or her for an informal meeting or to go to lunch or for coffee. If you feel comfortable, you can then ask them to help you in learning about the areas you are interested in. Most people are quite flattered to be asked to help and mentor someone, so they are not likely to turn you down. If they do, you may consider contacting them in the future.

A few things to keep in mind:

> ➤ Be very clear about how much help you need. Most of us are too busy to dedicate time to an involved process, so stick with a lunch or coffee once a month, or so.

> ➤ Don't use your mentor as a "dumping" ground for all the problems you face at work or school; stay focused on learning about specific areas you think the person can help you with.

> ➤ Express your appreciation for their time and support, and send thank you notes or emails after each meeting.

> ➤ Take the responsibility to keep the relationship going if you feel you are benefiting from it.

Although you may feel most comfortable with just one or two people, it is always helpful to have a broad network.

SELF-ASSESSMENT 10-1:   MY PERSONAL MISSION STATEMENT

One of the most important aspects of leadership development is self-knowledge and awareness of your priorities and values. You can use the information in Self-assessment 4-1 to review your values and keep those in mind as you complete this exercise.

Step 1: What Do I Want to Be When I Grow Up?

What do I want to be known for?

If there was one thing I would like people to remember me for, what would that be?

Kind, loving. service to others

What should my epitaph say about me?

When I retire, what I would like my most important accomplishment to be?

Step 2: My Personal Mission
Based on the results of the self-assessment about values in Chapter 4, and the answers to the questions above, write your personal mission statement. There is no right or wrong answer!
For information on how to write a mission statement see http://www.tgci.com/magazine/98fall/mission.asp
For a step-by-step tutorial on developing your personal mission statement, based on Franklin Covey principles, see http://www.franklincovey.com/missionbuilder/
Once you have developed your mission statement, keep it accessible. It can guide you when you are having trouble making decisions and in setting the path for your development as a leader.

Leadership in Action: Colleen Barrett— The soul of Southwest Airlines

"Learn from your mistakes; take the initiative; and listen to your heart" (The power of persistence, 2002) are simple and powerful words from Colleen Barrett, the CEO of Southwest Airlines since 2001 and its corporate secretary since 1978; she is planning to retire in 2008. Barrett has been with the airline almost since the beginning when Texas businessman Rollin King and attorney Herb Kelleher founded the company. The no-frills, low-cost airlines has had 34 consecutive profitable years (Fisher, 2007), an accomplishment unmatched by any other airline in the world. For many years now, Barrett has been credited with being responsible for the company's culture (one of her titles around the company is Queen of Hearts), which she describes as "fun, spirited, zesty, hard-working, and filled with love. Love is a word that isn't used too often in corporate America, but we've used it at Southwest from the beginning" (Shinn, 2004: 18).

Barrett flies to all of the company's locations to meet individually with employees and sends them all birthday card; managers and others make a point of acknowledging significant events in their employees' lives. For her, these actions are just being part of the family (Shin, 2003). In addition to a supportive culture, Southwest is deliberate about developing leaders and leadership. First, Barrett describes, "we are very, very disciplined about hiring and we're very, very disciplined about mentoring and coaching . . . We're a very forgiving about company in terms of good honest mistakes, but we're not forgiving about attitude and behavior and demeanor" (Fisher, 2007: 18). Barrett suggests that developing employees and maintaining the culture starts with the hiring process and by carefully selecting people and being very clear about expectations and company culture (Cohen and Rao, 2006). Programs to develop leaders range from formal leadership training for everyone, including frontline employees, to presentation by outside consultants, leadership briefings, and communications about leadership in company bulletins. Managers and company leaders also make a point to include the topic of leadership in their regular interactions and strive to demonstrate the principles the company embraces (Shin, 2003). The goal of training and development at Southwest is to perpetuate the culture and leadership style that have been effective. Barrett says that they are not shy about closely monitoring their employees, getting rid of people who do not fit in, promoting those who represent the spirit of the company, and holding their leaders and managers accountable (Cohen and Rao, 2006). She refers to one of the company's sayings that indicates the importance of role modeling and accountability: "First yourself, and then everybody else" (Cohen and Rao, 2006).

The concept of fit between the person and the company is central to Southwest's success. Through careful hiring and training, the company makes sure that those who do not fit well do not get hired or do not stay long. Caring about others, authenticity, and maybe most importantly, a sense of humor are prerequisites for being successful at Southwest. Barrett manages that fit partly through the company's Culture Committee, a group she created that is made up of a team of 100 employees who preach and teach the company's unique culture (Medley, 2006). In addition, local culture committee's members are further entrusted with the task for maintaining and strengthening the Southwest SPIRIT (always in capital letters). The culture even has its own language, which includes "Southwest Family," "Servant Leadership," and "New Hires," all used as proper nouns to indicate their importance to the company (Medley, 2006).

Although Barrett is the culture queen at Southwest, every company leader and employee is in charge of that culture. Through strong training programs, promotions from within, the telling and retelling of many stories, for which the company cofounder and past CEO Herb Kelleher was famous, the culture is ever present. The company offices are decorated with memorabilia that further reinforce Southwest ideals. Kelleher has assured that current and upcoming leadership are in place and guarantee "life after Herb" (Medley, 2006). Barrett plays a further role herself in developing leaders, mentoring anyone who has "a passion for what he or she does or who has a desire to learn" (Shin, 2003), and she empowers her followers to do the same. She states, "When New Hires ask me all the time 'how are you going to keep the culture?' I say, 'I'm not. You are.'" (Medley, 2006).

QUESTIONS

1. How does Southwest develop its leaders?
2. What is the role of culture and fit in success of the company?

Sources: Cohen, A. and J. Rao, 2006. "Creating a great spirit of service at Southwest airlines," *Babson Insight*, April. http://www.babsoninsight.com/contentmgr/showdetails.php/id/868 (accessed September 1, 2007); Fisher, S., 2007. "Flying off into the sunset: An airline icon plans to slow down," *The Costco Connection*, September: 17–19; Medley, M., 2006. "The culture queen," *Motto.* http://www.whatsyourmotto.com/articles/culturequeen.aspx (accessed September 1, 2007); "The power of persistence," 2002. Fast Company. http://www.fastcompany.com/fast50_02/people/persistence/barrett.html (accessed September 1, 2007); Shin, S., 2003. "LUV Colleen," *BizEd*, March/April: 18–23.

References

Abbott, G. N., B. W. Stening, P. W. B. Atkins, and A. M. Grant. 2006. Coaching expatriate managers for success: Adding value beyond training and mentoring. *Asia Pacific Journal of Human Resources* 44:295–317.

Ackerson, L. 1942. *Children's behavior problems: Relative importance and intercorrelations among traits.* Chicago: University of Chicago Press.

Adeyemi-Bello, T. 2003. The impact of leaders' characteristics on the performance of organizational members: An exploratory study. *Work Study* 52 (6): 286–289.

Adler, N. 2006. The arts and leadership: Now that we can do anything, what will we do? *Academy of Management Learning and Education* 5:486–499.

Adler, N. J. 1991. *International dimensions of organizational behavior.* 2nd ed. Boston: PWS-Kent.

Agarwal, R., C. M. Angst, and M. Magni. 2006. The performance effects of coaching: A multilevel analysis using hierarchical linear modeling. University of Maryland Robert H. Smith School Research paper no. RHS 06–031.

Alderfer, C. P. 1969. An empirical test of a new theory of human needs. *Organizational Behavior and Human Performance* 4:142–175.

Alderman, L. 2005. Simul-chief: Nissan executive may run Renault, too. *New York Times,* January 18, C8.

Allen, N. J., and T. D. Hecht. 2004. The "romance of teams": Toward and understanding of its psychological underpinnings and implications. *Journal of Occupational Organisational Psychology* 77:439–461.

Allen, T. H. 1981. Situational management roles: A conceptual model. *Dissertation Abstracts International,* publ. nr. 42, 2A: 465.

———. 1990. An investigation of Machiavellian and imaged interaction. *Communication Research Reports* 7 (2): 116–120.

Alluto, J. A., and L. G. Hrebeniak. 1975. Research on commitment to employing organizations: Preliminary findings on a study of managers graduating from engineering and MBA programs. Paper presented at the National Academy of Management Annual Conference, August, New Orleans.

Alspach, G. 2004. Wanna grow old? Then lose the attitude. *Critical Care Nurse* 24 (1): 8–9.

Alves, J. C., K. J. Lovelace, C. C. Manz, D. Matsypura, F. Toyasaki, and K. Ke. 2006. A cross-cultural perspective of self-leadership. *Journal of Managerial Psychology* 21:338–359.

Amble, B. 2006. Women still rare in Europe's boardrooms. *Management Issues,* June 20. http://www.management-issues.com/2006/8/24/research/women-still-rare-in-europes-boardrooms.asp (accessed June 19, 2007).

American Psychiatric Association. 2000. *Diagnostic and statistical manual of mental disorders (DSM-IV-TR).* 4th ed. Washington, DC: American Psychiatric Association.

AmEx's Ken Chenault talks about leadership, integrity and the credit card business. 2005. *Knowledge@Wharton,* April 20. http://knowledge.wharton.upenn.edu/article.cfm?articleid=1179 (accessed July 16, 2007).

Anders, G. 2001. Slack off. *Fast Company,* August, 27–30.

Anderson, C. 1997. Values-based management. *Academy of Management Executive* 11 (4): 25–46.

Anderson, C. R., D. Hellriegel, and J. W. Slocum. 1977. Managerial response to environmentally induced stress. *Academy of Management Journal* 20 (2): 260–272.

Anderson, C. R., and C. E. Schneier. 1978. Locus of control, leader behavior and leader performance among management students. *Academy of Management Journal* 21.690–698.

Anderson, J. 2007. Stepping lively at Credit Suisse; workaholic American named to lead Swiss financial services company. *New York Times,* February 16. http://query.nytimes.com/gst/fullpage.html?res=9B0DE4DE143EF935A25751C0A9619C8B63 (accessed January 8, 2008).

Andolšek, D. M., and J. Štebe. 2004. Multinational perspective on work values and commitment. *International Journal of Cross Cultural Management* 4 (2): 181–209.

Antonakis, J., B. J. Avolio, and H. Sivasubramaniam. 2003. Context and leadership: An examination of the nine-factor full-range leadership theory using the Multifactor Leadership Questionnaire. *Leadership Quarterly* 14:261–295.

Antonakis, J., A. T. Cianciolo, and R. J. Sternberg. 2004. *The nature of leadership.* Thousand Oaks, CA: Sage.

Aragon-Correa, J. A., F. Matias-Reche, and M. E. Senise-Barrio. 2004. Managerial discretion and corporate commitment to the natural environment. *Journal of Business Research* 57:964–975.

Arfken, D. E., S. L. Bellar, and M. M. Helms. 2004. The ultimate glass ceiling revisited: The presence of women on corporate boards. *Journal of Business Ethics* 50:177–186.

Argyris, C. 1991. Teaching smart people how to learn. *Harvard Business Review,* May–June, 99–109.

Armour, S. 2007. Hi, I'm Joan, and I'm a workaholic. *USA Today,* May 23, 1b.

Astley, W. G., and P. S. Sachdeva. 1984. Structural sources of intraorganizational power: A theoretical synthesis. *Academy of Management Review* 9:104–113.

Auden, W. C., J. D. Shackman, and M. H. Onken. 2006. Top management team, international risk management factor and firm performance. *Team Performance Management* 12:209–216.

Aune, R. K., and L. L. Waters. 1994. Cultural differences in deception: Motivation to deceive in Samoans and North Americans. *International Journal of Intercultural Relations* 18:159–172.

Avolio, B. J. 2005. *Leadership development in balance: Made/born.* Mahwah, NJ: Lawrence Erlbaum.

———. 2007. Promoting more integrative strategies for leadership theory-building. *American Psychologist* 62:25–33.

Avolio, B. J., and W. L. Gardner. 2005. Authentic leadership development: Getting to the root of positive forms of leadership. *Leadership Quarterly* 16:315–338.

Avolio, B. J., W. L. Gardner, F. O. Walumbwa, F. Luthans, and D. R. May. 2004. Unlocking the mask: A look at the process by which authentic leaders impact follower attitudes and behaviors. *Leadership Quarterly* 15:801–823.

Ayman, R. 1993. Leadership perception: The role of gender and culture. In *Leadership theory and research: Perspectives and directions,* ed. M. M. Chemers and R. Ayman, 137–166. New York: Academic Press.

Ayman, R., and M. M. Chemers. 1983. Relationship of supervisory behavior ratings to work group effectiveness and subordinate satisfaction. *Journal of Applied Psychology* 68:338–341.

———. 1991. The effect of leadership match on subordinate satisfaction in Mexican organizations: Some moderating influences of self-monitoring. *International Review of Applied Psychology* 40:299–314.

Ayman, R., M. M. Chemers, and F. E. Fiedler. 1995. The contingency model of leadership effectiveness: Its levels of analysis. *Leadership Quarterly* 6 (2): 147–167.

Ayman-Nolley, S., R. Ayman, and J. Becker. 1993. Gender affects children's drawings of a leader. Paper presented at the annual meeting of the American Psychological Association, August, Chicago.

Baker, B. 2006. John W Hickenlooper: Major of Denver. http://www.citymayors.com/mayors/denver_mayor.html (accessed June 17, 2007).

Ballinger, G. A., and F. D. Schoorman. 2007. Individual reaction to leadership succession in workgroups. *Academy of Management Review* 32 (1): 118–136.

Bandura, A. 1977. Self-efficacy: Toward a unifying theory of behavioral change. *Psychological Review* 84:191–215.

———, ed. 1995. *Self-efficacy in changing societies.* New York: Cambridge Press.

Baron, R. A. 1989. Personality and organizational conflict: Effects of the type A behavior pattern and self-monitoring. *Organizational Behavior and Human Decision Processes* 44:281–296.

Baron, R. A., J. H. Neuman, and D. Geddes. 1999. Social and personal determinants of workplace aggression: Evidence for the impact of perceived injustice and the type A behavior pattern. *Aggressive Behavior* 25 (4): 281–296.

Barrett, A. 2003. Staying on top. *Business Week,* May 5, 60–68.

Barrick, M. R., and M. Mount. 1991. The five big personality dimensions and job performance: A meta-analysis. *Personnel Psychology* 44 (1): 1–76.

———. 1993. Autonomy as a moderator of the relationship between the Big Five personality dimensions and job performance. *Journal of Applied Psychology* 78:111–118.

Barry, D. 1991. Managing the bossless team. *Organizational Dynamics* 19 (4): 31–47.

Barsoux, J. L., and P. Lawrence. 1991. The making of a French manager. *Harvard Business Review,* July–August, 58–67.

Bartlett, C. A., and S. Ghoshal. 1989. *Managing across borders: The transnational solution.* Boston: Harvard Business School Press.

———. 1992. Managing across borders: New organizational responses. *Sloan Management Review* 28 (9): 3–13.

Basadur, M. 2004. Leading others to think innovatively together: Creative leadership. *Leadership Quarterly* 15:103–121.

Bass, B. M. 1960. *Leadership, psychology, and organizational behavior.* New York: Harper and Row.

———. 1985. *Leadership and performance beyond expectations.* New York: Free Press.

———. 1990a. *Bass and Stogdill's handbook of leadership.* 3rd ed. New York: Free Press.

———. 1990b. From transactional to transformational leadership: Learning to share the vision. *Organizational Dynamics* 18 (3): 19–36.

———. 1997. Does the transactional-transformational leadership paradigm transcend organizational and national boundaries? *American Psychologist* 52 (3): 130–139.

———. 1999. On the taming of charisma: A reply to Janice Beyer. *Leadership Quarterly* 10 (4): 541–553.

Bass, B. M., and B. J. Avolio. 1990. Developing transformational leadership: 1992 and beyond. *Journal of European Industrial Training* 14:21–27.

———. 1993. Transformational leadership: A response to critiques. In *Leadership theory and research: Perspectives and directions,* ed. M. M. Chemers and R. Ayman, 49–80. San Diego, CA: Academic Press.

Bass, B. M., and P. Steidlmeier. 1999. Ethics, character, and authentic transformational leadership behavior. *Leadership Quarterly* 10:181–217.

Bates, T. W. 2005. Asset sales, investment opportunities, and the use of proceeds. *Journal of Finance* 60:105–135.

Battley, S. 2007. Executive coaching myths. *Leader to Leader* 44 (Spring): 20–25.

Bauer, T. N., and S. G. Greene. 1996. Development of the leader-member exchange: A longitudinal test. *Academy of Management Journal* 39:1538–1567.

Bebchuk, L. A., and J. Fried. 2004. *Pay without performance: The unfulfilled promise of executive compensation.* Cambridge, MA: Harvard University Press.

Becker, J., R. Ayman, and K. Korabik. 1994. Gender and self/subordinate discrepancies in perceptions of leadership: Understanding the impact of behavioral content, organizational context, and self-monitoring. Working paper. Chicago: Illinois Institute of Technology.

Bedeian, A. G., and A. A. Armenakis. 1998. The cesspool syndrome: How dreck floats to the top of declining organizations. *Academy of Management Executive* 12 (1): 58–63.

Bedeian, A. G., and D. V. Day. 2004. Can chameleons lead? *Leadership Quarterly* 15:687–718.

Begley, P. 2006. Self-knowledge, capacity and sensitivity: Prerequisites to authentic leadership by school principals. *Journal of Educational Administration* 44, 570.

Belet, D. 2007. Are "high potential" executives capable of building learning-oriented organisations? Reflections on the French case. *Journal of Workplace Learning* 19:465–475.

Bennis, W. G. 1992. *Leaders on leadership.* Boston: Harvard Business Review Books.

———. 2003. News analysis: It's the culture. *Fast Company,* August, 73. http://www.fastcompany.com/magazine/73/nyt.html (accessed September 30, 2004).

Bennis, W. G., and B. Nanus. 1985. *Leaders: The strategies for taking charge.* New York: Harper and Row.

Beyer, J. M. 1999a. Taming and promoting charisma to change organizations. *Leadership Quarterly* 10 (2): 307–330.

———. 1999b. Two approaches to studying charismatic leadership: Competing or complementary. *Leadership Quarterly* 10 (4): 575–588.

Bianchi, S. M. 2000. Maternal employment and time with children: Dramatic change or surprising continuity? *Demography* 37:401–414.

Bigoness, W. J., and G. L. Blakely. 1996. A cross-national study of managerial values. *Journal of International Business Studies* 27 (4): 739–752.

Bird, C. 1940. *Social psychology.* New York: Appleton.

Black, J. 2004. Always the optimist. *Inc.*, August, 95–98.

Bligh, M. C., and G. D. Hess. 2007. The power of leading subtly: Alan Greenspan, rhetorical leadership, and monetary policy. *Leadership Quarterly* 18:87–104.

Block, P. 1987. *The empowered manager.* San Francisco, CA: Jossey-Bass.

———. 1993. *Stewardship: Choosing service over self-interest.* San Francisco, CA: Berrett-Koehler.

Blundell, M. 2007. How McDonald's tracks morale at the front line. *Strategic Communication Management* 11 (4): 10.

Boal, K. B., and J. M. Bryson. 1987. Charismatic leadership: A phenomenological and structural approach. In *Emerging leadership vistas*, ed. J. G. Hunt, B. R. Baliga, H. P. Dachler, and C. A. Schriesheim, 11–28. Lexington, MA: D. C. Heath.

Boerner, S., S. A. Eisenbeiss, and D. Griesser. 2007. Follower behavior and organizational performance: The impact of transformational leadership. *Journal of Leadership and Organizational Studies* 13:15–26.

Bono, J. E., and R. Ilies. 2006. Charisma, positive emotion and mood contagion. *Leadership Quarterly* 17:317–334.

Bording, C., T. Bartram, and G. Casimir. 2007. The antecedents and consequences of psychological empowerment among Singaporean IT employees. *Management Research News* 30 (1): 34–46.

Bowers, D. G., and S. E. Seashore. 1966. Predicting organizational effectiveness with a four-factor theory of leadership. *Administrative Science Quarterly* 11:238–263.

Bowles, H. R., and K. L. McGinn. 2005. Claiming authority: Negotiating challenges for women leaders. In *The psychology of leadership: New perspectives and research*, ed. D. M.

Messick and R. M. Kramer, 191–208. Mahwah, NJ: Lawrence Erlbaum.

Boyle, M. 2001. How the workplace was won. *Fortune*, January 8, 139–146.

Bozionelos, N. 2004. The Big Five of personality and work involvement. *Journal of Managerial Psychology* 19 (1–2): 69–72.

Brant, J. 2004. Lucky Junki. *Inc.*, October, 109–116.

Bray, C. 2005. Executives on trial: Ex-director at Tyco testifies on loans. *Wall Street Journal*, February 1, C4.

Bray, D. W., and D. L. Grant. 1966. The assessment center in the measurement of potential for business management. *Psychological Monographs* 80 (17): 1–27.

Brazil, J. J. 2007. Mission: Impossible? *Fast Company*, March. http://www.fastcompany. com/magazine/114/features-mission-impossible.html (accessed August 21, 2007).

Breen, B. 2002. David Rockwell has a lot of nerve. *Fast Company*, November, 76–84.

———. 2004. The six myths of creativity. *Fast Company*, December, 75–78.

Brodsky, N. 2006. The one thing you can't delegate. *Inc.*, April, 61–62.

Broverman, I., S. Vogel, D. Broverman, F. Clarkson, and P. Rosenkrantz. 1975. Sex-role stereotypes: A current appraisal. *Journal of Social Issues* 28:29–78.

Brown, M. C. 1982. Administrative succession and organizational performance: The succession effect. *Administrative Science Quarterly* 29:245–273.

Brown, M. E., and L. K. Treviño. 2006a. Ethical leadership: A review and future directions. *Leadership Quarterly* 17:595–616.

———. 2006b. Socialized charismatic leadership, values congruence, and deviance in work groups. *Journal of Applied Psychology* 91:954–962.

Brown, N. 1998. *The destructive narcissistic pattern.* Westport, CT: Praeger.

Bryant, A. 1995. Worker ownership was no paradise. *International Herald Tribune*, March 23, 16.

Bryman, A. 1992. *Charisma and leadership.* London: Sage.

Bu, N., T. J. Craig, and T. K. Peng. 2001. Acceptance of supervisory direction in typical workplace situations: A comparison of U.S., Taiwanese, and PRC employees. *International*

Journal of Cross-Cultural Management 1 (2): 131–152.

Buchanan, L. 1999. The smartest little company in America. *Inc.*, January, 43–54.

———. 2001. Managing one-to-one. *Inc.*, October 16, 82–88.

Buchanan, R. 2004. The salary report. *Business Mexico*, August, 40–43.

Buckingham, M. 2005. The Frankenleader fad. *Fast Company*, September, 93–94.

Burke, C. S., K. C. Stagl, C. Klein, G. F. Goodwin, E. Salas, and S. M. Halpin. 2006. What type of leadership behaviors are functional in teams? A meta-analysis. *Leadership Quarterly* 17:288–307.

Burke, W., E. A. Richley, and L. DeAngelis. 1985. Changing leadership and planning processes at the Lewis Research Center, National Aeronautics and Space Administration. *Human Resource Management* 24:81–90.

Burlingham, B. 2003. The coolest small company in America. *Inc.*, January, 65–74.

Burns, J. M. 1978. *Leadership*. New York: Harper and Row.

Butler, R. J., and D. C. Wilson. 1990. *Managing voluntary and non-profit organizations: Strategy and structure*. London: Rutledge.

BW: The best managers. 2005. *Business Week*, January 10, 68.

BW: The cleanup crew. 2005. *Business Week*, January 10, 72.

BW: The fallen managers. 2005. *Business Week*, January 10, 78–80.

BW: Repeat performers. 2005. *Business Week*, January 10, 68.

Bycio, P., R. D. Hackett, and J. S. Allen. 1995. Further assessments of Bass's (1985) conceptualization of transactional and transformational leadership. *Journal of Applied Psychology* 80:468–478.

Byrne, J. A., and H. Timmons. 2001. Tough times for a new CEO: How Ken Chenault of AmEx is tested in ways few could have imagined. *Business Week*, October 29, 64–68.

Caligiuri, P. M. 2000. The Big Five personality characteristics as predictors of expatriate's desire to terminate the assignments and supervisor-rated performance. *Personnel Psychology* 53 (1): 67–88.

Callanan, G. A. 2004. What would Machiavelli think? An overview of the leadership challenges in team-based structures. *Team Performance Management* 10 (3–4): 77–83.

Cameron, D. 2007. Pilots at American slam option packages executive compensation. *Financial Times*, January 18, 18.

Cameron, K. 2006. Good or bad: Standards and ethics in managing change. *Academy of Management Learning and Education* 5:317–323.

Campbell, D. J., and G. J. Dardis. 2004. The "Be, Know, Do" model of leader development. *Human Resource Planning* 27 (2): 26–39.

Canabou, C. 2001. Have kid, won't travel. *Fast Company*, October, 48.

———. 2002. John Wood turns the page. *Fast Company*, December, 126–130.

———. 2003a. Fast talk. *Fast Company*, September, 58.

———. 2003b. Time for a turnaround. *Fast Company*, January, 56–61.

Canabou, C., and A. Overholt. 2001. Smart steps. *Fast Company*, March, 98–102.

Carbonara, P. 1998. Mervyn's calls in the SWAT team. *Fast Company*, April–May, 54.

Carl, D., V. Gupta, and M. Javidan. 2004. Power distance. In *Culture, leadership, and organizations: The GLOBE study of 62 countries*, ed. R. J. House, P. J. Hanges, M. Javidan, P. W. Dorfman, and V. Gupta, 513–563. Thousand Oaks, CA: Sage.

Carli, L. L. 1999. Gender, interpersonal power, and social influence. *Journal of Social Issues* 55:81–99.

———. 2001. Gender and social influence. *Journal of Social Issues* 57:725–741.

Carlyle, T. 1907. *Heroes and hero worship*. Boston: Adams.

Carpenter, M. A., M. A. Geletkanycz, and W. G. Sanders. 2004. Upper echelons research revisited: Antecedents, elements, and consequences of top management team composition. *Journal of Management* 30: 749–778.

Cartwright, D. C. 1965. Influence, leadership, control. In *Handbook of organizations*, ed. J. G. March, 1–47. Chicago: Rand McNally.

Carvell, T. 1998. By the way, your staff hates you. *Fortune* 138 (6): 200–212.

Casimir, G. 2001. Combinative aspects of leadership style: The ordering and temporal spacing of leadership behaviors. *Leadership Quarterly* 12 (3): 245–278.

Catalyst. 2002. Women in leadership: A European business imperative. http://catalystwomen. org/files/exe/WICLEUexesum.pdf (accessed July 20, 2007).

————. 2007. 2006 Census of women in Fortune 500 corporate officer and board positions. http://www.catalyst.org/pressroom/ press_ releases/2006_Census_Release.pdf (accessed June 26, 2007).

Chaleff, I. 1995. *The courageous follower: Standing up to and for our leaders.* San Francisco, CA: Berrett-Koehler.

Chandler, S. 2004. Execs take companies' cash as privilege. *Arizona Republic,* September 19, D1, D5.

Chappelow, C. T. 2004. 360-degree feedback. In *The Center for Creative Leadership: Handbook of leadership development.* 2nd ed. Ed. C. D. McCauley and E. Van Velsor, 58–84. San Francisco, CA: Jossey-Bass.

Chattodadhyay, P., M. Tluchowska, and E. George. 2004. Identifying the ingroup: A closer look at the influence of demographic dissimilarity on employee social identity. *Academy of Management Journal* 29:180–202.

Chemers, M. M. 1969. Cross-cultural training as a means for improving situational favorableness. *Human Relations* 22:531–546.

————. 1993. An integrative theory of leadership. In *Leadership theory and research: Perspectives and directions,* ed. M. M. Chemers and R. Ayman, 293–320. New York: Academic Press.

————. 1997. *An integrative theory of leadership.* Mahwah, NJ: Lawrence Erlbaum.

————. 2000. Leadership research and theory: A functional integration. *Group Dynamics: Theory, Research and Practice* 4 (1): 27–43.

Chemers, M. M., R. B. Hays, F. Rhodewalt, and J. Wysocki. 1985. A person-environment analysis of job stress: A contingency model explanation. *Journal of Personality and Social Psychology* 3:628–635.

Chemers, M. M., S. Oskamp, and M. A. Costanzo. 1995. *Diversity in organizations.* Thousand Oaks, CA: Sage.

Chemers, M. M., and G. J. Skrzypek. 1972. An experimental test of the contingency model of leadership effectiveness. *Journal of Personality and Social Psychology* 24: 172–177.

Chen, C. C., and E. Van Velsor. 1996. New directions for research and practice in diversity leadership. *Leadership Quarterly* 7:285–302.

Chen, Y. F., and D. Tjosvold. 2006. Participative leadership by American and Chinese managers in China: The role of relationships. *Journal of Management Studies* 43:1727–1752.

Cherrington, D. J., S. J. Condies, and J. L. England. 1979. Age and work values. *Academy of Management Journal,* September, 617–623.

Cherry, J., and J. Fraedrich. 2000. An empirical investigation of locus of control and the structure of moral reasoning: Examining the ethical decision-making processes of sales managers. *Journal of Personal Selling and Sales Management* 20 (3): 173–188.

Chester, A. 2005. Kenneth Chenault, AMEX CEO, speaks on leadership. *Wharton Journal,* March 28. http://media.www.whartonjournal. com/media/storage/paper201/news/2005/ 03/28/News/Kenneth.Chenault.Amex.Ceo. Speaks.On.Leadership-904135.shtml (accessed July 14, 2007).

Cho, T. S., and W. Shen. 2007. Changes in executive compensation following an environmental shift: The role of top management team turnover. *Strategic Management Journal* 28:747–754.

Christensen, L. M. 1997. Making strategy: Learning by doing. *Harvard Business Review* 75 (6): 141–156.

Christie, R., and F. L. Geis. 1970. *Studies in Machiavellianism.* New York: Academic Press.

Church, G. J. 1997/1998. Man of the year. *Time,* December 29/January 5. http://www. time.com/time/special/moy/grove/ runnergreenspan.html (accessed December 29, 2004).

Cleyman, K. L., S. M. Jex, and K. G. Love. 1993. Employee grievances: An application of the leader-member exchange model. Paper presented at the 9th Annual Meeting of the Society of Industrial and Organizational Psychology, Nashville, TN.

Collins, J. 2001. *Good to great.* New York: Harper Business.

Colvin, G. 2001a. The anti-control freak. *Fortune,* November 26, 60.

————. 2001b. The great CEO pay heist. *Fortune,* June 25. http://money.cnn.com/

magazines/fortune/fortune_archive/2001/06/25/305448/index.htm (accessed December 18, 2007).

———. 2007. Undercutting CEO power. *Fortune*, March 5, 42.

Conger, J. A. 1989. *The charismatic leader: Behind the mystique of exceptional leadership.* San Francisco, CA: Jossey-Bass.

———. 1990. The dark side of leadership. *Organizational Dynamics* 19:44–55.

———. 1991. Inspiring others: The language of leadership. *Academy of Management Executive* 5 (1): 31–45.

———. 1992. *Learning to lead: The art of transforming managers into leaders.* San Francisco, CA: Jossey-Bass.

———. 1999. Charismatic and transformational leadership in organizations: An insider's perspective on these developing streams of research. *Leadership Quarterly* 10:145–179.

———. 2004. Developing leadership capability: What's inside the black box? *Academy of Management Executive* 18 (3): 136–139.

Conger, J. A., and R. N. Kanungo. 1987. Toward a behavioral theory of charismatic leadership in organizational settings. *Academy of Management* 12:637–647.

———. 1988. The empowerment process: Integrating theory and practice. *Academy of Management Review* 13 (3): 471–482.

———. 1998. *Charismatic leadership in organizations.* Thousand Oaks, CA: Sage.

Conlin, M. 2007. Do us a favor, take a vacation. *Business Week*, May 21, 88.

Conyon, M. J., and S. I. Peck. 1998. Board control, remuneration committees, and top management compensation. *Academy of Management Journal* 41 (2): 146–157.

Cooper, C. D., T. A. Scandura, and C. A. Schriesheim. 2005. Looking forward but learning from the our past: Potential challenges to developing authentic leadership theory and authentic leaders. *Leadership Quarterly* 16:475–493.

Cooper, N. 2007. Looking after your leaders. *Personnel Today*, April 24, 24–26.

Cordery, J. 2004. Another case of the Emperor's new clothes? *Journal of Occupational and Organizational Psychology* 77:481–484.

Cornwell, J. M. 1983. A meta-analysis of selected trait research in the leadership literature. Paper presented at the Southeastern Psychological Association, August, Atlanta, GA.

Cotts, C. 2003. All the wrong moves. *Village Voice*, May 14. http://www.villagevoice.com/print/issues/0320/cotts.php (accessed September 22, 2004).

Covey, S. R. 1991. *Principle centered leadership.* New York: Fireside/Simon and Schuster.

Covin, J. G., and D. P. Slevin. 1988. The influence of organization structure on the utility of an entrepreneurial top management style. *Journal of Management Studies* 25 (3): 217–234.

Cronin, T. E. 1984. Thinking and learning about leadership. *Presidential Studies Quarterly* Winter: 22–24, 33–34.

———. 1987. Leadership and democracy. *Liberal Education* 73 (2): 35–38.

Crouch, A., and P. Yetton. 1987. Manager behavior, leadership style, and subordinate performance: An empirical extension of Vroom-Yetton conflict rule. *Organizational Behavior and Human Decision Processes* 39:384–396.

Cullen, J. B., K. P. Parboteeah, and M. Hoegl. 2004. Cross-national differences in managers' willingness to justify ethically suspect behaviors: A test of institutional anomie theory. *Academy of Management Journal* 47:411–421.

Cummings, B. 2004. The best bosses: The Whipcracker. *Fortune Small Business*, October 1. http://www.fortune.com/fortune/print/0,15935,697855,00.html (accessed November 15, 2004).

Cunningham, J. B., and J. MacGregor. 2000. Trust and the design of work: Complementary constructs in satisfaction and performance. *Human Relations* 53:1575–1591.

Customer service. 2007. http://www.superquinn.ie/Multi/default.asp?itemId=305 (accessed July 25, 2007).

Cyert, R. M., and J. G. March. 1963. *A behavioral theory of the firm.* Upper Saddle River, NJ: Prentice Hall.

Daft, R. L. 2008. *The leadership experience.* 4th ed. Forth Worth, TX: Harcourt College Publishers.

Daloz Parks, S. 2005. *Leadership can be taught: A bold for a complex world.* Boston: Harvard Business Press.

Dana, J. A., and D. M. Bourisaw. 2006. Overlooked leaders. *American School Board Journal*, June, 27–30.

Daniels, C. 2001. Does this man need a shrink? *Fortune*, February 5, 205–208.

Dansereau, F., Jr., G. B. Graen, and W. J. Haga. 1975. A vertical dyad linkage approach to leadership within formal organizations: A longitudinal investigation of the role making process. *Organizational Behavior and Human Performance* 13:46–78.

Darla Moore's full-court press. 2000. *Inc.com*, January. http://www.inc.com/articles/2000/01/16336.html (accessed June 27, 2007).

Dash, E. 2007a. Executive pay: A special report. http://www.nytimes.com/2007/04/08/business/yourmoney/08pay.html?ref=business (accessed January 8, 2008).

———. 2007b. Executive pay: Has the exit sign ever looked so good? *New York Times*, April 8. http://www.nytimes.com/2007/04/08/business/yourmoney/08axe.html?ref=businessspecial (accessed January 8, 2008).

Davis, J. H., F. D. Schoorman, and L. Donaldson. 1997. Toward a stewardship theory of management. *Academy of Management Review* 22:20–47.

Day, D. V. 2000. Leadership development: A review in context. *Leadership Quarterly* 11:581–613.

Day, D. V., P. Gronn, and E. Salas. 2004. Leadership capacity in teams. *Leadership Quarterly* 15:857–880.

Day, D. V., and R. G. Lord. 1988. Executive leadership and organizational performance: Suggestions for a new theory and methodology. *Journal of Management* 14:453–464.

Day, D. V., and D. J. Schleicher. 2006. Self-monitoring at work: A motive-based perspective. *Journal of Personality* 74:683–714.

Day, D. V., D. J. Schleicher, A. L. Unckless, and N. J. Hiller. 2002. Self-monitoring personality at work: A meta-analytic investigation of construct validity. *Journal of Applied Psychology* 87:390–401.

Day, D. V., S. J. Zaccaro, and S. M. Halpin, eds. 2004. *Leader development for transforming organization: Growing leader for tomorrow*. Mahwah, NJ: Lawrence Erlbaum.

De Bono, E. 1992. *Serious creativity: Using the power of lateral thinking to create new ideas*. New York: Harper Business.

———. 1999. *Six Thinking Hats*. Rev. ed. Boston: Back Bay Books.

De Cremer, D. J., and D. van Knippenberg. 2002. How do leaders promote cooperation? The effects of charisma and procedural fairness. *Journal of Applied Psychology* 87:858–866.

Dekmejian, R. H., and M. J. Wyszomirski. 1972. Charismatic leadership in Islam: The Mahdi of the Sudan. *Comparative Studies in Society and History* 14:193–214.

Delbecq, A. 2001. "Evil" manifested in destructive individual behavior: A senior leadership challenge. *Journal of Management Inquiry* 10:221–226.

Den Hartog, D. N., R. J. House, P. J. Hanges, S. A. Ruiz-Quintanilla, and P. W. Dorfman. 1999. Culture-specific and cross-culturally generalizable implicit leadership theories: Are attributes of charismatic/transformational leadership universally endorsed? *Leadership Quarterly* 10:219–256.

Denhardt, J. V., and K. B. Campbell. 2006. The role of democratic values in transformational leadership. *Administration and Society* 38:556–573.

Denhardt, R. B., and J. V. Denhardt. 2006. *The dance of leadership*. Armonk, NJ: M. E. Sharpe.

Dent, E. B., M. E. Higgins, and D. M. Wharff. 2005. Spirituality and leadership: An empirical review of definitions, distinctions, and embedded assumptions. *Leadership Quarterly* 16:625–653.

Denton, D. K. 2007. Using intranets as a training and empowerment tool. *Training and Development Methods* 21 (1): 217–222.

Derr, C. B. 1987. Managing high potentials in Europe: Some cross-cultural findings. *European Management Journal* 5:72–80.

Deutschman, A. 2004. Inside the mind of Jeff Bezos. *Fast Company*, August. http://www.fastcompany.com/magazine/85/bezos_1.html (accessed July 25, 2007).

———. 2005. Change or die. *Fast Company*, May. http://www.fastcompany.com/magazine/94/open_change-or-die.html (accessed June 19, 2007).

———. 2007. The three keys to change. *Fast Company*, January. http://www.fastcompany.com/articles/2007/01/change-or-die.html (accessed August 22, 2007).

Dickins, D., and R. Houmes. 2007. Much ado about nothing? *Financial Analysts Journal* 63:28–32.

Dicocco, J. 2006. Crew captain. *Builders and Leaders* (Boston University School of Management), Fall, 12–16.

Digman, J. M. 1990. Personality structure: Emergence of the five-factor model. *Annual Review of Psychology* 41:417–440.

Dillon, P. 1998. Is selling out "selling out"? *Fast Company*, February–March, 92–95.

———. 2004. Perceptive, adaptable, and remarkably low-key, eBay chief executive Meg Whitman rides e-tail's hottest segment. *Christian Science Monitor*, March 10. http://www.csmonitor.com/2004/0310/p11s01-wmgn.htm (accessed July 12, 2007).

D'Intino, R. S., M. G. Goldsby, J. D. Houghton, and C. P. Neck. 2007. Self-leadership: A process of entrepreneurial success. *Journal of Leadership and Organizational Studies* 13:105–120.

Dobbins, G. H., W. S. Long, E. J. Dedrick, and T. C. Clemons. 1990. The role of self-monitoring and gender on leader emergence: A laboratory and field study. *Journal of Management* 16 (3): 609–618.

Donaldson, T. 1994. Global business must mind its morals. *New York Times*, February 13, F11.

Dorfman, P. W., J. P. Howell, S. Hibino, J. K. Lee, U. Tate, and A. Bautista. 1997. Leadership in Western and Asian countries: Commonalities and differences in effective leadership processes across cultures. *Leadership Quarterly* 8 (3): 233–274.

Dose, J. J. 1999. The relationship between work values similarity and team-member and leader-member exchange relationships. *Group Dynamics* 3 (1): 20–32.

Dow Jones. 2005. VentureOne survey finds that venture-backed companies managed by women receive only small fraction of investment activity. http://www.dj.com/Pressroom/PressReleases/Other/Europe/2005/0308_Europe_DowJonesNewswires_3756.htm (accessed July 20, 2007).

Downey, H. K., J. E. Sheridan, and J. W. Slocum Jr. 1975. Analysis of relationships among leader behavior, subordinate job performance and satisfaction: A path-goal approach. *Academy of Management Journal* 18:253–262.

Duarte, N. T., J. R. Goodson, and N. R. Klich. 1994. Effects of dyadic quality and duration on performance appraisal. *Academy of Management Journal* 37:499–521.

Duff, C. 1993. "Jack the ripper": A CEO for a new era prospers by practicing the art of firing. *Wall Street Journal*, January 11, A1, A4.

Duncan, W. J., K. G. LaFrance, and P. M. Ginter. 2003. Leadership and decision making: A retrospective application and assessment. *Journal of Leadership and Organizational Studies* 9 (4): 1–20.

Dupriez, P., and S. Simmons, eds. 2000. *La resistance culturelle: Fondements, applications et implications du management intercultural.* Brussels: DeBoeck & Larcier.

Dvir, T., D. Eden, B. J. Avolio, and B. Shamir. 2002. Impact of transformational leadership on follower development and performance in a field experiment. *Academy of Management Journal* 45:735–744.

Eagly, A. H. 2005. Achieving relational authenticity in leadership: Does gender matter? *Leadership Quarterly* 16:459–474.

Eagly, A. H., and L. L. Carli. 2004. Women and men as leaders. In *The nature of leadership*, ed. J. Antonakis, A. T. Cianciolo, and R. J. Sternberg, 279–301. Thousand Oaks, CA: Sage.

Eagly, A. H., M. C. Johannesen-Schmidt, and M. van Engen. 2003. Transformational, transactional, and laissez-faire leadership styles: A meta-analysis comparing women and men. *Psychological Bulletin* 95:569–591.

Eagly, A. H., and B. T. Johnson. 1990. Gender and leadership style: A meta-analysis. *Psychological Bulletin* 108:233–256.

Eagly, A. H., and S. J. Karau. 2002. Role congruity theory of prejudice toward female leaders. *Psychological Review* 109:573–598.

Eagly, A. H., S. J. Karau, and M. G. Makhijani. 1995. Gender and the effectiveness of leaders: A meta-analysis. *Psychological Bulletin* 117: 125–145.

Eagly, A. H., M. G., Makhijani, and B. G. Klonsky. 1992. Gender and the evaluation of leaders: A meta-analysis. *Psychological Bulletin* 111:3–22.

Early, C., and E. Mosakowski. 1996. Experimental international management research. In *Handbook for international management research*, ed. B. J. Punnett and O. Shenkar, 83–114. Oxford: Blackwell.

Edelhauser, K. 2007. Steve Case takes on health care. *Entrepreneur.com*, July 18. http://www.

entrepreneur.com/ebusiness/article181860.html (accessed August 12, 2007).

EEOC. 2006. Sexual harassment charges. http://www.eeoc.gov/stats/harass.html (accessed July 6, 2007).

Elkins, T., and R. T. Keller. 2003. Leadership in research and development organizations: A literature review and conceptual framework. *Leadership Quarterly* 14:587–606.

Ellerbee, L. 1999. My biggest mistake. *Inc.*, January, 81.

Emmons, R. A. 1987. Narcissism: Theory and measurement. *Journal of Personality and Social Psychology* 52:11–17.

Employees of big firms post lower job satisfaction. 2006. *Wall Street Journal*, November 13, 30.

Endrissat, N., R. W., Muller, and S. Kaudela-Baum. 2007. En route to an empirically-based understanding of authentic leadership. *European Management Journal* 25(3), 207.

Erdogan, B., R. C. Linden, and M. L. Kramer. 2006. Justice and leader-member exchange: The moderating role of organizational culture. *Academy of Management Journal* 49:394–406.

Erickson, R. J. 1995. The importance of authenticity for self and society. *Symbolic Interaction* 18:121–144.

Ernst, C., and A. Martin. 2007. Experience counts: Learning lessons from key events. *Leadership in Action* 26 (6): 3.

Estow, S., J. P. Jamieson, and J. R. Yates. 2007. Self-monitoring and mimicry of positive and negative social behaviors. *Journal of Research in Personality* 41:425–433.

Evans, M. G. 1996. R. J. House's path-goal theory of leader effectiveness. *Leadership Quarterly* 7 (3): 305–309.

Executive pay watch. 2007. http://www.aflcio.org/corporatewatch/paywatch/ (accessed July 24, 2007).

Fairhurst, G. T., and R. A. Sarr. 1996. *The art of framing: Managing the language of leadership.* San Francisco, CA: Jossey-Bass.

Fanelli, A., and V. F. Misangyi. 2006. Bringing out charisma: CEO charisma and external stakeholders. *Academy of Management Review* 31:1049–1061.

Farh, J. L., P. M. Podsakoff, and B. S. Cheng. 1987. Culture-free leadership effectiveness versus moderators of leadership behavior: An extension and test of Kerr and Jermier's "substitutes for leadership" model in Taiwan. *Journal of International Business Studies* 18 (3): 43–60.

Farrel, G. 2005. A CEO and a gentleman. *USA Today—Money*. http://www.usatoday.com/money/companies/management/2005-04-24-chenault-usat_x.htm (accessed July 14, 2007).

Farzad, R. 2007. The change agent. *Business Week*, May 28, 57.

Fenn, D. 1998. Built for speed. *Inc* (September), 61–71.

Fiedler, F. E. 1967. *A theory of leadership effectiveness.* New York: McGraw-Hill.

———. 1978. The contingency model and the dynamics of the leadership process. In *Advances in experimental social psychology.* Vol. 2. Ed. L. Berkowitz, 59–112. New York: Academic Press.

———. 1992. The role and meaning of leadership experience. In *Impact of leadership*, ed. K. E. Clark, M. B. Clark, and D. P. Campbell, 95–105. Greensboro, NC: Center for Creative Leadership.

———. 1993. The leadership situation and the black box in contingency theories. In *Leadership theory and research: Perspectives and directions*, ed. M. M. Chemers and R. Ayman, 2–28. New York: Academic Press.

———. 1995. Cognitive resources and leadership performance. *Applied Psychology: An International Review* 44 (1): 5–28.

Fiedler, F. E., and M. M. Chemers. 1974. *Leadership and effective management.* Glenview, IL: Scott-Foresman.

———. 1984. *Improving leadership effectiveness: The leader match concept.* 2nd ed. New York: John Wiley.

Fiedler, F. E., and J. E. Garcia. 1987a. *Improving leadership effectiveness: Cognitive resources and organizational performance.* New York: John Wiley.

———. 1987b. *New approaches to leadership: Cognitive resources and organizational performance.* New York: John Wiley.

Fields, M. 2006. Ford fights back. http://media.ford.com/newsroom/release_display.cfm?release=22464 (accessed August 23, 2007).

Finkelstein, S., and D. C. Hambrick. 1988. Chief executive compensation: A synthesis and reconciliation. *Strategic Management Journal* 9:543–558.

_____. 1990. Top management team tenure and organizational outcomes: The moderating role of managerial discretion. *Administrative Science Quarterly* 35:484–503.

_____. 1996. *Strategic leadership: Top executives and their effects on organizations.* Minneapolis-St. Paul, MN: West Publishing.

Fisher, A. 1998. Success secret: A high emotional IQ. *Fortune* 138 (8): 293–298.

_____. 2007. The trouble with MBAs. *Fortune*, April 30, 49.

Fisher, K. 1993. *Leading self-directed work teams.* New York: McGraw-Hill.

Fishman, C. 2001. A dose of change. *Fast Company*, August, 50–52.

Fleishman, E. A. 1953. The measurement of leadership attitudes in industry. *Journal of Applied Psychology* 37:153–158.

Fleishman, E. A., and E. F. Harris. 1962. Patterns of leadership behavior related to employee grievance and turnover. *Personnel Psychology* 15:43–56.

Flint, P. 2006. The American way. *Air Transport World*, September, 40–48.

For Anne M. Mulcahy, leadership is about learning. 2001. *Knowledge@Wharton*, July 4. http://knowledge.wharton.upenn.edu/article.cfm?articleid=389 (accessed September 8, 2007).

Ford Foundation. 2007. Our mission. http://www.fordfound.org/about/mission (accessed January 8, 2008).

Forde, C., G. Slater, and D. A. Spencer. 2006. Fearing the worst? Threat, participation and workplace productivity. *Economic and Industrial Democracy* 27 (3): 369–378.

Forsythe, J. 2005. Leading with diversity: Washington Mutual. http://www.nytimes.com/marketing/jobmarket/diversity/wamu.html (accessed July 13, 2007).

Foster, T. 2004. Using delegation as a developmental tool: Methods and benefits. *Training Journal*, May, 28–32.

Founder of Oxygen media passes along tips for moms who want to be entrepreneurs. 2005. *Startup Nation*, May 7. http://www.startupnation.com/pages/radio/RD_May7_2005_GerryLaybourne.asp (accessed June 27, 2007).

Fowers, B. J., and B. J. Davidov. 2006. The virtue of multiculturalism: Personal transformation, character, and openness to the other. *American Psychologist* 61:581–594.

Fox, L. 2001. Meg Whitman. *Salon.com*, November 27. http://archive.salon.com/people/bc/2001/11/27/whitman/index.html (accessed January 8, 2008).

Franklin, R. 2003. The surge in female entrepreneurs. *BW Online*, May 15. http://www.businessweek.com/smallbiz/content/may2003/sb20030515_4950_sb010.htm (accessed October 28, 2004).

Frauenheim, E. 2007. Taking the measure of Agilent. *Workforce Management*, January. http://www.workforce.com/section/10/feature/24/62/46/index.html (accessed January 8, 2008).

French, J. R. P., and B. H. Raven. 1968. The basis of social power. In *Group dynamics*. 3rd ed. Ed. D. Cartwright and A. Zander, 259–269. New York: Harper and Row.

Frey, R. 1993. Empowerment or else. *Harvard Business Review*, September–October: 80–94.

Frink, D. D., and G. R. Ferris. 1999. The moderating effects of accountability on the conscientiousness performance relationship. *Journal of Business and Psychology* 13 (4): 515–524.

Fromartz, S. 1998. The right staff. *Inc.*, October 20, 125–132.

Fry, L. W. 2003. Toward a theory of spiritual leadership. *Leadership Quarterly* 14:693–727.

_____. 2005. Introduction to *The Leadership Quarterly* special issue: Toward a paradigm of spiritual leadership. *Leadership Quarterly* 16:619–622.

Fulmer, R. M., and M. Goldsmith. 2000. *The leadership investment: How the world's best organization gain strategic advantage through leadership development.* New York: AMACOM.

Furnham, A., and P. Stringfield. 1993. Personality and occupational behavior: Myers-Briggs type indicator correlates of managerial practices in two cultures. *Human Relations* 46 (7): 827–848.

Galinski, A. D., D. H. Gruenfeld, and J. C. Magee. 2003. From power to action. *Journal of Personality and Social Psychology* 85:453–466.

Gallagher, B. M. 2006. Commencement address at University of Maryland. http://national.unitedway.org/files/pdf/speeches/UniversityMarylandCommencement.pdf (accessed July 26, 2007).

Galton, R. 1869. *Hereditary genius.* New York: Appleton.

Gardner, L., and C. Stough. 2002. Examining the relationship between leadership and emotional intelligence in senior-level managers. *Leadership and Organizational Development Journal* 23 (1/2): 68–78.

Gardner, W. L., B. J. Avolio, F. Luthans, D. R. May, and F. Walumbwa. 2005. "Can you see the real me?" A self-based model of authentic leader and follower development. *Leadership Quarterly* 16:343–372.

Garibaldi de Hilal, A. V. 2006. Brazilian national culture, organizational culture and cultural agreement. *Journal of Cross-Cultural Management* 6:139–167.

Geiger, S. W., and L. H. Cashen. 2007. Organizational size and CEO compensation: The moderating effect of diversification in downscoping organizations. *Journal of Managerial Issues* 19:233–254.

Gelfand, M., D. P. S. Bhawuk, L. H. Nishii, and B. J. Bechtold. 2004. Individualism and collectivism. In *Culture, leadership, and organizations: The GLOBE study of 62 countries*, ed. R. J. House, P. J. Hanges, M. Javidan, P. W. Dorfman, and V. Gupta, 437–512. Thousand Oaks, CA: Sage.

George, B. 2007. *True north*. San Francisco, CA: Jossey-Bass.

George, B., and W. Kopp. 2007. Open debate. *Fast Company*, April, 112.

George, J. M. 2000. Emotions and leadership: The role of emotional intelligence. *Human Relations* 53 (8): 1027–1055.

George, W. 2003. *Authentic leadership*. San Francisco, CA: Jossey-Bass.

Gerstner, C. R., and D. V. Day. 1994. Crosscultural comparisons of leadership prototypes. *Leadership Quarterly* 5:121–134.

Ghiselli, E. E. 1963. Intelligence and managerial success. *Psychological Reports* 12:898.

Gibson, F. W. 1992. Leader abilities and group performance as a function of stress. In *Impact of leadership*, ed. K. E. Clark, M. B. Clark, and D. P. Campbell, 333–343. Greensboro, NC: Center for Creative Leadership.

Glaser, J. E. 2006. *The DNA of leadership*. Avon, MA: Platinum Press.

Glass, D. C. 1983. Behavioral, cardiovascular, and neuroendocrine responses. *International Review of Applied Psychology* 32:137–151.

Gockel, A. 2004. The trend toward spirituality in the workplace: Overview and implications for career counseling. *Journal of Employment Counseling* 41:156–167.

Gohm, C. L. 2003. Mood regulation and emotional intelligence: Individual differences. *Journal of Personality and Social Psychology* 84:594–607.

Goldstein, I. L. 1986. *Training in organizations: Needs assessment, development, and evaluation*. Monterey, CA: Brooks/Cole.

Goldstein, L. 2000. Whatever space works for you. *Fortune*, July 10, 269–270.

Goleman, D. 1995. *Emotional intelligence: Why it can matter more than IQ*. New York: Bantam Books.

———. 1998. *Working with emotional intelligence*. New York: Bantam Books.

———. 2004. What makes a leader? *Harvard Business Review* 82 (1): 82–91.

Goleman, D., R. E. Boyatzis, and A. McKee. 2002. *Primal leadership: Realizing the power of emotional intelligence*. Boston: Harvard Business School Press.

Golob, U., and J. L. Bartlett. 2007. Communication about corporate social responsibility: A comparative study of CSP report in Australia and Slovenia. *Public Relations Review* 33:1–9.

Gordon, M. 2004. Mickey Drexler's redemption. *New York Magazine*, November 29. http://newyorkmetro.com/nymetro/news/bizfinance/biz/features/10489/index1.html (accessed February 7, 2005).

Gould, E. 2007. Boom times for banks in Venezuela. *New York Times*, June 15. http://www.nytimes.com/2007/06/15/business/worldbusiness/15venezbank.html?n=Top%2fReference%2fTimes%20Topics%2fPeople%2fC%2fChavez%2c%20Hugo (accessed June 22, 2007).

Graen, G. B. 2006. In the eye of the beholder: Cross-cultural lesson in leadership from Project GLOBE. *Academy of Management Perspectives* 20 (4): 95–101.

Graen, G. B., and J. R. Cashman. 1975. A role-making model of leadership in formal organizations: A developmental approach. In *Leadership frontiers*, ed. J. G. Hunt and L. L. Larson, 143–165. Kent, OH: Kent State University Press.

Graen, G. B., and W. Shiemann. 1978. Leader-member agreement: A vertical dyad linkage approach. *Journal of Applied Psychology* 63:206–212.

Graen, G. B., and M. Uhl-Bien. 1991. The transformation of work group professionals into self-managing and partially self-designing contributors: Toward a theory of leadership-making. *Journal of Management Systems* 3 (3): 33–48.

———. 1995. Relationship-based approach to leadership: Development of leader-member exchange (LMX) theory of leadership over 25 years: Applying a multilevel-multidomain perspective. *Leadership Quarterly* 6:219–247.

Grant, P. 2005. Charter communication CEO quits amid board unhappiness. *Wall Street Journal*, January 19, Eastern edition, B3.

Green, S. G., and T. Mitchell. 1979. Attributional processes of leaders in leader-member interactions. *Organizational Behavior and Human Performance* 23:429–458.

Greenleaf, R. K. 1998. *The power of servant leadership*. San Francisco, CA: Berrett-Koehler.

Greenwald, J. 1992. Is Mr. Nice guy back? *Time*, January 27, 43.

Griffin, R. W. 1979. Task design determinants of effective leader behavior. *Academy of Management Review* 4:215–224.

Gronn, P. 1999. Substituting for leadership: The neglected role of the leadership couple. *Leadership Quarterly* 10 (1): 41–62.

Grzelakowski, M. 2005. *Mother leads best*. Chicago: Dearborn Trade Publishing.

Gull, G. A., and J. Doh. 2004. The transmutation of the organization: Toward a more spiritual workplace. *Journal of Management Inquiry* 13:128–139.

Gunther, M. 1998. The Internet is Mr. Case's neighborhood. *Fortune* 137 (6): 68–80.

Gupta, A. K. 1984. Contingency linkages between strategy and general manager characteristics: A conceptual examination. *Academy of Management Review* 9 (3): 399–412.

———. 1986. Matching managers to strategies: Point and counterpoint. *Human Resource Management* 25 (2): 215–234.

———. 1988. Contingency perspectives on strategic leadership: Current knowledge and future research directions. In *The executive effect: Concepts and methods for studying top managers*, ed. D. C. Hambrick, 141–178. Greenwich, CT: JAI Press.

Hackman, J. R., ed. 1990. *Groups that work (and those that don't): Creating conditions for effective teamwork*. San Francisco, CA: Jossey-Bass.

———. 2005. Rethinking team leadership or team leaders are not music directors. In *The psychology of leadership: New perspectives and research*, ed. D. M. Messick and R. M. Kramer, 115–142. Mahwah, NJ: Lawrence Erlbaum.

Hackman, J. R., and G. R. Oldham. 1980. *Work redesign*. Reading, MA: Addison-Wesley.

Haleblian, J., and S. Finkelstein. 1993. Top management team size, CEO dominance, and firm performance: The moderating roles of environmental turbulence and discretion. *Academy of Management Journal* 36:844–863.

Haley, F. 2004. Mutual benefits. *Fast Company*, October, 98–99.

Haley, U., and S. A. Stumpf. 1989. Cognitive traits in strategic decision making: Linking theories of personality and cognition. *Journal of Management Studies* 26:467–477.

Hall, E. T. 1973. *The silent language*. Garden City, NY: Anchor Press, Doubleday.

———. 1976. *Beyond culture*. Garden City, NY: Anchor Press, Doubleday.

Hall, R. N. 1977. *Organizations, structure, and process*. 2nd ed. Upper Saddle River, NJ: Prentice Hall.

Halpin, A. W., and B. J. Winer. 1957. A factorial study of the leader behavior descriptions. In *Leader behavior: Its description and measurement*, ed. R. M. Stogdill and A. E. Coons. Columbus: The Ohio State University, Bureau of Business Research.

Hambrick, D. C. 1987. The top management team: Key to strategic success. *California Management Review* 29:88–108.

———. 2007. Upper echelons theory: An update. *Academy of Management Review* 32 (2): 334–343.

Hambrick, D. C., and S. Finkelstein. 1987. Managerial discretion: A bridge between polar views of organization. In *Research in organizational behavior*. Vol. 9. Ed. L. L. Cummings and B. L. Staw, 349–406. Greenwich, CT: JAI Press.

Hambrick, D. C., and P. A. Mason. 1984. Upper echelon: The organization as a reflection of its top management. *Academy of Management Review* 9:193–206.

Hammer, M., and J. Champy. 1993. *Reengineering the corporation: A manifesto for business revolution*. New York: Harper Business.

Hammonds, K. H. 2001. How do you structure success? *Fast Company*, April, 58.

_____. 2004. GE smackdown. *Fast Company*, July, 32.

Hannan, M. T., and J. H. Freeman. 1977. The population ecology of organizations. *American Journal of Sociology* 82:929–964.

Hansemark, O. C. 2003. Need for achievement, locus of control and prediction of business start-ups: A longitudinal study. *Journal of Economic Psychology* 24:301–319.

Hardy, C. 1985. The nature of unobtrusive power. *Journal of Management Studies* 22:384–399.

Harris, P. R., R. T. Moran, and S. V. Moran. 2004. *Managing cultural differences.* 6th ed. Amsterdam: Elsevier.

Harrison, J. S., and R. E. Freeman. 2004. Democracy in and around organizations: Is organizational democracy worth the effort? *Academy of Management Executive* 18 (3): 49–53.

Hautala, T. M. 2006. The relationship between personal and transformational leadership. *Journal of Management Development* 25:777–794.

Hayes, T., H. Roehm, and J. Catellano. 1994. Personality correlates of success in total quality manufacturing. *Journal of Business and Psychology* 8 (4): 397–411.

Hedlund, J., G. B. Forsythe, J. A. Horvath, W. M. Williams, S. Snook, and R. J. Sternberg. 2003. Identifying and assessing tacit knowledge: Understanding the practical intelligence of military leaders. *Leadership Quarterly* 14:117–140.

Heifetz, R. A. 1994. *Leadership without easy answers.* Boston: Belknap Press of Harvard University Press.

Heiftetz, R. A., and M. Linsky. 2002. *Leadership on the line: Staying alive through the dangers of leading.* Boston: Harvard Business School Press.

Helfat, C. E., D. Harris, and P. J. Wolfson. 2006. The pipeline to the top: Women and men in the top executive rank of U.S. corporations. *Academy of Management Perspectives* 20 (4): 42–64.

Helgesen, S. 1995. *The female advantage: Women's way of leadership.* New York: Doubleday, Currency.

Hemphill, J. K., and A. E. Coons. 1957. Development of the leader behavior description questionnaire. In *Leader behavior: Its description and measurement,* ed. R. M. Stogdill and A. E. Coons. Columbus: The Ohio State University, Bureau of Business Research.

Henderson, J. P., and P. Nutt. 1980. The influence of decision style on decision-making behavior. *Management Science* 26:371–386.

Herman Miller culture. 2007. http://www. hermanmiller.com/CDA/SSA/Category/ 0,,a10-c680,00.html (accessed August 25, 2007).

Hershey, P., and K. H. Blanchard. 1977. *Management of organizational behavior.* 3rd ed. Upper Saddle River, NJ: Prentice Hall.

Hess, P. W. 2007. Enhancing leadership skills development by creating practice feedback opportunities in the classroom. *Journal of Management Education* 31:195–213.

Hewlett, S. A. 2007. *Off-ramps and on-ramps.* Boston: Harvard Business School Press.

Hickson, D. J., C. R. Hinings, C. A. Lee, R. E. Scheneck, and J. M. Pennings. 1971. A strategic contingencies theory of intra-organizational power. *Administrative Science Quarterly* 16:216–229.

Himelseten, L., and S. A. Forest. 1977. Breaking through. *Business Week* (February, 17), 64–70.

Hindo, B. 2007. At 3M, a struggle between efficiency and creativity. *Business Week,* June 11, 8.

Hira, N. A. 2007. You raised them, now manage them. *Fortune,* May, 38–43.

Hirsch, J. S. 1993. New hotel clerks provide more than keys. *Wall Street Journal,* March 5, B1, B2.

Hirst, G., L. Mann, P. Bain, A. Pirola-Merlo, and A. Richter. 2004. Learning to lead: The development and testing of a model of leadership learning. *Leadership Quarterly* 15:311–327.

Hodson, R., V. J. Roscigno, and S. H. Lopez. 2006. Chaos and the abuse of power: Workplace bullying in organizational and interactional context. *Work and Occupation* 33 (4): 382–416.

Hofman, M. 2000. The metamorphosis. *Inc.,* March 1, 53–60.

_____. 2001. It takes all kinds. *Inc.,* July, 70–75.

Hofmann, D. A., and F. P. Morgeson. 1999. Safety-related behavior as a social exchange: The role of perceived organizational support and leader-member exchange. *Journal of Applied Psychology* 84 (2): 286–296.

Hofstede, G. 1992. *Culture and organizations.* London: McGraw-Hill.

_____. 1996. An American in Paris: The influence of nationality on organization theories. *Organization Studies* 17:525–537.

_____. 1997. *Culture and organizations: Software of the mind; intercultural cooperation and its importance for survival.* New York: McGraw-Hill.

_____. 2001. *Culture's consequences: Comparing values, behaviors, institutions, and organizations across organizations.* Beverly Hills, CA: Sage.

Hogg, M. A. 2005. Social identity and leadership. In *The psychology of leadership: New perspectives and research*, ed. D. M. Messick and R. M. Kramer, 53–80. Mahwah, NJ: Lawrence Erlbaum.

Holland, K. 2007. How diversity makes a team click. *New York Times*, April 22. http://select.nytimes.com/search/restricted/article?res=F20D10FD3D5A0C718EDDAD0894DF404482 (accessed June 27, 2007).

Hollander, E. P. 1979. Leadership and social exchange processes. In *Social change: Advances in theory and research*, ed. K. Gergen, M. S. Greenberg, and R. H. Willis. New York: Winston-John Wiley.

Holson, L. M. 2004a. Eisner says Ovitz required oversight daily. *New York Times*, November 17, C1, C12.

_____. 2004b. Ovitz testifies he was sabotaged at Disney. *New York Times*, October 27, C1, C4.

Holstein, W. J. 2007. What consultants may not know about leadership. *New York Times*, April 1. http://select.nytimes.com/search/restricted/article?res=F20E1EFA3A540C728CDDAD0894DF404482# (accessed June 15, 2007).

Homans, G. C. 1950. *The human group.* New York: Harcourt, Brace.

Hooijberg, R., and J. Choi. 1999. From Austria to the United States and from evaluating therapists to developing cognitive resources theory: An interview with Fred Fiedler. *Leadership Quarterly* 10:653–665.

Hoppe, M. H. 2004. Cross-cultural issues in the development of leaders. In *The Center for Creative Leadership: Handbook of leadership development*. 2nd ed. Ed. C. D. McCauley and E. Van Velsor, 331–360. San Francisco, CA: Jossey-Bass.

Houghton, J. D., T. W. Bonham, C. P. Neck, and K. Singh. 2004. The relationship between self-leadership and personality: A comparison of hierarchical factor structures. *Journal of Managerial Psychology* 19:427–454.

Houghton, J. D., and C. P. Neck. 2002. The revised self-leadership questionnaire: Testing a hierarchical factor structure for self-leadership. *Journal of Managerial Psychology* 17:672–691.

House, R. J. 1971. A path-goal theory of leader effectiveness. *Administrative Science Quarterly* 16:321–339.

_____. 1977. A 1976 theory of charismatic leadership. In *Leadership: The cutting edge*, ed. J. G. Hunt and L. L. Larson, 189–204. Carbondale: Southern Illinois University Press.

_____. 1996. Path-goal theory of leadership: Lessons, legacy, and a reformulated theory. *Leadership Quarterly* 7:323–352.

_____. 1999. Weber and the neo-charismatic leadership paradigm: A response to Beyer. *Leadership Quarterly* 10:563–574.

House, R. J., and R. N. Aditya. 1997. The social scientific study of leadership: Quo vadis? *Journal of Management* 23:409–473.

House, R. J., and G. Dessler. 1974. The path-goal theory of leadership: Some post hoc and a priori tests. In *Contingency approaches to leadership*, ed. J. G. Hunt and L. L. Larson, 29–55. Carbondale: Southern Illinois University Press.

House, R. J., and A. C. Filley. 1971. Leadership style, hierarchical influence, and the satisfaction of subordinate role expectations: A test of Likert's influence proposition. *Journal of Applied Psychology* 55.422–492.

House, R. J., P. J. Hanges, M. Javidan, P. W. Dorfman, and V. Gupta. 2004. *Culture, leadership and organizations: The GLOBE study of 62 countries.* Thousand Oaks, CA: Sage.

House, R. J., M. Javidan, P. W. Dorfman, and M. S. De Luque. 2006. A failure of scholarship: Response to George Graen's critique of GLOBE. *Academy of Management Perspectives* 20 (4): 102–114.

House, R. J., M. Javidan, P. Hanges, and P. Dorfman. 2002. Understanding cultures and implicit leadership theories across the globe: An introduction to project GLOBE. *Journal of World Business* 37:3–10.

House, R. J., and T. R. Mitchell. 1974. Path-goal theory of leadership. *Contemporary Business* (Fall), 81–98.

House, R. J., and B. Shamir. 1993. Toward the integration of transformational, charismatic and visionary leadership. In *Leadership theory and research: Perspective and directions*, ed. M. M. Chemers and R. Ayman, 81–107. New York: Academic Press.

Howell, J. M. 1988. Two faces of charisma: Socialized and personalized leadership in organizations. In *Charismatic leadership: The illusive factor in organizational effectiveness,* ed. J. Conger and R. Kanungo, 213–236. San Francisco, CA: Jossey-Bass.

Howell, J. M., and B. J. Avolio. 1992. The ethics of charismatic leadership: Submission or liberation. *Academy of Management Executive* 6 (2): 43–54.

Howell, J. M., and K. E. Hall-Merenda. 1999. The ties that bind: The impact of leader-member exchange, transformational and transactional leadership, and distance on predicting follower performance. *Journal of Applied Psychology* 84 (5): 680–694.

Howell, J. P. 1997. "Substitutes for leadership: Their meaning and measurement"—an historical assessment. *Leadership Quarterly* 8 (2): 113–116.

Howell, J. P., D. E. Bowen, P. W. Dorfman, S. Kerr, and P. M. Podsakoff. 1990. Substitutes for leadership: Effective alternatives to ineffective leadership. *Organizational Dynamics* 19:21–38.

Humphrey, R. H. 2002. The many faces of emotional leadership. *Leadership Quarterly* 13:493–504.

Hunt, J. G. 1999. Transformation/charismatic leadership's transformation of the field: An historical essay. *The Leadership Quarterly* 10, 129–144.

Hunter, D. 2006. Leadership resilience and tolerance of ambiguity in crisis situations. *Business Review* 5 (1): 44–50.

Hutchinson, L. R., and N. F. Skinner. 2007. Self-awareness and cognitive style: Relationships among adaptation-innovation, self-monitoring, and self-consciousness. *Social Behavior and Personality* 35:551–560.

Hymowitz, C. 1988. Five main reasons why managers fail. *Wall Street Journal,* May 2, B1.

———. 1998. Some managers are more than bosses: They're leaders too. *Wall Street Journal,* November 8, B1.

Ibarra, H. 1993. Personal networks of women and minorities in management: A conceptual framework. *Academy of Management Review* 18:56–87.

Ilgen, D. R., J. R. Hollenbeck, M. Johnson, and D. Jundt. 2005. Teams in organizations: From input-process output models to IMIO modes. In *Annual review of psychology.* Vol. 56. Ed. S. T. Fiske, D. L. Schacter, and A. E. Kazdin, 517–543. Palo Alto, CA: Annual Reviews.

IWDC—International Women Democracy Center. 2007. *Fact sheet.* http://www.iwdc.org/resources/fact_sheet.htm (accessed June 27, 2007).

Jaffe, E. D., I. D. Nebenzahl, and H. Gotesdyner. 1989. Machiavellianism, task orientation, and team effectiveness revisited. *Psychological Reports* 64 (3): 819–824.

James, W. 1880. Great men, great thoughts, and their environment. *Atlantic Monthly* 46:441–459.

Jansen, K. J., and A. Kristof-Brown. 2006. Toward a multidimensional theory of person-environment fit. *Journal of Management Issues* 18:193–212.

Javidan, M., and R. J. House. 2001. Cultural acumen for the global manager: Lessons from project GLOBE. *Organizational Dynamics* 29:289–305.

Jawahar, I. M. 2001. Attitudes, self-monitoring, and appraisal behavior. *Journal of Applied Psychology* 86 (5): 875–883.

Jenkins, W. O. 1947. A review of leadership studies with particular reference to military problems. *Psychological Bulletin* 44:54–79.

Jensen, S. M., and Luthans, F. 2006. Entrepreneurs as authentic leaders: Impact on employees' attitudes. *Leadership and organization development journal* 27, 646.

Johnson, M. 1996. Still a man's world at the top, survey says. *Arizona Republic,* 18 October, E1, E2.

Jones, D. 2007. P&G CEO wields high expectation but no whip. *USA Today,* February 19.

Jones, E. E., and K. E. Davis. 1965. From acts to dispositions: The attribution process in person perception. In *Advances in experimental social psychology.* Vol. 2. Ed. L. Berkowitz, 219–266. New York: Academic Press.

Jones, R. A., A. E. Rafferty, and M. A. Griffin. 2006. The executive coaching trend: Toward more flexible executives. *Leadership and Organizational Development Journal* 27: 583.

Jones, S. 1998. Emergency surgery for MedPartners. *Business Week,* March 9, 81.

Joo, B. K. 2005. Executive coaching: A conceptual framework from an integrative review of practice and research. *Human Resource Development Review* 4 (4): 462–488.

Joyce, A. 2005. Big bad boss tales. *Washington Post,* May 29, F01.

Juarez, V., S. Childress, and E. Hoffman. 2005. 12 women leaders on life. *Newsweek/MSNBC.com.* http://www.msnbc.msn.com/id/9712114/site/newsweek/page/0/ (accessed July 24, 2007).

Judge, P. C. 2001. Suddenly the world changes. *Fast Company,* December, 131–132.

Judge, T. A., A. E. Colbert, and R. Ilies. 2004. Intelligence and leadership: A quantitative review and test of theoretical propositions. *Journal of Applied Psychology* 89 (3): 542–552.

Judge, T. A., C. A. Higgins, C. J. Thoresen, and M. R. Barrick. 1999. The Big Five personality traits, general mental ability, and career success across the life span. *Personnel Psychology* 52 (3): 621–652.

Judge, T. A., J. A. LePine, and B. L. Rich. 2006. Loving yourself abundantly: Relationship of the narcissistic personality to self- and other perceptions of workplace deviance, leadership and task and contextual performance. *Journal of Applied Psychology* 91:762–776.

Judge, T. A., R. F. Piccolo, and R. Ilies. 2004. The forgotten ones? The validity of consideration and initiation of structure in leadership research. *Journal of Applied Psychology* 89 (1): 36–51.

Judson, A. S. 1991. *Changing behavior in organizations: Minimizing resistance to change.* Cambridge, MA: Basil Blackwell.

Jung, A. 2007. How to succeed in 2007. http://money.cnn.com/popups/2006/biz2/howtosucceed/40.html (accessed August 12, 2007).

Jung, D. I., B. M. Bass, and J. Sosik. 1995. Collectivism and transformational leadership. *Journal of Management Inquiry* 2:3–18.

Kabasakal, H., and M. Bodur. 2004. Human orientation in societies, organizations, and leaders attributes. In *Culture, leadership, and organizations: The GLOBE study of 62 countries,* ed. R. J. House, P. J. Hanges, M. Javidan, P. W. Dorfman, and V. Gupta, 564–601. Thousand Oaks, CA: Sage.

Kacmar, K. M., L. A. Witt, S. Zivnuska, and S. M. Gully. 2003. The interactive effect of leader-member exchange and communication

frequency on performance ratings. *Journal of Applied Psychology* 88:764–772.

Kacmar, K. M., S. Zivnuska, and C. D. White. 2007. Control and exchange: The impact of work environment on the work effort of low relationship quality employees. *Leadership Quarterly* 18:69–84.

Kahn, J. 1998. The world's most admired companies. *Fortune* 138 (8): 218.

Kaiser, R. B., and R. B. Kaplan. 2006. The deeper work of executive development: Outgrowing sensitivities. *Academy of Management Learning and Education* 5:463–483.

Kang, H. R., H. D. Yang, and C. Rowley. 2006. Factors in team effectiveness: Cognitive and demographic similarities of software development team members. *Human Relations* 59:1681–1711.

Kanter, R. M., and R. I. Corn. 1993. Do cultural differences make a business difference? Contextual factors affecting cross-cultural relationship success. *Journal of Management Development* 13 (2): 5–23.

Kark, R., B. Shamir, and G. Chen. 2003. The two faces of transformational leadership: Empowerment and dependency. *Journal of Applied Psychology* 88:246–255.

Katz, D., and R. L. Kahn. 1966. *The social psychology of organization.* New York: John Wiley.

Katz, N. 2001. Sports teams as a model for workplace teams: Lessons and liabilities. *Academy of Management Executive* 15 (3): 56–67.

Katzenbach, J. R., and D. K. Smith. 1993. *The wisdom of teams: Creating the high-performance organization.* New York: Harper Business.

Kaufman, G., and P. Uhlenberg. 2000. The influence of parenthood on the work effort of married men and women. *Social Forces* 78:931–949.

Kegan, R., and L. L. Lahey. 2001. *How the way we talk can change the way we work: Seven languages for transformation.* San Francisco, CA: Jossey-Bass.

Keinan, G., and M. Koren. 2002. Team up type As and Bs: The effects of group composition on performance and satisfaction. *Applied Psychology: An International Review* 51 (3): 425–445.

Keller, L. M., T. J. Bouchard Jr., R. D. Arvey, N. L. Segal, and R. V. Dawis. 1992. Work values: Genetic and environmental influences. *Journal of Applied Psychology* 77:79–88.

Kellerman, B. 2004. *Bad leadership: What it is, how it happens, why it matters.* Boston: Harvard Business School Press.

Kellett, J. B., R. H. Humphrey, and R. G. Sleeth. 2002. Empathy and complex task performance: Two routes to leadership. *Leadership Quarterly* 13:523–544.

Kelley, H. H. 1967. Attribution theory in social psychology. In *Nebraska symposium on motivation 1967*, ed. D. Levine, 192–238. Lincoln: University of Nebraska Press.

Kelly, K., and M. Marr. 2005. Boss-Zilla. *Wall Street Journal*, September 26, A5, Europe edition.

Keltner, D. J., and Robinson. 1996.

Kemmelmeier, M., E. Burnstein, K. Krumov, P. Genkova, C. Kanagawa, M. S. Hirshberg, H. P. Erb, G. Wieczorkowska, and K. A. Noels. 2003. Individualism, collectivism, and authoritarianism in seven societies. *Journal of Cross-Cultural Psychology* 34:304–322.

Kempster, S. 2006. Leadership learning through lived experience: A process of apprenticeship? *Journal of Management and Organization* 12:4–22.

Kennedy, J. C. 2002. Leadership in Malaysia. *Academy of Management Executive* 16 (3): 15–26.

Kennedy, J. K., Jr. 1982. Middle LPC leaders and the contingency model of leadership effectiveness. *Organizational Behavior and Human Performance* 30:1–14.

Kernis, M. H. 2003. Toward a conceptualization of optimal self-esteem. *Psychological Inquiry* 14:1–26.

Kerr, J., and J. W. Slocum. 1987. Managing corporate culture through reward systems. *Academy of Management Executive* 1:99–108.

Kerr, S., and J. M. Jermier. 1978. Substitutes for leadership: Their meaning and measurement. *Organizational Behavior and Human Performance* 22:395–403.

Kets de Vries, M. F. R. 1993. *Leaders, fools, and imposters: Essays on the psychology of leadership.* San Francisco, CA: Jossey-Bass.

Kets de Vries, M. F. R., and D. Miller. 1986. Personality, culture, and organizations. *Academy of Management Review* 11:266–279.

Khandwalla, P. N. 1976. Some top management styles, their context, and performance. *Organization and Administrative Science* 74:21–52.

Kharif, O. 2003. Anne Mulcahy has Xerox by the horns. *Business Week*, May 29. http://www.businessweek.com/technology/content/may2003/tc20030529_1642_tc111.htm?chan=search (accessed September 8, 2007).

Kickul, J., S. W. Lester, and W. Belgio. 2004. Attitudinal and behavioral outcomes of psychological contract breach: A cross-cultural comparison of the United States and Hong Kong Chinese. *International Journal of Cross-Cultural Management* 4 (2): 229–252.

Kiley, D. 2007. The new heat on Ford. *Business Week*, June 4, 32.

Kim, K., F. Dansereau, S. Kim, and K. S. Kim. 2004. A multiple-level theory of leadership: The impact of culture as a moderator. *Journal of Leadership and Organizational Studies* 11:78–92.

Kipnis, D. 1972. Does power corrupt? *Journal of Personality and Social Psychology* 24:33–41.

Kipnis, D., S. M. Schmidt, and I. Wilkinson. 1980. Why do I like thee: Is it your performance or my orders? *Journal of Applied Psychology* 66:324–328.

Kirkpatrick, S. A., and E. A. Locke. 1991. Leadership: Do traits matter? *Academy of Management Executive* 5 (2): 48–60.

Kirschenbaum, J. 2001. Failure is glorious. *Fast Company*, October, 35–38.

Kisfalvi, V., and P. Pitcher. 2003. Doing what feels right: The influence of CEO character and emotion on top management team dynamics. *Journal of Management Inquiry* 12:42–66.

Kiviat, B. 2007. A whole new crew. *Time-CNN*, March 15. http://www.time.com/time/magazine/article/0,9171,1599694,00.html (accessed July 25, 2007).

Klein, H. J., and J. S. Kim. 1998. A field study of the influence of situational constraints, leader-member exchange, and goal commitment on performance. *Academy of Management Journal* 41:88–95.

Klidas, A., P. T. van den Berg, and C. P. M. Wilderom. 2007. Managing employee empowerment in luxury hotels in Europe. *International Journal of Service Industry Management* 18:70–83.

Kluger, A. N., and A. DeNisi. 1996. The effects of feedback interventions on performance: A historical review, a meta-analysis, and a preliminary feedback intervention theory. *Psychological Bulletin* 119:254–284.

Komaki, J. 1986. Toward effective supervision: An operant analysis and comparison of managers at work. *Journal of Applied Psychology* 71:270–278.

Konrad, A. M. 2006. Engaging employees through high-involvement work practices. *Ivey Business Journal*, March–April, 1–6.

Kotin, J., and M. Sharaf. 1976. Management succession and administrative style. *Psychiatry* 30:237–248.

Kotter, J. P. 1985. *Power and influence.* New York: Free Press.

———. 1990. *A force for change: How leadership differs from management.* New York: Free Press.

———. 1996. *Leading change.* Boston: Harvard Business School Press.

Kouzes, J. M., and B. Z. Posner. 1993. *Credibility: How leaders gain and lose it, why people demand it.* San Francisco, CA: Jossey-Bass.

———. 2003a. *Encouraging the heart: A leader's guide to rewarding and recognizing others.* San Francisco, CA: Jossey-Bass.

———. 2003b. *The leadership challenge.* San Francisco, CA: Jossey-Bass.

———. 2007. *The leadership challenge: How to get extraordinary things done in organizations.* San Francisco, CA: Jossey-Bass.

Kraar, L. 1994. The overseas Chinese: Lessons from the world's most dynamic capitalists. *Fortune* 130 (9): 91–114.

———. 1995. Acer's edge: PC to go. *Fortune* 132 (9): 187–204.

———. 1999. Asia's businessman of the year. *Fortune* 139 (2): 27.

Kraemer, H. 2003. Keeping it simple. *Health Forum Journal*, Summer, 16–20.

Krech, D., and R. S. Crutchfield. 1948. *Theory and problems of social psychology.* New York: McGraw-Hill.

Krishnan, S. 2005. Wipro is private employer no. 1. *Rediff.com.* http://www.rediff.com/money/2005/feb/10wipro.htm (accessed February 11, 2005).

Krisner, S. 2004. GE smackdown. *Fast Company*, July, 32.

Kriss, E. 1998. So you want to be an *Inc.* 500 CEO? *Inc.*, October 20, 25–26.

Kroll, L., and A. Fass. 2007. The world's billionaires. *Forbes.com*, March 8. http://www.forbes.com/2007/03/07/billionaires-worlds-richest_

07billionaires_cz_lk_af_0308billie_land.html (accessed August 6, 2007).

Kupfer, A. 1998. The real king of the Internet. *Fortune* 138 (5): 84–93.

Kurtz, D. L., L. E. Boone, and C. P. Fleenor. 1989. *CEO: Who gets to the top in America?* East Lansing: Michigan State University Press.

Kurtz, R. 2004. Knowing when to say when. *Inc.*, July, 65–71.

LaBarre, P. 1998. These leaders are having a moment. *Fast Company*, September, 86–88.

———. 2001. Marcus Buckingham thinks your boss has an attitude problem. *Fast Company*, August, 88–98.

———. 2007. Leap of faith. *Fast Company*, June. http://www.fastcompany.com/magazine/116/features-leap-of-faith.html (accessed August 12, 2007).

Lam, W., X. Huang, and E. Snape. 2007. Feedback-seeking behavior and leader-member exchange: Do supervisor-attributed motives matter? *Academy of Management Journal* 50:348–363.

Laurent, A. 1983. The cultural diversity of Western conceptions of management. *International Studies of Management and Organizations* 13 (1–2): 75–96.

Lawler, E., and C. Worley. 2006. *Built to change.* San Francisco, CA: John Wiley.

Lawler, E. E., III, and S. A. Mohrman. 1987. Quality circles: After the honeymoon. *Organizational Dynamics* 15 (Spring): 42–54.

Lawler, E. E., III, S. A. Mohrman, and G. E. Ledford Jr. 1995. *Creating high performance organizations: Practices and results of employee involvement and total quality management in Fortune 1000 companies.* San Francisco, CA: Jossey-Bass.

Lawlor, C. 2006. De La Salle running wild again as prep football season passes halfway mark. *USA Today*, October 11. http://www.usatoday.com/sports/preps/football/2006-10-10-midseason report_x.htm (accessed January 8, 2008).

Lawrence, R. L., D. A. Deagen, and A. Debbie. 2001. Choosing public participation methods for natural resources: A context specific guide. *Society and Natural Resources* 14: 57–872.

Leading by omission. 2005. http://mitworld.mit.edu/video/308 (accessed January 8, 2008).

Leban, W., and C. Zulauf. 2004. Linking emotional intelligence abilities and transformational leadership styles. *Leadership and Organization Development* 25:554–564.

Lee, E., and R. Turner. 2004. Celebrity entrepreneurs. *Inc.*, December, 73.

Lennox, R. D., and R. N. Wolfe. 1984. Revision of the self-monitoring scale. *Journal of Personality and Social Psychology* 46 (6): 1349–1364.

Lepsinger, R., and A. D. Lucia. 1997. *The art and science of 360 degree feedback.* San Francisco, CA: Jossey-Bass/Pfeiffer.

Levy, O. 2005. The influence of top management team attention patterns on global strategic posture of firms. *Journal of Organizational Behavior* 26:797–819.

Lewin, K. 1951. *Field theory in social science.* New York: Harper and Row.

Lewin, K., and R. Lippit. 1938. An experimental approach to the study of autocracy and democracy: A preliminary note. *Sociometry* 1:292–300.

Lewin, K., R. Lippit, and R. K. White. 1939. Patterns of aggressive behavior in experimentally created social climates. *Journal of Social Psychology* 10:271–301.

Liden, R. C., and G. Graen. 1980. Generalizability of the vertical dyad linkage model of leadership. *Academy of Management Journal* 23:451–465.

Lieberson, S., and J. F. O'Connor. 1972. Leadership and organization performance: A study of large corporations. *American Sociological Review* 37 (2): 117–130.

Lim, B. C., and R. E. Ployhart. 2004. Transformational leadership: Relationship to the Five-Factor model and team performance in typical and maximum contexts. *Journal of Applied Psychology* 89:610–621.

Limerick, D. C. 1990. Managers of meaning: From Bob Geldof's band aid to Australian CEOs. *Organizational Dynamics* 18 (4): 22–33.

Litzky, B. E., K. A. Eddleston, and D. L. Kidder. 2006. The good, the bad, and the misguided: How managers inadvertently encourage deviant behaviors. *Academy of Management Perspectives* 20 (1): 91–103.

Livers, A. B., and K. A. Caver. 2004. Leader development across race. In *The Center for Creative Leadership: Handbook of leadership development.* 2nd ed. Ed. C. D. McCauley and E. Van Velsor, 304–330. San Francisco, CA: Jossey-Bass.

Lohrke, F., A. G. Bedeian, and T. B. Palmer. 2004. The role of top management teams in formulating and implementing turnaround strategies: A review and research agenda. *International Journal of Management Reviews* 5–6:63–90.

London, M. 2002. *Leadership development: Paths to self-insight and professional growth.* Mahwah, NJ: Lawrence Erlbaum.

London, M., and T. J. Mauer. 2004. Leadership development: A diagnostic model for continuous learning in dynamic organizations. In *The nature of leadership,* ed. J. Antonakis, A. T. Cianciolo, and R. J. Sternberg, 222–245. Thousand Oaks, CA: Sage.

Lord, R. G., C. L. De Vader, and G. M. Alliger. 1986. A meta-analysis of the relation between personality traits and leadership perceptions: An application of validity generalization procedures. *Journal of Applied Psychology* 71:402–410.

Lord, R. G., and K. J. Maher. 1991. *Leadership and information processing.* London: Routledge.

Lowney, C. 2005. *Heroic leadership: Best practices from a 400-year-old company that changed the world.* Chicago: Loyola Press.

Lowrey, Y. 2006. Women in business: A demographic review of women's business ownership. *Small Business Research Summary*, August. http://www.sba.gov/advo/research/rs280.pdf (accessed July 16, 2007).

Lubin, R. 2002. Long-term organizational impact of destructively narcissistic managers. *Academy of Management Executive* 16 (1): 127–138.

Luthans, F. 1989. Successful vs. effective real managers. *Academy of Management Executive* 2 (2): 127–132.

———. 2002. The need for and meaning of positive organizational behavior. *Journal of Organizational Behavior* 23:695–706.

Luthans, F., and B. J. Avolio. 2003. Authentic leadership: A positive developmental approach. In *Positive organizational scholarship,* ed. K. S. Cameron, J. E. Dutton, and R. E. Quinn, 241–261. San Francisco, CA: Barrett-Koehler.

Luthans, F., and D. L. Lockwood. 1984. Toward an observation system for measuring leader behavior in natural settings. In *Leaders and managers: Internal perspectives on managerial behavior and leadership,* ed. J. G. Hunt, D. Hosking, C. A. Schreishrim, and R. Stewart, 117–141. New York: Pergamon Press.

Lutz, S. 1992. A "lifetime" of accomplishments by age 38. *Modern Healthcare*, March 2, 41–44.

Magee, J. C., D. H. Gruenfeld, D. J. Keltner, and A. D. Galinski. 2005. Leadership and the psychology of power. In *The psychology of leadership: New perspectives and research*, ed. D. M. Messick and R. M. Kramer, 275–293. Mahwah, NJ: Lawrence Erlbaum.

Mai-Dalton, R. 1993. Managing cultural diversity on the individual, group, and organizational levels. In *Leadership theory and research: Perspective and directions*, ed. M. M. Chemers and R. Ayman, 189–215. New York: Academic Press.

Malekzadeh, A. 1995. How leaders manage the six strategic forces. Unpublished manuscript.

Mallello, M. 2005. Executive pay: Crying all the way to the bank. *Forbes.com*, May.

Malveaux, J. 2005. The planet's chief diversity officer. *Focus on Diversity and Inclusion* 1 (2): 1–2. http://www.jbcinstitute.org/pdfs/FOCUS%20Newsletter.pdf (accessed June 19, 2007).

Manville, B., and J. Ober. 2003. Beyond empowerment: Building a company of citizens. *Harvard Business Review* 81 (1): 48–53.

Manz, C. C. 1992. Self-leading work teams: Moving beyond self-management myths. *Human Relations* 11:1119–1140.

Manz, C. C., and C. Neck. 1999. *Mastering self-leadership: Empowering yourself for personal excellence.* 2nd ed. Upper Saddle River, NJ: Prentice Hall.

———. 2004. *Mastering self-leadership: Empowering yourself for personal excellence.* 3rd ed. Upper Saddle River, NJ: Prentice Hall.

Manz, C. C., and H. P. Sims Jr. 1991. Superleadership: Beyond the myth of heroic leadership. *Organizational Dynamics* 19 (4): 18–35.

———. 2001. *The new superleadership: Leading others to lead themselves.* San Francisco, CA: Berrett-Koehler Publisher.

Marchetti, M. 2005. Stepping in for Superman. *Fast Company*, September. http://www.fastcompany.com/magazine/98/open_playbook.html (accessed August 12, 2007).

Markels, A. 1998. Power to the people. *Fast Company*, February–March, 155–165.

Marquez, J. 2007a. Goldman Sachs: Optimas award winner for general excellence. *Workforce Management*, March 26, 22–23.

———. 2007b. Goldman Sachs University's 5 tips for creating a learning culture. *Workforce Management*, March 26.

Marsh, H. W., G. E. Richards, and J. Barnes. 1987. A long-term follow-up of the effects of participation in an Outward Bound program. *Personality and Social Psychology Bulletin* 12:475–492.

Marshall, R., J. Talbott, and D. Bukovinsky. 2006. Employee empowerment works at small companies, too. *Strategic Finance*, 88 (3): 34–39.

Marsick, V. J., E. Turner, and L. Cederholm. 1989. International as a team. *Management Review* 78 (3): 46–49.

Martin, J. 1997. Mercedes: Made in Alabama. *Fortune* 136 (1): 150–158.

Martinez, S., and P. W. Dorfman. 1998. The Mexican entrepreneur: An ethnographic study of the Mexican empressario. *International Studies in Management and Organizations* 28 (Summer): 97–123.

Maruca, R. F. 2001. Masters of disaster. *Fast Company*, April, 81–96.

Massey, M. E. 1986. *The past: What you are is where you were when.* Schaumburg, IL: Video Publishing House.

Mathur, A., Y. Zhang, and J. P. Meelankavil. 2001. Critical managerial motivational factors: A cross-cultural analysis of four culturally divergent countries. *International Journal of Cross-Cultural Management* 1 (2): 251–267.

Matviuk, S. 2007. A study of leadership prototypes in Colombia. *Business Review* 7:14–19.

Maull, S. 2005. Tyco execs' trial to start with tight focus. *Arizona Republic*, January 18, D5.

Maune, D. J. 1999. The glass ceiling and the glass escalator: Occupational segregation and race and sex differences in managerial promotions. *Work and Occupations* 26:483–509.

Mayo, A., and N. Nohria. 2006. *Paths to power: How insider and outsiders shaped American business Leadership.* Boston: Harvard Business School Publishing Corporation.

McAllister, D. J. 1995. Affect- and cognition-based trust as foundations for interpersonal cooperation in organizations. *Academy of Management Journal* 38:24–59.

McCain, J. 2004. In search of courage. *Fast Company*, September, 51–56.

McCall, M. W., and M. M. Lombardo. 1978. *Leadership: Where else can we go?* Durham, NC: Duke University Press.

_____. 1983. Off the track: Why and how successful executives get derailed. Technical Report No. 21. Center for Creative Leadership, Greensboro, NC.

McCall, M. W., Jr., M. M. Lombardo, and A. M. Morrison. 1988. *The lessons of experience: How successful executives develop on the job.* San Francisco, CA: New Lexington Press.

McCauley, C. D. 2001. Leader training and development. In *The nature of organizational leadership*, ed. S. J. Zaccaro and R. J. Klimoski, 347–383. San Francisco, CA: Jossey-Bass.

McCauley, C. D., and C. A. Douglas. 2004. Developmental relationships. In *The Center for Creative Leadership: Handbook of leadership development.* 2nd ed. Ed. C. D. McCauley and E. Van Velsor, 85–115. San Francisco, CA: Jossey-Bass.

McCauley, C. D., and E. Van Velsor, eds. 2004. *The Center for Creative Leadership: Handbook of leadership development.* 2nd ed. San Francisco, CA: Jossey-Bass.

McCauley, L. 2000. Unit of one: Don't burn out. *Fast Company*, May, 101–132.

McClelland, D. C. 1975. *Power: The inner experience.* New York: Irvington.

McCrae, R. R. 1993. Moderated analyses of longitudinal personality stability. *Journal of Personality and Social Psychology* 65 (3): 577–585.

McFarland, K. R. 2007. Lesson from the anti-mentor. *Business Week*, June 11, 86.

McGregor, J. 2004a. Putting customers first. *Fast Company*, October, 80–88.

_____. 2004b. Rocky Mountain High. *Fast Company*, July, 59–63.

_____. 2005a. Competing on culture. *Fast Company*, March. http://www.fastcompany.com/magazine/92/clear-leader-extra.html (accessed June 18, 2007).

_____. 2005b. Gospels of failure. *Fast Company*, February. http://www.fastcompany.com/magazine/91/gospels.html (accessed June 19, 2007).

_____. 2007. The 25 most innovative companies: The leaders in nurturing culture of creativity. *Business Week*, May 14, 52.

Meindl, J. R., and S. B. Ehrlick. 1987. The romance of leadership and the evaluation of organizational performance. *Academy of Management Journal* 30:90–109.

Meister, J. C. 2006. Grading executive education. *Workforce Management*, December 11, 1, 27.

Menon, S. T. 2001. Employee empowerment: An integrative psychological approach. *Applied Psychology: An International Review* 50 (1): 153–180.

Menon, S. T., and L. C. Hartmann. 2002. Generalizability of Menon's empowerment scale: Replication and extension with Australian data. *International Journal of Cross-Cultural Management* 2 (2): 137–153.

Meyerson, H. 2003. I'm a CEO, so I'm worth millions. *Mercury News*, April 23. http://www.mercurynews.com/mld/mercurynews/5695986.htm?lc (accessed December 28, 2004).

Meyerson, M. 1997. What it means to lead. *Fast Company*, February–March, 99.

Michael, J. 2003. Using the Myers-Briggs type indicator as a tool for leadership development? Apply with caution. *Journal of Leadership and Organizational Studies* 10 (1): 68–81.

Michie, S., and J. Gooty. 2005. Values, emotions, and authenticity: Will the real leader please stand up? *Leadership Quarterly* 16:441–457.

Mieszkowski, K. 1998. Barbara Waugh. *Fast Company*, December, 146–154.

Miller, D. M. 1987. The genesis of configuration. *Academy of Management Review* 12:686–701.

Miller, D. M., and C. Droge. 1986. Psychological and traditional determinants of structure. *Administrative Science Quarterly* 31:539–560.

Miller, D. M., and P. H. Freisen. 1982. Structural change and performance: Quantum vs. piecemeal-incremental approaches. *Academy of Management Journal* 25:867–892.

Miller, D. M., M. F. R. Kets de Vries, and J. M. Toulouse. 1982. Top executive locus of control and its relationship to strategy-making, structure, and environment. *Academy of Management Journal* 25 (2): 237–253.

Miller, D. M., E. R. Lack, and S. Asroff. 1985. Preference for control and the coronary-prone behavior pattern: "I'd rather do it myself." *Journal of Personality and Social Psychology* 49:492–499.

Miller, D. M., and J. Toulouse. 1986. Chief executive personality and corporate strategy and structure in small firms. *Management Science* 32:1389–1409.

Miner, J. B., and N. R. Smith. 1982. Decline and stabilization of managerial motivation over a

20-year period. *Journal of Applied Psychology* 67 (June): 298–305.

Mintzberg, H. 1973. *The nature of managerial work*. New York: Harper and Row.

Mintzberg, H., J. B. Quinn, and J. Voyer. 1995. *The strategy process*. Englewood Cliffs, NJ: Prentice Hall.

Mischel, W. 1973. Towards a cognitive social learning reconceptualization of personality. *Psychological Review* 80:252–283.

Mishel, L. 2006. CEO pay-to-minimum wage ratio soars. *Economic Policy Institute*, June 27. http://www.epinet.org/content.cfm/webfeatures_snapshots_20060627 (accessed July 24, 2007).

Misumi, J. 1985. *The behavioral science of leadership*. Ann Arbor: University of Michigan Press.

Misumi, J., and M. F. Peterson. 1985. The performance-maintenance (PM) theory of leadership: Review of a Japanese research program. *Administrative Science Quarterly* 30:198–223.

Mitchell, T. R., and R. E. Wood. 1980. Supervisor's responses to subordinate poor performance: A test of an attributional model. *Organizational Behavior and Human Performance* 25:123–138.

Montesino, M. 2003. Leadership/followership between people in a developed and a developing country: The case of Dominicans in NYC and the Dominicans on the island. *Journal of Leadership and Organizational Studies* 10:82–93.

Moore, A. 2006. Ali Moore speaks to Cisco Systems senior vice president Howard Charney. *Lateline Business*, September 14. http://www.abc.net.au/lateline/business/items/200609/s1741472.htm (accessed August 12, 2007).

Moore, T. 1987. Personality tests are back. *Fortune* 121 (5): 30, 74–82.

Morf, C. C., and F. Rhodewalt. 2001. Unraveling the paradoxes of narcissism: A dynamic self-regulatory processing model. *Personality Inquiry* 12:177–196.

Morrison, A. M., and M. A. Von Glinow. 1990. Women and minorities in management. *American Psychologist* 45:200–208.

Mosadegh-Rad, A. M., and M. H. Yarmohammadian. 2006. A study of relationship between managers' leadership style and employees' job satisfaction. *Leadership in Health Service* 19 (2): 11–28.

Moshavi, D., F. W. Brown, and N. G. Dodd. 2003. Leader self-awareness and its relationship to subordinate attitudes and performance. *Leadership and Organizational Development Journal* 24 (7–8): 407–418.

Mount, I. 2004. Be fast, be frugal, be right. *Inc.*, January, 64–70.

Moxley, R. S. 2000. *Leadership and spirit*. San Francisco, CA: Jossey-Bass.

Muio, A. 1999. Mint condition. *Fast Company*, December, 330.

Mumford, M. D., and B. Licuanan. 2004. Leading for innovation: Conclusions, issues, and directions. *Leadership Quarterly* 15:163–171.

Mumford, M. D., S. J. Zaccaro, M. S. Connelly, and M. A. Marks. 2000a. Leadership skills: Conclusions and future directions. *Leadership Quarterly* 11:155–170.

Mumford, M. D., S. J. Zaccaro, F. D. Harding, T. O. Jacobs, and E. A. Fleishman. 2000b. Leadership skills for a changing world: Solving complex problems. *Leadership Quarterly* 11:11–35.

Munk, N. 1998. Gap gets it. *Fortune* 138 (3): 68–82.

Munter, M. 1993. Cross-cultural communication for managers. *Business Horizons* 36 (May–June): 69–78.

Murphy, S. E., and E. A. Ensher. 1999. The effects of leaders and subordinate characteristics in the development of leader-member exchange quality. *Journal of Applied Social Psychology* 29:1371–1394.

Murphy, S. E., and R. E. Riggio, eds. 2003. *The future of leadership development*. Mahwah, NJ: Lawrence Erlbaum.

Murray, S. 1997. BP alters atmosphere amid turnaround. *Wall Street Journal*, September 17, A19.

Myers, D. 2006. *Setting the table: The power of hospitality in restaurants, business, and life*. New York: Harper Collins.

Nadkarni, S., and P. D. Perez. 2007. Prior conditions and early international commitment: The mediating role of domestic mindset. *Journal of International Business Studies* 38:160–177.

Nahavandi, A. 1983. The effect of personal and situational factors on satisfaction with leadership. PhD diss., University of Utah, Salt Lake City.

———. 1993. Integrating leadership and strategic management in organizational theory. *Canadian Journal of Administrative Sciences* 10 (4): 297–307.

Nahavandi, A., and E. Aranda. 1994. Restructuring teams for the re-engineered organization. *Academy of Management Executive* 8 (4): 58–68.

Nahavandi, A., and A. R. Malekzadeh. 1988. Acculturation in mergers and acquisitions. *Academy of Management Review* 13:79–90.

———. 1993a. Leader style in strategy and organizational performance: An integrative framework. *Journal of Management Studies* 30 (3): 405–425.

———. 1993b. *Organizational culture in the management of mergers.* New York: Quorum Books.

———. 1999. *Organizational behavior: The person-organization fit.* Upper Saddle River, NJ: Prentice Hall.

Nahavandi, A., P. J. Mizzi, and A. R. Malekzadeh. 1992. Executives' type A personality as a determinant of environmental perception and firm strategy. *Journal of Social Psychology* 13 (1): 59–68.

Nahavandi, F. 1988. *Aux sources de la revolution Iranienne.* Paris: Editions L'Harmattan.

Nahavandi, H. 1994. *Le voile dechire de l'Islamisme.* Paris: Premiere Ligne.

Neck, C. P., and J. D. Houghton. 2006. Two decades of self-leadership theory and research: Past developments, present trends, and future possibilities. *Journal of Managerial Psychology* 21:270–295.

Nelton, S. 1997. Leadership for the new age. *Nation's Business,* May, 18–27.

Nemanich, L. A., and R. T. Keller. 2007. Transformational leadership in an acquisition: A field study of employees. *Leadership Quarterly* 18:49–68.

Neubert, M. J., and J. C. Wu. 2006. An investigation of the generalizability of the Houghton and Neck revised self-leadership questionnaire to a Chinese context. *Journal of Managerial Psychology* 21:360–373.

New Zealand Human Rights Commission. 2007. http://www.hrc.co.nz/index.php?p=13856 (accessed July 6, 2007).

Newstetter, W. I., M. J. Feldstein, and T. M. Newcomb. 1938. *Group adjustment.* Cleveland, OH: Western Reserve University Press.

Nicholls, J. R. 1985. A new approach to situational leadership. *Leadership and Organization Development Journal* 6 (4): 2–7.

Nocks, J. 2007. Executive coaching: Who needs it? *Physician Executive,* March–April, 46–48.

Nonis, S. A., and D. R. Hoyt. 2004. Coping strategies used by managers in the People's Republic of China: Relationship with personal characteristics and job outcomes. *Journal of Asia-Pacific Business* 5 (3): 45.

Norman, W. T. 1963. Toward an adequate taxonomy of personality attributes: Replicated factor structure in peer nomination personality ratings. *Journal of Abnormal and Social Psychology* 66:547–583.

Nutt, P. 1986. Decision style and strategic decisions of top executives. *Technological Forecasting and Social Change* 30:39–62.

———. 1988. The effects of culture on decision making. *OMEGA International Journal of Management Science* 16:553–567.

Offermann, L. R., C. J. Schroyer, and S. K. Green. 1998. Leader attributions for subordinate performance: Consequences for subsequent leader interaction behaviors and ratings. *Journal of Applied Social Psychology* 28 (13): 1125–1139.

Ohlott, P. J. 2003. Answering the call: Job assignments that grow leaders. *Leadership in Action* 23 (5): 19–21.

———. 2004. Job assignments. In *The Center for Creative Leadership: Handbook of leadership development.* 2nd ed. Ed. C. D. McCauley and E. Van Velsor, 151–182. San Francisco, CA: Jossey-Bass.

Ones, D. S., and C. Viswesvaran. 1999. Relative importance of personality dimensions of expatriate selection: A policy capturing study. *Human Performance* 12 (3–4): 275–294.

O'Reilly, B. 1994. J&J is on a roll. *Fortune* 130 (13): 178–192.

O'Reilly, C. A., III, and B. G. M. Bain. 2007. Setting the CEO's pay: It's more than simple economics. *Organizational Dynamics* 36:1–12.

Osborn, R. N., J. G. Hunt, and L. R. Jauch. 2002. Toward a contextual theory of leadership. *Leadership Quarterly* 13:797–837.

Overholt, A. 2001. Unit of one: Open to women. *Fast Company,* August, 66.

———. 2002. The art of multitasking. *Fast Company,* October, 118–125.

———. 2004. Cuckoo for customers. *Fast Company,* June, 86–87.

_____. 2005 Jumpstart. *Fast Company,* January, 55.

Ozaralli, N. 2003. Effects of transformational leadership on empowerment and team effectiveness. *Leadership and Organizational Development Journal* 24 (5–6): 335–345.

Pagano, B., and E. Pagano. 2004. *The transparency edge: How credibility can make or break you in business.* Chicago: McGraw-Hill.

Panitz, E. 1989. Psychometric investigation of the MACH IV scale measuring Machiavellianism. *Psychological Reports* 64 (3): 963–968.

Papadakis, V. M., and P. Barwise. 2002. How much do CEOs and top managers matter in strategic decision making. *British Journal of Management* 13:83–96.

Parker, C. P. 1999. The impact of leaders' implicit theory of employee participation on tests of the Vroom-Yetton model. *Journal of Social Behavior and Personality* 14 (1): 45–62.

Paton, N. 2006. Half of U.S. firms have no women at the top. *Management Issues,* December 1. http://www.management-issues.com/2007%2F8%2F31%2Fresearch%2Fhalf-of-us-firms-have-no-women-at-the-top.asp (accessed January 8, 2008).

Paulhus, D. L., and K. M. Williams. 2002. The dark triad of personality: Narcissism, Machiavellianism, and psychopathy. *Journal of Research in Personality* 36:556–563.

Paunonen, S. V. 2003. Big Five facts of personality and replication predictions of behavior. *Journal of Personality and Social Psychology* 84:411–424.

Pawar, B. S., and K. K. Eastman. 1997. The nature and implications of contextual influences on transformational leadership: A conceptual examination. *Academy of Management Review* 22:80–109.

Pelled, L. H., and K. R. Xin. 1997. Birds of a feather: Leader-member demographic similarity and organizational attachment in Mexico. *Leadership Quarterly* 8:433–450.

_____. 2000. Relationship demography and relationship quality in two cultures. *Organization Studies* 21 (6): 1077–1094.

Pellegrini, E. K., and T. A. Scandura. 2006. Leader-member exchange (LMX), paternalism, and delegation in the Turkish business culture: An empirical investigation. *Journal of International Business Studies* 37:264–279.

People to watch. 2001. *Fortune,* January 8, 34.

Pescosolido, A. T. 2002. Emergent leaders as managers of group emotion. *Leadership Quarterly* 13:583–599.

Peters, L. H., D. D. Hartke, and J. T. Pohlmann. 1985. Fiedler's contingency theory of leadership: An application of the meta-analysis procedure of Schmitt and Hunter. *Psychological Bulletin* 97:274–285.

Peterson, G. 2005. Ford's Nancy Gioia: Hybrid Queen. *Vehicle Voice,* December 29. http://blog.vehiclevoice.com/2005/12/fords_nancy_gioia_hybrid_queen.html (accessed July 22, 2007).

Peterson, M. F., and J. G. Hunt. 1997. International perspective on international leadership. *Leadership Quarterly* 8:203–231.

Peterson, R. S., D. B. Smith, P. V. Martorana, and P. D. Owens. 2003. The impact of chief executive officer personality on top management team dynamics: One mechanism by which leadership affects organizational performance. *Journal of Applied Psychology* 88:795–809.

Pettigrew, A. 1973. *The politics of organizational decision making.* London: Tavistock.

Pew Global Attitudes Project. 2004. *A global generation gap: Adapting to a new world.* Washington, DC: Pew Research Center. http://peoplepress.org/commentary/display.php3?AnalysisID=86 (accessed December 18, 2007).

Pfeffer, J. 1981. *Power in organizations.* Marshfield, MA: Pitman.

_____. 1983. Organizational demography. In *Research in organizational behavior,* ed. L. L. Cummings and B. W. Staw, 299–357. Greenwich, CT: JAI Press.

_____. 1998. *The human equation: Building profits by putting people first.* Cambridge: Harvard Business School Press.

Phampraha, S., and S. Chansrichawla. 2007. Leadership-supported mentoring: The key to enhancing organisational commitment and retaining newcomers. *International Journal of Management and Decision Making* 8:394.

Piccolo, R. F., and J. A. Colquitt. 2006. Transformational leadership and job behaviors: The mediating role of core job characteristics. *Academy of Management Journal* 49:327–340.

Pink, D. H. 2002. Just like the rest of us. *Fast Company,* October, 41–44.

Podsakoff, P. M., and S. B. MacKenzie. 1997. Kerr and Jermier's substitutes for leadership model: Background, empirical assessment, and suggestions for future research. *Leadership Quarterly* 8:117–125.

Poggioli, S. 1998. Turkish feminism. *National Public Radio*, March 7, Weekend edition.

Popper, M. 2002. Narcissism and attachment patterns of personalized and socialized charismatic leaders. *Journal of Social and Personal Relationships* 19:797–809.

———. 2005. Main principles and practices of leader development. *Leadership and Organization Development Journal* 26:62–75.

Posner, B., and J. Kouzes. 1993. Psychometric properties of leader practices inventory: Updated. *Educational and Psychological Measurement* 53:191–199.

Powell, G. N., D. A. Butterfield, and J. D. Parent. 2002. Gender and managerial stereotypes: Have the times changed? *Journal of Management* 28:177–193.

Prendergast, C. 1993. The theory of "Yes Men." *American Economic Review* 83 (4): 757–770.

President Bush's cabinet. 2007. http://www. whitehouse.gov/government/cabinet.html (accessed July 6, 2007).

Price, T. L. 2003. The ethics of authentic transformational leadership. *Leadership Quarterly* 14:67–81.

Prospero, M. A. 2004. The business of politics. *Fast Company*, October, 57–64.

Puffer, S. M. 1994. Understanding the bear: A portrait of Russian business leaders. *Academy of Management Executive* 8 (1): 41–54.

Pugh, D. S., D. J. Hickson, C. R. Hinings, and C. Turner. 1968. Dimensions of organization structure. *Administrative Science Quarterly* 13:65–105.

Rafferty, A. E., and M. A. Griffin. 2004. Dimensions of transformational leadership: Conceptual and empirical extensions. *Leadership Quarterly* 15:329–354.

Raghavan, A. 2005. More CEOs say "Nay" to serving on boards. *Asian Wall Street Journal*, January 31, M11.

Rahim, M. A., D. Antonioni, K. Krumov, and S. Ilieva. 2000. Power, conflict, and effectiveness: A cross-cultural study in the United States and Bulgaria. *European Psychologist* 5 (1): 28–33.

Ralston, D. A., D. J. Gustafson, F. M. Cheung, and R. H. Terpstra. 1993a. Differences in managerial values: A study of U.S., Hong Kong, and PRC managers. *Journal of International Business Studies* 2:249–275.

Ralston, D. A., D. J. Gustafson, R. H. Terpstra, D. H. Holt, F. M. Cheung, and B. A. Ribbens. 1993b. The impact of managerial values on decision-making behavior: A comparison of the United States and Hong Kong. *Asia Pacific Journal of Management* 10 (1): 21–37.

Randolph, W. A., and M. Sashkin. 2002. Can organizational empowerment work in multinational settings? *Academy of Management Executive* 16 (1): 102–115.

Raskas, D. F., and D. C. Hambrick. 1992. Multifunctional managerial development: A framework for evaluating the options. *Organizational Dynamics* 21 (AutuMN1): 5–17.

Raskin, R., and C. S. Hall. 1979. A narcissistic personality inventory. *Psychological Reports* 45:590.

Rastogi, R., and V. Dave. 2004. Managerial effectiveness: A function of personality type and organisational components. *Singapore Management Review* 26 (2): 79–87.

Reave, L. 2005. Spiritual values and practices related to leadership effectiveness. *Leadership Quarterly* 16:655–687.

Reeves, R. 2006. Our fetish for feedback. *Management Today*, June 25.

Reimers, J. M., and J. E. Barbuto Jr. 2002. A frame exploring the effects of Machiavellian disposition on the relationship between motivation and influence tactics. *Journal of Leadership and Organizational Studies* 9 (2): 29–41.

Reingold, J. 2003. Still angry after all these years. *Fast Company*, October, 89–94.

———. 2005. Hondas in space. *Fast Company*, February, 74–79.

Repetti, A., and R. Prélaz-Droux. 2003. An urban monitor as support for a participative management of developing cities. *Habitat International* 27 (4): 653–662.

Rice, R. 1978a. Construct validity of the least preferred coworker. *Psychological Bulletin* 85:1199–1237.

———. 1978b. Psychometric properties of the esteem for least preferred coworker (LPC) scale. *Academy of Management Review* 3:106–118.

Rich, L. 2005. Hands-on managing: Playing well with others. *Inc.*, January, 29–32.

Roberts, N. C., and R. T. Bradley. 1988. Transforming leadership: A process of collective action. *Human Relations* 38:1023–1046.

Rogers, A. 1994. Is he too cautious to save IBM? *Fortune* 130 (7): 78–88.

Rokeach, M. 1973. *The nature of human values*. New York: Free Press.

Rosenman, R. H., and M. Friedman. 1974. Neurogenic factors in pathogenesis of coronary heart disease. *Medical Clinics of North America* 58:269–279.

Rosenthal, S. A., and T. L. Pittinsky. 2006. Narcissistic leadership. *Leadership Quarterly* 17:617–633.

Rosier, R. H. 1994. *The competency model handbook*. Vol. 1. Boston: Linkage.

———. 1995. *The competency model handbook*. Vol. 2. Boston: Linkage.

Ross, S. M., and L. R. Offerman. 1997. Transformational leaders: Measurement of personality attributes and work group performance. *Personality and Social Psychology Bulletin* 23:1078–1086.

Rotter, J. B. 1966. Generalized expectancies for internal versus external control of reinforcement. *Psychological Monographs* 80 (1): Whole No. 609.

———. 1971. External control and internal control. *Psychology Today*, June, 42.

Rubin, R. S., L. K. Bartels, and W. H. Bommer. 2002. Are leaders smarter or do they just seem that way? Exploring perceived intellectual competence and leadership emergence. *Social Behavior and Personality* 30:105–118.

Rubinkan, M. 2007. Teamsters still foaming over ejection by brewery Yuengling. *Philly.com*, May 29. http://www.phillyburbs.com/pb-dyn/news/103-05282007-1353974.html (accessed January 8, 2008).

Ruderman, M. N. 2004. Leader development across gender. In *The Center for Creative Leadership: Handbook of leadership development*. 2nd ed. Ed. C. D. McCauley and E. Van Velsor, 271–303. San Francisco, CA: Jossey-Bass.

Ryan, M. K., and S. A. Haslam. 2007. The glass cliff: Exploring the dynamics surrounding the appointment of women to precarious leadership positions. *Academy of Management Review* 32:549–572.

Rychlak, J. F. 1963. Personality correlates of leadership among first level managers. *Psychological Reports* 12:43–52.

Ryerson-Cruz, G. 2004. Scrushy's successor at HealthSouth tries to pick up pieces.

Tennessean.com, December 20. tennessean.com/business/archives/04/12/63085234.shtml?Element_ID=63085234 (accessed December 28, 2004).

Salancik, G. R., and J. Pfeffer. 1977a. Constraints on administrator discretion: The limited influence of mayors in city budgets. *Urban Affairs Quarterly* 12 (4): 475–496.

———. 1977b. Who gets power and how they hold onto it: A strategic-contingency model of power. *Organizational Dynamics* 5 (Winter): 3–21.

Salas, E., K. Stagl, and C. S. Burke. 2004. 25 years of team effective in organizations: Research themes and emerging needs. In *International review of industrial and organizational psychology*. Vol. 19. Ed. C. L. Cooper and I. T. Robertson, 47–91. New York: John Wiley.

Salovey, P., and J. Mayer. 1990. Emotional intelligence. *Imagination, Cognition, and Personality* 9:185–211.

Salter, C. 2000a. Designed to work. *Fast Company*, March, 255.

———. 2000b. What's your mission statement? *Fast Company*, July, 48–50.

———. 2002. Diversity without excuses. *Fast Company*, September, 44.

———. 2004. Mr. inside speaks out. *Fast Company*, September, 92–93.

San Antonio, D. M., and D. T. Gamage. PSALM for empower educational stakeholders: Participatory school administration, leadership, and management. *The International Journal of Education* 21, 254.

Sanchez, M. 2004. The charm of the status quo in Venezuela. *Washington Post*, August 14, A21.

Sanders, W. M. G., and M. A. Carpenter. 1998. Internationalization and firm governance: The roles of CEO compensation, top team composition, and board structure. *Academy of Management Journal* 41:158–178.

Sashkin, M. 2004. Transformational leadership approaches. In *The nature of leadership*, ed. J. Antonakis, A. T. Cianciolo, and R. J. Sternberg, 171–196. Thousand Oaks, CA: Sage.

Scandura, T. 1999. Rethinking leader-member exchange: An organizational justice perspective. *Leadership Quarterly* 10 (1): 25–40.

Scandura, T., and P. Dorfman. 2004. Leadership research in an international and cross-cultural context. *Leadership Quarterly* 15:277–307.

Schein, E. H. 2004. *Organizational culture and leadership*. San Francisco, CA: Jossey-Bass.

Schlender, B. 1997. On the road with Chairman Bill. *Fortune* 135 (10): 72–81.

Schmitt, D. P., J. Allik, R. R. McCrae, and V. Benet-Martinez. 2007. The geographic distribution of the Big Five personality traits: Patterns and profiles of human self-description across 56 nations. *Journal of Cross-Cultural Psychology* 38:173–212.

Schoeff, M. 2007. P&G places a premium on international experience. *Workforce Management*, October 10–12. http://www.workforce.com/archive/feature/24/33/52/index.php?ht=p%20g%20international%20experience%20p%20g%20international%20experience (accessed June 27, 2007).

Schriesheim, C. A., S. L. Castro, and C. C. Cogliser. 1999. Leader-member exchange (LMX) research: A comprehensive review of theory, measurement, and data-analytic practices. *Leadership Quarterly* 10 (1): 63–113.

Schriesheim, C. A., and S. Kerr. 1974. Psychometric properties of the Ohio State University Leadership scales. *Psychological Bulletin* 81:756–765.

Schriesheim, C. A., B. J. Tepper, and L. Tetrault. 1994. Least-preferred co-worker score, situational control and leadership effectiveness: A meta-analysis of contingency model performance predictions. *Journal of Applied Psychology* 79:561–574.

Schwartz, N. D. 2001. What's in the cards for Amex? *Fortune*, January 22, 58–70.

———. 2007. Wall Street's man of the moment. *Fortune* 155 (4): 74.

Schwartz, S. H. 2005. Sex differences in value priorities: Cross-cultural and multimethod studies. *Journal of Personality and Social Psychology* 89:1010–1028.

Scott-Ladd, B., and C. C. A. Chan. 2004. Emotional intelligence and participation in decision making: Strategies for promoting organizational learning and change. *Strategic Change* 13:95–105.

Seibert, S. E., and M. L. Kraimer. 2001. The five-factor model of personality and career success. *Journal of Vocational Behavior* 58 (1): 1–21.

Seibert, S. E., S. R. Silver, and W. A. Randolph. 2004. Taking empowerment to the next level: A multiple-level model of empowerment,

performance, and satisfaction. *Academy of Management Journal* 47:332–349.

Seid, J. 2006. 10 best-paid executives: They're all men. *CNNMoney.com*. http://money.cnn.com/2006/10/03/news/newsmakers/mpwpay/index.htm (accessed May 17, 2007).

Seigel, R. 2005. Labor dispute disrupts U.S. men's soccer plans. *All Things Considered*, January 14. http://www.npr.org/templates/story/story.php?storyId=4285620 (accessed January 19, 2005).

Seligman, M. E. P. 2002. *Authentic happiness: Using the new positive psychology to realize your potential for lasting fulfillment*. New York: Free Press.

Seligman, M. E. P., and M. Csikszentmihalyi. 2000. Positive psychology. *American Psychologist* 55:5–14.

Sellers, P. 1996. Cocktails at Charlotte's with Martha and Darla. *Fortune* 134 (3): 56–57.

———. 1997. Don't mess with Darla. *Fortune* 136 (5): 62–72.

———. 1998. The 50 most powerful women in American business. *Fortune* 138 (7): 76–98.

———. 2000a. The 50 most powerful women in business. *Fortune*, October 16, 131–160.

———. 2000b. Big, hairy, audacious goals don't work—just ask P&G. *Fortune*, April 3, 39–44.

———. 2004. eBay's secret. *Fortune*, October 25, 161–178.

Seltzer, J., and B. M. Bass. 1990. Transformational leadership: Beyond initiation of structure and consideration. *Journal of Management* 16:693–703.

Semler, R. 1989. Managing without managers. *Harvard Business Review* 67 (5): 76–84.

———. 1993. *Maverick! The success story behind the world's most unusual workplace*. London: Century.

———. 1996. Mr. Price is on the line. *Fortune* 134 (11): 70–88.

Senge, P. M. 2006. *The fifth discipline: The art and practice of the learning organization*. New York: Doubleday.

Shamir, B. 1991. The charismatic relationship: Alternative explanations and predictions. *Leadership Quarterly* 2:81–104.

———. 1999. Taming of charisma for better understanding and greater usefulness: A response to Beyer. *Leadership Quarterly* 10 (4): 555–562.

Shamir, B., M. B. Arthur, and R. J. House. 1994. The rhetoric of charismatic leadership: A theoretical extension, a case study and implications for research. *Leadership Quarterly* 5:25–42.

Shamir, B., R. J. House, and M. B. Arthur. 1993. The motivational effects of charismatic leadership: A self-concept-based theory. *Organization Science* 4:1–17.

Shamir, B., and J. M. Howell. 1999. Organizational and contextual influence on the emergence and effectiveness of charismatic leadership. *Leadership Quarterly* 10 (2): 257–283.

Shamir, B., E. Zakay, E. Breinin, and M. Popper. 1998. Correlates of charismatic leaders' behavior in military units: Subordinates' attitudes, unit characteristics, and superiors' appraisals of leader performance. *Academy of Management Journal* 41:387–409.

Sherman, S. 1994. Leaders learn to heed the voice within. *Fortune* 130 (4): 92–100.

Shin, S. J., and J. Zhou. 2003. Transformational leadership, conservation, and creativity: Evidence from Korea. *Academy of Management Journal* 46:703–714.

Shinn, S. 2004. The Maverick CEO. *BizEd*, January/February, 16–21.

Sightler, K. W., and M. G. Wilson. 2001. Correlates of the imposter phenomenon among undergraduate entrepreneurs. *Psychological Reports* 88 (3): 679–689.

Silver, S., W. A. Randolph, and S. Seibert. 2006. Implementing and sustaining empowerment: Lesson learned from comparison of a for-profit and a nonprofit organization. *Journal of Management Inquiry* 15:47–58.

Simerly, R. L. 2003. An empirical examination of the relationship between management and corporate social performance. *International Journal of Management* 20:353–359.

Singer, P. 1969. Toward a re-evaluation of the concept of charisma with reference to India. *Journal of Social Research* 12 (2): 13–25.

Singh, J. 2006. Employee disempowerment in a small firm (SME): Implications for organizational social capital. *Organizational Development Journal* 24 (1): 76–86.

Slocum, J. W., Jr., and D. Hellreigel. 1983. A look at how managers' minds work. *Business Horizons*, July–August, 58–68.

Smith, M. A., and J. M. Canger. 2004. Effects of supervisor "Big Five" personality on subordinate attitudes. *Journal of Business and Psychology* 18 (4): 465–481.

Smith, P. B. 2002. Culture's consequences: Something old and something new. *Human Relations* 55:119–135.

Smith, T. W., and F. Rhodewalt. 1986. On states, traits, and processes: A transactional alternative to the individual difference assumption in type A behavior and psychological reactivity. *Journal of Research in Personality* 20:229–251.

Snyder, M. 1974. The self-monitoring of expressive behavior. *Journal of Personality and Social Psychology* 30:526–537.

Song, J. H. 1982. Diversification strategies and the experience of top executives of large firms. *Strategic Management Journal* 3:377–380.

Sonnenfeld, J. 2007. The real scandal at BP. *Business Week*, May 14, 98.

Sosik, J. J. 2005. The role of personal values in the charismatic leadership of corporate managers: A model and preliminary field study. *Leadership Quarterly* 16:221–244.

Sosik, J. J., B. J. Avolio, and D. Jung. 2002. Examining the relationship of self-presentation attributes and impression management to charismatic leadership. *Leadership Quarterly* 13:217–242.

Sparrowe, R. T., and R. C. Liden. 1997. Process and structure in leader-member exchange. *Academy of Management Review* 22 (2): 522–552.

Spears, M. C., D. F. Parker, and M. McDonald. 2004. Globalization attitudes and locus of control. *Journal of Global Business* 15 (29): 57–66.

Spector, B. 1987. Transformational leadership: The new challenge for U.S. unions. *Human Resource Management* 26:3–16.

Spector, P. E. 1982. Behavior in organizations as a function of employee's locus of control. *Psychological Bulletin* 91 (3): 482–497.

Speizer, I. 2005. State of the sector: Executive education. *Workforce Management*, March, 57–63.

———. 2007. Back to school: Exec programs see resurgence. *Workforce Management*, January 15, 19–23.

Spencer, R. J. 1995. Success with self-managed teams and partnering. *Journal for Quality and Participation* 18 (4): 48–54.

Srivastava, A., K. M. Bartol, and E. A. Locke. 2006. Empower leadership in management teams: Effects on knowledge sharing, efficacy, and performance. *Academy of Management Journal* 49:1239–1251.

Starbuck, W. H., A. Greve, and B. L. T. Hedberg. 1978. Responding to crisis. *Journal of Business Administration* 9 (2): 111–127.

Starck, G., M. Fottler, M. Wheatley, and P. Sodomka. 2002. Spirituality and effective leadership in healthcare: Is there a connection? *Frontiers of Health Services Management* 18:3–45.

Steptoe, S. 2007. Building a better mouse. *Time.com,* June 14. http://www.time.com/time/globalbusiness/article/0,9171,1633077,00.html (accessed July 17, 2007).

Sternberg, R. J., ed. 2000. *Handbook of intelligence.* New York: Cambridge University Press.

_____. 2002a. Creativity as a decision. *American Psychologist* 57:376.

_____, ed. 2002b. *Why smart people can be so stupid.* New Haven, CT: Yale University Press.

_____. 2007. A systems model of leadership. *American Psychologist* 62:34–42.

Sternberg, R. J., G. B. Forsythe, J. Hedlund, J. A. Horvath, R. K. Wagner, W. M. Williams, S. A. Snook, and E. Grigorenko. 2000. *Practical intelligence in everyday life.* New York: Cambridge University Press.

Sternberg, R. J., and T. I. Lubart. 1995. *Defying the crowd: Cultivating creativity in a culture of conformity.* New York: Free Press.

Stewart, T. A. 1998a. Why leadership matters. *Fortune* 137 (4): 82.

_____. 1998b. The cunning plots of leadership. *Fortune* 138 (5): 165–166.

Stewart-Belle, S., and J. A. Lust. 1999. Career movement of female employees holding lower-level positions: An analysis of the impact of the type A behavior pattern. *Journal of Business and Psychology* 14 (1): 187–197.

Stinson, J. E., and T. W. Johnson. 1975. The path-goal theory of leadership: A partial test and suggested refinement. *Academy of Management Journal* 18:242–252.

Stogdill, R. M. 1948. Personal factors associated with leadership: A survey of the literature. *Journal of Psychology* 25:35–71.

_____. 1974. *Handbook of leadership.* New York: Free Press.

Strauss, G., and B. Hansen. 2005. CEO pay "business as usual." *USA Today,* March 30. http://www.usatoday.com/money/companies/management/2005-03-30-ceo-pay-2004-cover_x.htm (accessed July 26, 2007).

Strube, M. J., and J. E. Garcia. 1981. A meta-analytical investigation of Fiedler's contingency model of leadership effectiveness. *Psychological Bulletin* 90:307–321.

Strube, M. J., C. W. Turner, D. Cerro, J. Stevens, and F. Hinchey. 1984. Interpersonal aggression and the type A coronary-prone behavior pattern: A theoretical distinction and practical implications. *Journal of Personality and Social Psychology* 47:839–847.

Strube, M. J., and C. Werner. 1985. Relinquishment of control and the type A behavior pattern. *Journal of Personality and Social Psychology* 48:688–701.

Sullivan, M. 2004. Cambodia's new king ascends the throne. *All Things Considered,* October 29. http://www.npr.org/templates/story/story.php?storyId=4133660 (accessed December 18, 2007).

Suutari, V. 2002. Global leader development: An emerging research agenda. *Career Development Journal* 7:218–233.

Swan, K. 2000. Difference is power. *Fast Company,* July, 258–266.

Szilagyi, A. D., and H. P. Sims. 1974. An exploration of the path-goal theory of leadership in a health care environment. *Academy of Management Journal* 17:622–634.

Taft, D., and G. Singh. 2003. Executive compensation: A comparison of United States and Japan. *Compensation and Benefits Review* 35 (3): 68–78.

Taggar, S., and R. Ellis. 2007. The role of leaders in shaping formal team norms. *Leadership Quarterly* 18:105–120.

Tahmincioglu, E. 2004. Back from the brink. *Workforce Management* 5 (46). http://www.workforce.com/section/09/feature/23/90/10/index.html (accessed December 28, 2004).

Tallarico, C. M., and D. Gillis. 2007. Latest count of women in Canada's largest business shows marginal progress. http://www.catalystwomen.org/pressroom/press_releases/2006CanCensus.pdf (accessed June 19, 2007).

Tannen, D., ed. 1993. *Gender and conversational interaction.* Oxford: Oxford University Press.

Tannenbaum, A. S., and R. A. Cooke. 1974. Control and participation. *Journal of Contemporary Business* 3 (4): 35–46.

Taylor, A., III. 2006. Ford's fight for survival. *CNNmoney.com*, January 20. http://money.cnn.com/2006/01/20/news/companies/pluggedin_fortune/index.htm (accessed August 23, 2007).

Teagarden, M. B., M. C. Butler, and M. A. Von Glinow. 1992. Mexico's Maquiladora industry: Where strategic human resource management makes a difference. *Organizational Dynamics* 20 (3): 34–47.

Tepper, B. J., and P. M. Percy. 1994. Structural validity of the multifactor leadership questionnaire. *Educational and Psychological Measurement* 54:734–744.

Thach, E. C. 2002. The impact of executive coaching and 360 feedback on leadership effectiveness. *Leadership and Organization Development Journal* 23:205–214.

Thomas, A. B. 1988. Does leadership make a difference to organizational performance? *Administrative Science Quarterly* 33:388–400.

Thomas, K. M. 2001. The truth about mentoring minorities: Race matters. *Harvard Business Review* 79:98–112.

Tierney, T. J. 2006. *The non-profit sector's leadership deficit.* The Bridespan Group. http://www.bridgespangroup.org/kno_articles_leadershipdeficit.html (accessed July 26, 2007).

Ting, S., and E. W. Hart. 2004. Formal coaching. In *The Center for Creative Leadership: Handbook of leadership development.* 2nd ed. Ed. C. D. McCauley and E. Van Velsor, 116–150. San Francisco, CA: Jossey-Bass.

Tischler, L. 2002. Monica Luechtefeld makes the net click. *Fast Company,* November, 122–128.

_____. 2003. Bank of (middle) America. *Fast Company*, March, 104–109.

_____. 2004. IBM's management makeover. *Fast Company*, November, 112–113.

_____. 2005. Extreme jobs (and the people who love them). *Fast Company*, April, 54.

_____. 2006. Hospitality. Sweet. *Fast Company*, September. http://www.fastcompany.com/magazine/108/next-60seconds.html (accessed July 14, 2007).

Tjosvold, D., W. C. Wedley, and R. H. G. Field. 1986. Constructive controversy: The Vroom-Yetton model and managerial decision making. *Journal of Occupational Behavior* 7:125–138.

Tomlinson, R. 2000. Europe's new business elite. *Fortune*, April 3, 177–184.

_____. 2004. The new king of beers. *Fortune,* October 18, 233–238.

Tornow, W. W., and M. London, eds. 1998. *Maximizing the value of 360 degree feedback: A process for successful individual and organizational development.* San Francisco, CA: Jossey-Bass.

Tosi, H. L., V. F. Misangyi, A. Fanelli, D. A. Waldman, and F. J. Yammarino. 2004. CEO charisma, compensation, and firm performance. *Leadership Quarterly* 15:405–420.

The top 25 managers of the year. 2002. *Business Week,* January 14, 53–72.

Townsend, J., J. S. Phillips, and T. J. Elkins. 2000. Employee retaliation: The neglected consequence of poor leader-member exchange relations. *Journal of Occupational Health Psychology* 5 (4): 457–463.

Transparency International. 2006. Transparency International: Corruption perception index—2006. http://www.transparency.org/policy_research/surveys_indices/cpi/2006 (accessed January 8, 2008).

Triandis, H. C. 1993. The contingency model in cross-cultural perspective. In *Leadership theory and research: Perspectives and directions*, ed. M. M. Chemers and R. Ayman, 167–188. New York: Academic Press.

_____. 1995. *Individualism and collectivism.* Boulder, CO: Westview Press.

_____. 2004. The many dimensions of culture. *Academy of Management Executive* 18 (1): 88–93.

Triandis, H. C., P. Carnevale, M. Gelfand, C. Robert, S. A. Wasti, T. Probst, E. S. Kashima, et al. 2001. Culture and deception in business negotiations: A multilevel analysis. *International Journal of Cross-Cultural Management* 1 (1): 73–90.

Trice, H. M., and J. M. Beyer. 1993. *The cultures of work organizations.* Upper Saddle River, NJ: Prentice Hall.

Trompenaars, A. 1994. *Riding the waves of culture: Understanding culture and diversity in business.* London: Nicholas Brealey.

Trompenaars, A., and C. M. Hampden-Turner. 2001. *21 leaders for the 21st century.* Chicago: McGraw-Hill.

Trompenaars, A., and P. Woolliams. 2003. *Business across cultures.* Chichester: Capstone.

Truby, M. 2003. Bill Ford Jr. carries on family traditions. *Detroit News.* http://www.detnews.com/2003/specialreport/0306/09/f05-186877.htm (accessed March 31, 2005).

Trucco, T. 2007. Meetings; rope climbing? Passé. Treasure hunts? Cool. *New York Times,* April 16. http://select.nytimes.com/search/restricted/article?res=F10813FC3A5B0C758D-DDAD0894DF404482 (accessed September 13, 2007).

Tsui, A. S., and C. A. O'Reilly. 1989. Beyond simple demographic effects: The importance of relationship demography in superior-subordinates dyads. *Academy of Management Journal* 32:402–423.

Tsurumi, R. 1982. American origins of Japanese productivity: The Hawthorne experiment rejected. *Pacific Basin Quarterly* 7 (Spring–Summer): 14–15.

Tuggle, K. 2007. Marathon man. *Fast Company,* February, 54.

Turnley, W. H., and M. C. Bolino. 2001. Achieving desired images while avoiding undesired images: Exploring the role of self-monitoring in impression management. *Journal of Applied Psychology* 86 (2): 351–360.

Tyabji, H. 1997. What it means to lead. *Fast Company,* February–March, 98.

Tyson, A. S. 2002. Antiwar views split along generation gap. *Christian Science Monitor,* November 6. http://www.csmonitor.com/2002/1106/p01s01-ussc.htm (accessed November 12, 2004).

Uhl-Bien, M., R. Marion, and B. McKelvey. 2007. Complexity leadership theory: Shifting leadership from the industrial age to knowledge era. *Leadership Quarterly* 18:298–318.

Underwood, R. 2004. The creative impulse. *Fast Company,* December, 43–48.

U.S. House of Representatives. 2007.

U.S. Senate. 2007. Biographical directory. http://www.senate.gov/general/Features/bioguide.htm (accessed June 26, 2007).

Useem, J. 2001. It's all yours Jeff. Now what? *Fortune,* September 17, 64–68.

Useem, M. 2001. *Leading up: How to lead your boss so you both win.* New York: Crown Business/Random House.

Vakola, M., I. Tsausis, and I. Nikolaou. 2004. The role of emotional intelligence and personality variables on attitudes toward organizational change. *Journal of Managerial Psychology* 19:88–99.

Van der Vegt, G. S., J. S. Bunderson, and A. Oosterhof. 2006. Expertness diversity and interpersonal helping in teams: Why those who need the most help end up getting the least. *Academy of Management Journal* 49:877–893.

VanSandt, C. V., and C. P. Neck. 2003. Bridging ethics and self-leadership: Overcoming ethical discrepancies between employee and organizational standards. *Journal of Business Ethics* 43:363–388.

Vecchio, R. P. 1983. Assessing the validity of Fiedler's contingency model of leadership effectiveness: A closer look at Strube and Garcia. *Psychological Bulletin* 93:404–408.

Venezuela. 2002. Report on *Morning Edition, National Public Radio,* January 28.

Vidal, B. J., and M. Möller. 2007. When should leaders share information with their subordinates? *Journal of Economics and Management Strategy* 16:251–283.

Villa, J. R., J. P. Howell, P. Dorfman, and D. L. Daniel. 2003. Problems with detecting moderators in leadership research using moderated multiple regression. *Leadership Quarterly* 14:3–23.

Vroom, V. H. 1964. *Work and motivation.* New York: John Wiley.

Vroom, V. H., and A. G. Jago. 1988. *The new leadership: Managing participation in organizations.* Upper Saddle River, NJ: Prentice Hall.

Vroom, V. H., and P. W. Yetton. 1973. *Leadership and decision making.* Pittsburgh, PA: University of Pittsburgh Press.

Wakabayashi, M., G. B. Graen, M. R. Graen, and M. C. Graen. 1988. Japanese management progress: Mobility into middle management. *Journal of Applied Psychology* 73:217–227.

Waldman, D. A., M. Javidan, and P. Varella. 2004. Charismatic leadership at the strategic level: A new application of upper echelons theory. *Leadership Quarterly* 15:355–380.

Walker, M. C. 2006. Morality, self-interest, and leaders in international affairs. *Leadership Quarterly* 17:138–145.

Walker, R. 1997. Back to the farm. *Fast Company*, February–March, 110–122.

Wall, S. J. 2005. The Protean organization: Learning to love change. *Organizational Dynamics* 24:37–46.

Wallace, D. 2003. The soul of a sports machine. *Fast Company* 75 (October): 100–104.

Walsh, T. 1996. CEOs: Greenspan by a landslide. *Fortune* 133 (5): 43.

Walters, J. 2006. Across the board innovator. *Governing*, November, 42.

Walumbwa, F. O., and J. J. Lawler. 2003. Building effective organization: Transformational leadership, collectivist orientation, work-related attitudes, and withdrawal behavior in three emerging economies. *International Journal of Human Resource Management* 14:1083–1101.

Walumbwa, F. O., J. J. Lawler, and B. J. Avolio. 2007. Leadership, individual differences, and work-related attitudes: A cross-cultural investigation. *Applied Psychology* 56:212–230.

Warner, R. 2001. Where is the next frontier of innovation? *Fast Company*, September, 128–132.

Watson, W. E. 2006. Type A personality characteristics and the effect on individual and team academic performance. *Journal of Applied Social Psychology* 36:1110–1128.

Wayne, S. J., M. Shore, and R. C. Liden. 1997. Perceived organizational support and leader-member exchange: A social exchange perspective. *Academy of Management Journal* 40 (1): 82–111.

Weierter, S. J. M. 1997. Who wants to play follow the leader? A theory of charismatic relationships based on routinized charisma and follower characteristics. *Leadership Quarterly* 8 (2): 171–193.

Weil, E. 1998. Every leader tells a story. *Fast Company*, June–July, 38–40.

Weiner, N., and T. A. Mahoney. 1981. A model of corporate performance as a function of environment, organization, and leadership influences. *Academy of Management Journal* 24:453–470.

Weiss, H. M., and S. Adler. 1984. Personality in organizational research. In *Research in organizational behavior*. Vol. 6. Ed. B. Staw and L. Cummings, 1–50. Greenwich, CT: JAI Press.

Weiss, R. M., and V. W. Gantt. 2004. *Knowledge and skill development in non-profit organizations*. London: Ebbie Bowers Publishing.

Weiss, T. 2006. Live chat with Oxygen's Gerry Laybourne. *Forbes.com*, October 18. http://www.forbes.com/leadership/2006/10/18/leadership-tv-oxygen-lead-manage-cx_tw_1018laybourne.html (accessed June 27, 2007).

Welch, J., and S. Welch. 2007. When to talk, when to balk. *Business Week*, April 30, 102.

Wellner, A. S. 2004. Managing: Who can you trust? *Inc.*, October, 39–40.

———. 2007. Eye on the prize. *Inc.*, January, 40–41.

Wilson, D. C. 2006. When equal opportunity knocks. *Gallup Management Journal*, April 13.

Winning the waiting game for women CEOs. 2006. *Christian Science Monitor*, August. http://www.csmonitor.com/2006/0829/p08s02-comv.html (accessed June 19, 2007).

Winters, M. F. 2007. CEOs who get it. *Leadership Excellence*, April 4.

Wiscombe, J. 2007a. Toyota: Driving diversity. *Workforce Management*, January. http://www.workforce.com/section/09/feature/24/62/58/index.html (accessed July 6, 2007).

———. 2007b. What's behind the wheel at Toyota. *Workforce Management*, January. http://www.workforce.com/archive/feature/24/62/58/246260.php?ht=toyota%20toyota (accessed July 6, 2007).

Wofford, J. C., and L. Z. Liska. 1993. Path-goal theories of leadership: A meta-analysis. *Journal of Management* 19:858–876.

Wolff, S. B., A. T. Pescosolido, and V. U. Druskat. 2003. Emotional intelligence as the basis of leadership emergence in self-managing teams. *Leadership Quarterly* 13:505–522.

Wood, J., and T. Vilkinas. 2007. Characteristics associated with CEO success: Perception of CEOs and their staff. *The Journal of Management Development* 26:213.

World Fact Book: Malaysia. 2007. https://www.cia.gov/library/publications/the-world-factbook/geos/my.html#People (accessed June 16, 2007).

World Fact Book: Singapore. 2007. https://www.cia.gov/library/publications/the-world-factbook/geos/sn.html#People (accessed June 16, 2007).

WorldBlu list of most democratic places to work. 2007. http://www.worldblu.com/scorecard/list2007.php (accessed July 11, 2007).

Worley, C. G., and E. E. Lawler III. 2006. Designing organizations that are built to change. *Sloan Management Review* 48 (1): 19–23.

Wren, J. T. 2006. A quest for a grand theory of leadership. In *The quest for a general theory of leadership*, ed. G. R. Goethals and G. L. J. Sorenson, 1–38. Cheltenham, UK: Edward Elgar.

Wylie, I. 2003. Can Philips learn to walk the talk? *Fast Company*, January, 44–45.

———. 2004a. Please, displease me. *Fast Company*, December, 90–91.

———. 2004b. Parma-splat! *Fast Company*, March, 34.

Yammarino, F. J., and B. M. Bass. 1990. Long-term forecasting of transformational leadership and its effects among naval officers: Some preliminary findings. In *Measures of leadership*, ed. K. E. Clark and M. B. Clark, 151–169. Greensboro, NC: Center for Creative Leadership.

Yammarino, F. J., A. J. Dubinsky, L. B. Comer, and M. A. Jolson. 1997. Women and transformational and contingency reward leadership: A multiple-levels-of-analysis perspective. *Academy of Management Journal* 40:205–222.

Yan, J., and J. G. Hunt. 2005. A cross-cultural perspective on perceived leadership effectiveness. *International Journal of Cross-Cultural Management* 5:49–66.

Yang, C. 2005. Another Case entirely. *Business Week*, April 11. http://www.businessweek.com/magazine/content/05_15/b3928093.htm (accessed August 12, 2007).

Yasai-Ardekani, M. 1986. Structural adaptations to environments. *Academy of Management Review* 11:9–21.

———. 1989. Effects of environmental scarcity and munificence on the relationship of context to organizational structure. *Academy of Management Journal* 32:131–156.

Yoshida Group. 2007. http://www.yoshidagroup.com/index (accessed June 22, 2007).

Yuengling, D. 2007 Message from the president. http://www.yuengling.com/message.htm#more (accessed June 22, 2007).

Yukl, G. 1999. An evaluation of conceptual weaknesses in transformational and charismatic leadership theories. *Leadership Quarterly* 10 (2): 285–305.

Yukl, G., and C. M. Falbe. 1990. Influence tactics in upward, downward, and lateral influence attempts. *Journal of Applied Psychology* 75:132–140.

———. 1991. The importance of different power sources in downward and lateral relations. *Journal of Applied Psychology* 76:416–423.

Zaccaro, S. J. 2007. Trait-based perspectives of leadership. *American Psychologist* 62:6–16.

Zaccaro, S. J., and D. Banks. 2004. Leader visioning and adaptability: Bridging the gap between research and practice on developing the ability to manage change. *Human Resource Management* 43:367–380.

Zaleznik, A. 1990. The leadership gap. *Academy of Management Executive* 4 (1): 7–22.

Zander, A. 1983. The value of belonging to a group in Japan. *Small Group Behavior* 14:7–8.

Zeiger-Hill, J. 2006. Discrepancies between implicit and explicit self-esteem: Implications for narcissism and self-esteem instability. *Journal of Personality* 74:119–143.

Zellner, W. 2003. What was Don Carty thinking? *Business Week*, May 5, 32.

Zhou, J., and J. M. George. 2001. When job dissatisfaction leads to creativity: Encouraging the expression of voice. *Academy of Management Journal* 44 (4): 682–696.

———. 2003. Awakening employee creativity: The role of leader emotional intelligence. *Leadership Quarterly* 14:545–568.

Zinnbauer, B. J., K. I. Pargament, and A. B. Scott. 1999. The emerging meaning of religiosity and spirituality: Problems and prospects. *Journal of Personality* 67:889–919.

Zolli, A. 2006. Demographics: The population hourglass. *Fast Company*, March. http://www.fastcompany.com/magazine/103/open_essay-demographics.html (accessed June 26, 2007).

Author Index

Subject Index